INSIGHT GUIDES

VIETNAM

T 20000

DISCOVERY
CHANNEL

APA PUBLICATIONS L

Part of the Langenscheidt Publishing Group

ABOUT THIS BOOK

Editorial

Editor
Scott Rutherford
Editorial Director
Brian Bell

Distribution

UK & Ireland
GeoCenter International Ltd
The Viables Centre, Harrow Way
Basingstoke, Hants RG22 4BJ
Fax: (44) 1256 817988

United States
Langenscheidt Publishers, Inc.
46–35 54th Road, Maspeth, NY 11378
Fax: (1) 718 784-0640

Canada
Thomas Allen & Son Ltd
390 Steelcase Road East
Markham, Ontario L3R 1G2
Fax: (1) 905 475-6747

Australia
Universal Press
1 Waterloo Road
Macquarie Park, NSW 2113
Fax: (61) 2 9888-9074

New Zealand
Hema Maps New Zealand Ltd (HNZ)
Unit D, 24 Ra ORA Drive
East Tamaki, Auckland
Fax: (64) 9 273-6479

Worldwide
Apa Publications GmbH & Co.
Verlag KG (Singapore branch)
38 Joo Koon Road, Singapore 628990
Tel: (65) 6865-1600. Fax: (65) 6861-6438

Printing

Insight Print Services (Pte) Ltd
38 Joo Koon Road, Singapore 628990
Tel: (65) 6865-1600. Fax: (65) 6861-6438

©2003 Apa Publications GmbH & Co.
Verlag KG (Singapore branch)
All Rights Reserved
First Edition 1992
Fourth Edition 1999
Updated 2001
Reprinted 2003

CONTACTING THE EDITORS
We would appreciate it if readers
would alert us to errors or out-
dated information by writing to:
Insight Guides, P.O. Box 7910,
London SE1 1WE, England.
Fax: (44) 20 7403-0290.
insight@apaguide.demon.co.uk

NO part of this book may be reproduced,
stored in a retrieval system or transmitted
in any form or means electronic, mech-
anical, photocopying, recording or otherwise, without prior written permission of
Apa Publications. Brief text quotations
with use of photographs are exempted
for book review purposes only. Information has been obtained from sources
believed to be reliable, but its accuracy
and completeness, and the opinions
based thereon, are not guaranteed.

www.insightguides.com

This guidebook combines the interests and enthusiasms of two of the world's best-known information providers: Insight Guides, whose titles have set the standard for visual travel guides since 1970, and the Discovery Channel, the world's premier source of nonfiction television programming.

Insight Guides' editors provide practical advice and general understanding about a place's history, culture, and people. Discovery Channel and its extensive website, www.discovery.com, help millions of viewers explore their world from the comfort of their home and also encourage them to explore it firsthand.

In this, the fourth edition of *Insight Guide: Vietnam*, our writers and photographers travel the length and breadth of this simultaneously enchanting and confounding nation. Outside of the cities of Ha Noi and Ho Chi Minh, much of the country is not for those looking for ease of travel. But for the traveller seeking an extraordinary experience, Vietnam awaits.

Map Legend

—··	International Boundary
—·—	National Park/Reser
----	Ferry Route
✈ ✈	Airport: Internationa Regional
🚌	Bus Station
P	Parking
❶	Tourist Information
✉	Post Office
✝ ✝	Church/Ruins
✝	Monastery
☾	Mosque
✡	Synagogue
🏰	Castle/Ruins
∴	Archaeological Site
∩	Cave
🗿	Statue/Monument
★	Place of Interest

The main places of interest in the Places section are coordinated by number with a full-colour map (e.g. ❶), and a symbol at the top of every right-hand page tells you where to find the map.

Left: Ha Long Bay

How to use this book

The book is carefully structured to convey an understanding of Vietnam and its culture and to guide readers through its sights and attractions:

◆ The Features section, with a yellow colour bar, covers the country's history and culture in lively authoritative essays written by specialists.

◆ The Places section, with a blue bar, provides full details of all the sights and areas worth seeing. The chief places of interest are coordinated by number with specially drawn maps.

◆ The Travel Tips listings section, with an orange bar, at the back of the book, offers a convenient point of reference for information on travel, accommodation, restaurants, and other practical aspects of the country. Information can be located quickly using the index printed on the back cover flap, which also serves as a handy bookmark.

The contributors

This new edition, which builds on the first edition edited by **Helen West**, was managed and edited by **Scott Rutherford**, who has overseen many of our Asian and Pacific titles.

Contributing to this edition, with updated material and new information on Hanoi and northern Vietnam was Bangkok-based **Susan Cunningham**, who has also contributed to Apa's Thailand guide. The southern part of the country, including Ho Chi Minh (Saigon), was covered by **Sharon Owyang**, a frequent contributor who worked on *Insight Guide: China*. The central region, including Hue and Da Nang, was updated by Chiang Mai-based **Andrew Forbes** and **David Henley**, who have helped with several Insight Guides.

Catherine Karnow and **Jim Holmes** provided much of the photography, while **Mariko Fujinaka** tidied up the text.

Previous contributors to the guide include **Tim Larimer**, **Andy Soloman**, **Diana Reid**, **Tran Van Dinh**, **Tim Page**, **Kim Naylor**, **Nguyen Tan Dac**, **Jean-Leo Dugast**, **Bill Wassman**, **Alain Evrard**, **Joseph Lynch**, and **Zdenek Thoma**.

CONTENTS

Maps

Vietnam **136**

Hanoi **142**

Beyond Hanoi **162**

Hai Phong/Ha Long **178**

Northern Vietnam **186**

Central Vietnam **234**

Hue **241**

Hoi An **260**

Southern Vietnam **266**

Nha Trang **271**

Da Lat **281**

Ho Chi Minh **288**

Introduction

A Resilient Place **15**

History

Decisive Dates **20**

The First 4,000 Years **25**

The Anti-Colonial Struggle **39**

Limping into a New Century.... **49**

Features

Geography **61**

People **69**

Religion **83**

Performing Arts **97**

Literature and Art **105**

Cuisine **123**

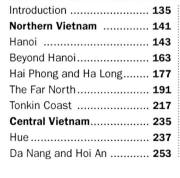

Hill-tribe harvest in northern Vietnam.

Travel Tips

Getting Acquainted . . 338

Planning the Trip 339

Practical Information . 343

Getting Around 351

Where to Stay 355

Eating Out 362

Attractions 365

Festivals 367

Shopping 368

Language 370

Further Reading 371

◆ **Full Travel Tips index is on page 337**

Insight on ...

Festivals 92

Temples............................ 118

Hill Tribes 212

Hue Citadel 248

Information panels

Vietnam's Name.................... 35

Water Puppets 101

The Language..................... 117

Co Loa.............................. 159

Preservation 247

Places

Introduction 135

Northern Vietnam 141

Hanoi 143

Beyond Hanoi..................... 163

Hai Phong and Ha Long........ 177

The Far North..................... 191

Tonkin Coast 217

Central Vietnam................. 235

Hue 237

Da Nang and Hoi An 253

Southern Vietnam 265

Nha Trang 271

Da Lat 278

Ho Chi Minh 289

Beyond Ho Chi Minh 307

Mekong Delta..................... 319

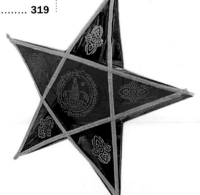

A RESILIENT PLACE

The Vietnamese are an adaptable and pragmatic people,
with a national sense of being that has humbled great powers

In the early 1400s, the Chinese invaded Vietnam, one of many such invasions over the centuries. The Chinese were soundly defeated by the Vietnamese. Le Loi, emperor of Vietnam, might have had the Chinese prisoners killed. He chose otherwise. Le Loi apologised to the Chinese court for defeating its army, made peace with China, and then provided the defeated Chinese troops with horses and ships for their return north. Le Loi knew that, although momentarily defeated, China would never, ever disappear from Vietnam's future or memory.

Perhaps more than anything else, the presence of its leviathan neighbour to the north has shaped the nature and outlook of the Vietnamese mind. Centuries of fending off China's invasions, while at the same time not making China *too* angry, has given the Vietnamese a pragmatism, patience, and solid sense of national identity. In fact, the Vietnamese have an uncanny and unusually deep feeling of national identity and of nation-building. Had the French and Americans seriously pondered Vietnamese history, the inevitable futility of their military efforts in the 1950s and 1960s would have been more self-evident and at an earlier stage.

Vietnamese offer a modern slogan: *Vietnam is a country, not a war.* But for much of the post-World War II years, until 1975, Vietnam was nearly synonymous with war, first with the French and later the Americans. Vestiges of the war remain in the bomb craters, old military hardware, and labyrinths of tunnels where entire villages endured the fighting. The craters have been converted into fish ponds and the tunnels turned into tourist traps. Memories of the war are fading. More than 60 percent of Vietnamese today are less than 25 years old, born after the Vietnam War's end. They are the first generation in many not to know war in their homeland.

"All men are created equal. They are endowed by their creator with certain inalienable rights, among these are life, liberty and the pursuit of happiness". The meaning is familiar to every American as the foundation of the American constitution. But the words above are in the Declaration of the Democratic Republic of Vietnam, written in 1945 by Ho Chi Minh, a Communist revolutionary who was influenced by the American constitution and its ambitions.

The Vietnamese government is unabashedly Communist. It is a Leninist regime, nevertheless, that sometimes transcends the Cold War stereotype of grey, static, and anchored by a cult-of-personality leadership. While it has been at times harshly oppressive, Vietnam's Communism is occasionally, though hesitatingly, pragmatic.

PRECEDING PAGES: temple detail from Ha Tien, southern Vietnam; boats on Vinh Ha Long, northern Vietnam; Hanoi religious shop; Song Huong (Perfume River), Hue.
LEFT: vendor at a Mekong Delta market, southern Vietnam.

"Vietnam's Communist Party... voiced a common yearning for equality and betterment" reported a typically lucid article in *The Economist* in 1995. "Few communist parties so harnessed themselves to national ideals. Its cruelty might have been feared, but its daring and tenacity for a cause most Vietnamese supported – national independence – was admired".

The struggling pragmatism of Vietnam's government comes against great odds. When the Americans pulled out and the South was reunified ("liberated" has passed from pragmatic usage) with the North, the Hanoi government immediately turned southern Vietnam into a Soviet-style economy. The result nearly left a carcass of a nation. By the mid-1980s, the country's economy was destitute. Inflation exceeded 800 percent. Large parts of the rural population were starving or nearly so. Its neighbour to the north, China, had beaten up Vietnam earlier by invading Vietnam's northern provinces. Moreover, Vietnam itself had been internationally ostracised by its own invasion of the Khmer Rouge-controlled Cambodia. But unlike elsewhere in Asia, saving face is not an obsessive concern of the Vietnamese. Admitting that their socialisation of the South was in error, the government shifted course towards a free-market economy with its *doi moi,* or new reform policy. The move was essential, but it is still finding its feet and it may not succeed.

Vietnam remains one of the poorest countries in the world, with a per capita annual income of around US$300. Yet on the streets of Hanoi or Ho Chi Minh one does not sense a wretchedness or fatalism of poverty often encountered elsewhere in the Third World. Everywhere there is the hum of activity, of a hard-working people anxious to build their country and lives. There is a future to be made and the Vietnamese intend to make it, corruption and the reactionary impediments of the central government notwithstanding. And the Vietnamese drive like they work: looking only ahead, ignoring traffic to the sides, and stopping for nothing.

For even as the country repeats its mantra – a country, not a war – its long history of conflict has left the people with a natural tendency to be wary of foreigners, to value self-reliance, and to do things their own way with an innate pride and a national awareness that this impoverished land was able to defeat great powers and superior technology. And, too, throughout Vietnam's history is a thread of victimisation – that it was foreigners who caused all of Vietnam's problems. Yet, with the pragmatism of Emperor Le Loi more than half a millennium ago, the Vietnamese will define their future, perhaps with resounding finesse. ❑

RIGHT: young girl in Ho Chi Minh, the former Saigon, in southern Vietnam.

Decisive Dates

BEGINNINGS

2879 BC: Legendary founding of the Van Lang Kingdom by the first Hung Vuong.

2879–258 BC: Hung dynasty.

1800–1400 BC: Phung Nguyen culture, the Early Bronze Age.

200 BC–AD 938: Chinese rule.

210 BC: Kingdom of Au Lac established. Chinese general Chao Tuo founds Nan Yueh (Nam Viet).

AD 39: Trung sisters lead a rebellion against Chinese.

AD 43: Trung sisters' rebellion is crushed by the

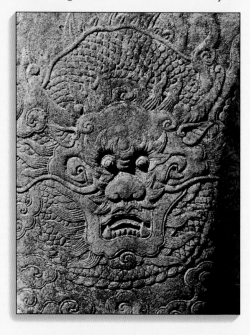

Chinese general Ma Yuan, and subsequently, the Viet people are placed under direct Chinese administration for the first time.

542–544: Ly Bi leads uprising against China's Liang dynasty to create independent kingdom of Van Xuan.

939–967: Ngo dynasty.

968–980: Dinh dynasty.

970–975: Dinh Bo Linh gains Chinese recognition of Nam Viet's independence by establishing a tributary relationship with China's Song dynasty.

980–1009: Tien Le dynasty.

1009–1225: Ly dynasty.

1225–1400: Tran dynasty.

1400–1428: Ho dynasty.

1428–1776: Le dynasty.

DIVISION AND REUNIFICATION

16th century: Decadence of Le dynasty leads to the country's division into two rival principalities.

1543: Descendants of the Le dynasty occupy the country's southern capital after a series of fierce battles. The southern court is founded near Thanh Hoa.

1592: The death of Mac dynasty's last king, Mac Mau Hop, ends the war.

1672: Lord Trinh consents to partition the country at the Linh River.

early 1770s: Struggle between French and Chinese factions begin with the court.

1776–92: Tay Son Uprising.

1792–1883: Nguyen dynasty.

1861: French forces capture Saigon. The French defeat the Vietnamese army and gain control of Gia Dinh and surrounding provinces. Six years later, the entire southern part of the country is annexed as a French colony.

1862: The Treaty of Saigon cedes three southern provinces to the French.

1893: Emperor Ham Nghi and Phan Dinh Phung organise a royalist movement and stage an unsuccessful uprising at Ha Tinh.

1904: Japanese victory over Russia convinces Vietnamese that Western power is no longer invincible.

1907: Eastward Movement is established by Phan Boi Chau and Cuong De. French authorities discover the scheme and negotiate with Japan to extradite all Vietnamese students.

1919: Ngyuen Ai Quoc (later known as Ho Chi Minh) attempts to present a programme for Vietnamese rights and sovereignty at the Versailles Peace conference but is turned away.

1920: Ho Chi Minh participates in the founding of the French Communist Party.

1923: Ho Chi Minh goes to Moscow to be trained as an agent of the Communist International.

1930: Ho Chi Minh successfully rallies several Communist groups and becomes the founder of the Indochinese Communist Party.

WORLD WAR II AND AFTER

1939: World War II begins.

1945: Japan overthrows French colonial rule and renders Vietnam "independent" but under Japanese "protection". The Japanese surrender to the Allies some months later.

1942–43: Ho Chi Minh imprisoned in China.

1943: Ho Chi Minh is released and recognised as the chief of the Viet Minh.

1945: Japan surrenders and the Viet Minh commences the August Revolution, gaining effective control over much of Vietnam. In September Ho Chi Minh declares Vietnam's independence in Hanoi.

1946: Ho Chi Minh visits Paris during negotiations with France; hostilities begin following violation of agreements.

1951: Ho merges Viet Minh with the Lien Viet and announces the formation of the Workers Party (Lao Dong), a disguise for the Communist Party that had officially disbanded, but was still active.

NORTH-SOUTH DIVIDE

1954: Geneva Accord divides Vietnam at the 17th parallel. South Vietnam is led by Prime Minister Ngo Dinh Diem, and North Vietnam under the Communist Ho Chi Minh.

1955: Diem refuses to hold general elections. Start of Second Indochina War. DIrect United States aid to South Vietnam begins.

1959: Group 559 established to infiltrate South Vietnam via the Ho Chi Minh Trail.

1960: National Liberation Front of South Vietnam (NLF) is formed. During the 1960s, the southern Communist movement – the Viet Cong – grows stronger.

1962: United States military personnel in Vietnam total about 3,200.

1963: Ngo Dinh Diem, president of South Vietnam, is overthrown and assassinated.

1965: United States begin bombing military targets in North Vietnam. First United States ground combat troops land in Vietnam at Da Nang.

1968: My Lai massacre. Tet Offensive includes a raid on the American embassy that stuns and embarrasses the United States.

1969: Ho Chi Minh dies without seeing his efforts completed. Peace negotiations drag on in Paris between 1968 and 1973.

1973: Paris Peace Agreement aims to put an end to hostilities. The last United States troops depart from Vietnam in March.

1975: In April, North Vietnamese troops enter Saigon. The South Vietnamese government surrenders.

A UNIFIED VIETNAM

1976: Vietnam is officially reunified.

1977: Vietnam is admitted to the United Nations.

1978: Vietnam signs friendship treaty with the Soviet Union. The invasion of Cambodia by Vietnamese troops and the subsequent so-called "Chinese lesson" were to augur a new cycle of war, which was to absorb most of Vietnam's post-war energies.

LEFT: dragon motif on Nguyen mausoleum, Hue.
RIGHT: the legendary Ho Chi Minh in the 1950s.

1978–9: Vietnamese forces begin invasion of Cambodia. The Cambodian government of Pol Pot is overthrown when Phnom Penh, the capital of Cambodia, falls to Vietnamese forces.

1979: China retaliates by invading Vietnam. After less than 3 months, Chinese forces withdraw.

1982: Fifth National Party Congress.

ECONOMIC SHIFTS

1986: Sixth Party Congress. Programme of socio-economic renovation called *doi moi* is launched.

1987: Law on Foreign Investment is passed.

1988: New contract system is implemented to encourage Vietnamese farmers to cultivate their land. Rice

production experiences an immediate upsurge.

1989: Vietnamese troops leave Cambodia.

1990: Vietnam adopts a new course in foreign affairs, and peace talks in China take place. Diplomatic relations established with the European Union.

1991: China relations normalised.

1993: Restrictions on Vietnam borrowing from IMF and Asian Development Bank are lifted.

1994: Trade embargo lifted by the United States.

1995: Diplomatic ties are restored with the US, and a US embassy opens in Hanoi. Vietnam is admitted to the Association of Southeast Asian Nations (ASEAN).

1997: Economic reforms of 1996 stall. Foreign investors and companies leave in large numbers.

2000: Continuing economic stagnation. ❑

THE FIRST 4,000 YEARS

Dynasties rose and fell as Vietnam coalesced into a nation constantly tempered by the ancient weight of the Middle Kingdom – China – to the north

V ietnam's ancient history reads like a book of legend, but with many of the pages torn or missing due to a lack of early historical records. And like any ancient nation, Vietnam's earliest history has been generously embellished with legend and fairy tales. However, by melding Chinese and Vietnamese historical records together with Vietnamese folklore and recent archaeological discoveries, some of the missing pages have come to light.

The first threads of Vietnam's history are inextricably intertwined with the history of the country that looms to the north and is the most significant in the psyche of the Vietnamese people: China. Indeed, the outside force Vietnamese fear today is this most ancient of kingdoms that threatened Vietnam's existence repeatedly throughout history.

From the earliest records of civilisation, what is now Vietnam faced repeated incursions from China, even as late as 1979 when Chinese forces crossed the border in retaliation for Vietnam's earlier invasion into Cambodia. This history has left Vietnamese people with a suspicion of foreigners and perhaps with something of a martyr complex. Even today, when discussing poverty in the Vietnamese countryside, many people lay blame with America, or the French colonialists, or the centuries of fighting off the Chinese.

The Vietnamese have not been without their own territorial ambitions, however. Vietnamese history books tend to ignore the country's own invasions of neighbouring lands. Over the years, the country has had designs on what are now Cambodia and Laos, and there were early and lengthy conflicts between the northern and southern parts of Vietnam. Long before Ho Chi Minh sought to unify the country under the banner of Communism, the Viet people of what is now northern Vietnam had their eyes on – and eventually conquered – the Champa kingdom

in the southern part of Vietnam. Interestingly enough, the ancient historical and geographical divisions of north and south – of Tonkin and Champa – were geographically similar to the United Nations-defined demilitarised zone that divided North and South Vietnam after World War II until reunification in 1975.

DONG SON CULTURE

Extending from northern Vietnam into Cambodia, Laos, and even Indonesia, the Dong Son culture, named after a small village in northern Vietnam, produced exquisite bronze works as early as 300 BC. Often decorated with human and animal figures, Dong Son bronze was cast using wax models. Most exemplary were ceremonial "kettle" drums (the largest was found in Bali; *see photo on page 26)* and elaborate axes. Spirals are a notable motif in Dong Son bronze. The Dong Son were seafarers who ventured throughout Southeast Asia, but they also turned northern Vietnam's Song Hong, or Red River, region into a rice-growing region.

PRECEDING PAGES: pagoda of Thien Mu, Hue.
LEFT: dancing Cham *uma* stone image.
RIGHT: ancient Cham tower near Cam Ranh.

Hung Vuong dynasty

Nearly 5,000 years ago, if the stories are correct, the southern Viet kingdom of Xich Qui was divided into 100 principalities, each governed by one of the 100 sons. The eldest son was crowned as king of Lac Viet, naming himself Hung Vuong, while Lac Viet was renamed Van Lang. His kingdom of Van Lang was the most powerful around, encompassing most of present-day northern and central Vietnam. The kingdom of Van Lang prospered under the rule of 18 successive Hung kings during the 1st millennium BC – the dynasty of Hung Vuong, founded in the present-day

dynasty in 208 BC. His capital was located near present-day Guangzhou (Canton).

China's influence

Nam Viet progressively entered the Chinese sphere of influence. In exchange for periodic tributes to the court of the Han emperor, Nam Viet received protection against foreign invasion. Less than a century later, however, the Han emperor Wudi sent his mighty armies to conquer Nam Viet. Despite the defending Nam Viet army's fierce resistance – a quality that continued through to the 20th century – Nam Viet yielded to the Han invaders.

province of Vinh. But like all kingdoms, this one eventually fell to another, that of Thuc Phan, king of neighbouring Au Viet, in 258 BC.

Thuc Phan (calling himself An Duong Vuong), established the new kingdom of Au Lac, putting his capital at Phuc An, where a spiral citadel was built. The remains of the citadel are in the present-day village of Co Loa, to the north of Hanoi.

Fifty years later, the kingdom fell to the northern hordes of an ambitious general, Trieu Da, who was from the south of China. Trieu Da founded the independent kingdom of Nam Viet, which included much of present-day southern China, and established the Trieu

THE TRUNG SISTERS

Heroes of Vietnam's first independence movement, sisters Trung Trac and Trung Nhi were of northern Vietnamese aristocracy. The husband of Trung Trac, the elder sister, was killed by the Chinese for plotting to overthrow them. Trung Trac took over leadership of the movement, and she and her sister led other nobles to Lien Lau and forced the Chinese to flee. They proclaimed themselves queens of a nation extending north from Hue into southern China. The sisters and their modest army were overwhelmed by Chinese forces near present-day Hanoi. Facing defeat, they committed suicide by drowning in the Song Hong (Red River), in AD 43.

The first Chinese occupation lasted half a century, until AD 42. After Trieu Dau's defeat, the country became a Chinese protectorate under the new name of Giao Chi. Highly qualified administrators were appointed as governors to rule the country, but their efforts to introduce Chinese literature, arts and agricultural techniques met with fierce resistance from the Viet people. Greatly frustrated by long decades of Chinese influence and culture, the Vietnamese not only guarded their existing national identity but fought fiercely to preserve it. Finally, in AD 39, the oppressive rule and injustices of a cruel

governor, To Dinh, provoked a victorious armed revolt against the Chinese authorities led by two sisters, Trung Trac and Trung Nhi, heroines known as Hai Ba Trung. Their reign, however, was short-lived (see box at left). Three years later, the superior strategies and arms of the Chinese armies brought the country again under Chinese control.

The fall of the Trung sisters marked the second period of Chinese occupation. Nam Viet was administered as a Chinese province and a campaign was launched against the kingdom

LEFT: an example of a large, Dong Son-era drum.
ABOVE: traditional theme of simple pleasures.

THE DRAGON AND THE IMMORTAL

Both the Chinese and Viet cosmology viewed the world through the concept of the Five Elements: metal, wood, water, fire and earth, sometimes represented by the Five Regions of Centre, South, North, East, and West. The Centre was represented by the earth and the colour yellow, the South by fire and the colour red, the North by water and the colour black, the East by wood and the colour green, the West by metal and the colour white.

From ancient times, a kingdom controlled the heart of the Asian continent, its rulers basing their power on these concepts of the Five Elements and Five Regions. Known as the Middle Kingdom, or Chung Hoa, its power centre was located in the territory of Five Mounts (Ngu Linh) and was peopled by many races but dominated by the Han and the Viet. While the Han were ethnically homogeneous, the Viets incorporated hundreds of tribes. The Viets settled south of the Yellow River and developed an agricultural culture, whereas the Han, in the northwest, became expert in hunting and battle skills.

The Viet chief ruled the Five Mounts territory, and there were three consecutive rulers: Toai Nhan, who discovered fire; Phuc Hi, who discovered the I Ching and domesticated wild animals; and Shen Nong, who cultivated wild plants for domestic use and taught his people to grow rice. The Viets regarded themselves as descendants of these three. The last ruler, Shen Nong, is the direct link to the Viet.

By the end of Shen Nong's era, the Han had invaded the Five Mounts territory. Their chief proclaimed himself Huangdi, the Yellow Emperor of the centre, in accordance with the Five Elements concept, and China's first true emperor. His son, Sung Lam, succeeded his father to become Lac Long Quan, Dragon Lord of the Mighty Seas. He married the beautiful Princess Au Co, descendant of the Immortals of the High Mountains. Their union gave birth to 100 sons and the Kingdom of Bach Viet, whose 100 principalities extended from the lower Yangzi to the north of Indochina. The kingdom prospered. But the Lord of the Dragon and the Princess of the Mountains, convinced that the difference in their origins would always deny them earthly happiness, separated. Half of the children returned with their mother to the mountains, the others followed their father to the eastern sea.

The symbolism of Lac Long Quan's descendance from the Dragon Lord and Au Co from the Immortals holds significance for the Vietnamese, as the Dragon symbolises the *yang* and Immortal the *yin*. Thus, the Vietnamese believe they are descendants of Tien Rong, the Immortal and the Dragon, and these symbols constitute the Vietnamese people's earliest totems.

of Champa, in the south. This period of Chinese occupation ended abruptly when a scholar named Ly Bon led an armed revolt and succeeded in chasing out the Chinese. Ly Bon took control of the territory, naming it Van Xuan and founding the Ly dynasty, which lasted until the Chinese once again regained supremacy in 545.

The particularly troubled era that followed was marked by frequent outbreaks of violent battles between Chinese and Vietnamese. It ended with the third period of Chinese occupation from 603 until 938. The Chinese made concerted efforts to establish their culture

transferred the capital to Co Loa, which had been the capital of the Au Lac kingdom, thus affirming continuity of the traditions of the Lac Viet people. Ngo Quyen spent the six years of his reign fighting revolts. After his death in 967, the kingdom fell into chaos. For more than 20 years, the country remained fragmented and the external threat from China's Song dynasty loomed large to the north on the border.

Dinh dynasty (968–980)

The most powerful of the feudal lords, Dinh Bo Linh, reunified the fragmented country under the name of Dai Co Viet and took the

and civilisation in Nam Viet, which they renamed An Nam. Still, numerous insurrections broke out despite the solid administrative structure imposed by the Chinese government of the Tang dynasty.

Ngo dynasty (939–967)

Disorder accompanied the decline of the Tang dynasty in China, giving the Vietnamese the chance for which they had long waited. In a protracted war that ended with the celebrated naval battle of Bach Dang, east of Hai Phong, Ngo Quyen vanquished the Chinese invaders and founded the first Vietnamese dynasty in 939. He named the country Dai Viet and

imperial title of Dinh Tien Hoang De (The First August Emperor Dinh). Well aware of the Chinese Song dynasty's military might, Dinh Bo Linh negotiated a non-aggression treaty in exchange for tributes payable to the Chinese every three years. This set the foundation of future relations with China that were to last for many centuries.

Dinh Tien Hoang established a royal court and a hierarchy of civil and military servants. He instated a rigorous justice system and introduced the death penalty to serve as a deterrent to all who threatened the new order in the kingdom. He organised a regular army divided into 10 *dao,* or military corps. Security and order were progressively re-established, inaugurating a new era of *thai binh* (peace).

However, Tien Hoang's reign was not to last long. He was assassinated in 979 by a palace guard, who saw "a star falling into his mouth" – a celestial omen heralding promotion. But the heir to the throne was only six years old and would not survive the mounting and pernicious intrigues of the court.

Tien Le dynasty (980–1009)

Le Hoan dethroned the throne's heir and proclaimed himself king as Le Dai Hanh. He retained the capital in Hoa Lu and succeeded

to consolidate the Viet nation. He developed the road network in order to better administer the country's regions. However, a succession of local revolts assured 24 years of difficult rule until Le Dai Hanh died. In the ensuing period, the monk Khuong Viet managed to establish Buddhism as a long-overdue stabilising pillar of the kingdom.

Ly dynasty (1009–1225)

The Ly dynasty, which reigned over the country for more than two centuries, was the first of the enduring national dynasties. Ly Cong Uan was a disciple of a monk, Van Hanh, who helped

in warding off several Chinese invasions by the Song court but continued paying them tributes every three years in exchange for friendly relations. With peace finally assured on the northern border, he sought to pacify the south. In 982, Le Dai Hanh launched a military expedition against the Champa kingdom. The conquest of this northern part of the Champa kingdom brought about a marked Cham influence on Vietnamese culture, particularly in the fields of music and dance.

Le Dai Hanh's reign marked the first attempt

LEFT: depicting the big cat (China) receiving tribute from servile mice (Vietnam). **ABOVE:** men of letters.

TEMPLE OF LITERATURE

In 1070, a national college was founded by King Ly Thai Tong to educate future mandarins based in large part on Confucian ideals. The college, known as Van Mieu and designated the Temple of Literature when the capital was transferred to Hue at the beginning of the 18th century, has been restored and still stands in Hanoi. Knowledge of the Confucian classics, as well as the mastery of literary composition and poetry, were the main requirements of the rigorous three-year course, which culminated in a very competitive diploma examination. Architecturally, Van Mieu reflects Chinese influence and contains ritual bronzes in Chinese styles.

him rise to power. Assuming the name Ly Thai To, the new sovereign inaugurated his dynasty with a change of capital. Ly Thai To had seen the apparition of an ascending dragon on the site of the future capital and so decided to name it Thang Long (Ascending Dragon), near present-day Hanoi (Ha Noi). In 1054, one of his successors, King Ly Thanh Ton, renamed the country Dai Viet.

During the Ly dynasty, Buddhism flourished as the national religion. Buddhist masters, who acted as supreme advisors, assisted the Ly

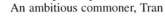

MILITARY WIZARDS

The Tran dynasty is known for its many brilliant military victories, especially a notable one against Kublai Khan's much larger Mongol armies from the north.

Tran dynasty (1225–1400)

An ambitious commoner, Tran Canh, married the Ly dynasty's last queen and shrewdly manoeuvered his way to power to found the Tran dynasty. Buddhism, which had become predominant under the Ly dynasty, continued to play an important role, but it was subsequently weakened by co-existence with Confucianism, Daoism and various other popular beliefs. The century-old competitive examination system introduced during the first period of Chinese

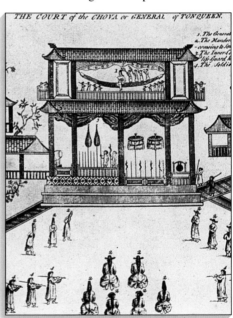

kings in their rule. Several Ly kings led Buddhist sects and founded some 150 monasteries in the region of Thang Long. The Ly dynasty consolidated the monarchy by setting up a centralised government and establishing a tax system, a judiciary system, and a professional army. Important public works, including the building of dykes and canals, were undertaken in order to develop agriculture and settle the population.

The monarchist centralisation – influenced by Confucian notions – endowed the king with three roles: absolute monarch and religious chief of the empire; mediator between the people and heaven; and father of the nation.

occupation underwent draconian revisions. An administration incorporating both the reigning king and the heir to the title of the previous reign was adopted to ensure its continuity. The country's territorial ambitions to the south continued. The king's sister married the king of Champa in 1307, thus extending territory southward with the peaceful annexation of the Hue region and at the same time inaugurated the politics of diplomatic marriage.

Ho dynasty (1400–1428)

The king's marriage to the aunt of a minister, Le Qui Ly, was to prove a fatal move for the Tran dynasty. Taking full advantage of his aunt's union, Le Qui Ly shrewdly manoeuvered his way to power. He eventually assumed control of the kingdom and founded a dynasty under his ancestral name of Ho.

During his reign, the army was reorganised and reinforced. Taxes were revised and ports opened to trading ships, which were obliged to pay duties. Under a new fiscal system, coins were taken out of circulation and replaced with bank notes. Restrictions were imposed on land ownership. The exam system for administrators was modified to demand more practical knowledge of the peasant life, mathematics, history, Confucian classics, and literature.

Vietnamese national identity – Vietnamese literature, artistic and historical works were either burned or taken to China and replaced by the Chinese classics in all the schools.

The Chinese style of dress and hair were imposed on Vietnamese women. Most local religious rites, festivals and costumes were replaced or banished by the Chinese. Moreover, private fortunes were confiscated and taken to the Chinese court.

Le dynasty (1428–1776)

The Vietnamese found a new leader in the person of Le Loi, a man renowned for his

Legal reforms were undertaken and a medical service established.

His reign prompted yet another attack from China. Well aware that Ho had usurped the throne, the Chinese Ming-dynasty emperor sent 5,000 soldiers under the pretext of helping the movement faithful to the deposed Tran dynasty. The Ming intervention led to the fall of the Ho dynasty in 1407. During the short period of Chinese occupation that followed, the Vietnamese suffered inhumane exploitation. The Chinese resolutely strove to destroy the

LEFT: Chinese influence, and the Tonkin royal court.
ABOVE: old print of traditional village in the Hue area.

courage and generosity. Under the title Prince of Pacification, he organised a resistance movement from his village and waged a guerrilla war against the enemy. By employing a strategy of surprise attacks targeting his adversary's weakest points, Le Loi managed to further weaken the enemy and at the same time avoid combat with the superior Chinese forces. His enforcement of strict military discipline ensured that no pillaging was carried out by his troops in the regions under his control, making him a very popular hero.

Le Loi founded the Le dynasty in 1428 and became king under the name of Le Thai To. He renamed the country Dai Viet and immediately began the task of its reconstruction after the devastation caused by the war. He reduced his army from 250,000 to 10,000 men and adopted a rotation system that enabled soldiers to return to the countryside to work and help boost food production. The legal system was reorganised and the penal system revised. A new college was founded to educate future administrators, with admission based entirely on merit and not on social or family status.

Le Thai To died in 1443, leaving the throne to his son, Le Thai Tong, whose sudden death not long after was followed by a decade of confusion and plots within the royal court. This

troubled period ceased when Le Thanh Tong began his 36-year reign and the country prospered as never before. He revised the fiscal system, encouraged agriculture, and placed great emphasis on customs and moral principles. A writer himself, he wrote the first volume of Vietnamese history.

Le Thanh Tong was by no means only a recorder of history, nor was the dynasty solely one of pacification. His reorganised army won an easy victory over the southern Champa army in 1471. His farmer-soldiers excelled not only on the battlefields but also in the fields by setting up militarised agricultural communities wherever they went. In this way the national territory was gradually expanded southward, until finally the Champa kingdom was completely absorbed and assimilated.

Secession wars

The increasing decadence of the Le dynasty in the late 16th century led to the country's division into two rival principalities as corrupt and useless kings succeeded Le Thanh Tong. Mac Dang Dung, a shrewd and scheming adviser at the court, seized control of the country and founded the Mac dynasty. Descendants of the Le dynasty rallied around Nguyen Kim and Trinh Kiem, looking for a way to overthrow Mac Dang Dung. After fierce battles, they succeeded in occupying the country's southern capital, and in 1543 they founded the southern court near Thanh Hoa, 120 km (75 miles) south of Hanoi. The war continued indecisively until the death of the dynasty's last king, Mac Mau Hop, in 1592.

In an effort to restore law and order to the territory controlled by the Macs, Trinh left the southern court under the temporary control of Nguyen Kim's nephew, Nguyen Hoang, and set out for the north. After pacifying the north and re-establishing the Le authority in Hanoi, Lord Trinh returned to find Nguyen Hoang well entrenched in the southern court as lord and master of all, and liking where he was.

In 1672, after repeated tentative attempts failed to remove Nguyen Hoang, Trinh finally consented to the partition of the country at the Linh River. It was not, however, until after half a century of civil war that the Trinh and Nguyen lords eventually agreed to a period of co-existence. This respite lasted for more than a century, during which time the Le emperors

TAY SON UPRISING

The Tay Son brothers – Nguyen Nhac, Nguyen Lu and Nguyen Hue – led an insurrection that was initially local in scope but became country-wide in the 1770s. Provoked by the corruption rife within the disintegrating imperial court, the uprising was a peasant insurrection that grew into a force against the leading Le lords, easily defeating them. By the mid-1780s, the brothers had gained control of much of the country. From 1788 until 1793, they each ruled part of Vietnam. But they failed to ease the fundamental land issues that brought them to power and were unseated by the future emperor Gia Long in 1793.

played no more than a passive and ceremonial role. But rebellion fermented in the country, including the Tay Son uprising *(see box on opposite page)*.

Nguyen Hue pronounced himself Emperor Quang Trung and overran the Chinese troops in a swift campaign. He then pacified the northern part of the country, from the Chinese border to Hai Van Pass in the country's centre, north of Da Nang, and devoted his energies to national rehabilitation, administrative reorganisation, and economic

NEW SCRIPT

The 17th century saw the phasing out of Chinese and *nom* scripts and the introduction of Romanised *quoc ngu*. The *quoc ngu* script remains in use today.

Behaine, Bishop of Adran. The Ming Chinese, who had fled the Qing takeover of the Chinese imperial court and settled in the Mekong Delta region, regarded Nguyen Anh as the leader who could safeguard their settlement in the newly annexed territory of Dai Viet. The Tay Son suspected the Ming were Nguyen Anh's sympathisers, and this suspicion intensified after the leading Tay Son generals, Tap Dinh and Ly Tai, fled to Nguyen Anh's camp. After suffering defeat at the hands of their former

development. Unfortunately, his promising reign was cut short by his premature death not long after, in 1792.

Nguyen dynasty (1792–1883)

Nguyen's successor, Nguyen Anh, was supported by Nguyen royalists who saw him as the legitimate heir in the south. With their backing, Nguyen Anh took up the fight against the Tay Son brothers and after Quang Trung's death extended control over the country with the aid of a French missionary, Pigneau de

LEFT: early European residences in old Saigon.
ABOVE: French officers in Da Nang, 1830s.

generals in the Mekong region, the Tay Son army exacted their revenge and massacred thousands of the Chinese settlers.

De Behaine saw an opportunity to expand the Catholic Church's influence and negotiated a promise of military aid for Nguyen Anh from the French government in exchange for territorial and commercial rights in the country. However, the French were busy with their own internal disputes and the promised aid never materialised. Undaunted, the bishop organised funds and recruited troops himself. Training in Western military techniques proved invaluable to Nguyen Anh and his army, and it probably facilitated victory in 1801 when he subdued the Tay Son and proclaimed himself emperor. A power struggle between French and Chinese factions began within the court.

Although Nguyen Anh owed his accession to power to the French, he was nevertheless very suspicious of France's designs on his country, and so under his reign the court's Chinese faction took precedence. He came to rely more on the assistance of Confucian mandarins than the Catholic missionaries in the consolidation of his empire, not the last time national pride would win.

The reunified and newly renamed Viet Nam extended from the Chinese frontier to the Ca

Mau Peninsula at the country's southernmost tip. Serious efforts were made to codify the law and develop the national administration along Confucian principles. Hue became the country's new administrative capital.

The Nguyen dynasty's absolutism was reflected in the extraordinary development of Hue as the most beautiful city of Vietnam. Elaborate palaces, mausoleums, temples and pagodas were successively built here, all in keeping with the harmony of cosmic order. The Nguyen kings also extended Vietnam's border into Laos and Cambodia, incorporating parts of these two kingdoms as new vassal states of their empire. Conversely, they closed the country to Western penetration from the seas, fearing that the opening of the kingdom and the expansion of trade links would undermine the structure of the monarchy.

Meanwhile, Prince Canh, Nguyen Anh's eldest son, accompanied de Behaine to France during his negotiations with the French government. The prince was later educated at a missionary school in Malacca and converted to Catholicism. This made Canh the first Viet prince to be educated under Western ideas and teachers. Military leaders within Nguyen Anh's army realised the superiority of modern Western military technology and so wished to utilise Canh's knowledge to rebuild the country after the war. The prince was regarded by many as the one who could modernise Dai Viet and bring it into industrialisation.

While the issue of Gia Long's successor was being discussed in the imperial court before his death, the power struggle between the French and Chinese factions resumed. Military generals, including Nguyen Thanh, the governor of Thang Long, and Le Van Duyet, the governor of Gia Dinh (Saigon), supported the French and wanted Canh as the heir. However, most of the court ministers belonged to the Chinese faction and supported Canh's younger brother, Mien Tong.

Again, it was the conservative Chinese faction that triumphed. Prince Canh reportedly died of measles at the age of 21. This prognosis was refuted by missionaries close to the court, who reported to the French mission that he had died of poisoning.

Once Mien Tong was crowned as Emperor Minh Mang, the French–Chinese divide officially ended. Most of Canh's followers were either demoted or executed. Gen. Nguyen Thanh was forcefully administered poison and Gen. Le Van Duyet's tomb was desecrated.

In the meantime, the Catholic missions had accelerated their proselytising, provoking Minh Mang into an anti-Catholic policy.

An opportunity for peace, and with it, a chance to modernise and industrialise the country, was lost. It would not be the last time. Religious rivalries, political factions and foreign intervention would embroil Vietnam in tragic war once again. ❑

LEFT: the young Prince Canh. **RIGHT:** map of Tonkin Gulf and northern Vietnam dated 1653.

By Many Names

The name Vietnam has become as synony-mous with war as Agincourt, Waterloo, Get-tysburg, Normandy and Bosnia. Yet few know the significance of the name. The country has been known as Vietnam (in the Vietnamese language, it is spelled in two words, Viet Nam) for only about 200 years. The first national name of Van Lang was given to the country by the Hung, or Lac, eth-nic group, inventors of the wet-rice cultivation tech-nique and the bronze drums still used today by the Muong minority. The Lac were followed by the Au, or Tay Au, who arrived from China. The two people integrated and formed the new kingdom of Au Lac. Then came the Viet, or Yue, an ethnic group emi-grating from the coast of China around 2,500 years ago. They came with other ethnic groups of the Bach Viet (the 100 Viet principalities of ancient China) on a long southward march towards the Indochinese peninsula, a migration from the north that would continue for more than 15 centuries.

The name Vietnam first appeared when Emperor Gia Long wanted to rename the country Nam Viet in the early 19th century. Seeking the Chinese emperor's approval of the new national name, Gia Long sent his ambassador to China. He pleaded for the reunification of the old land of An Nam and the new land of Viet Thuong, and for permission to change the ancient name of An Nam to Nam Viet.

After consulting his court, the Chinese emperor decided that the name Nam Viet would bring to mind the ancient kingdom of Nam Viet Dong, which had included the two Chinese provinces. The pro-posed name of Nam Viet might lead to misunder-standings or even conceal territorial ambitions.

The problem was solved by simply reversing the order of the two words to Viet Nam: the people *(viet)* of the South *(nam)*.

Etymologists and anthropologists have defined the origins of the Viet people by separating the components of the original Chinese character for Viet. On the left side of this ideogram is a charac-ter pronounced *tau* in Vietnamese, meaning to run. On the right is the complementary component pro-nounced *viet*, with the meaning and profile of an axe. This component carries with it the particle *qua*, which signifies a lance or javelin, the tools of a hunter. This ideographic analysis depicts the Viet as a race known since antiquity as a migratory, hunting people. The word *viet* is the Vietnamese pronunciation of a Chinese character meaning

beyond or far, and with the sense of crossing or going through. The character *nam*, meaning south, probably served to differentiate between the Viets in the north who remained in China and those who had left and headed south.

A long history of foreign invaders branded Viet-nam with different names. Marco Polo skirted the coast of Vietnam in 1292. In his writings appears the name Caugigu, which corresponds to Giao Chi Quan, Vietnam's name under the Han dynasty, from 111 BC to AD 203. This name was trans-formed to Kutchi by the Malays and later to Kotchi by the Japanese. The Portuguese in turn named it Cauchi Chine, to distinguish it from Cauchi or

Kutchi in India, also known as Cochin. This name was again summoned by French colonialists who called southern Vietnam Cochin China. These names, when written or pronounced in the occi-dental manner, evoked a far more ancient name, Cattigara, which first appeared on a map drawn by Ptolemy, the Greek mathematician and geographer.

Since the earliest antiquity, the Indochinese peninsula has played a major role in international trade relations and migrations, forming the link between India and China. This connection between the two ancient civilisations explains the name Indochina, first coined by the Danish geographer Konrad Malte-Burn (1775–1826) and still used today by some to refer to the region. ❑

THE ANTI-COLONIAL STRUGGLE

The Vietnamese fight against Western powers for over a century helped to
prop up Marxist arguments for the revolutionary struggle in Communism

Emperor Minh Mang's anti-Catholic policy gave the French a pretext to intervene in Vietnam. The old cycle of invasion-and-occupation began anew, but this time from afar. The landing of a French party in Da Nang (called Tourane by the French) in 1858 heralded the beginning of colonial occupation that would last almost a century. The French government wanted to establish a strategic and religious sphere of influence in Indochina (present-day Vietnam, Laos, and Cambodia), but their demands to install a French consulate and commercial attache in Da Nang were rejected by the Vietnamese imperial court in Hue. The French responded to the slap by occupying Da Nang.

In 1861, the French took Saigon. Six years later the entire southern part of the country, rechristened by the French as Cochin China, was annexed as a French colony. The French later extended control to the north in 1883. The central part of Vietnam, renamed by the French as Annam, and the north, or Tonkin, became French protectorates.

Of course, the Vietnamese were no happier living under French domination than they had been under the Chinese. In 1893, Emperor Ham Nghi and Phan Dinh Phung organised a royalist movement – Can Vuong – and staged an unsuccessful uprising at Ha Tinh, about midway between Hanoi and Da Nang. The Can Vuong movement survived until one of its leaders was killed by a Vietnamese traitor. Emperor Duy Tan's abortive attempt in 1916 to form a revolutionary movement resulted in his replacement as sovereign by Khai Dinh.

By the beginning of the 20th century, various nationalist resistance movements had formed. One was composed almost entirely of aristocrats, intellectuals, and young people led by radical Confucian scholars such as Phan Boi Chau, Phan Chau Trinh, and Cuong De, Prince

PRECEDING PAGES: young Emperor Duy Tan and court.
LEFT: French troops entering Hung Hoa in 1884.
RIGHT: the child-emperor of Annam, Duy Tan.

Canh's great-grandson. In an effort to break from royalist thinking, they embraced the idea of democracy. This resistance movement was greatly influenced by the Japanese victory over Russia in 1904, for it convinced the Vietnamese that Western power was no longer invincible. Phan Boi Chau and Cuong De established the

Eastward Movement in 1907 and secretly sent students to study in Japan. French authorities, discovering the scheme, negotiated with Japan to extradite all Vietnamese students, but Japanese officials helped some of them escape to China.

When the exiled Vietnamese in China witnessed the 1911 revolution led by Sun Yat-sen in China, some were convinced Vietnam was ready for the same kind of coup. They formed the Vietnam Quoc Dan Dang Party, which later became the leading revolutionary party in the struggle against the French. The revolutionaries were not yet united, however. A rift widened between the Westernised reformer Phan Chu Trinh and the nationalist Phan Boi

Chau. Phan Chu Trinh opposed appealing for foreign help to unseat the French colonialists: he believed Vietnam could regain independence through the democratic process. In 1915 he went to Paris to rally Vietnamese exiles and radical French politicians to support the Vietnamese struggle against colonial rule.

Nationalism intensified in Vietnam, especially after World War I, but tentative uprisings failed to obtain any concessions from the French. The Russian Revolution of 1917, while

ALUMNI

Vo Nguyen Giap, professor of history and the general who defeated both France and the United States after World War II, attended the same high school as Ho Chi Minh.

agent of the Communist International. He enjoyed the special privileges afforded him by his Soviet mentors and wholeheartedly espoused Stalin statesmanship.

In 1924, Ho Chi Minh was sent to China as a delegate to the Communist Party of China, where he contacted young Vietnamese revolutionaries and founded the Association of Vietnamese Youth, a group that would compete with other organisations for the liberation of the country. Some recruits were sent to Moscow for

not provoking anything similar in Vietnam at the time, nonetheless had a tremendous impact on shaping Vietnamese history, primarily because of its influence on a young revolutionary, Nguyen That Thanh, later to be known as Ho Chi Minh. (Although he changed his name much later, we shall use the more familiar Ho Chi Minh throughout.)

Ho Chi Minh, under the alias Nguyen Ai Quoc, was working with Phan Chu Trinh on an anti-colonial petition put forward at the Versailles Conference in 1919. Ho became involved with French intellectuals who formed the French Communist Party in 1920. He went to Moscow to be trained as a *kominternshik*, an

training, and others became affiliated with the Chinese Communist party. This situation fostered internal conflict within Vietnam's Communist party, between the pro-Chinese and pro-Soviet factions, for many decades.

In the same year, Emperor Khai Dinh died, and his son Bao Dai, then aged 12, ascended to the throne. Bao Dai was sent to France for his education and returned to Vietnam in 1932. The Vietnamese waited to see if the French would adopt more liberal politics, but it became clear they would make no real concessions.

In 1930, on the Comintern's instruction, Ho Chi Minh successfully rallied several communist groups and founded the

Indochinese Communist Party. For the first time in history, a revolutionary party was systematically formed with the unlimited financial and ideological support of an aspiring superpower. Also in 1930, under the leadership of Nguyen Thai Hoc, the Quoc Dan Dang, inspired by the Chinese Kuomintang, launched a military revolt. Later, communist groups following the same path of armed revolt, known as the Nghe Tinh Soviets movement, staged a series of peasant uprisings.

Unhappy with the instability, the French retaliated by taking severe measures against the fledgling movements. The apparent calm that

allowed to continue administering Vietnam. In 1945, realising that allied victory was inevitable, Japan overthrew the French, imprisoned their civil servants, and rendered Vietnam "independent" under Japanese "protection", with Bao Dai as chief of state.

The Japanese surrender later in the year was the opening that Ho Chi Minh had eagerly anticipated. Earlier, the Central Committee of the Indochinese Communist Party had met in southern China and announced the formation of the Revolutionary League for the Independence of Vietnam, which later became known as the Viet Minh. Ho Chi Minh used the Viet

reigned after the reprisals shattered with the first battles of World War II. In Asia, most coastal cities of China fell under the advancing Japanese forces, and in Vietnam, the Japanese rapidly occupied key regions in 1940.

World War II

For Vietnam, the explosion of World War II in 1939 was an event as significant as the French occupation of Da Nang in 1858. The pro-Nazi Vichy government of France accepted the Japanese occupation of Indochina, but it was

Minh as an instrument to apply his revolutionary strategy. In its creation he finally achieved "the union of diverse Vietnamese nationalist groups under communist direction", a goal that he had been working towards since announcing it as his immediate task to the Comintern in 1924.

At first, the Chinese Nationalist authorities supported the Viet Minh, but they later got wise to Ho's new political affiliation and imprisoned him and created a rival organisation. However, they soon realised that Ho's organisation was in fact needed and so released him in 1943. Moreover, they recognised Ho as the chief of the Viet Minh, and it was around this time that he adopted the name of Ho Chi Minh.

LEFT: Tonkin (north Vietnam) mandarin and escorts.
ABOVE: Hang Bo Street, Hanoi, in the late 1930s.

Around the same time, Ho's principal collaborator, Vo Nguyen Giap, set up guerrilla units in several regions of northern Vietnam and created an intelligence network. Communist cells were organised throughout the country under the supervision of Truong Chinh, the young secretary-general of the Indochinese Communist Party. These later became of inestimable value to Ho after Japan's sudden surrender in 1945. Here was the *thoi co* – the opportune moment – in which to launch the general insurrection.

Ho's resolute certainty of victory is reflected in the conclusion of one of his poems: "In

Party and the Viet Minh as intermediaries, Ho Chi Minh endeavoured to become the dominant political force by occupying as much territory as possible.

Start of revolution

The so-called August Revolution began on 16 August 1945, when the Viet Minh announced the formation of a National Committee of Liberation for Vietnam. Three days later, Ho's guerrilla forces took Hanoi. Hue's turn came four days later when Bao Dai's government was besieged and "asked" to hand over the royal seal. Bao Dai abdicated, believing that the Viet

1945, the work will be accomplished". But, of course, in 1945, the work had really just begun.

At the end of World War II, Vietnam faced a political void, as Bao Dai's government existed in name only. Apart from a handful of French civil servants and troops, whom the Japanese had imprisoned prior to France's removal, Bao Dai had no supporting troops – his own or those of outsiders – in Indochina.

Chinese Nationalist forces entered Vietnam as far as the 16th parallel, at Da Nang, to accept the Japanese surrender. The British assumed control of the south. By the middle of August, chaos and uncertainty reigned once again. Using the clandestine Indochinese Communist

THE LAST EMPEROR

Nguyen Vinh Thuy ascended the throne in 1926, taking the title Bao Dai, or Keeper of Greatness. The French kept tight reins on Bao Dai until the Japanese forced France from Vietnam in 1945. The Japanese retained Bao Dai as a figurehead, and when the Viet Minh took power in August 1945, they asked Bao Dai to resign but to link himself to the Viet Minh movement as "Citizen Prince Nguyen Vinh Thuy". Disillusioned, Bao Dai fled to Hong Kong in 1946, where he led a sybarite's life until 1949, when he returned as sovereign. Known as a playboy emperor, Bao Dai took little interest in affairs of state. He retired in 1955 and moved to France.

Minh was a national front supported by the former European allies. Ho's forces now controlled Saigon and practically all the surrounding rural areas. Ho announced the formation of a provisional government in Hanoi, and in early September he proclaimed himself president of the new Democratic Republic of Vietnam.

However, Ho found himself in a strategically vulnerable position when the allied forces arrived. He camouflaged the existence of the communist elements within the

CATALYST

After a skirmish between French and Vietnamese troops, a French cruiser shelled Hai Phong in 1946, killing nearly 6,000 Vietnamese and igniting hostilities.

only 291 members, including 37 from the opposition, turned up. When asked to explain the poor turnout, one Viet Minh minister announced that the absentees had been arrested for criminal offences. The country's first national constitution was approved by 240 votes to one.

France finally recognised the Democratic Republic of Vietnam as a free state, within the French union. However, relations rapidly deteriorated. Hostilities mounted and reached a peak with the French bombing of Hai Phong

Viet Minh and sought support from both the Chinese and the French. In an unprecedented move, the Indochinese Communist Party announced its dissolution in November, although, in reality, it continued to function.

Ho then prepared to negotiate Vietnam's future status with France. In the general elections, organised in early 1946, the Viet Minh won the majority of seats in the first National Assembly. Ho's government was approved at the assembly's first session in March, but at the second session in October,

LEFT: Vietnamese, Cambodian, and Laotians in China plot against France. **ABOVE:** Giap planning the war.

port, east of Hanoi. In December 1946, Ho ordered a general offensive against the French in Hanoi and at French garrisons in northern and central Vietnam. The decade-long war for independence had begun.

War of resistance

The war for national independence that began after the Japanese occupation constitutes a confused period of contemporary Vietnamese history. Thousands of Vietnamese took up arms against the French, yet few knew the identity and allegiance of their new leader and his party. The population did not entirely understand the historical events happening in their country, nor could they imagine the consequences that were to follow. At face value, Ho Chi Minh's new party appeared to consist of nationalists fighting for the common cause of national independence against the known enemy. And indeed, today, as the country increasingly adopts what it calls a market-oriented economy and dumps some of its communist system, the wars of resistance are stressed to have been fought by nationalists.

On Ho's orders, Vo Nguyen Giap launched a general offensive against the French forces,

HO'S IMPORTANCE

Amongst all the 20th-century revolutionaries, Ho Chi Minh's importance is that he waged the longest – and most devastating – battle against Western powers.

aggressor nation that had threatened Vietnam's independence, was now an ally and supplied the young republic with military equipment, substantial provisions, and further aid to develop the Viet Minh army.

On his side, Ho attempted to increase his government's base of nationalist support. At the beginning of 1951, he merged the Viet Minh with the Lien Viet, or Patriotic Front, into a new league for the National Union of Vietnam, and he announced the formation of the Workers Party

but in the face of superior fire power, Ho's troops were forced to retreat to the countryside. They adopted Mao Zedong's guerrilla strategy of a "people's war and people's army" by attacking and sabotaging isolated French units, rather than becoming embroiled in large-scale battles. It was a tactic reminiscent of Le Loi's against Chinese forces in the 15th century and one that would be used against the Americans.

The emergence of Communist China towards the end of 1949 favoured the communist-dominated struggle. After Ho's guerrillas had wiped out several French posts on the Chinese border, China and Vietnam established direct contact for the first time. China, the old

(Lao Dong), a disguise for the Communist Party that officially had disbanded but in reality was still active. The nationalists and non-communists were forced to choose between the new regime or the French colonialists. Giap's forces progressively extended their territory.

By the spring of 1953, several divisions were training in Laos and had joined forces with the pro-communist Pathet Lao.

In May of 1954, the French base at Dien Bien Phu *(see Northern Vietnam chapter, page 195)* suffered a humiliating defeat after a heavy artillery attack from Giap's forces, who used bicycles to carry supplies. The French forces in northern Vietnam evacuated to below the

16th parallel, at Da Nang. The war officially ended on 20 July, after long negotiations in Geneva. In finally gaining full national independence, Vietnam lost its unity. The Geneva Agreement signed in August divided the country at the 17th parallel, pending general elections scheduled for the middle of 1956.

The northern part of the country became the Democratic Republic of Vietnam – North Vietnam – under the leadership of the Lao Dong party; the southern part became the Republic of South Vietnam.

The last French troops left Vietnam and Indochina in April 1956. Bao Dai made a last

appeal on behalf of the royalists. He asked Ngo Dinh Diem to become prime minister of what would become South Vietnam. Diem was a curious choice, a Catholic in a predominately Buddhist country who had been away from Vietnam for two decades and returning in the midst of a nationalist uprising.

In fraudulent elections, Bao Dai was deposed by Diem, marking the end of the Nguyen dynasty and the beginning of the Republic of South Vietnam. But rather than stability, things

LEFT: Gen. Giap's Vietnamese forces take Dien Bien Phu from the French army. **ABOVE:** Ho Chi Minh in the field during the early 1950s.

THE LEGACIES OF WAR

Of course, Vietnam is a country and not a war. For the past quarter century the country has sought to move beyond the decades of conflict that defined its history and outlook. And while the war against first the French and then the Americans is history, its importance is considerable as a turning point not only in Vietnam's history but in those of the world's superpowers, especially the United States.

Militarily, the Vietnam War solidly redefined the nature of war, especially in regards to conflict between a technologically endowed army and a low-technology adversary. The guerrilla war of the Viet Cong, drawing from history (Vietnamese resistance against occupying China in the 15th century and American resistance against the British in the 18th century), redefined the nature and history of warfare.

From 1965 onwards, the United States not only brought more than half a million troops to Vietnam, but it undertook an immense construction program that built deep-water ports, air bases, roads, bridges, and pipelines. Helicopters not only introduced a new type of warfare but they tripled the survival rate (on the American side) of the wounded over World War II. By the end of the war, there were 4 to 5 support personnel for every American soldier in combat.

On the North Vietnamese side, a resilience based on a village-centred agricultural system and minimal industrial strength (North Vietnam produced just 20 percent of the electrical power of a single American generating plant) permitted it to carry on a war despite concentrated bombing and a technologically superior opponent. The United States brought in supplies via deep-water ports and 3,000-metre-long (10,000-ft) airfields while the North Vietnamese used the so-called Ho Chi Minh Trail through Laos and Cambodia. Supplies brought south along the dirt-road route took from three to six months via vehicle, bicycle, and foot. In 1968, non-food require-ments of all communist forces in South Vietnam totalled 120 tons daily, just five times the amount required by a single division of American troops.

The end of the war in 1975 brought peace and reunification to Vietnam. In the United States, it redefined politics, military strategy and theory, and social agendas. America became more introspective.

The aggregate cost of the war is estimated at US$200 billion. Around 900,000 North Vietnamese and Viet Cong troops were killed; South Vietnamese Army deaths were 200,000, and 50,000 Americans were killed. It is estimated that more than 1,000,000 Vietnamese civilians died on both sides.

would only get worse, setting the stage for Vietnam's next conflict.

The North-South divide

The elections stipulated by the Geneva Agreement never occurred. From 1954 to 1974, the two Vietnams had no diplomatic, cultural, or commercial relations with each other. Immediately after the Geneva Agreement, a virtual state of war existed between the two divided parts of the country. North Vietnam's intensified armed and revolutionary activities made the prospect of reunification through free elections increasingly unlikely.

himself on a street corner in Saigon (now called Ho Chi Minh). As his image blazed across the world's television screens and newspapers, the flames that consumed him were burned into the consciousness of Vietnamese, Americans, and the international community.

This signaled the beginning of the end for Diem's regime. Diem and his brother were murdered five months later in Saigon's Cho Lon district by Diem's own officers following a coup d'état, which was supported by the American government.

The following years witnessed a succession of coups d'état. Several generals and civilians

Meanwhile, the United States had reinforced Diem's troops, in effect turning South Vietnam into an American military protectorate.

In December 1960, the National Liberation Front of South Vietnam (NLF) was formed and began launching revolutionary activities against the unstable regime in the south. This southern communist movement, christened the Viet Cong, grew stronger in the early 1960s.

Facing mounting pressures, Diem ordered repressive measures against the Buddhist establishment. This move provoked a wave of suicides by Buddhist monks, who set fire to themselves in protest. In June 1963, Thich Quang Duc, a 66-year-old monk, immolated

took turns presiding over the unstable and corrupt Saigon regime.

The beginning of 1965 marked the escalation of direct American involvement in Vietnam, when US President Lyndon Johnson decided to send large numbers of troops to Vietnam. By the end of 1967, there were more than 500,000 American and 100,000 allied troops (mostly coming from Korea, Australia, and New Zealand) in Vietnam.

What many consider the war's turning point came in 1968, when the Viet Cong launched surprise attacks on Saigon and other cities throughout the south during the Lunar New Year, Tet. This Tet Offensive included a raid on the American embassy in Saigon that stunned and embarrassed the United States, who began to see the war as futile. Domestic opposition in the United States increasingly took on political and social legitimacy. Eventually, Johnson announced he would not run for re-election.

His successor, Richard Nixon, had promised a secret plan to end the war during the election campaign, but this turned out to be nothing more than turning the bulk of fighting over to the South Vietnamese.

In 1969, Ho Chi Minh died without seeing his work completed, and peace negotiations dragged on in Paris between 1968 and 1973.

On 30 April 1975, the northern army entered Saigon as the last American troops and diplomats fled by helicopter from the American embassy. The Communist Party's long struggle for power under the banner of national liberation and reunification finally ended in their complete victory.

Vietnam was now independent of foreign troops and control, and it could set its sights on unification. But there would not be peace, nor freedom from foreign influence, for years to come. Vietnam became militarily involved by occupying neighbouring Cambodia and in military battles with China itself. ❑

The 1973 Paris Peace Agreement aimed to put an end to hostilities. The Americans pulled out their troops, but the two warring Vietnamese sides lost no time in violating the agreement. In 1975, as the Communist forces steadily moved south and the Saigon regime finally crumbled, the US Congress refused to offer additional military aid, in effect ending South Vietnam's ability to continue the war. The North's leadership launched its final offensive against South Vietnam.

LEFT: North Vietnamese MiG-17 in American sights in 1967; US pilot captured by North Vietnamese militia.
ABOVE: communists enter Presidential Palace, 1975.

AGREEMENT AND PRIZES

Two episodes encouraged serious peace talks: the US had found détente with both Moscow and Beijing, and North Vietnam had failed in a spring 1972 offensive. Secret 1972 talks in Paris between US Secretary of State Henry Kissinger and North Vietnam's Le Duc Tho (who later oversaw the offensive that took Saigon in 1975 and Cambodia in 1978) led to a ceasefire, the release of prisoners, the withdrawal of US forces, and political negotiations amongst the Vietnamese. The war continued, however, even after the Americans left in May 1973. Both Kissinger and Le Duc Tho received the 1973 Nobel Prize for Peace, which Le Duc Tho declined.

Đại tướng Võ Nguyên Giáp chụp ảnh lưu niệm với chiến sỹ Điện Biên

LIMPING INTO A NEW CENTURY

The atmosphere in Vietnam today is one of a country trying to move ahead on one foot, the other shackled by rusty chains of government bureaucracy

A bright future seemed to stretch before socialist Vietnam after 1975, with the communist leadership making great plans for the rehabilitation of the country and the long years of war finally at an end. But a series of strategic blunders made – and later admitted – by the Hanoi leaders shattered all hope for a new era in Vietnam's history.

The party leadership, under the pressure of the northern conservative factions, dissolved the Revolutionary Provisional Government of South Vietnam and the National Liberation Front of South Vietnam.

In July 1976, Vietnam was officially reunified, thus breaking the fragile dual balance between the two parts of the country. A radical programme of socialist construction was put forward at the Communist Party congress. It called for the rapid socialisation of the southern economy, with the forced collectivisation of agriculture, small industry and commerce. This rapidly led to an unprecedented economic disaster, provoking new waves of refugees trying to flee the country. Further sapping the nation's resources was the internment of the south's intellectual and governmental leaders, along with other highly skilled and educated people, in so-called re-education camps.

Just a couple of years after the reunification of Vietnam, the country found itself in open conflict with neighbouring Cambodia (then known as Kampuchea) and on a collision course with China – once again – less than two years later.

In 1978, Vietnam signed a friendship treaty – in fact, a security pact – with the Soviet Union at the same time as its relations with China went into decline. Once again, Vietnam was entangled in the bloc politics of the communist powers and their proxies. The invasion of Cambodia by Vietnamese troops at the end of

1978 and the subsequent so-called "Chinese lesson" *(see box below)* were to augur a new cycle of war that was to absorb most of Vietnam's post-war energies and delay its long-overdue recovery.

Vietnam's all-out alliance with the Soviet Union did nothing, in the long run, to help

VIETNAM'S OWN AGGRESSION

In the late 1970s, as relations with China deteriorated, Vietnam sought to set up a close alliance with new – and Marxist – governments in Laos and Cambodia, then called Kampuchea. But the Khmer Rouge government in Cambodia turned Vietnam down, and in no time there were fierce fire-fights between Cambodia and Vietnam along their common border. Vietnam invaded Cambodia in December 1978 with 200,000 troops, removing the Khmer Rouge government. For a month in early 1979, Chinese troops crossed into northern Vietnam, inflicting heavy damage. Because of their invasion of Cambodia, Vietnam was internationally ostracised until 1989.

LEFT: a war veteran of the 1954 Dien Bien Phu battle, which ended France's presence in Vietnam.
RIGHT: the residue of war peppers the countryside in both the north and south.

boost Vietnam's position internationally. And for the next decade, the presence of Vietnamese troops in Cambodia remained a central issue in the international arena, around which a coalition of nations – China, the United States, and the members of ASEAN (Association of South East Asian Nations) – managed to enrol international support to isolate Vietnam.

Meanwhile, the Khmer resistance rendered Vietnam's control over Cambodia into a no-win dilemma. A coalition government in Cambodia, established in 1982 with Prince Norodom Sihanouk as president and with Khmer Rouge participation, received growing

Economic shifts and *doi moi*

New economic policies introduced earlier in 1979 had managed to bring some respite on the domestic front without improving the chronic weaknesses of Vietnam's economy. The 1980s, however, saw the domestic economy worsen. People were starving, and there wasn't enough rice to go around. Meat was rationed, and people stood in line for monthly and weekly allotments of food. It was only in 1986, following the Soviet example of *glasnost* and *perestroika,* that the party decided to launch the country on an ambitious programme of socio-economic renovation called *doi moi.*

support from the international community. The coalition occupied Cambodia's seat at the United Nations while at the same time Vietnam lost most of its hard-earned international sympathy from the wars with France and the United States.

The Cambodian war was a costly stalemate. At the Fifth Party Congress in 1982, the old guard, under the guidance of party secretary general Le Duan, obstinately maintained Vietnam's course, hoping that, against all odds, it could consolidate its political and military edge in Cambodia and at the same time stabilise Vietnam's own internal economic and social situation.

Under the new leadership of Nguyen Van Linh, the motto of the party was then "to change or to die". A new contract-system was implemented in 1988 to encourage Viet-namese farmers to cultivate their land, and as a result rice production witnessed an immediate upsurge in 1989. Progress was also recorded in the sector of manufactured goods and commodities exports.

Until the end of 1988, socialist Vietnam followed the path of Soviet *perestroika*, but the Vietnamese leaders were soon to discover the bold and unchartered nature of Soviet leader Mikhail Gorbachev's "new thinking" and its social and political consequences. A surge of domestic turmoil in China and the collapse of communism in Europe in the late 1980s was a severe shock for Vietnam's leaders, who feared the impact of these events upon their regime. While reaffirming the Communist Party's commitment to reform, Nguyen Van Linh repeatedly rejected any idea of political pluralism for Vietnam.

STUNNING NEWS

The Tiananmen Square massacre in China and the collapse of the Warsaw Pact in Europe in the late 1980s no doubt stunned Hanoi's communist leaders.

Withdrawal of Vietnamese troops from Cambodia in September 1989 cleared the way for the political settlement of the Cambodian conflict. The peace process was

socialism in the Soviet Union and Eastern Europe contributed to the worsening economic crisis in Vietnam, as former members of the now-defunct Soviet bloc, besieged with domestic crises, were no longer in any position to continue their economic help to Vietnam and other client states such as Cuba. It was in this uncertain context that, in mid-1990, Vietnam adopted a new course in foreign affairs. Vietnam's top leaders secretly visited China in order to mend fences with Beijing. With Vietnamese forces

a difficult one involving the efforts of all the parties directly and indirectly involved: the former Soviet Union, China, ASEAN countries, the United States, Japan, France, and Australia. In September 1990, a UN plan was finally endorsed calling for the setting up of a Supreme National Council, a ceasefire, and the cessation of foreign military assistance to the Khmer factions under a UN-control mechanism contingent upon the organisation of free general elections in Cambodia.

Meanwhile, the continuing demise of

withdrawn from Cambodia, it seemed that the three-decade-old American embargo against Vietnam would finally be lifted. However, political pressure from the US Senate hinged the end of the embargo on the full accounting of all missing American servicemen from the Vietnam War.

The foreigners return

Meanwhile, European and Asian companies flooded into Vietnam seeking investment opportunities in what many proclaimed as the last economic frontier. Hanoi and Ho Chi Minh (the former Saigon) became boom towns – hotels were renovated and new ones built,

LEFT: contemporary soldiers in their reading room.
ABOVE: patriotism in the old quarter of Hanoi.

international airline service increased, and telecoms and other infrastructures upgraded.

In late 1992, Americans working on the search for US servicemen listed as missing in action from the war were convinced that Vietnamese authorities were cooperating sufficiently in the search. American businesses lobbied the administration of US President George Bush to lift the trade embargo. The United States then permitted American companies to open representative offices in Vietnam.

> ### LEADERSHIP WISH
>
> The challenge for Vietnam's leadership over the past decade has been to retain its firm grip on power at the same time as the country develops economically.

economy and opening the door to foreigners; some who want to limit foreign investment to Asian countries; and some who want to slow down reform, fearing the party is losing control. The country's leaders are ageing, yet there are no clear indications that anybody is ready – or being groomed – to replace them. For now, the leadership appears to have little to fear in the way of political or social opposition. This is primarily because the country's economy has been steadily moving up, and people throughout the

In 1993, the new American administration of Bill Clinton allowed the release of International Monetary Fund loans to Hanoi. Foreign investment in Vietnam increased. In early 1994, the United States lifted its trade embargo, and in the following year Clinton restored diplomatic ties and an embassy was opened in Hanoi. In 1995, Vietnam became a full member of ASEAN, putting behind it the international ostracism of the 1980s.

Elusive consensus

Within the government and the Communist Party today there are divisions of thinking: some who want to continue liberalising the

country feel as if their lives are improving, however gradually. The country's growth increased at a pace of about 8 percent a year throughout much of the 1990s. Income levels are still low – the average per capita income is about US$250 a year – yet there are pockets of wealth developing in the urban centres. And because costs for basic needs – food, housing, and schooling – are still relatively low, people in the cities have begun to enjoy a better lifestyle. Inflation, which had been spiralling out of control in the 1980s, is now at about 20

ABOVE: disco scene in hip Ho Chi Minh.

RIGHT: foreign businessmen on the slow road in Hanoi.

percent a year – still high, but not crippling. Vietnam is now one of the world's largest exporters of rice, and the country is pinning hopes of future economic revival on a fledgling offshore oil-and-gas industry, though the oil glut that greeted the 21st century pushed oil development to the background.

This is not to say there aren't problems. Much of the country – particularly rural areas – is still mired in poverty.

Nearly 80 percent of the population lives outside the urban areas, and many live without running water or electricity; private telephones are uncommon. While Ho Chi Minh City and Hanoi appear to be humming with modern motorcycles and cars, in fact, a bicycle is still a luxury for most rural people.

Ahead is a widening gap between rich and poor as a wealthy class emerges. People from the countryside are flooding the cities looking for jobs; they find few places to live and little support from the government. As Vietnam begins to adopt a market economy, the socialist safety net is unravelling, meaning the elderly, veterans, and the uneducated are losing some benefits to which they have grown accustomed.

State agencies and state-owned companies – notoriously bloated and inefficient – are having

DOI MOI DUD

In the early 1990s, opportunities and possibilities for a "new" Vietnam seemed unlimited as the government declared a stance of *doi moi*, ostensibly intended to reinvigorate and move the country's economy forward. Unfortunately, by the end of the 1990s the programme was a big, resounding dud.

The inability of the government to allow market forces to define the economy, along with an institutionalised and pernicious corruption, led many foreign companies – European, North American, and Asian – to abandon the country as the 21st century began. In 1998 alone, 19 foreign banks closed their doors in Vietnam, ostensibly because of the region's economic woes. In 1998, more than 120 foreign companies – excluding banks and law firms – left Vietnam, up from 70 in 1997. While the professed excuse for the foreigners' exit was the region's economy, it was well known and acknowledged that corruption, diaphanous "special" fees, opaque regulations, and high operating costs (telephone fees are among the world's highest) led many foreign businesses, large and small, to simply give up and leave. The trend will probably accelerate unless Vietnamese authorities are more willing to let parts of the country's economy and society operate beyond the leaders' and Communist Party's control.

to cull their workforces to compete in the market economy, adding to an increasing problem of unemployment. The population, too, is young – more than two-thirds of Vietnamese are under the age of 30. Many college graduates are unable to find jobs.

The government still controls the press, as well, and there are no free elections. Any criticism of the party or government is forbidden, and political dissidents are still thrown in jail. Still, newspapers in Vietnam have nonetheless become livelier, writing about crime, government corruption, police scandals, and social issues like prostitution, drug abuse,

Aids, labour unrest, and health care. Yet stories are strictly censored, especially if they touch on the government or its leaders.

Corruption is rampant in business – foreigners and Vietnamese alike complain they are nickel-and-dimed to death, with bureaucrats at all levels demanding "tokens" in order to get paperwork completed, licences approved, offices opened. In fact, by the end of the 1990s many Western companies had become so fed up with the corruption and constantly changing regulations that they abandoned operations in the country and went home.

However, Vietnam, finally free of the military conflicts that for so long impoverished the people, has adopted a convoluted course of economic reform that may now be so far along that its leaders cannot control it, as much as they promulgate Byzantine regulations and restrictions that are changed yet again almost immediately. The infusion of foreign capital over the past decade has nurtured something of a consumer society, where young people, especially, have become materialistic.

New century uncertainties

Vietnam still feels threatened from the north. In the late 1990s, it pushed Laos, its neighbour, to improve air strips as possible emergency bases for the Vietnamese air force should China and Vietnam once again clash. At the same time, Vietnam sweetened its relationship with Moscow. In exchange for a 50-percent interest in a new oil refinery, Russia wrote off Vietnam's $15 billion decades-old debt.

In 1999, daring dissent came from within the Communist Party's ranks. Retired Gen. Tran Do, a Party member, called for political reform – considered a blatant criticism of government policies – to ensure economic development in Vietnam. The general was expelled from the Party. Shortly afterwards, a second general, Pham Hong Son, criticised the Communist Party and the government, scolding party and government officials who live luxurious, opulent lives in one of the world's poorest nations. In 2000, social pressures led to open unrest in the Central Highlands. Poverty and corruption remain endemic, and Vietnam's future remains uncertain. ❑

SIGNIFICANT ISLES

A possible flashpoint of conflict in Southeast Asia is the Spratly Islands – coral reefs, really – peppering the South China Sea midway between Vietnam and the Philippines. Barely breaking the ocean's surface, the largest of the Spratly's 12 main isles is Itu Aba at 36 hectares (90 acres). Spratly Island itself is but 275 metres (900 ft) by 450 metres (1,500 ft) in size. France held the islands until World War II, when Japan used them as a submarine base. Since then, China, Taiwan, the Philippines, Malaysia, and Vietnam have all claimed these islands by stationing small garrisons on one or more islet, all of which sit atop a potentially rich oil field.

LEFT: foreign companies are increasingly wary.
RIGHT: mausoleum of Ho Chi Minh in Hanoi.

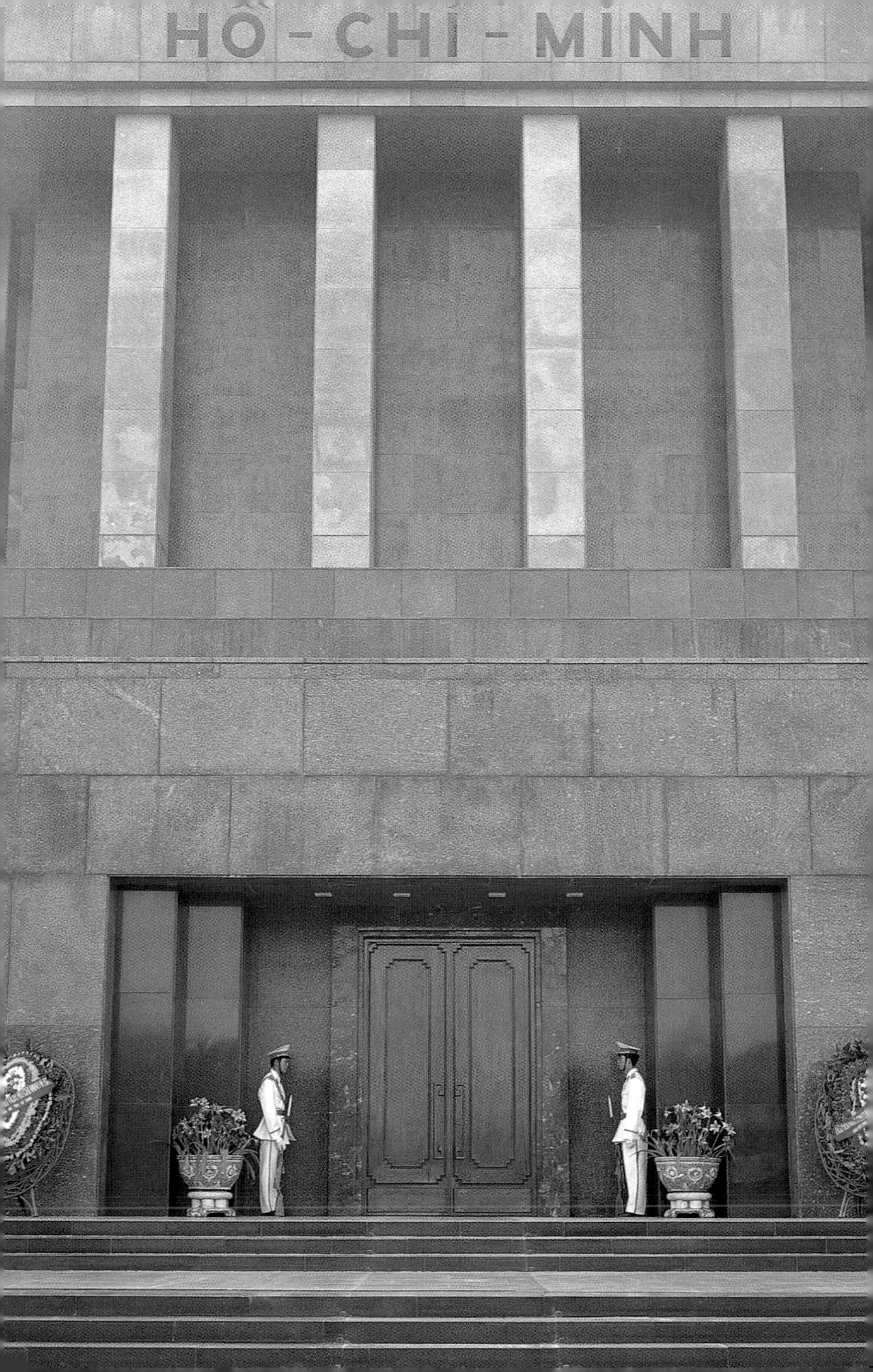
HỒ - CHÍ - MINH

THE LAND AND ITS NATURE

While its contours and coast rival that of Thailand, Vietnam's bewitchments also

include exceedingly rare fauna, a challenging climate, and universally dismal roads

Shaped like an immense and elongated letter S, Vietnam stretches the length of the Indochinese peninsula, bordering the Bien Dong, or the South China Sea, to the east. Its 3,730-km (2,320-mile) frontier shares a 1,150-km (715-mile) border with China in the north, and to the west, a border of 1,650 km (1,000 miles) with Laos and 930 km (600 miles) with Cambodia. Mountains and forests make up more than three-quarters of Vietnam's total land area. With an area of 327,500 sq. km (126,500 sq. miles), Vietnam's territory also encompasses a vast sea area, including a large continental shelf and a string of thousands of islands stretching from Vinh Bac Bo, or the Tonkin Gulf, to the Gulf of Thailand. These include the disputed Spratly (Truong Sa) and Paracel (Hoang Sa) islands, which China and other Southeast Asian nations also claim, mostly because of rich oil reserves deep underground. The isles themselves are hardly islands *(see box on page 54).*

As the crow flies, Vietnam stretches 1,650 km (1,000 miles) from Mong Cai in the north to Ha Tien in the south. At its widest point in the north, Vietnam is just 600 km (370 miles) across; at its narrowest part, in the centre, it is 50 km (30 miles) wide. The 2,500-km (1,500-mile) coastline is dotted with beautiful beaches.

On the same latitude as Bombay, Hawaii, and Mexico City, Vietnam is a land endowed with great physical beauty and diversity. The fertile imaginations of some geographers have likened the country, with its three regions – Bac Bo (north), Trung Bo (centre) and Nam Bo (south) – to a set of scales, the north and south constituting two balancing baskets of rice supplied by rich deltas of the north's Song Hong (Red River) and the south's Mekong.

Chains of mountains and profoundly carved valleys separate Vietnam from China to the north, geography that has not impeded China's

numerous invasions of Vietnamese territory. The country's highest summit, Fan Si Pan, rises to 3,160 metres (10,370 ft) over the Hoang Lien Son mountain range, in the province of Lao Cai near the Chinese border.

The plains of Cao Bang, Lang Son, and Vinh Yen and the valleys watered by the Lo, Chay,

Cau, Luc, Nam, and Cung rivers occupy the northern part of the country, extending over the immense delta of the Song Hong, or Red River, home to 90 percent of northern Vietnam's population. The Song Hong flows from its source in the Yunnan region of China across the north of Vietnam and then southeast to its coastal mouth near Hai Phong.

Central Vietnam forms a long convex curve, within which are small plains wedged between the South China Sea and the high plateaus of the Truong Son mountains. This terrain is characterised by dunes and lagoons in the east towards the coast and terraces of ancient alluvial deposits towards the mountains. The lime-

---

PRECEDING PAGES: boat crossing the Mekong; the pass at Hai Van, central Vietnam. **LEFT:** Ha Long Bay. **RIGHT:** extracting coal near Ha Long Bay.

stone peaks of Pu Sam Sao stretch along the border with Laos. The Central Highlands between Da Nang and Da Lat are rich in volcanic basalt soil and constitute one of Vietnam's most important forest areas, in addition to tea- and coffee-growing regions.

The Mekong River, known as Cuu Long Giang, or the River of Nine Dragons, is one of the longest rivers in Asia at 4,180 km (2,600 miles). The Mekong flows from its source in the mountains of Tibet across China, through Burma (Myanmar) into Laos and northern Thailand, and then across Cambodia before flowing through southern Vietnam into the

the Equator, gives rise to a complex and humid climate that varies from region to region. The average temperature of 22°C (72°F) varies slightly from one season to another, but like anywhere, it is prone to sudden changes. A persistent dampness tends to make the temperature feel cooler.

Northern Vietnam's climate is influenced by the winds of central Asia, which gives rise to a climate similar to that of China. Generally, two distinct seasons prevail in Vietnam. From November to April, the northern part of Vietnam experiences a relatively cold and humid winter. This is precipitated by invading polar

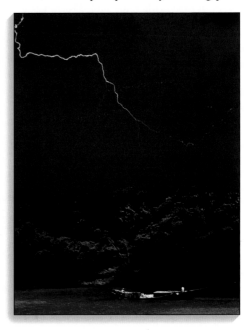

South China Sea. Over many centuries, the Mekong's deposits collected on a shallow, undersea shelf forming an immense, low-lying alluvial plain – the Mekong Delta – which now extends over 75,000 sq. km (29,000 sq. miles). These alluvial deposits do not accumulate on the natural delta but rather at the mouth of the Mekong and around the Ca Mau Peninsula in Vietnam's extreme south, where the deposits contribute to enlarging Vietnam by dozens of square metres annually.

Climate

Vietnam's location in the Southeast Asian monsoon zone, between the Tropic of Cancer and

SOUTHEAST ASIA'S RIVER

More than 810,000 sq. km (310,000 sq. miles) of Southeast Asia are drained by the Mekong River. Geographers divide the river into two parts: the upper Mekong in China and the lower Mekong, beginning at the border of Burma and Laos before reaching the ocean nearly 2,400 km (1,500 miles) later. Among Asian rivers, only the Chang Jiang (Yangze) in China and the Ganges in India have larger flows. The management and development of the river's lower extents is under the auspices of the Committee for Coordination of Investigations of the Lower Mekong Basin, which consists of Laos, Cambodia, Thailand, and Vietnam.

air currents that sweep into Vietnam from Siberia and China, often bringing temperatures down to 0°C (32°F) in the mountainous regions lying north and east of Hanoi, and with a fine, chilly drizzle throughout most of the winter months. Summer, from May to October, is characterised by higher temperatures and heavy rain, and often typhoons.

The northern and central regions of the country experience their hottest months during June, July, and August.

The climate varies from north to south in the

WOODY LIMITS

Rainforests are few in Vietnam, and forests of a single species of tree are rare, limited mostly to pine trees found in the highlands and coastal mangrove forests.

rainy season from May to October. There is a relatively dry season from November to February and a dry season from February to April before the rains.

The south experiences its hottest months from March to May, when temperatures may reach 35°C (95°F).

The rains, affected by the monsoon winds arriving across the ocean and the geographical position and relief of the various regions, are often abundant. Between May and December, the warm and humid summer monsoon brings

central part of the country. The area near the northern provinces has a climate that is almost identical to that of the Red River Delta, whereas towards the south the central provinces have more in common climatically with the Mekong Delta area. In Hue, in the centre of the country, the cold season lasts from November to March, with almost continual drizzle falling for periods of up to a week.

Southern Vietnam's climate is characterised by a relatively constant temperature, sudden changes during the monsoon, and a punctual

higher temperatures, a humidity of between 80 and 100 percent, and heavy rain to most of the country. During this season, violent typhoons often ravage the southern coastline between Nha Trang and Ca Mau, causing considerable damage. High plateau regions are usually much cooler than the coastal areas, with a marked drop in nightly temperatures year-round.

Flora and fauna

The country's topographical diversity is matched only by the diverse species of flora and fauna in its mountains, forests, plains, and plateaus. In prehistoric times, much of Vietnam was covered by dense forest. Tropical forests

LEFT: monsoon flooding on the Mekong; lightning near Hue. **ABOVE:** water buffalo are essential.

still cover around 40 percent of the country and contain more than 700 identified plant species, constituting a rich source of oils, resins, some precious woods, timber, and medicinal plants. Over several centuries, exploitation of the environment has greatly reduced Vietnam's forested regions, which have virtually been halved since 1945 alone.

War, chemical defoliation during the Vietnam War, and an ever-increasing population growth have greatly accelerated this deforestation. Precious hardwoods are being felled in massive quantities for export. However, this wholesale depletion of forest could cost the

country far more as flooding and erosion take their environmental toll, much as happened in the 1980s in Thailand with devastating effects.

Despite efforts to reverse this alarming trend, the government's reforestation programme, which replants some 1,600 sq. km (620 sq. miles) annually, is not enough to cover the annual forest losses of 2,000 sq. km (770 sq. miles).

Vietnam's wildlife is, in general, identical to that of Bengal and the Malaysian peninsula. It includes species extinct in other parts of Asia amongst its 273 species of mammals, 180 species of reptiles, 273 species of birds, and hundreds of species of fish and invertebrates. Among these are elephant, wild buffalo, rhinoceros, antelope, tapir, monkey, wild boar, tortoise, crocodiles, and hornbills. In the 1990s, a previously unknown species of mammal was found in Vietnam: an antelope living in Nghe An Province, near Laos. Moreover, the horns of a bovine thought to be extinct were found near the Cambodian border, in Dak Lak Province.

Environment

The country's development is putting new pressures on an already fragile environment. A growing population – now estimated to be approaching 80 million – means that there are more demands on Vietnam's land.

Since the 1980s, the government has wrestled with how much rice-growing land to convert into industrial use. The forests continue to be threatened by the slash-and-burn farming techniques of the highlands regions often practised by hill tribes, which in turn creates more erosion and flooding.

Much of the country was sprayed with chemical defoliants – such as Agent Orange – during the years of the American involvement in the war in an attempt to deprive the Viet Cong of ground protection and cover. The resulting contamination to the food chain was devastating. In the 20 years since the end of the war, however, the contamination of land has continued as farmers have doused their crops with noxious chemicals. Along with rural decline, the cities are overcrowded also, with garbage piling up and water sources polluted by industrialisation, and with factories dirtying the air. ❑

LOST WORLD DISCOVERIES

Despite war and industrialisation, Vietnam harbours some unique sanctuaries. In 1992, biologists studying the Vu Quang rainforest along the Laos border northwest of Vinh uncovered the skull of a previously unknown species of antelope, *Pseudoryx nghetinhensis*, which looks more like an onyx and is called *saola* in Vietnamese. In 1994, two live specimens of the 100-kg (220-lb) animal were captured. Since then, other previously unknown species of animals have been discovered in the remote rainforest, including the giant muntjac, a deer-like animal with large canine teeth. The government has expanded the area protected by the reserve and halted logging.

LEFT: drying sea horses for use as medicine.
RIGHT: chartering a boat among Ha Long's islands.

THE VIETNAMESE

Settled at the crossroads between China to the north and Southeast Asia,
Vietnam's population reflects an eclectic swirl of races awash in many cultures

Although 90 percent of Vietnam's population lists its ethnicity as *kinh* – the commonly accepted term for the indigenous race – in reality most Vietnamese have evolved from a mixture of races and ethnicities over thousands of years.

That mixture is quite naturally the result of repeated invasions from outside Vietnam, particularly from China, along with continual migrations within Vietnam, most commonly from north to south. So in Vietnam today there are the predominant kinh but also dozens of distinct minority groups, including the Cham and Khmer of the south, two groups whose own kingdoms were long ago vanquished by invading Vietnamese armies from the north.

Minority groups have been among the last to share in the prosperity under Vietnam's recent economic renovation – with one exception. Ethnic Chinese, who as recently as the late 1970s were ostracised if not run out of the country because of tensions arising during a brief northern border clash with China, have not only benefited from Vietnam's recent economic progress but, in many ways, have fuelled an economic revival, particularly in Ho Chi Minh, Vietnam's entrepreneurial centre.

Other minority groups have not been so fortunate. Usually living in remote, undeveloped, mountainous regions with little fertile ground for agriculture, their existence is worlds removed from the hustle of Vietnam's urban centres.

Viet origins

Studies of folk songs from the hill regions of northern Vietnam, and from the coastal area in the northern part of central Vietnam, affirm that the Vietnamese originated in the north's delta of the Song Hong (Red River). These agricultural, fishing, and hunting people were probably animistic. Their dress, although unique in Indochina, is also found in certain Pacific island

cultures. The scenes – mostly of nautical, dance and war themes – depicted on ancient bronze drums reveal a notable similarity to the mystical traditions of the Dayaks of Borneo and the Batak of Sumatra. In fact, artefacts of five races have been uncovered in Vietnam: the Melanesians, Indonesians, Negritos, Australoids, and

Mongoloids. The most predominant of these were the Indonesians and Mongoloids.

Throughout monsoon Asia, which includes northern Vietnam, a shared culture existed from a very early era as evidenced by its tools, vocabulary, and certain essential rites and traditions such as the blackening of teeth, water festivals, bronze drums, kites, tattooing, betel nut and cajeput, pole houses, cockfighting, and mulberry cultivation.

The times of the prehistoric Vietnam are retained in the collective memory of the Vietnamese people through numerous tales, legends, and popular songs that recount at length the traditions, customs, and manners of this people,

---

PRECEDING PAGES: students at flight attendant school.
LEFT: young violin student in Hanoi.
RIGHT: theatre performers in traditional costume.

The concept of tourism is new to Vietnam. Even before reaching the country, you may encounter attitudes in official representatives at embassies and consulates that will try your patience. However, firmness, perseverance, and diplomacy will achieve a great deal more than losing your cool. Indeed, patience is a necessity in this long-suffering country.

If misunderstandings arise and things do not seem to be going the way you anticipated, or if you don't feel you're getting what you paid for, raising your voice, shouting, and loudly criticising the offending party will only result in loss of face all round and make matters worse. If you have a complaint to make, do so in a manner that will not be taken as threatening or insulting.

On the whole, the Vietnamese are very friendly, polite, hospitable, and helpful. Like anywhere else in the world, these attributes take a back seat during rush-hour traffic and in the battle for space on overcrowded public transport – situations that bring out the worst in everyone.

Very direct questions about one's age, family status, and income are quite natural topics of conversation and not considered rude or personal. Vietnamese who have not had much exposure to foreign visitors are often very shy but curious, and those who speak English or French enjoy an opportunity to converse with foreigners and make friends. Be sensitive to anyone who may appear ill at ease or not wish to be seen talking to a foreigner, as locals have been arrested for less and the past is hard to shake off. (Secret police do exist here.)

A gentle handshake is usual when meeting, but public demonstrations of close affection are not quite accepted. People in the north are generally more reserved and have had less exposure to Westerners than those in the south.

As anywhere, tips are much appreciated, but bear in mind that whatever you do sets a precedence for those who follow. The average wage is very low. A small donation is much appreciated when you visit a temple or pagoda – there is always a little contribution box for this. It is a matter of courtesy to ask before taking someone's photograph, and to ask permission to take photographs in religious buildings, although permission is usually granted. Proper and modest dress is expected when you visit religious places.

In the south, particularly, you will be approached by beggars. If you give anything, do so discreetly; otherwise, you will be plagued by a very persistent and ever-increasing following. It is very difficult to ignore these people, whether their plight is genuine or not, but in the long run it does not help to foster an attitude whereby foreigners are seen as a soft touch and preyed upon.

including the making of large and elaborately ornamented bronze kettle drums, which have been discovered as far south as Bali *(see photograph on page 26).*

Continuing studies on the origins of the Vietnamese people show that the people who settled on the Indochinese peninsula and its bordering regions most likely came from southern and eastern China, the high plateaus of Central Asia, islands in the South Pacific, and perhaps other parts of the world. Thus, Vietnam can be considered a proverbial melting pot into which major Asiatic and Oceanic migrations converged.

Ancient migrations

It is most likely that the first inhabitants of Vietnam originated from several ethnic groups. The most important of these were the Hung, or Lac, specialists in wet-rice cultivation and inventors of the bronze drums, and who inhabited the Song Hong Delta and central regions of Vietnam, and the Muong, who came from the high, wooded plateaus and mountainous regions.

Two major Viet emigrations from the coastal and southern provinces of the Chinese empire added to this population. The first occurred during the 5th century BC at the fall of the Viet kingdom of the low Yangze valley, and the second during the 3rd century BC, when the Au, or Au Tay, from Quangxi invaded the northern part of Vietnam.

They progressively established themselves in the coastal regions, gradually making their way inland via rivers until they eventually reached the high regions, which were inhabited by the native Lac people in the delta and the Muong at Hoa Binh and Thanh Hoa, just south of present-day Hanoi.

The Vietnamese population's southward expansion from northern Vietnam brought an important native Malayo-Indonesian element to the fair-skinned contingent from the valleys into central Vietnam in 982, reaching Hue in 1306, Quang Ngai in 1402, Binh Dinh in 1470, Phu Yen in 1611, Ba Ria in 1623, Nha Trang in 1653, Bien Hoa in 1658, Saigon in 1674, Phan Rang in 1693, Phan Thiet in 1697, and finally Ha Tien in the southernmost province of the Mekong Delta in 1714.

In this southward expansion, they overran the kingdoms of Champa and part of Cambodia. By 1714, the Viet empire extended from the Chinese frontier to the Gulf of Thailand.

Several thousands of years ago, the Viet tribes moved from China in the southern (*nam*) direction towards the Song Hong (Red River)

of the Yangze when they merged with the first native occupants of the Red River Delta around the third century BC to found the Kingdom of Au Lac.

The numerous centuries of intermingling between these races has produced the Vietnamese people of today.

In their search for vital living space, this vigorous, tenacious, and courageous people crossed the mountain ranges of central Indochina and more than 3,000 km (1,800 miles) in their move to the south. They crossed

LEFT: the universal piano lesson.
ABOVE: relaxing in the cool of the evening.

CONTRADICTION

The country's standard of living ranks amongst the lowest in the world. Despite a protracted effort to revive the rural economy, disastrous economic polices coupled with the drain of more than 50 percent of the country's budget on its occupation forces in Cambodia for so many years have had devastating effects on Vietnam's economy. In an effort to revive the ailing economy, the country has opened its doors to encourage foreign investment and tourism, but the effort has been shackled by bureaucratic bungles, corruption, and suspicions. Still, one will find the average Vietnamese open to new ideas and entrepreneurial zest.

Delta. They settled in a beautiful land surrounded by high mountains, deep waters, thick forests, and narrow plains. Inspired by the wonders of nature, the Viet soon realised that only with blood, sweat, tears, and sharp eyes could they preserve their newly acquired *dat* (earth) and *nuoc* (water).

To succeed, for centuries the Vietnamese have had to be conscious of the forces around them – the seen and the unseen, the favourable and the hostile – and to understand their nature and intentions and to resist them if necessary and co-exist with them if possible but never to provoke their anger.

namese culture, are actually borrowed from the Chinese, who colonised Vietnam 2,000 years ago. Among the colonialists were the usual tyrants and exploiters, but, along with these, there were compassionate administrators and dedicated teachers who brought with them religions, philosophies, organisational skills, and especially their written characters, the *chu han*.

This influence from the Chinese created the possibility of losing a Viet identity and independence but also the opportunity of assimilating and adapting the best of Chinese civilisation and culture. (In some ways, it is a process that continues today, as the proud

To make sense of this immense web of influences and the matrix of powers ruling existence, the Vietnamese have looked to what is in heaven, on earth, and amongst the people themselves. To penetrate the mysteries of heaven, to understand the workings and movements of the earth, and to establish relationships with other people, Vietnamese traditionally have sought to know the way in which things emerge, exist, progress, disappear, and re-emerge. They seek the religions. In Vietnamese, they are *ton giao*, the highest and most elevated knowledge, or *dao giao*, the knowledge of the Way, or simply, Dao.

These words and concepts, like much in Viet-

BRIBES TO MAKE ENDS MEET

Low wages in government and the civil service account for a nagging problem of corruption, as bureaucrats at all levels look to supplement their meagre incomes. Bankers, for example, often charge people extra if they want larger-denomination *dong* notes when withdrawing money. Doctors sometimes insist on separate payments to treat patients or insist that patients buy medicine from them. Teachers routinely extract bribes from students in exchange for good grades. At government ministries, licences and permissions often require a "special payment". The government criticises these practices and has prosecuted high-profile cases, but they persist.

Vietnamese now open the doors to foreigners, attempting to learn the best from other cultures and societies while maintaining their hard-fought independence.)

The early attempts at making the best of Chinese domination were honed within the village, the *cha* (later called *xa*) that is the foundation of Vietnamese life. The village's economic and commercial activities, in which all inhabitants participate, are concentrated on growing food, especially rice, which requires constant observation of nature, the

CHAM PRESERVATION

Today, the Cham people preserve their customs, language, and script with a religion that is a modified form of Hinduism.

identified ethnic groups.) Vietnam's one million Chinese constitute another important minority group. Only about 3,000 have kept their Chinese nationality, however, while the rest, referred to in Vietnam as *hoa*, have adopted Vietnamese nationality.

On the whole, whether naturalised or not, many Chinese remain loyal to the costumes and traditions of their country of origin. Mostly shopkeepers and traders, they settled in Ho Chi Minh City's Cho Lon district, which has long flourished as the Chinese

precise coordination of cultivation, and a bonding communal effort.

The Chinese

The Viet, or Kinh, form the majority of Vietnam's people, representing about 90 percent of the population. Numerous ethnic minorities inhabit the mountainous regions that cover almost two-thirds of Vietnam. (At the end of the 20th century, a small tribe of fewer than 100 members was found in a northern province, a tribe distinct from previously

community's primary commercial centre in southern Vietnam.

Hill-tribe minorities

The ethnic minorities living in the mountainous regions in central and southern Vietnam form another important group. Called Montagnards by the French, these tribes include the Muong, Ra De, Jarai, Banhar, and Sedang living in the high plateaus of the west. Totalling around 700,000 people, they have always opposed foreign influence and only recently have begun to integrate more into the national life.

The Cham and Khmer number around

LEFT: Amerasians are offspring of American fathers and Vietnamese mothers. **ABOVE:** Cho Lon food stall.

400,000. The Chams inhabit the Phan Rang and Phan Thiet regions in southern Vietnam, east of Ho Chi Minh City, while Khmer are found in the Mekong Delta. Chams once possessed a brilliant culture that lasted for several centuries. Its vestiges can still be seen in Nha Trang's Po Nagar ruins and the shrines and monasteries at Dong Duong, and also in the temples, towers, and large-scale irrigation systems found in central Vietnam. Most of the architectural and sculptural traces relate to their religious beliefs, linked with

> **ANCESTRAL WORSHIP**
>
> An ancestral altar has the central position in a Giai home. Each vase of incense represents a divinity such as the sky, the earth, the ancestors, or the god of the home.

Lang Son, Bac Thai, Quang Ninh, Ha Giang, and Tuyen Quang, and in the Dien Bien Phu region. Their villages, or *ban,* are located in valleys near flowing water, where they build their traditional houses, usually on stilts. They cultivate rice, soybeans, cinnamon, tea, tobacco, cotton, indigo, fruit trees, and bamboo on the mountainsides above the village. The influence of Viet culture is evident in their dialect and customs, which distinguish them from the other Tay-Tai speaking groups.

ancient legend and polytheist in nature. Its prevailing image was that of a woman regarded as the mother of the country who gave birth to the dynastic rulers. Large blocks of vertical-standing stones symbolising the God of the Earth represented another Cham cult. Later, Hinduism and Indian culture would influence the Chams, as can be seen in *lingga* images; Mahayana Buddhism, too, also became an important influence.

The highlands and midland regions of northern Vietnam are home to many ethnic minorities and diverse tribes, including the Tay, who number just under a million and are found in village groups in the provinces of Cao Bang,

The Nung, in many aspects similar to the Tay, share the same language, culture, and customs, often living together in the same villages where they are referred to as Tay Nung. Numbering about 340,000, they live in Cao Bang and Lang Son provinces.

There are about 76,000 Tai living along the Song Hong, in the northwest of Vietnam, often together with other ethnic minorities. Their bamboo or wooden stilt houses are constructed in two distinct styles. The Black Tai build homes shaped like tortoise shells, while the White Tai construct rectangular dwellings. The women wear long, black sarongs and short tops with silver buttons. They are very skilled weavers and produce beautiful embroidery using motifs of flowers, birds, animals, and dragons.

The San Chi, numbering more than 77,000, live in village groups mainly in Ha Giang, Tuyen Quang, and Bac Thai provinces, but they are also found in certain regions of Lao Cai, Yen Bai, Vinh Phu, Ha Bac, and Quang Ninh provinces. They are of the Tay-Tai language group and arrived from China at the beginning of the 19th century. San Chi ritual dances reflect the life of the community. Groups of boys and young girls perform traditional love songs in festivities that can last all night.

The Giai, also of the Tay-Tai language group, number about 30,000 and emigrated from China about 200 years ago. Their villages are often built very close to those of the Tay, Nung, and Tai. The Giai believe the universe has three levels, with humans in the middle between the highest level of heaven and the lowest level, a vile place inhabited by sinners. The Giai have numerous proverbs and maxims that constitute a kind of moral code.

The Lao number about 7,000 and belong to the Tay-Tai language group. They are actually

LEFT: glances from Black Tai girls in north Vietnam.
ABOVE: Muong woman's attire.

NAMES: LAST COMES FIRST

There are only approximately 140 Vietnamese family names in use today. The most common are Nguyen, Pham, Phan, Tran, and Le. Children take the father's family name, though people with the same family name need not have the same origin. In fact, most Vietnamese surnames are the same as one of the 16 imperial families, or dynasties, that have ruled in Vietnam: Thuc, Trung, Trieu, Mai, Khuc, Ly, Phung, Kieu, Ngo, Dinh, Le, Tran, Ho, Mac, Trinh, and Nguyen (listed in chronological order). While a person today with one of these family names may be a descendent, the name was probably acquired otherwise: a voluntary change of name to show loyalty to the current monarch; an imposed name change when a new dynasty rose to power, especially if the old family name was the same as the former – and now disgraced – royal family; or as a reward or honour bestowed upon a person or family by the reigning ruler.

Only around 30 of the 140 or so family names used in Vietnam are actually of Vietnamese origin. For the most part, family names are of Chinese (Khong, Luu, Truong, Lu, Lam), Cambodian (Thach, Kim, Danh, Son), or ethnic minority origins (Linh, Giap, Ma, Deo).

Vietnamese names follow the structure of family name-middle name-given name. Most of the time, Vietnamese address each other by their given names.

Traditionally, the most common middle names are Van (meaning an educated person or scholar) for men and Thi (meaning a woman) for women. Some language experts suggest that these middle names derive from Malay influences, in which traditionally *van* means "son of" and *thi,* "daughter of". In recent times, however, Vietnamese have taken more meaningful middle names. A middle name may also indicate the order of a child within the family (Ba for first son of first wife, Manh for the first son of second wife, Trong for a second son, etc.) or the children of a particular brother (Thuc indicates a son of a younger brother).

Today, most given names are chosen for their meaning, often derived from objects or themes of nature such as geographical features (rivers, mountains), flora, fauna, precious gems, or the seasons. Sometimes children within the same family will have given names from the same category, for example, the seasons or flowers. Contrary to Western traditions, the Vietnamese usually will avoid the given names of ancestors or relatives out of respect.

Another tradition that runs contrary to Western ways is the order of learning a stranger's name. Nicknames or given names are usually learned first; only when trust is established is the family name shared with another.

closer to the Tai minority than their Laotian namesakes across the border. They are found along the Vietnam-Laos border in the Song Ma district of Son La Province and around Dien Bien Phu and Phong Tho in Lai Chau Province. Their homes are built on stilts in the form of a tortoise shell, like those of the Black Tai. Their traditional costume also resembles that of the Tai, and their elaborate rice-growing techniques are similar to those of the Tai. They are also skilled craftspeople, particularly in ceramics, weaving, and embroidery.

The Lu also belong to the Tay-Tai language group. They number around 3,000 and are found in the Phong Tho and Sin Ho districts of Lai Chau Province in well-arranged villages of 40 to 60 dwellings. They arrived from China and occupied the Dien Bien Phu area as part of the Bach Y migrations in the first century AD. The Lu's famous Tam Van Citadel, dedicated to Buddha, was noted by the Black Tai on their arrival in the 11th and 12th centuries.

The Hmong, who number more than 400,000, are found in villages known as *giao* throughout the highlands of 11 provinces: Cao Bang, Lang Son, Bac Thai, Ha Giang, Tuyen Quang, Lao Cai, Yen Bai, Son La, Lai Chau, Hoa Binh, and Thanh Hoa. Due to their wars

ROLL CALL

Over 2,000 years ago, imperial edicts in Vietnam required that local administrators establish family registries in which they recorded all names, marriages, births, and deaths within a family. Known as *gia pha* (family history), such registries have their origin in ancient China and are found elsewhere in Asia, including Japan. The oldest recovered *gia pha* in Vietnam is dated AD 1026. Family registries are more common in the northern and central parts of the country. Vietnamese names typically follow the structure of family name, middle name, and given name last *(see box on previous page)*. Vietnamese usually call one another by their given names.

with the feudal Chinese in the north, Hmong emigrated to Vietnam from the southern Chinese kingdom of Bach Viet at the end of the 18th and beginning of the 19th century. Once in Vietnam, they settled in northwestern provinces. Maize is their main staple, but rice is often grown on terraces watered with the aid of an irrigation system. Hemp is grown as the main textile material, and cotton is also cultivated in some villages. Poppy and Job's tears are among the plants cultivated for medicinal purposes. Fruit such as plums, peaches, and apples produced by the Hmong is highly valued throughout the country, although transportation problems make selling the produce difficult. They collect gentian, cardamom, honey, fungi, bamboo, and many medicinal herbs from the forests, which constitute an important source of income.

As skilled artisans, the Hmong produce a variety of items, including handwoven indigo-dyed cloth, paper, silver jewellery, leather goods, baskets, baby carriers, kitchen utensils, and embroidery. Many of these are increasingly sold to tourists.

The Hmong have no written language. Their legends, songs, folklore, and proverbs have been passed down from one generation to the next through the spoken word. They have

to women. Catholic missionaries attempted to convert the Hmong at the beginning of the 20th century, and although some churches were built at Sa Pa and Nghia Lo, the evangelical efforts didn't succeed.

The Dao first arrived from China in the 18th century. Part of the Hmong-Dao language group, the Dao number about 35,000 and are found in the mid- and lower-regions of Thanh Hoa Province, living in large villages or small isolated hamlets, cultivating rice using the slash-and-burn method. The Dao are very skilled artisans. They make their own paper, used primarily for writing family genealogies,

developed a varied culture, rich in popular knowledge concerning the nature of society – extolling liberty, justice, charity, the work ethic, and virtue, and condemning laziness, meanness, hypocrisy, and lying.

Totemism – the veneration of symbolic objects – is still evident in Hmong culture in which spirit worship, animist rites, and even exorcism are still practised. Buddhism, Dao-ism, and Confucianism have left their mark on some Hmong societies, introducing beliefs in reincarnation and the idea that men are superior

LEFT: Hmong at a village's sacrificial pledge to central government, 1960s. **ABOVE:** Dao and Meo women.

official documents, and religious books. For centuries, the Dao have used Chinese characters to record their genealogies, rhymes, folk tales, humourous tales, fables, and popular songs. The women plant cotton, which they weave then dye with indigo. Their embroidery is worked directly onto the cloth from memory, the traditional designs fixed in their minds.

Central Highlands

The Jarai, or Gia Rai, are located in the provinces of Gia Lai, Kon Tum, and Dak Lak, and in the north of Phu Khanh. They belong to the Malay-Polynesian language group and arrived in the Tay Nguyen highlands from the coast a little less than 2,000 years ago. They live a sedentary lifestyle in villages known as *ploi*, or sometimes *bon*. Jarai villages, with at least 50 homes, are built around a central *nga rong*, a communal house.

The community is composed of small matriarchal families, with each family an economically independent unit within the village. A council of elders, with a chief, directs village matters. The chief is responsible for all the village's communal activities.

Jarai cultivate fruit trees, rice, beans, and other cereals and raise buffalo, goats, chickens, and pigs, primarily to offer as sacrifices to their

various gods and spirits. Oxen, horses, and elephants are raised as working animals, and horses are also used to hunt wild boar.

Young girls take the incentive in choosing a marriage partner, making their approach through an intermediary. The promise of marriage is sealed with the exchange of bronze bracelets, with the ceremony proceeding in three steps. First, the bracelet-exchanging rite is performed in front of the two families and the intermediary. Then the young couple's nightly dreams are interpreted, a ritual that predicts their future prospects. Finally, the actually wedding ceremony is held at the home of the man's parents.

Jarai funerals are extremely complex affairs with endless rites, particularly in connection with the careful construction of the burial house. Carved wooden sculptures representing men, women, and birds are placed inside it. Jarai believe the deceased is transformed into a spirit and joins ancestors in another world.

The Ra De, or E De, found mainly in Dak Lak Province, number more than 140,000. Like the Jarai, they belong to the Malay-Polynesian language group. They live in wooden longhouses, built on stilts, in villages known as *buon,* with as few as 20 and as many as 70 dwellings. Each longhouse shelters a large matriarchal family under the authority of a *koa sang,* the most senior and respected woman. She directs community affairs, settles internal conflicts, and is also responsible for the safekeeping of all the communal heirlooms, bronze gongs, ancient jars used for preparing rice beer, a large seat carved from a single tree trunk reserved for the *khoa sang*, and special stools reserved for hosts and musicians. The village's autonomous organisation is run by the *po pin ea,* the chief who is elected to take care of communal affairs.

The Ra De employ the slash-and-burn techniques to clear the land for agriculture. Rice, the main crop, is cultivated along with sugar cane, melons, cotton, and tobacco.

Nearly every village has its own forge to produce and repair metal farming implements. Basketry, somewhat rudimentary pottery, and indigo cloth are produced by the Ra De for their own use. ❑

CHINESE ROOTS

Much as English has substantial linguistic roots in Latin, so too does Vietnamese have a solid foundation in the ancient Chinese language, called in Vietnamese *tieng Han* or *chu nho.* (This would not be unexpected, given the Vietnamese origins in southern China and the centuries of Chinese-Vietnamese connection.) Ideas can often be expressed two ways in contemporary Vietnamese: one might use the more high-brow or "learned" Han words or else the regular or ordinary Vietnamese. Context determines the usage; informal conversation would use the plain form, while a scholarly essay would ascend to the Han.

LEFT: 19th-century Meo tribeswomen.
RIGHT: court mandarin in his imperial finery.

RELIGION

*Predominantly Buddhist, Vietnam's spiritual foundations are rich and deep,
also embracing Confucianism, Daoism, animism, and Catholicism*

Foremost in the Vietnamese religious hierarchy – regardless of the dogmatic undergirding – is a heaven above, which the Vietnamese (who have a tendency to humanise everything, in order to better deal with it) called *Ong Troi*, the honourable Heaven with a masculine cast. They approach him with food offerings, requests, complaints, and prayers. In principle, Ong Troi is the keeper of human fate and in charge of all the unseen powers and vague mysteries of the universe.

Together, the gods of the earth, water, and mountains define and transform the geomantic structures and rules that determine – in the same way that the Chinese use *feng shui* – the orientation of houses, businesses, cities, graves, and temples and configure the good and bad luck of families, communities, and nations.

Between heaven and earth, but never separate from them, is the human being, both male and female, the dead and the living, the ancestors and the descendants.

Each of the realms – heaven, earth, and human – has its own rules, regulations, modes of transformations, elements of good, bad, ugly, and beautiful, and above all, its own deities. These deities are everywhere – in stones, trees, lakes, and animals – and they are praised, fed, housed, and revered with ritual offerings and appropriate behaviour. The richness and variety of these worlds and their manifestations has preoccupied, confused, and even dazzled the traditional Vietnamese, often leaving them little sense of space or privacy to eat, sleep and make love – the basic human needs.

This perception results from the Vietnamese sense of awe for the visible and invisible forces of nature, their observation and interpretation of these forces, and the ways and means they have found to compromise and co-exist with them, or resist them. Above all, the belief is grounded in their intimate relationship with the land on

which they live, procreate, and bury their dead, in their deep faith in the continuity of the Viet nation, and in their sacred mission to defend and build their land and water *(dat* and *nuoc)*. The secret wish of all Vietnamese is to attain *nhan* – a word borrowed from the Chinese meaning "contemplating the moon through a

SACRED PLACES

In addition to the traditional pagodas *(chua)* and communal houses *(dinh)* found in common villages, there are smaller places of worship where both the benevolent and malevolent divinities and spirits are worshipped. These temples include the *den*, which is typically used to commemorate a deified emperor who offered particular help or safety to the village, or perhaps to a national hero; the *mieu*, which is usually situated on an elevated piece of land and is reserved for the cult of both benevolent and malevolent gods and spirits; and finally the *ban*, where all divinities of nature and life not worshipped elsewhere are worshipped.

PRECEDING PAGES: monk at Giac Vien Pagoda, Ho Chi Minh City. **LEFT:** Buddha image. **RIGHT:** small roadside shrine with incense sticks.

window" – laughing off the glory and the burden of the day and instead immersing one's self in the serenity of a moonlit night.

When the Chinese imposed their rule on Vietnam, they brought along their agricultural know-how and their books on religion, philosophy, and other ideas, written in one of the most complicated scripts of all time. While today a roman script is used, having replaced the adopted Chinese script, the Vietnamese once loved these Chinese characters, which visually and stylistically

HINDU BELIEFS

Hinduism was brought to Vietnam by Indian merchants about 1,000 years ago. The Champa empire in central Vietnam worshipped Shiva, later converting to Islam.

generations, including Hinduism and Islam brought from India, and Christianity imported from Europe and America.

As in other societies, religion and politics have never been far removed from one another in Vietnamese society. Under Communist rule, the religious faithful have sometimes faced persecution, and churches and pagodas were shuttered. In recent years, however, the government has loosened its restrictions and there has been a resurgence of religious interest within the coun-

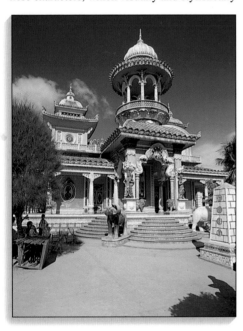

represented the meaning and feeling attached to each word.

Although the Vietnamese fought against Chinese political domination and economic exploitation, they selectively screened and assimilated what they considered the best of Chinese culture.

The Chinese teachers, some of whom were administrators, were usually accompanied by Confucian scholars, Buddhist masters, Daoist wanderers and even I-Ching diviners. The Vietnamese absorbed much of what they had to offer, melding them into their lives. All of these religious influences persist in Vietnam today, as do the religions introduced in later

try. Pagodas are crowded with the faithful and curious on holidays and on important dates of the lunar calendar; schools for training Buddhist monks have been allowed to open; and Catholic churches are filled.

Yet, there are still signs of restraint. An example is the government preference of particular Buddhist organisations or sects over others. For example, some Buddhist monks are loyal to a rival sect that existed in South Vietnam before the end of the Vietnam War in 1975, but which was then outlawed by the Communists when they installed their own state church. Some monks and lay people associated with that particular outlawed sect were arrested and imprisoned, not for religious reasons, authorities say, but because they ostensibly tried to organise anti-government movements under the guise of helping flood victims. There is little evidence that today the outlawed Buddhist organisation has much of a following in Vietnam.

Any government restraints are low-key. Like the emperor Minh Mang's anti-Catholic policies and South Vietnam's President Ngo Dinh Diem's jailing of Buddhists in earlier years, any crackdowns today on dissident Buddhists would only call attention to them and turn them into symbols of repression.

teacher. Confucius was more of a moral and ethical guide than a spiritual leader. He refused to discuss life after death, as well as the unseen or the mystical, and he was primarily interested in a social order based upon compassion, etiquette, loyalty, knowledge, and trust.

Confucianism reached Vietnam through the Chinese over 2,000 years ago. It became the official doctrine of the imperial government examinations, the first of which was held in 1706 and the last in 1919.

The Vietnamese monarchy recruited its high officials according to the results of these competitive examinations, which were in theory

Confucianism

As an ideology, Confucianism has endured longer than any other belief system, in both the East and West, and its influence, sometimes as just a remnant, has crossed many national borders into all parts of the world. It is based on the teachings of Confucius, born around 550 BC and who lived at a time of great political turmoil. As a teacher and unsolicited adviser to kings, he compiled rules and ideas to define the relationships between ruler and subject, parents and children, husband and wife, student and

open to anyone except actors and women. Many, however, learned Confucianism at home from their parents. The examinations, which also required knowledge of Buddhism, Daoism, and Tan Giao, were extremely competitive. From 1075 to 1919 – more than 800 years – just slightly over 2,000 doctorate degrees were granted.

Those who earned their degrees received a hat and tunic from the emperor and were welcomed home as wise scholars with great pomp and ceremony by the entire population. Those who failed the examinations went quietly home to their villages and earned their redemption, and living, as teachers. In this

LEFT: Tay An Pagoda, Chau Doc; Khmer monk in the south. **ABOVE:** retreat near Hue; Hoi An temple.

way, villagers were indirectly introduced to the teachings of Confucianism.

For over 2,000 years, Confucianism has remained a pillar of the Vietnamese moral and spiritual establishment. By the time Vietnam regained its independence from China, it possessed a large number of Vietnamese scholars with almost a millennium of institutional Confucian studies behind them. Officially and pragmatically, the Vietnamese imperial dynasties adopted Confucianism because of its ability to sustain a system of social order, but without much repression, and for its code of social mobility based on merit.

Buddhism

Vietnamese Buddhism is a fascinating blend of several branches of Buddhism. Introduced across the sea from India and overland from China, Buddhism extended the question of knowledge from the social order and rules of Confucianism to the general human condition. In this Buddhism, existence is unhappiness; unhappiness is caused by selfish cravings. Unhappiness ends when the selfish cravings – which can be destroyed – end. Attaining this last of the truths could be done by following the steps of the so-called eight-fold path: right understanding, right purpose (aspiration), right

CAO DAI DIVINITY

The Cao Dai sect began when an obscure Vietnamese official in the French colonial government received a message from a "superior spirit" – Cao Dai, meaning High Terrace or Supreme Being – in the early 1920s. Cao Daism attempts to bring all faiths, including Buddhism, Daoism, Confucianism, Islam, and Christianity, under one supreme deity. Many figures are revered by the Cao Dai sect, extending to a diverse collection such as Sun Yat-sen, Napoleon Bonaparte, and Winston Churchill. Appealing primarily to peasants, Cao Daism gained political influence following World War II. Estimates are that there are several million members of the sect.

speech, right conduct, right vocation, right effort, right alertness, and right concentration. "Right" means conforming to the Four Noble Truths. Central to Buddhism is the concept of Brahman, the Absolute origin, the equivalent of the Chinese *taiqi (tai chi)*.

Vietnamese have embraced Buddhism for more than 2,000 years; today, it is the predominant spiritual belief in Vietnam. To Vietnamese Buddhists, Brahman represents the unknown and unknowable, the source and embodiment of reality, knowledge, and bliss.

More than 1,000 years ago, a Vietnamese Buddhist master was sent to the Japanese court to teach Buddhist music. From the 2nd century

AD to the 10th century, two popular sects – the A-Ham (Agama) and the Thien (Dhyana in Sanskrit and Zen in Japanese) – competed peacefully for Vietnamese followers and believers. Gradually, Thien prevailed, despite its exacting practice that requires continual training in self-discipline and in mastering the focused "techniques" of breathing, meditation, and right concentration.

Thien is one of the many sects of Mahayana Buddhism widely observed in China, Japan, Korea, and Vietnam. Less dogmatic than others, it is receptive to the diverse cultural and social conditions of different countries and of differ-

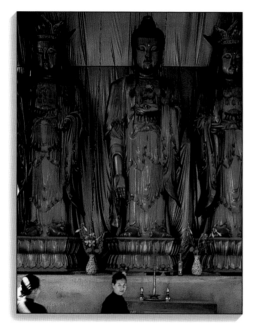

ent eras. The other branch of Buddhism, the Hinayana or Theravada (found in Sri Lanka, Burma, Thailand, Laos, Cambodia, and parts of southern Vietnam), is more orthodox yet co-exists with Mahayana.

In practically every Vietnamese village, from north to south, one finds a *chua* (pagoda) and a *dinh* (communal house). The villagers worship Buddha in the chua, which is cared for by resident monks. On the first and 15th days of the lunar months, villagers visit the chua, bringing flowers, joss sticks, and fruit for the Buddha.

LEFT: Cao Dai temple in Tay Ninh, southern Vietnam.
ABOVE: images in a Buddhist temple.

TET NEW YEAR

Tet Nguyen Dan (Festival of the First Morning of the Year) is Vietnam's most important festival and is the beginning of the lunar year. Embodied in Tet is the whole spectrum of Vietnamese mythology and of one's place within family, with one's ancestors, and with the universe. It is a mixture of Buddhism, Daoism, and Confucianism.

Tet rites begin a week before the lunar New Year. This is the time for the gods to return to the Kingdom of Heaven and present their annual report on the state of earthly matters to the Jade Emperor before returning to earth on New Year's Eve. During the gods' week-long journey to Heaven, the Vietnamese guard themselves against bad spirits. In the countryside, they erect a *cay neu* (signal tree), a high bamboo pole with a sonorous clay tablet with a piece of yellow cloth attached to the top, in front of the home.

With malevolent spirits now deflected, the Vietnamese prepare the *banh chung,* or glutinous rice cakes stuffed with pork, fat, beans, and dried onion. Another indispensable feature, even for the poorest families, is a tree branch of peach blossom, the *cahn dao.* During Tet, branches of peach blossom can cost more than a day's average wages. In southern and central Vietnam, the peach blossom is replaced by *canh mai,* a branch of yellow apricot blossom.

For maximum security against any possible intrusion by demons and bad spirits, the Vietnamese traditionally lit firecrackers to thwart the notorious devils Na A and his terrible wife, who cannot bear noise and light. However, firecrackers had turned the cities and countryside into a battle zone; in 1995, firecrackers were outlawed. Ingenious Vietnamese turned to tape recordings of firecracker noise.

After all these precautions have been taken, the Vietnamese calmly await the arrival of spring. The first day of Tet is for the worship of ancestors, who are ceremoniously welcomed back from heaven on New Year's Eve during the Giao Thua, the transition between the old and new year.

Elaborately prepared food offerings, together with the perfume of burning sandalwood, incense, and *thai tien,* a type of fragrant white narcissus that blooms during Tet, await the ancestors at the altar. At midnight on the last day of the old year, all human problems, war, political intrigue, and commercial transactions are left behind. A temporary general truce is declared between human beings and spirits.

All events – whether favourable or unfavourable – that take place on the first day of Tet are believed to affect the course of one's life for the year ahead.

They also attend services at the pagoda on the evenings of the 14th and 30th days of the month to repent for wrongs committed and vow to act in the right, proper way. Buddhist practices at the village level are not exactly those of Zen, which requires guidance by a well-trained master, but rather are a mixture of Zen and Amitabha, commonly called Pure Land and a devotional faith. It is believed that Amitabha achieved Buddhahood on the express condition that he receive all who sincerely call upon his name at

THE BODHISATTVA

The compassionate *bodhisattva* *(bo tat)*, who postpones entrance to Nirvana through loving concern for the salvation of others, is at the heart of Amitabha Buddhism.

good deeds will ensure a happy and joyful present life and a safe delivery to the land of absolute bliss, the Pure Land, after death.

Daoism

Dao Te Ching, the *Book of the Way and its Power,* begins: "The Dao that can be told is not the eternal Dao".

Dao is the highest and most active level of an otherwise static consciousness, the general law of the motion of the universe and of all things. It is both energy and matter, and the moment when the

death and so carry them to the Western Paradise, where they may seek the ultimate perfection (Nirvana) under happier auspices than found on earth.

The practice of Amitabha Buddhism consists essentially of concentrating the mind through a self-absorption and chanting the name of Buddha. Those who practise Pure Land Buddhism must abstain from killing, stealing, banditry, lying, adultery, wrong speech and intoxicants. Its adherents are expected to recite the name of Amitabha Buddha, the Amitabha Sutra, and perform good deeds to gain merit for self and family. They believe that merits accumulated through

contradictory forces of *yin* and *yang* fuse in temporary harmony to provide people and things with a sense of direction. In Chinese writing, it is represented by a character meaning 'way' or 'path'.

An important book of reference for Daoists and Buddhists alike is the *I Ching,* or *The Book of Changes,* which uses symbols – simplified and stylised in signs and codes – to integrate a number of separate systems into a seemingly "mysterious" whole. It contains 64 triangles and hexagons arranged in broken and unbroken lines that, along with its basic text, represent "the process of vast and never-ending cosmic change. These endless chains of actions and interaction assemble and divide the myriad objects proceeding from and flowing into *taiqi,* the Still Reality underlying the worlds of form, desire and formlessness". In the Chinese characters for I Ching, the word "I" represents a lizard, perhaps a chameleon.

In villages where Buddhism, Confucianism, animism, and other forms and places of worship co-existed, Daoist priests were also welcome. In these villages, special places of worship known as *dien,* or *tinh,* are found. Introduced to Vietnam at about the same time as Confucianism, Vietnamese Daoism does not have the hierarchy of schools and systems as

ancestors. Although many traditional beliefs and superstitions have waned, ancestor worship remains of high moral and social significance within Vietnamese society.

On anniversaries of deaths and on traditional festival days, the relatives of the deceased gather together. The eldest son of the deceased presides over the ceremonial offerings of food and incense, then the entire family visits the grave of the deceased. The ceremony ends with family members prostrating themselves before the altar and burning paper "money", which provides the dead with funds to make their life happier in the other world.

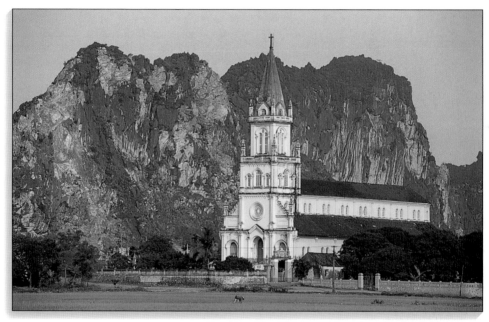

in China. On the philosophical level, it is expressed in the thoughts and poetry of both Confucian and Buddhist intellectuals. However, Daoist priests and their places of worship are found in villages among the common people. At this level, Daoist practices become a maze of superstitions, magic manifestations, and mystic healings.

Ancestor worship

Within many Vietnamese homes and inside all pagodas, one can find an altar dedicated to

LEFT: Giac Lam Pagoda, Ho Chi Minh City.
ABOVE: Catholic church south of Hanoi.

Failing to worship one's ancestors is considered an act of grave filial impiety that condemns the ancestors to a life of hellish wandering and subsisting on charity.

Christianity

To this universe with its rainbow of institutionalised religions, philosophies, and animistic beliefs came Catholicism. The first Western missionaries set foot in Tonkin, in northern Vietnam, in 1533, followed later in central Vietnam in 1596.

But theirs was only a brief stay. It was not until 1615 that the first permanent Christian missions were founded – in Hoi An, Da Nang, and Hanoi – by the Portuguese Jesuits. The introduction of this highly organised and culturally alien religion generated, unavoidably, misunderstanding and conflict. Yet Catholicism contributed two major transformations to Vietnamese culture: the romanisation of the written language and the introduction of Western scientific methods and logic.

Many Vietnamese from all classes of society converted to Catholicism. This development worried the mandarins and ruling classes, who saw the new religion as a threat to the traditional order of society and its rites, particularly the belief of heaven *(nam giao)*

and ancestor worship. Between 1712 and 1720, a decree forbidding Christianity was enforced in the north. In the south, foreign missionaries were sent packing in 1750 when Christianity was forbidden.

Levels of tolerance towards Christianity varied among leaders. Under Emperor Minh Mang, who viewed Christianity as "the perverse religion of Europeans" that "corrupts the heart of men", a decree was enforced forbidding the entry of Christian missionaries to Vietnam. Thieu Tri, who reigned for a time afterwards, was more tolerant, but his successor, Tu Duc, reinforced the prohibition of Christianity. This period of persecution lasted until

the mid-1860s, when a treaty ceded territory and commercial rights to the French and granted freedom for Christians to practise their faith. Between 1882 and 1884, another wave of persecution hit the Catholic church, and many followers paid with their lives. The persecution ended in 1885 with the French conquest of the entire country.

After the signing of the Geneva Agreement in 1954 and the division of the country, over half a million Catholics fled North Vietnam for the tolerance of the former South Vietnam.

Since the reunification of Vietnam in 1975, the Catholic Church has lived under the written law of the Socialist Republic of Vietnam, which guarantees the freedom of religion or non-religion under an official Marxist–Leninist ideology. All Catholic schools in the country have been nationalised. Churches are crowded on Sundays and on religious holidays.

The Hanoi government has loosened its restrictions on the Catholic Church in the past decade. Seminarians have been allowed to be ordained, and parishes have been allowed to teach children the faith. In heavily Catholic areas, such as Dong Nai Province, just north of Ho Chi Minh City, the countryside is dotted with churches in the midst of a rebuilding frenzy. However, the government can still veto who the Vatican names as a cardinal in Vietnam, in part because the Vatican had once attempted to nominate a relative of the former South Vietnam leader Ngo Dinh Diem.

Islam

Vietnam's small Muslim community consists mainly of ethnic Chams and South Asians. A 10th-century stele inscribed in Arabic, found near the central coastal town of Phan Rang, provides the earliest record of Islam's presence in Vietnam. Although the Chams consider themselves as Muslim, their religious practices are not fully orthodox.

They don't make the pilgrimage to Mecca, and although they don't eat pork, Vietnamese Muslims drink alcohol; they pray only on Fridays, observe Ramadan for only three days instead of the normal full month, and their rituals co-exist with other animistic and Hindu-based worship. ❑

LEFT: Muslim men in southern Vietnam.
RIGHT: interior of the cathedral in Hue.

COLOURFUL FESTIVALS FOR ALL SEASONS

Festivals in Vietnam are a time of fun and plenty. The main festival of Tet is especially vibrant as the whole country joins together in celebration

Festivals are held throughout the year, but the most interesting take place in spring and autumn. Visitors wishing to join in should acquaint themselves with the lunar calendar. The most important festival for Vietnamese people is Tet, the lunar new year.

In the weeks before Tet, the streets are a frenzy as people buy food, presents, and the peach blossom and mandarin trees – without which no family Tet would be complete. On New Year's Eve, ceremonies are held to "close the year". Offerings to the ancestors are placed on the family altar and then burnt, the smoke carrying their respects to heaven. The weeks after Tet are a popular time for ceremonies outside the home and people gather at local temples or make a pilgrimage to places like the Perfume Pagoda. They have their fortunes told and present wishes for the coming year. These are written in Chinese on pink paper, which are displayed while joss sticks are burned.

The autumn equinox *(trung thu)* festival is for children. On the 15th day of the eighth lunar month, children are taken to water by day and to watch the moon at night. They carry simple toys and lanterns, making this a particularly charming festival.

◁ **DRAGON DANCING**
The colourful rong mua lan, or dancing dragon, is a centrepiece of Tet festivals in villages throughout the country. The dance scares away evil spirits.

△ **BURNT OFFERINGS**
On lunar New Year's Eve, families burn paper offerings to their ancestors. They often do so right on the pavement outside their house, so watch your feet!

◁ **AUTUMN FESTIVAL**
Beautifully crafted toys and candle-lit lanterns are the main feature of the children's festival, celebrated at the autumn equinox in mid-September.

△ **NEW YEAR WISHES**
Monks literate in Chinese characters write people's New Year wishes onto pink paper slips. These are then displayed in the pagoda or burned.

VILLAGE FESTIVALS

The best time to visit village festivals is just after Tet, a word which itself means "festival". During the first two lunar months (February and March), most villages organise a fete. Families visit the village pagoda and light incense to local deities and their ancestors. Young people play games, swinging on giant bamboo swings or playing "human chess" with people or metre-high models moving between squares marked on a courtyard. Villages near the Red River send boats to collect ceremonial water to offer to the water god, Ha Ba. Most spectacular of all, young men put on the elaborate costumes of the dancing dragon and dance among the revellers to the sound of beating drums. One of the most popular of these occasions is the *quan ho* festival at Lim village, near Hanoi. Here young couples sing love songs to each other in a fertility rite to welcome the spring.

▷ **INCENSE**
Incense offerings are made in the form of joss sticks. They are an essential part of all worship, both in the home and, as here, in temples and pagodas.

▽ **ANCESTORS' ALTARS**
Tet offerings to the ancestors include rice, betel nuts, false money, and pink "New Year's wish" papers. After incense is offered, paper items are burned.

▽ **PAGODA EFFIGIES**
Ancestor worship is the main religion of the Vietnamese, co-existing with Buddhist, Confucian, and Daoist practices. The ancestor cult is a homely affair but it is also celebrated publicly with effigies on pagoda altars.

PERFORMING ARTS

*Vietnam's eclectic performing arts, while having roots in China,
tell great tales of Vietnamese gods and heroes in time-honoured adventures*

According to the wise teacher Confucius, "personal cultivation begins with poetry, is made firm by the rule of decorum, and is perfected by music". Before Western influences penetrated into Asia, music had long played an integral part in religious ceremonies but was not used for public entertainment.

The Dong Son bronze drums, which depict dancers performing to the accompaniment of musical instruments, and the lithophone of Ndut Lien Krat, in the southern highlands of Vietnam, testify to the importance of musical and dance traditions in Vietnam for over 2,500 years. Along with the other arts, music received its share of Chinese influence over the years. It was also influenced by the music of the Hindu kingdom of Champa, in the southern part of present-day Vietnam, which the Viet dynasties gradually absorbed during their long southward march.

Court music had its beginnings during the Le dynasty (1428–1788), when a Vietnamese mandarin was asked to establish a system of court music, following that of the Ming dynasty in China. He organised the following categories of music, each to be played at different religious and social occasions: *giao nhac,* played as an offering at the Esplanade of Heaven during the emperor's triennial celebration of the Cult of Heaven; *mieu nhac,* played during ceremonies at the Court of Literature in honour of Confucius, and at anniversary commemorations for deceased emperors; *ngu tu nhac,* music of the Five Sacrifices; *cuu nhat giao trung nhac,* music for helping the sun and moon during an eclipse; *dai trieu nhac,* music for ordinary audiences; *dai yen cuu tau nhac,* music for large banquets; and *cung trung chi nhac,* or palace music.

Throughout the 15th to 18th centuries, Vietnamese leaders took great interest in unifying the diverse orchestrations.

Ceremonial and religious music

In the coastal provinces of central Vietnam, songs known as *hat ba trao* – songs for worshipping the ocean spirits – are a popular tradition. One, called the *hat chau van,* is an incantation used in hypnotising a person through musical tunes, rhythms, and lyrics.

Buddhist music falls into two styles: the *tan* or melismatic chant, and the *tung* or sutra prayers. The tan is accompanied by a string and percussion orchestra in syncopated rhythm, while the tung is a chant on knowledge and enlightenment and is recited by a monk and punctuated by strokes on a wooden slit-drum.

Chamber music, performed by small instrumental ensembles for selected audiences of intellectuals, was confined to major cities. The most popular, known as *a dao,* takes its name from a historical story from the 15th century, at the time of the Ming invasion from China. During the military struggle, all manner of weapons were used, including on one occasion a combi-

PRECEDING PAGES: backstage at a *cai luong* performance, Ho Chi Minh. **LEFT:** performer in Ho Chi Minh. **RIGHT:** traditional dancer.

nation of female beauty and music. A country girl from a Dao village in Hai Hung province, in northern Vietnam, used her charm – together with dance, song, and music – to distract the Ming soldiers and so gain time to allow her countrymen to organise a guerrilla attack. *Hat A Dao*, the Song of the Lady from the Dao village, was composed by a group of mandarin scholars to commemorate the heroine's beauty, talent, and patriotism.

Each region of Vietnam has its own musical tradition, as do the country's 50-plus ethnic minorities. But, generally, Vietnamese music falls into two basic groups: the *dieu kach,* or northern tune, with its Chinese influence, and the *dieu nam,* or southern tune, with the slower tempo and sentimentality of the Cham culture.

Folk music takes the form of tunes sung and composed by villagers illustrating their life in the countryside. This music falls into several broad categories: lullabies, known as *hat run* in the north, *ru em* in the centre, and *au o* in the south; work songs, or *ho;* and the eternal love songs, *ly.*

There are ho and ly songs for each region, and for each season, every type of work, and every leisure activity. Ho refers to calling people to work in a rising and prolonged voice. A

SUNG POETRY

Essentially, Hat A Dao is sung poetry performed at the home of a songstress. The audience takes famous poems and composes verses themselves, all sung to the rhythmic accompaniment of the *phach*, a bamboo instrument beaten with two wooden sticks, and the *dan day*, a long-necked lute with three strings. The audience registers approval by beating a drum. By the beginning of the 20th century, the Hat A Dao had gradually become a refuge for pleasure rather than a centre for song and poetry. Its counterparts, though lacking the same significance, include the *ca hue*, music-song of Hue, and the *dan tai tu*, music of the amateurs in southern Vietnam.

lead singer begins the chant, which is then taken up by others in the working party. The most cherished of the ho is one called Ho Mia Nhi, usually sung by young boatwomen on the Perfume River, in Hue. Structured like a poem, this ho's four lines express deep thoughts and feelings, suitable for a river's transient moods.

Theatre

The oldest recorded form of performance is the *tro he,* a farce created by Lieu Thu Tam under the Tien Le dynasty. During the Tran dynasty, two new types of theatre emerged: the *hat giau mat,* or masked performances, and the *hat coi tran,* or coat-less performances.

Today's theatre, a blend of court theatre, folk performances, and foreign influence, includes three types of performances: *cheo, hat tuong,* and *cai luong.* Cheo is as old as the Vietnamese nation itself. The word "cheo" is a distortion of *tieu,* the Chinese word for laughter. Cheo's origins can be found in the religious and social activities that are depicted on the engravings of Bronze Age drums and urns.

Developed from animistic customs, mime, dance, song, prayers, and poetry, cheo reached

CIVIC CHEO

Anti-establishment *hat cheo* educates peasants on how to expose the injustices of those in power. Under some rulers, cheo was forbidden and its performers prosecuted.

a flute. These are not the only sounds to be heard. To start the play, someone from the audience beats a large drum. When a performer sings well, this drum will be beaten by a member of the audience to register approval; when the performance is poor, however, then the drum's wooden barrel is struck.

The length of a performance is determined by how much the audience has paid, and this is represented by a burning incense stick. When approval is marked by the drum, incense tapers are laid in

its present form of technique by the 1100s. Performances usually are staged in front of a village community house or Buddhist pagoda. The troupe's equipment is carried from village to village in a single box, which also serves as a unique part of the stage setting, representing whatever is required of it. Cheo plays provide a framework within which the players improvise. The troupe is judged according to its ability to vary and renew a familiar theme. The musicians sit to the right of the stage area with drums, gongs, rattles, stringed instruments, and

LEFT: ancient image of Cham dancers, Da Nang.
ABOVE: dragon-dance troupe members on a break.

a pile in honour of the player, lengthening, in turn, the performance – and the fee.

The audience knows every detail of cheo, whose strict rules were set as early as 1500. Throughout a performance, the players explain events, stop to question the audience, and take replies. Melodies familiar to everyone symbolise certain life-cycle events: marriage, birth, death. And all gestures, including movements of the eyes and mouth, have a specific meaning. A chorus and a clown express emotional high points. The clown, wearing black makeup, interrupts the players to comment on their lies and tricks, make fun of them, and praise their good deeds. The audience often stops a player to demand a replay of an interesting or intriguing detail.

Unlike hat cheo, which is clearly and uniquely Vietnamese, hat tuong arrived from China in the 13th century under the Tran dynasty after the defeat of Mongol invaders. Among the war prisoners was a master of Chinese theatre, Ly Nguyen Cat, who later became a Vietnamese citizen and taught Chinese drama to the Vietnamese court. From China came face makeup, ceremonial costumes, masks, stylised gestures, percussion and wind-instrument music, and emphasis on the heroic and noble.

Hat tuong begins with a song introducing the the Cham culture. Today, the hat tuong orchestra includes cymbals, gongs, drums, tambourines, flutes, and an arsenal of stringed instruments: the *dan nguyet,* a moon-shaped lute; the *dan nhi,* a violin with a high register played by drawing two strings tight over a drum skin; the *thap luc,* a zither-like instrument with 16 strings plucked with the fingers; and the *dan bau,* whose single string, stretched over a long lacquered sound box, is both bowed and plucked to produce a variety of vibrato effects and long resonances of great subtlety. The result is truly exquisite.

Hat tuong originated as a theatre for the

drama's story line. Each player describes his character and role. The stage is nearly empty, except for special props representing the landscape: a branch for a forest, a painted wheel for a cart. The action, always dramatic, is guided by Confucian moral virtues and concepts – for example, loyalty to kings or devotion to parents. The orchestra sits on the stage's side, accompanying not only the singing but also details of the activity and movement on stage. In typical Vietnamese fashion, the hat tuong, although a copy of Chinese drama, was adapted to the Vietnamese character. Women replaced men in the female roles, and the orchestra was enlarged, incorporating Indian influences from elite. It allows criticism and flexibility, but in the end it is still a theatre for the moral and social status quo.

Cai luong, or renovated theatre, made its first appearance in the southern part of Vietnam in 1920. It interprets classical Chinese stories in a more accessible style. Influenced by the European stage, cai luong has evolved into its present spoken-drama form, abandoning the cumbersome epic style in favour of shorter acts, emotional and psychological play, and free dialogue. *(See photo on pages 94–95.)* ❑

ABOVE: bamboo instrument at Hanoi conservatory.
RIGHT: water-puppet performance in Hanoi.

Fluid Movements

The delta of the Song Hong, or Red River, of northern Vietnam is a low-lying plain that would be submerged in water during the rainy season every year if not for a vast series of dikes, the 7,000 km (4,500 miles) of levees that criss-cross the rice paddies and villages. The dikes were first built out of soil 1,000 years ago. Prior to that time, during the Ly dynasty of the 11th century, the Red River would swell each year like clockwork, spill over its banks, and flood much of the region.

communal house. Their techniques were closely guarded secrets. Even now, some elderly water-puppet masters are reluctant to pass on their secrets to younger generations. But the fear that the art will die out completely has persuaded some of the masters to teach apprentices.

Today, there are just a few troupes in Vietnam, with two in Hanoi. Many of the northern provinces have a touring troupe.

A performance usually consists of about 12 acts, each of them telling a mythological story about Vietnam and its history, while traditional musicians provide background music. One story, for example, tells the story of the tortoise that

The annual flooding of the lowlands inspired a form of entertainment to be found only in Vietnam, the water puppets. "The farmers did not know what to do during the flood season, so they created this form of art", explained the artistic director of Hanoi's leading puppetry troupe, which travels the globe exporting this bit of Vietnamese culture.

Water puppetry combines the Vietnamese love for mythology with the fierce nationalistic pride that is encouraged in the country.

The puppeteers stand behind a screen in water up to their waists, controlling the puppets' movements with long bamboo poles. Centuries ago, every village would have a troupe that would perform in a pond in front of the *dinh,* or

lived in Hanoi's Hoan Kiem Lake and supposedly emerged from the depths to provide the good King Ly Thai Tho with the sword he needed to fight off Chinese invaders. Other stories detail village life: the planting and harvesting of the rice crop, fishing, boat races.

Some have suggested that the puppets be mechanised. For one thing, some have argued, they are heavy, at times weighing 20 kg (45 lbs) and requiring up to four people to manoeuvre. For another, the puppets usually can perform just one movement at a time, limiting their repertoire. Directors have toyed with the idea of adding contemporary stories to the repertoire, but of course traditionalists resist changes. ❑

LITERATURE AND ART

The Vietnamese are among the world's most literate and poetic people,
and now their contemporary art is seducing collectors around the world

Art in Vietnamese is *my thuat,* which literally translated means "beauty skill". Vietnam's artists use traditional art to communicate their ideas through the mediums of music, literature, poetry, dance, theatre, painting, sculpture, and even architecture. Although Vietnam is a civilisation some 4,000 years old, the country has no great monument like Cambodia's Angkor Wat.

Many of Vietnam's ancient monuments have fallen prey to the ravages of war and the climate, as well as to neglect. However, despite the destructive forces of both nature and war, nothing has succeeded in destroying the vast legacy of art, crafts, architecture, theatre, music, and the written word.

Literature and poetry

Writers and poets have always occupied a place of high esteem in Vietnamese society. Well acquainted with struggle and hardship over the centuries, Vietnamese find their rich literary heritage a source of comfort, hope and inspiration. A seemingly endless wealth of oral storytelling traditions – consisting of myths, songs, legends, folk and fairy tales – constitutes Vietnam's most ancient literature. Later, as the society developed, scholars, Buddhist monks, kings, and court ministers (many of whom were talented writers and poets) wrote down their thoughts and epics using adopted Chinese characters *(chu nho).* This literature was greatly influenced by Confucian and Buddhist thought.

Even more poems and literary works were undertaken with the advent of *chu nom,* a complicated script based on chu nho. However, the Vietnamese found the romanised alphabet, introduced by foreign missionaries, to be a more accessible means of communicating, rather than the foreboding need to use the thousands of different ideograms in Chinese writing. Vietnamese literature was soon enriched

with new ideas of Western thought and culture. Indeed, Vietnamese literary prose and poetry was influenced by European literature, which introduced new ways of expressing ideas in novel ways – and, too, reflected the rising sentiment of nationalism.

During the 20th-century wars for Vietnamese

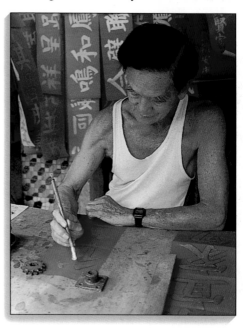

independence from outside powers, northern writers limited themselves mostly to stories meant to unify the people and to inspire the population during difficult times. Communist Party cadres strictly controlled publishing after the end of the Vietnam War in 1975 as well, and even today government censors must approve writings before publication.

However, in recent years control has been loosened somewhat. The publication in the early 1990s of *The Sorrow of War,* by a Vietnam War veteran from the north under the pseudonym of Bao Ninh *(see photo on next page),* was the first war novel to confront the gruesome realities of war and the psychological

---

PRECEDING PAGES: "Lucky or Not", by Le Thiet Cuong.
LEFT: "Girl with Banana Leaf," by Nguyen Quan.
RIGHT: calligrapher working on Chinese characters.

effects upon surviving soldiers. Another writer, Duong Thu Huong, has had her works translated, which include thinly veiled criticism of government and Communist Party officials. For a time, she was imprisoned for crimes against the socialist state.

Today, scribes with reputations for writing critically are presumed to be under close surveillance. Despite the appearance of a new period of openness, Party leaders have warned writers that they must focus on ideas that are of benefit to the nation. As one literary standard-bearer says, "We can write about problems, about negative things in society. But we

development in the long run. "We get rid of a lot of bad writers. Only the good ones can survive", he says. "Now people have other ways to use their creativity. Maybe instead of trying to write, they become good traders or businessmen. That is better for them and better for the country".

Above all else, poetry dominates the Vietnamese arts. The language of Vietnam is a natural tool for poetry, as each of its syllables can be pronounced in six tones to convey six meanings. By simply combining these tones and modulating certain words, a sentence turns into a verse; and plain speech becomes a song.

must also finish with optimism". An improved economy and increased contact with the outside world has meant that Vietnamese interest in Vietnamese literature, always intense, has declined somewhat. Today, there is television, translations of foreign works (American writer Sydney Sheldon is popular), and for children, comic books. (Kids are addicted to Japanese *anime*.) Still, it is not unusual to find people reading in their spare time, whether it be a cyclo driver waiting for a customer, a labourer from the country taking a tea break, or students at a cafe.

There are fewer writers nowadays, but a professor of literature thinks this is a positive

Another group of Vietnamese words made up of repeated syllables can cast a discreet shade on the meaning of words, conjuring up a particular colour, movement, attitude, or mood.

Vietnamese poetry falls into two major categories: *ca dao,* a popular folk song, oral in origin but collected and transcribed in written form; and *tho van,* the literary poetry written by kings, scholars, Buddhist monks, mandarins of the court, Daoist recluses, feminists, revolutionaries – even Marxists.

Poetry has become such an important medium of communication in Vietnam that even present-day political slogans must be written in verse to be effective.

The Tale of Kieu

Nearly every Vietnamese reads and remembers a few chapters of a 3,254-verse story published 200 years ago called *The Tale of Kieu*. Pupils begin studying it in the sixth grade. *Kieu* was written by one of Vietnam's most esteemed and respected forefathers, Nguyen Du, and is now considered the cultural window to the soul of the Vietnamese people. One may wonder how *Kieu* came to occupy its special position in Vietnamese literature. Why is the complex tale author, Nguyen Du, is the faithful interpreter of their hopes, and, too, the discreet confidant of their misfortunes. Born in the village of Nghi Xuan, in northern Vietnam's Ha Tinh Province, Nguyen Du came from an old aristocratic family of mandarins and scholars. His father was prime minister in the royal court of Emperor Le. Nguyen Du grew up in a country, under the nominal rule of the Le dynasty, torn by civil war. When he was 24, the Le dynasty, which his family had faithfully served for generations,

LITERATE READERS

For such an impoverished country, the literacy rate in Vietnam is quite high, estimated to be above 90 percent and reflective of the Vietnamese love of reading.

of a woman's personal misfortunes regarded by a whole people as the perfect expression of their essential nature, of their national soul? After all, the protagonist Kieu is a prostitute. "This shows", explains a Hanoi writer and critic, "how important the simple people are to Vietnamese. Our most important literary figure is not a king, not a warrior, not a hero, but a simple prostitute".

Regardless of age, gender, geography, or ideology, all Vietnamese perceive the epic as the heart and mind of their nation. To them, its

was overthrown by the peasant-based Tay Son revolution. After Gia Long, a descendant of the southern Nguyen warlords, defeated the Tay Son brothers and was declared emperor, Nguyen Du became an official of several northern provinces, distinguishing himself as an honest and able administrator. In 1806, at the age of 41, he was summoned to the capital of Hue to serve as high chancellor.

Having reunited Vietnam, Gia Long faced the problem of national security, foremost of which meant establishing diplomatic relations with China. All Vietnamese envoys to China were chosen from the cream of Vietnamese *literati*, as it was by intellectual, rather than mil-

LEFT: Bao Ninh, author of *The Sorrow of War*.
ABOVE: Temple of Literature gate, Hanoi.

THE TALE OF KIEU

The *Tale of Kieu*, considered by Vietnamese to be reflective of their national character, was adapted from a Chinese Ming-period novel.

Where bamboo covers case
Old manuscripts of countless price
Preserved in fragrant spice,
Sit by a lamp and study well
The story that they tell
How in the dynasty of Ming
When Jia-ching was the king
And all his empire was at rest,
Among those who were blessed
With learning was a man named Vuong.
He had a son, the young
Vuong-Quan, to carry on his name
And literary fame;
And two girls, Thuy-Van and Thuy-Kieu,
Who were as slim as two
Young poplar-trees, as pure as snow.

❖

But Kieu was yet more fair,
The elder's merits took the prize.
Like autumn seas her eyes,
Eyebrows like spring hills far away.
Flowers wished they were as gay;
The aspen shook with envying her.
One glance of Kieu's could stir
Cities or empires to revolt!
Her beauty had no fault,
Nor in her mind was any flaw
She'd write in verse, or draw,
Excel at playing on the lute,
And, choosing tunes to suit,
Compose songs for herself to sing.
One such, so sad a thing
The listeners wept, she called "Cruel Fate".

❖

It's always been the same:
Good fortune seldom came the way
Of those endowed, they say,
With genius and a dainty face,
What tragedies take place
Within each circling space of years!
"Rich in good looks" appears
to mean poor luck and tears of woe;
which may sound strange, I know,
but is not really so, I swear,
since Heaven everywhere
seems jealous of the fair of face.

itary, might that Vietnam sought to impress China. So Nguyen Du, already recognised as a great poet, was a natural choice to be emissary. After five years in China, he returned and devoted most of his time to literary pursuits until his 1820 death at the age of 53. A literary school founded in 1979 to train writers was named after Nguyen Du over the objections of government officials, who preferred to name the school after a war hero.

What makes *Kieu* as relevant today as it was two centuries ago is Nguyen Du's ability and courage to lay bare the whole spectrum of society. Vices and virtues, ugliness and beauty, nobility and trickery – all are entangled in a seemingly hopeless tragic comedy reflecting the true face of Vietnam. The prostitute Kieu also personifies the inherent contradiction faced by the Vietnamese.

"Within the span of a hundred years of human existence, what a bitter struggle is waged between talent and fate", lament the opening lines. And, in the conclusion, Nguyen Du writes, "When one is endowed with talent, do not rely upon it".

Deep in their hearts and behind their gracious modesty, the Vietnamese know they are not lacking in talent, *tai.* At the same time, they do not understand why this tai, which has helped them win independence from formidable foreign invasions and enabled them to develop a respectable culture and civilisation, has failed to bring them lasting peace and enduring prosperity. Unable to solve this paradox, most believe they are *oan,* a word meaning wronged and which appears throughout *Kieu.* Indeed, the epic explores the Buddhist notion of karmic fate and retribution.

The Vietnamese, like Kieu, see themselves as victims who are punished for crimes they are not aware that they have committed. (One might speculate that when the United States bombed Vietnam under the guise of stopping the spread of communism, peasants probably wondered why they, and not Moscow, received the brunt of the firepower.)

Even Vietnamese who fled their country after the war ended in the 1970s turn to the woes of Kieu for comfort, especially in the cultural isolation of a new land and language. Huynh Sanh Thong, a Vietnamese scholar at Yale University who translated *Kieu* into English, wrote in his introduction that immigrants "know most of its lines by heart, and when they recite them out loud, they speak their mother tongue at its finest. To the extent that the poem implies something at the core of the Vietnamese experience, it addresses [Vietnamese people] intimately as victims, as refugees, as survivors".

Art

After starring in countless war movies, Vietnam has found a certain peace in the pleasures of a different kind of artistic expression: painting. Upon arriving in Viet-

ART OR KITSCH?

Most art for sale hanging in the cramped, dim shops along Trang Tien in Hanoi and Dong Khoi in Ho Chi Minh is mass produced for the unsuspecting tourist.

Netherlands, Sweden, the US, Hong Kong, Japan, and Singapore. The most acclaimed artists' works fetch prices up to US$50,000.

Much of the work creating this international acclaim shares a gentle, lyrical quality – rarely is any self-indulgent anger expressed – while styles explored range from figurative to abstract and surrealist, at other times expressionist or realist. The abundance of this impressionist and figurative art in Vietnam is testament to the tenacious influence a foreign cultural her-

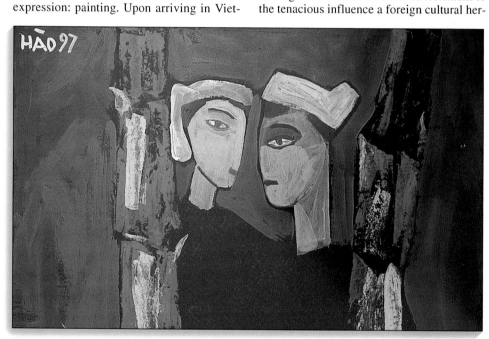

ABOVE: "Bamboo", by northern Vietnamese artist Truong Dinh Hao.

nam one of the first things a traveller may be surprised to discover is the country's vigorous contemporary art scene.

Away from well-trodden tourist streets, a dozen galleries are beginning to showcase the works of a small legion of talented artists who dedicate their life to the single-minded pursuit of artistic excellence. After decades of obscurity and isolation, these artists are making inroads into the international arena, with well-attended – and well-received – exhibitions in Australia, Denmark, France, Germany, Great Britain, the

itage has on a country. While China, Japan, and Korea share long painting histories, Vietnam's painting tradition emerged entirely from the French colonial imposition dating from the 19th century. Prior to this time, Vietnam's artistic achievements had been restricted to decorative arts for religious and communal purposes, with only a limited output of paintings, coloured embossments, and portraits on silk.

In spite of the largely destructive arrival of the French, new opportunities for creative achievement arose during the colonial period, with painting becoming the most developed artistic expression. Through this Western influx a unique French-Vietnamese amalgamation of cultures emerged, identifiable by four distinct periods: the first extending until 1925; the second from 1925 to 1945; the third from 1945 to 1980; and the last from 1980 until the present. The first period was notable for producing a small handful of Confucian scholars who would become the first European-educated painters.

In 1925, under the initiative of the French painter Victor Tardieu, the Ecole des Beaux-Arts de l'Indochine (EBAI) was founded in

MIXED COLOURS

Early works had a blend of culture and education in their European compositions completed in oil, while simultaneously retaining the quiet Vietnamese spirituality.

sion. To Ngoc Van, on the other hand, is attributed with using French impressionism, realism, and romanticism to create a locally styled impressionism injected with nationalist sentiments.

While the influence of these first graduates was felt in the 1930s, the artistic influence of the last group of notable graduates – Bui Xuan Phai, Nguyen Sang, and Nguyen Tu Nghiem – was not felt until the 1960s and 1970s.

Sang set about elevating the stature of the ordinary people through his skilful European-

Hanoi. Through its 18 courses of study offered over just 20 years, 128 painters and sculptors were taught in the European tradition.

The school was responsible for creating the "first generation" of Vietnamese masters, most notable of whom were Nguyen Gia Tri, Nguyen Phan Chanh, To Ngoc Van, Bui Xuan Phai, Nguyen Sang, and Nguyen Tu Nghiem. While Nguyen Gia Tri's works continue to generate acclaim for transforming the traditional decorative art form of lacquer to an Art Nouveau style depicting Vietnamese subjects and atmosphere, Nguyen Phan Chanh became renowned for his silk paintings of women expressed using his own form of Asian expres-

styled oil and lacquer portraits, which featured elements of folk paintings; Phai, Vietnam's most internationally renowned artist, left an enormous legacy of beautiful and sentimental works depicting Hanoi street scenes and humble subject matter. Nghiem has gained great credit for de-academising the painting language and generating a return to a national art by integrating old traditions into modern painting.

While not all of the above artists shared the same vision or produced the same style of painting, each shared a desire to champion a European modernism while remaining true to their Vietnamese spirit and heritage. Through their innovative use of traditional materials and their depiction of domestic themes in warm colours, all of these artists can be accredited with freeing Vietnamese painting from its colonial academism.

These philosophies were then passed onto their students at the Hanoi College of Fine Arts – the EBAI's successor – and the College of Applied Arts in Hanoi. The result today? Every Vietnamese painter has roots, in some way, instilled in the traditional European school of painting. Through this method of art education, somewhere between the French school and Asian aesthetic idea, Vietnamese art has

always being more open to foreign and artistic influence, the war tore apart the artistic community. Nearly everything from nudes to abstraction, even impressionism, was banned.

Meanwhile, in the north, artists influenced by the increasingly close relationship with Socialist Realist art of the Soviet Union, Eastern Europe, and China (prior to the 1970s) found themselves confined and bound to recording the solidarity of the large social movement. As such, this style of painting of politics, soldiers, and labourers has gained its own level of importance as a valuable witness to this complicated period of Vietnam's history.

emerged as something very unusual and absolutely unique in Asia.

While artists from the first two periods used their European technique to give shape and expression to their Vietnamese soul, after 1945 artists from the cities of Hanoi, Saigon, and Hue developed their own particular styles. Isolated through partition and continual war, artists in the south had few opportunities to witness directly the artistic heritage of the north and instead were increasingly exposed to the artistic trends of Europe and America. Despite

LEFT: Tran Van Thao, and Buu Chi's "The Testament".
ABOVE: hill-tribe women, watercolour on silk.

Creatively, however, it was fiercely criticised after 1975.

It was not until 1986, when *doi moi* (the policy of economic "renovation") began, that the artistic climate throughout the country began to flourish once again. With openness in economic and cultural intercourse and with the overall renovation in the political, economic, and social fields, Vietnamese art began to undergo dramatic changes with exhibitions and paintings being sold. Nowhere was this rebirth better captured than in the 1991 exhibition *Uncorked Soul,* organised by Plum Blossoms Gallery in Hong Kong in the first full-scale, post-war show of Vietnamese contemporary art outside of Vietnam. The exhibition not only introduced a span of Vietnamese art to the rest of Asia but highlighted the difficulties faced by artists during Ho Chi Minh's repression of the Aesthetic Humanism movement from the mid-1950s until the mid-1980s. (The Aesthetic Humanism movement was short-lived, from 1955–57, and sought cultural democratisation and political reform, led by intellectuals.)

Since then, the Vietnamese art scene has not looked back. While an indisputable wave of crass, commercialised art has infested the tourist market, over a dozen exciting young artists have emerged who are showcasing Viet-

Subtle experience

Looking back at the fertile soil of their traditions and realities, and with wounds still raw from their suffering and solitude, Vietnamese artists have much to discuss and share with an increasingly receptive audience.

Surprisingly, however, despite its decades of destructive influence on the country, war is rarely portrayed directly in Vietnamese art. Instead, there are reflections on the pain and sorrow caused by armed conflict.

Similarly, the bitterness, anger, angst, and inhumanity of war are not depicted. Instead, Vietnamese canvases are predominantly filled

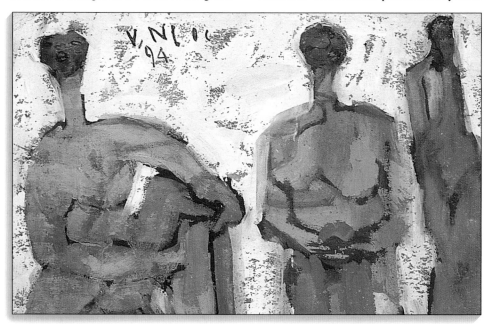

namese art to the international art world. With an increased individuality of artistic expression and greater contact and receptivity to international art currents – from the Paris school to native art, surrealism, abstraction, and the latest artistic currents in Asia, Europe, and America – the world is seeing an increasing spectrum of images, motifs, and methods being used.

This fourth and fifth generation of artists, who were educated after 1975, are now free from the constraints of a social or political agenda and enjoying artistic freedom. They are interested in portraying something more interesting, and so are representing more personal freedom.

with soulful characters in a variety of warm, soft shades depicted in smooth, sensuous, expressive lines, hinting at the more recent influence of Buddhism across the country. Portraying the beautiful is very important to the artists, who respect it and as such don't like to portray the violent, the strange, or the suffering.

Receiving international notoriety are the "Gang of Five" and "Five New Faces". These two groups of five artists are products of the same Hanoi College of Fine Arts class, 1987–90. The haunting yet sensuous and soulful works of Tran Quoc Tuan, Dinh Quan, Pham Ngoc Minh, Tran Quang Huy, and

Nguyen Quoc Hoi have gained recognition not only for their fresh style but also the international quality of their contemporary works.

The Gang of Five's first exhibition in 1990 brought Dang Xuan Hoa, Hong Viet Dung, Ha Tri Hieu, Tran Luong, and Pham Quang Vinh acclaim for their affinity at portraying everyday life by striving to wed tradition with modernity. Bold, fresh, and full of vitality and self-expression, each work is distinctive for the artist's idiosyncrasies. Despite the fact they don't exhibit together anymore, they have garnered enormous attention all over the region and are regarded as the most promising of the

against the French and in the first years after partition in the mid-1950s. The third generation graduated from art schools or were self taught during the "American" 1960s and 1970s. It consists of dynamic artists such as Trinh Cung, abstract artist Nguyen Trung, metaphorical surrealist Nguyen Quan, and the achingly melancholic works of Buu Chi, one of the country's most haunted artists.

Such sensibilities may be the reason Vietnamese art is attracting the eyes of international buyers, who now pay prices unthinkable 10 years ago. Prices have shot up very quickly, with a gouache painting on paper by one of the

new generation of artists. Other exciting artists to have emerged in recent years include Truong Dinh Hao, Van Ngoc, Hoang Hong Cam, abstract artist Tran Van Thao, Nguyen Thanh Chuong, Le Thiet Cuong, Do Quang Em and Le Quang Ha, each of whom bears his or her own unique style.

Already highly regarded and well established in the history books are the second-generation artists such as Tran Luu Hau, Le Cong Than, and Viet Hai, who trained at the Hanoi College of Fine Arts during the war

LEFT: "Bathing", a gouache by Van Ngoc.
ABOVE: gallery staff in Ho Chi Minh City.

GUARDED AESTHETICS

With Vietnamese artists now in the international art market, authorities are ever careful to oversee foreigners' perceptions of the country. Paintings with political overtones and opinions opposing the government's ideals are potential firecrackers, such as the works of Truong Tan. Blatantly depicting his own individual sexuality by confronting traditional family values and traditional hierarchy, his graphic works of irony are often hidden from public viewing. Eighteen of Truong's paintings were confiscated by the Ministry of Interior during an exhibition in 1995, an intervention not seen for 10 years. Generally, however, Vietnamese artists simply avoid such subjects.

"old masters" now selling in Vietnam for US$4,000, as opposed to US$200 a decade or so ago. While this phenomenon comes as no surprise to those in the industry, particularly the artists who have long been patiently waiting for recognition, to buy Vietnamese art solely for investment purposes is a risky speculative game, especially with faultless imitations of the older masters quite common on the open market.

This growing internationalisation can be credited with providing an international influence that is helping produce better quality, more mature works – not to mention the financial rewards that enable better working conditions, more motivation, and larger budgets to experiment with styles and techniques – the globalisation of the Vietnamese art market has created many negative changes as well.

With the influence of so many foreign cultures in Vietnam, it is not easy for the younger artists to remain true to their vision and their traditional style. As a result, the strong works they were producing some years ago are now coming under constant threat from being commercially "produced". Choosing which path to follow and developing their own style is an increasingly difficult challenge.

CONTEMPORARY GALLERIES

The best way to ensure your purchase is a genuine original painting by the artist being proposed is to purchase from reputable galleries. Hanoi boasts Red River Gallery (or Galerie Fleuve Rouge), a modern, well-lit gallery with large contemporary paintings. Tran Phuong Mai, the daughter of influential Hanoi poet, translator, and art critic/patron Duong Tuong Duong, opened Mai Gallery in 1993 in her parents' home using contacts she'd made through her father and her artist friends. They promote artists who have already achieved recognition as well as promising young painters who are still subject to controversy. Also in Hanoi is the tiny hole-in-the-wall gallery-atelier Salon Natasha. The workplace of self-trained Vietnamese artist Vu Dau Tau, the bohemian gallery is a popular meeting place with artists, who chat with the artist and his Russian wife.

Down in Ho Chi Minh City, Gallery Saigon gained notoriety as the first modern, Western gallery in the city and for being the first custom-built art gallery in Vietnam when it opened in 1995. It represents about 30 new and established artists from Hanoi and Ho Chi Minh, many of whom meet daily at the gallery, located within the grounds of the Museum of Ton Duc Thang. Others are Gallery Vietnam, on Dong Khoi, and Blue Space Contemporary Art Centre within the Fine Art Museum on Le Thi Hong Gam.

However, with 200 exhibitions a year, 300 art galleries nationwide, and over 1,500 arts association members, the best artists are also working even harder to pull themselves above the market's glut. In doing so, it is hoped the flooded market will correct itself and price inflation will go down. The best artists, though they use Western language and technique, still have their Asian soul and work full-time as professional artists, living proudly and with respect from society for their art.

COMPLEX AESTHETICS

The works of Vietnam's artists are becoming less homogeneous and more complex and experimental, ensuring their future in Asia's vibrant art scene.

examples of woodcuts are the Tranh Lang Ho village paintings. This art form – known as Ho village painting – existed from as early as the 11th century during the Ly dynasty. At first it was limited to black-and-white prints of the woodcuts, but after the 15th century, colour was introduced.

In accordance with the craft tradition, whole villages were given solely over to block printing. Many families in Ho village, located in Bach Ninh Province north of Hanoi, are collectively

Despite the financial temptations, the dedicated artists are constantly searching and injecting new styles and forms into Vietnam's contemporary art.

Crafts

Vietnamese folk art and crafts had gone into decline with the onset of French colonisation at the end of the 19th century. By the end of the 20th century, however, efforts were thriving to revive both. Two successful examples are woodcuts and lacquerware. The best

LEFT: studio producing fakes of famous paintings.
ABOVE: fine detail of inlaid lacquer work.

engaged in producing coloured prints of traditional themes.

The village craftsmen make their own paper and natural colours, and they prepare the blocks in variations of classic models depicting good luck signs, historical figures and battles, spirits, popular allegories, and social commentary.

Good fortune is symbolised by a corpulent pig decorated with garlands, often accompanied by a litter of suckling piglets. A hen surrounded by chicks symbolises prosperity. The cockerel, herald of the dawn, is the symbol of peace and courage. Social criticism is expressed by caricatures of mandarins, represented by croaking frogs and rats marching with drums and trumpets. Warriors are shown together with apes, tigers, and other animal spirits, all in splendid colours, with humour and optimism ridiculing the corrupt and powerful.

Objects made of lacquered wood have been found in tombs dating from the 3rd and 4th centuries. Today, lacquer *(son mai)* work – including paintings, screens, boxes, vases, trays, and chessboards – are fast becoming a main export item. Their quality is a result of the meticulous attention given to the preparation of the lacquer and to the designs of a thousand-year-old tradition.

Two types of lacquer are used. Varnish lac-

quer is obtained by mixing lacquer resin with *mu* oil, while pumice lacquer, a higher-quality and more durable lacquer, is produced by mixing lacquer resin with pine resin. Unlike varnish lacquer, pumice lacquer is rubbed and smoothed in water after painting to bring out a gloss finish.

Lacquer is prepared from the resin of the *cay son,* or lacquer tree, which is collected in the same way as latex. After being stored for a while, the resin is diluted with water and then the dark-brown surface layer known as *oil lac* is skimmed off. With the addition of various ingredients, this is used for the upper layer of lacquer paintings.

This high-quality lacquer is poured into a bamboo or wooden vessel and stirred vigorously with a wooden pestle for eight to ten hours. (If stirred in a plastic or iron vessel, the lacquer turns black.) A small amount of colophony, a resin, is added to render it more elastic and suitable for polishing. Normal paint added to lacquer will also produce a black or grey colour.

Special paints are needed for lacquer pictures: cinnabar for various hues of red; pure gold or silver applied as thin sheets or strips; blue gouache; several kinds of aniline dyes that produce carmine red or green; and the yellow dye obtained from the seeds of hydrangeas. Eggshell fragments yield the purest white colour, while fragments of mother-of-pearl, mollusc, and snail shell produce blue or violet.

Lacquer artists painstakingly select and prepare the boards for their pictures. These must be smooth, dry, and free of the smallest crack, scratch, or imperfection before they are coated with several layers of lacquer. This is followed by a thin layer of cotton fabric or silk, followed by another layer of lacquer.

The board is then left in a damp place for two or three days until dry, then coated with another layer of lacquer, a layer of lacquer putty, sawdust, and kaolin, which render the board uniformly smooth.

The dried surface is rubbed with wet pumice before another two to four layers of lacquer are applied and left to dry for several days between coats, then painstakingly rubbed for hours. Only after all this preparation is the board ready for painting.

If the artist uses egg or mollusc shells, he cuts the image in the upper layers of lacquer covering the fabric, smears the depression with black lacquer, which acts as a glue, and then taps the shell into position with a tiny hammer. More lacquer is applied, then tinted with the desired dye.

When this is quite dry, the picture is rubbed down thoroughly to bring out the texture of the shell with its numerous tiny cracks. The craftsman will continue rubbing the picture with the palm of his hand until the contours become outlined and the lacquer acquires transparency and sheen. ❑

LEFT: detail of temple's carving in wood.
RIGHT: page from Latin-Annamese religious text.

Language

In the Vietnamese language, the word for natural disaster is *thien tai,* from Chinese. The word for cheese is *pho mat,* from the French *fromage.* There are sounds and words from English and Russian too. Thousands of words in contemporary Vietnamese – as much as 80 percent of the language – come from Chinese, a reflection of the centuries of non-too-harmonious relations between Vietnam and its massive neighbour to the north, including the influence of Chinese literature.

There is the touch of French with words that entered the lexicon first during the colonial period of the 18th and 19th centuries, and later well into the 20th century. A dab of English was left by the Americans during the Vietnam War, and subsequent years of fraternisation with the former Soviet Union introduced Russian. In fact, expressions and nomenclature indicating 20th-century technology and ideas are often expressed with French, English, and Russian words. The newest foreign linguistic invasion – that of consumer marketers – is represented by Japanese. The word most commonly used to refer to a two-wheeled motorised vehicle, for example, is *honda.*

Variations: Distinct dialects within Vietnam reveal strong regional identities. Often northerners and southerners confess they cannot understand each other. Foreigners might need two translators, one to translate the foreign language into Vietnamese, another to translate the Vietnamese into another dialect. Some letters of the alphabet are pronounced differently, and the vocabularies of northerners and southerners contain distinct words. Even the syntax is different. In addition to Vietnamese, the country's many ethnic minorities speak their own distinct languages and dialects. In the Mekong Delta, for example, so many people speak the Khmer of Cambodia that local television has a Khmer-language broadcast.

Yet the country does share one language, a blend of several languages – ancient and modern – that has evolved through Vietnam's contact with other cultures. Its roots, while still debated, come from a mixture of Mon-Khmer, Thai, and Muong.

Written Vietnamese: Chinese influence during the first centuries of Vietnam's history led to the extensive use of Chinese characters known as *chu nho,* which replaced an ancient written script of Indian origin, preserved and used today only by the Muong minority.

After independence in the 10th century, scholars realised the necessity and advantages of developing a separate written Vietnamese language. Several tentative attempts were made to modify the characters of Chinese, but it was a 13th-century poet, Nguyen Thuyen, who managed to incorporate the previous efforts into a distinct, but very complicated, script known as *chu nom.*

Although standardised for popular literature, chu nom never received official recognition, and most Vietnamese writers continued using the more complicated Chinese calligraphy.

Today, however, Vietnam has a romanised alphabet, thanks to a French Jesuit missionary, Alexan-

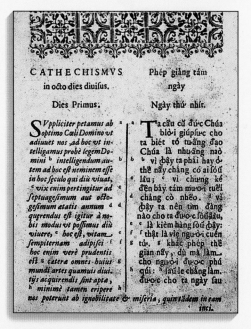

dre de Rhodes, who developed a script called *quoc ngu* in 1651.

Quoc ngu was, at first, used only by the Catholic Church and the colonial administration, gaining widespread popularity only in the early part of the 20th century. The study of quoc ngu became compulsory in secondary schools in 1906, and two years later, the royal court in Hue ordered a new curriculum entirely in quoc ngu. It became the national written language in 1919.

Now, only scholars use the traditional calligraphic chu nom to decipher ancient carvings and writings. And during holidays, such as the lunar new year *(Tet),* people buy scrolls written in Chinese characters for their homes. ❑

VIETNAMESE TEMPLES AND PAGODAS

Pagodas and temples reflect the cultural diversity of religious practice in Vietnam and are a focus of social, political and religious life

Each Vietnamese village has its own complex of temple buildings, including the *dinh* (communal house), where the village founder is venerated and the village council, an assembly of male leaders, traditionally met to debate local affairs.

The *chua* or pagoda is regarded as an important social centre for women, while the *den* and *mieu* are shrines to the ancestors of individual families. Vietnamese religious practice is eclectic, and this is reflected in the layout of the temple buildings. Large temple complexes may also include a *phuong dinh* (front hall); *ngoai cung* (central hall); a *noi cung* or main altar hall; and a *cay tien huong*, which acts as a gate to the main temple complex. The choice of temple gods also varies from one village to the next. In some temples, statues of Confucius sit alongside Daoist or Buddhist images. In the north, it is common to find Vietnam war heroes joining the statue line up. More than one dinh offers the chance to burn joss sticks before a life-size statue of Ho Chi Minh.

After 1945, religious activity was discouraged but since the 1980s there has been a revival and many Vietnamese have donated money towards temple renovations in their villages.

△ **LILY PONDS**
Water is an important design element of pagodas and lily flowers, symbolic of peace, enhance reflection.

▷ **SWASTIKAS**
The reversed swastika is an ancient Buddhist icon symbolising harmony.

▷ **CEREMONIAL BELLS**
Bronze bells bear Chinese inscriptions paying homage to the donor and describing village and temple history.

◁ **CHUA MOT COT**
First built in wood in 1049, Ha Noi's Chua Mot Cot (One Pillar Pagoda) was destroyed in 1954 and has since been rebuilt in sturdy concrete.

△ **GUARDIAN SOLDIERS**
Every temple gate has its *quan bao ve* or guardian soldiers, one malevolent and one benevolent, as pictured here at the Thien Mu pagoda in Hue.

▷ **BUDDHIST PRAYERS**
Worshippers attend services at the pagoda on the evenings of the 14th and 30th days of the lunar month to repent for wrongs and vow to act in the right way.

▽ **CHINESE ARCHITECTURE**
Chinese influence on Vietnam's culture is reflected in temple architecture and Chinese characters are common features of religious buildings.

▷ **MONASTIC WELCOME**
Monks and nuns, dressed in simple white or brown tunics, welcome visiting worshippers and are happy to sit over a cup of green tea, explaining in detail the history and the imagery of their pagoda.

THE IMPORTANCE OF INCENSE

Worship in pagodas is informal, as people come and go, chat to the monks, drink tea, and present offerings. But no one visits a pagoda without burning incense. On festival days, packets of joss sticks can be bought outside the pagoda building. One may burn the whole packet or a small number of sticks, depending on the occasion. But the number burned must be an odd number – it is taboo to burn an even number of sticks.

After lighting the incense, worshippers stand in contemplation before the altar for a few moments. They then make respectful bowing movements before placing the burning sticks in a small urn filled with fragrant ash. The rising smoke symbolises communication with the other world. It allows people to maintain contact with ancestors or present wishes to one of the many gods in the Vietnamese religious pantheon.

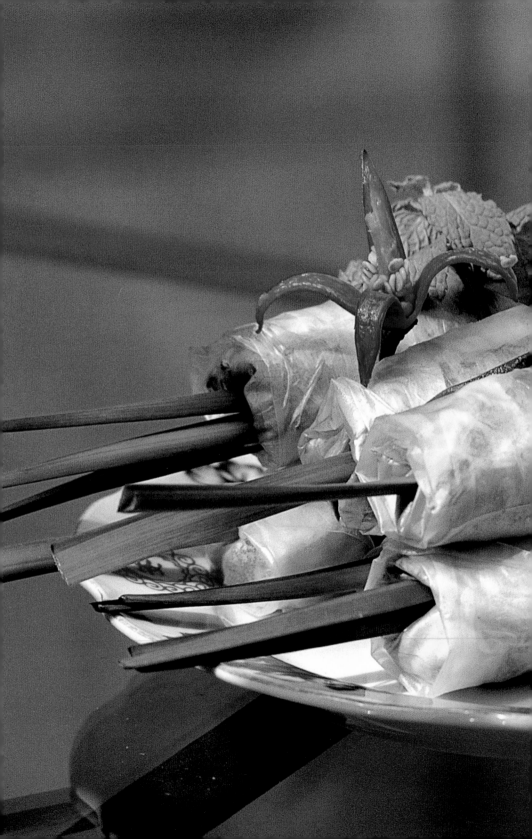

A FLAVOURFUL CUISINE

Much as the country has been divided by politics and culture, so too is Vietnam's
uncommonly healthy cuisine distinctive in its latitudinal differences

For the sociable Vietnamese, a well-stocked dining table is an important symbol of one's hospitality, and visitors to any home, from Can Tho in the Mekong Delta to Hanoi in the north, will be overwhelmed with generosity from the kitchen pantry. Even in the poorest villages where people subsist mainly on rice, people will scrape together whatever they have to give to their guests.

The cuisine itself varies greatly by region. Even dishes that are staples throughout Vietnam are prepared differently in the north, centre, and south. Vietnam's cuisine is like much of its culture in reflecting its many contacts with other cultures over the centuries – Chinese, Khmer, and French the most notable.

Rice (*com* in Vietnamese) is the staple of the diet and the basis of the country's agriculture. In fact, the changing fortunes in rice production reflect quite a bit about Vietnam's economy. In the early 1980s, Vietnam relied on imports to feed its people; as a result, entire provinces of people were starving.

Today, rid of its collectivised farms, Vietnam is now the third-largest rice exporter in the world – despite persistent fears that the country will run out of rice, which frequently causes the government to halt exports and impose quotas. Any Vietnamese over the age of 20 well remembers standing in long queues for rations of meat, and then stretching a monthly rice allotment to its limit.

The years of Chinese influence and occupation are evident in the use of chopsticks and the tendency to eat plain white rice separately with other foods rather than mixing them together.

On every table

Ubiquitous in Vietnamese cooking is the use of a fish sauce called *nuoc mam*. Set on every table like salt in Western countries or soy sauce in China, nuoc mam is used as an ingredient in many dishes, but it is also combined with other ingredients as a condiment called *nuoc cham*. Every cook has his or her own formula, but usually this dipping sauce consists of chilli, lime juice, garlic, sugar, and pepper and is used for a variety of snack-type foods. The fish sauce has something of a pungent

aroma and flavour that can take some getting used to, but it is nonetheless a complement to the subtle flavours of the food. Manufactured in coastal cities such as Phan Thiet and Phu Quoc, the fish sauce is made by fermenting anchovies and salt in large wooden barrels for about six months.

Vietnamese cooks use many fresh herbs – lemon grass, basil, coriander, mint, parsley, laksa leaf – as well as garlic, lime, and ginger. These ingredients lend the cuisine a subtlety of flavour that sets it apart from its neighbours.

French influence brought with it the *pâté* and baguettes sold in the markets and roadside stalls, and an appreciation of French food

PRECEDING PAGES: shrimp spring rolls, or *goi cuon*.
LEFT: fresh, local seafood in Ha Long, east of Hanoi.
RIGHT: Vietnamese food is focused on fresh foods.

shared by visitors and locals alike in the Vietnamese-run French restaurants.

The 3,000 km (1,800 miles) of Vietnam's coastline, innumerable rivers and waterways provide an ample and varied supply of fresh fish and seafood year-round. Fresh- and salt-water fish, shellfish, and crustaceans are eaten as the main source of protein in delicious dishes such as *cha ca,* a barbecued fish made in Hanoi, and in minced fish-meat cakes.

The Vietnamese have created very innovative dishes with pork, chicken, and beef, sometimes combining meat together with fish and seafood. Whether boiled, barbecued, grilled, stewed, or fried, the dishes are a delicious blend of flavours, textures, and influences.

A culinary primer

Here is a primer on some of the Vietnamese specialities visitors will likely encounter.

Cha gio (called *nem Saigon* in the north): small rolls of minced pork, prawn, crab meat, fragrant mushrooms, and vegetables wrapped in thin rice paper and deep fried until crisp. Cha gio is rolled in a lettuce leaf with fresh herbs and dipped in nuoc cham. It makes a thoroughly satisfying meal.

Cha lua: Wrapped in banana leaves before

CULINARY DIVIDES

Variations of taste and spice in Vietnamese food are quite distinctive, even if dishes are the same. Food in the north tends to be more bland, using fewer spices, herbs, and heaps of MSG. In the central part of the country, the food is quite hot but also boasts creative vegetarian cooking, particularly in Hue, where there are many Buddhists who follow a meatless diet. Southern cooking, familiar to Westerners who have eaten in Vietnamese restaurants in the West, tends to be more flavourful and creative than that of the north.

Many northerners complain they cannot eat southern food, claiming that the southern cooks dump sugar into

everything. Sugar is used in dishes such as *pho*, but not in great amounts. In general, southern food isn't sweeter – though coconut milk is often used – just more flavourful.

Southerners, too, don't care for northern food. The south has one essential advantage that diners cannot help but notice: better access to fresh fruits and vegetables – a wider variety of food is grown in the south and the growing seasons are longer. Tropical fruits and vegetables can be hard to find in the north and are often of poor quality. Many southern delicacies are served with raw, leafy vegetables, bean sprouts, and herbs, wrapped up in a do-it-yourself manner probably indigenous to the area.

cooking, this pork pate is served as a snack and on French bread for lunch.

Chao tom: A Hanoi speciality, this unusual appetiser is ground shrimp baked on sugar cane. The shrimp is removed from the sugar cane and rolled in rice paper with lettuce, cucumber, coriander (cilantro) and mint, and then everything is dipped in the obligatory fish sauce.

Cuon diep: Shrimp, noodles, mint, coriander and pork wrapped in lettuce leaves.

Goi ga: Similar to a chicken salad, goi ga is

> ### NOODLE TEMPTRESS
> If there is a dish that defines Vietnam, it is a simple broth of rice noodles called *pho*, sometimes referred to as the mistress of Vietnamese cuisine.

Mien ga: Another type of noodle dish, most popular in the south, mien ga is a soup of chicken, coriander, fish sauce, and scallions.

Banh cuon: A steamed rice pancake that is rolled around minced pork.

Canh chua: A sour soup by which Vietnamese cooks are judged. Often served with shrimp or fish head, the soup is a fragrant blend of sweet and tangy flavours, using tomato, pineapple, star fruit, bean sprouts, fried onion, bamboo shoots, coriander, cinnamon, and, of course, fish sauce.

shredded chicken marinated in onion, vinegar, mint, and, sometimes, peanuts.

Ga xao sa ot: Sauteed chicken cooked with lemon grass, fish sauce, garlic, onion, and chillis. Sometimes peanuts are added.

Bun bo: A Hue speciality, bun bo is fried beef, served over noodles with coriander, onion, garlic, cucumber, chillis and tomato paste.

Hu tieu: Also called Saigon soup, hu tieu is chicken, beef, pork, and shrimp served with a broth over rice noodles, with crab meat, peanuts, onion and garlic.

LEFT: central cuisine representative of Hoi An.
ABOVE: *pho*, a traditional and popular noodle soup.

Banh khoai: Called the Hue pancake, banh khoai is a speciality of that area and is something of an omelette. A batter of rice- and cornflour is fried with egg to make a pancake that is wrapped around pork or shrimp, onion, bean sprouts and mushrooms.

Pho, the noodle mistress

Vietnamese usually eat rice with their meals at home, three times a day. But when they go out, they often eat pho. Vietnamese use foods as a euphemism for their relationships. When you tire of rice (your wife or husband), you take pho (a lover). This analogy suggests a racy – if not spicy – connotation to what is really a simple food. Pronounced *foh,* the soup typically is eaten for breakfast or for a late-night snack, although many people take pho for lunch and dinner, as well.

While the number and variety of restaurants in Vietnam have grown dramatically in recent years, the ubiquitous pho stall is still one of the most popular kinds of eateries. On nearly every street, someone is selling pho – a broth of rice noodles topped with chicken or beef, fresh herbs, and onion. Sometimes, a raw egg yolk is added, and some pho aficionados like to add lime juice, hot peppers, or vinegar. It is usually served with *quay* – a fried piece of flour dough.

There are indoor pho shops with tables and wooden benches, stalls with tiny stools on the sidewalk, and vendors who carry pho in pots strapped to bamboo poles. None of them have menus or tablecloths or serve anything but pho. The floors are often dirty, the walls streaked with mildew. But the pho is always steaming hot and filling.

Pho is most popular in Hanoi, although it is widely eaten in Ho Chi Minh City and the other major cities as well. It is not consumed as much in the countryside, however, for it is somewhat of a luxury.

In fact, before the country began reforming its economy in the mid-1980s, pho was con-

sidered contraband. Pho stalls were illegal, as the government, which rationed meat and rice to families, considered it wasteful to use meat in pho. Often vendors would hide their shops in the backs of their houses and sell pho only to knowing customers. Police often raided the joints and confiscated the pho pots, chopping blocks and soup bowls.

Today, the shops are everywhere, and the best places have customers queuing up in long lines for their morning pho.

Typically, a pho shop sells either chicken or beef – not both. Pho is one of several kinds of noodles Vietnamese eat. *Bun,* usually served with beef, is not a soup but dry noodles. *My,* more common in the south, is a wheat noodle eaten like pho. *Mien* is similar to pho but eaten dry. Pho, however, is the most common. The recipe is fairly standard, although cooks do add their own variations. One pho chef in Hanoi, a woman in her sixties who has a prosperous business selling 1,000 bowls of beef pho every-day, said she cooks the ingredients "until I feel they are ready".

The chef oversees every aspect of the business, which means she has little time to sleep. She cooks from midnight into the early morn-ing, serves pho until early afternoon, and then heads to the market to purchase ingredients for the next day's pho.

She begins her day at midnight, putting on a large pot of water to boil with beef bones and pork bones. She adds fish sauce (used in almost all Vietnamese cooking), ginger, onion and star anise, and then lets the pot simmer for about five hours. "The secret", she says, "is boiling lots of beef and bones".

To serve pho, she takes a bowl, drops in some rice noodles, tops them with beef – raw or cooked, depending on the customer's taste – and pours broth over it. Then she adds some chopped onions, mint, basil, and pepper. Pho – like much of Vietnamese food, especially in the north – uses MSG, though customers wary of eating the additive can ask to have it left out. Often cooks ladle on a large amount of fat. To have that omitted from a serving, customers request *khong beo.* Pho is best, the cook con-fesses, in the late afternoon or evening, after the broth has simmered the longest.   ❑

LEFT: busy roadside stalls are popular.
RIGHT: drying Chinese vermicelli in the Mekong Delta.

PLACES

A detailed guide to the entire country, with principal sites clearly cross-referenced by number to the maps

Travel in Vietnam is anything but easy. After decades of war and with an economy that was subsequently throttled, the country's infrastructure – or lack of it – and pesky vendors at popular sights can test the most hardened traveller's patience. But Vietnam is truly one of those destinations where the inconveniences pale beside the remarkable, and where the beauty of its culture seduces all.

One expects to find the remnants of a war-shattered country, even after nearly three decades of peace, and indeed, one sometimes does. But the residue of war, in an odd irony, is now part of the country's tourism pull, whether for the Cu Chi tunnels outside of the former Saigon or the rusting heaps at a Hanoi war museum. But the war is history, and beyond the memories of war the bright tropical sun illuminates a coastline of serene, white-sand beaches and clear, blue waters, and mists veil forested mountains alive with exotic animals.

Northern Vietnam is anchored by Hanoi, an ancient city established nearly 1,000 years ago. This political capital clings to the rhetoric of a socialist system while at the same time embracing a government-controlled capitalism. The old villas and facades of the French colonial era give the city an ambience not found anywhere else in Asia.

Beyond Hanoi, the provinces of the vast Song Hong, or Red River, delta reflect the traditional agricultural culture upon which the economy is based. And beyond the delta's plains, the cooler mountain regions, populated by hill tribes, ascend towards the west and Laos and northward towards China.

Southwards, following the historical movement of the Viet people, the traveller finds a chain of coastal provinces washed by the South China Sea. In the old imperial city of Hue, an overwhelming sense of the past pervades the older streets. The antiquities don't end here. In the lands of the ancient kingdom of Champa further south are decaying sanctuaries, temples, and towers that testify to the conquest by the Viet people from the north.

Then there is the city of Ho Chi Minh. Often still called Saigon, it is reviving its long-time image as the clichéd hustling-and-bustling city of people on the make and on the go. Where Hanoi is quiet, Ho Chi Minh is frenetic. Where Hue has a subtle and refined beauty, Ho Chi Minh grabs by the lapels and shakes. If Hanoi is a city of earth tones, Ho Chi Minh is neon, all lit up in gaudy lights.

The country has moved far beyond a century of foreign domination and war, and the traveller will find that Vietnam is a land of the ascending dragon and a place finally at peace. ❑

PRECEDING PAGES: early morning voyage in Vinh Ha Long, east of Hanoi; Khai Ninh's tomb, one of many in Hue; night in downtown Ho Chi Minh, or Saigon.
LEFT: tomb of Emperor Tu Duc, in Hue.

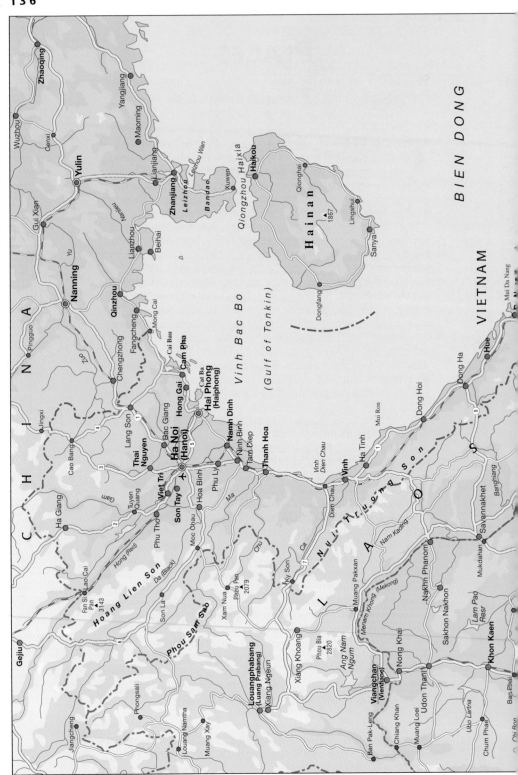

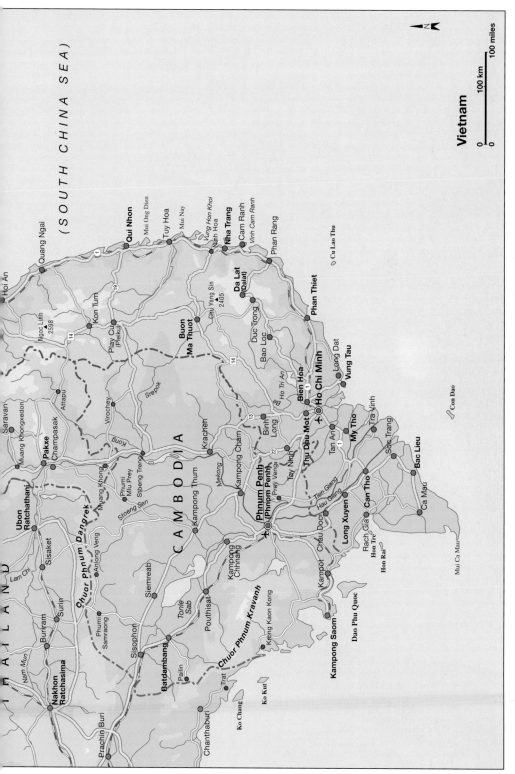

Vietnam

NORTHERN VIETNAM

*The northern provinces of Vietnam are fed by the Song Hong,
anchored by the city of Hanoi, and inhabited by hill tribes*

A journey through northern Vietnam begins in today's political and administrative capital of Hanoi, once the ancient capital of Thang Long. Visitors to Hanoi will encounter the cultures of both East and West, with the changing fortunes of history reflected in the architecture of its many traditional temples and pagodas, in the lingering presence of a French colonial past, and in the whir of construction as the city's blossoming modern towers rise above it all.

Beyond Hanoi and its populous suburbs are the picturesque provincial regions, with their chequerboard paddy fields of rice, the nation's agricultural staple and export earner and nourished by the delta of the Song Hong, or Red River. Green belts of trees and bamboo enclose the villages, where traditional communal houses, pagodas, and temples remain hidden from view.

Men, women, children, and buffalo toil together in the fields, seven days a week, and in all weather. The scene is one of tranquil beauty, but the hardship and toil of this life is obvious.

On the coast to the east, touching Vinh Bac Bo, or the Gulf of Tonkin, is the busy port of Hai Phong, the country's third-largest city and boasting Vietnam's only casino. Nearby, junks sail among the stunning scenery of Vinh Ha Long, an exquisite bay with its grottoes and caves and jutting rocks often shrouded in a mysterious, bewitching fog.

The northern territory, near the Chinese border, is home to ethnic tribes living in mountainous areas, and there is a booming border trade amidst isolated forest retreats.

Throughout the north, the pagodas come alive with festivals – both religious and nationalistic – that have honoured spirits, gods, and war heroes for centuries. This is a seductive countryside, the kind that leaves one with the desire of never leaving. There are waterfalls, rainforests, mountain trails, and village craftspeople making woodcarvings, pottery, embroidery, and lacquered wood.

Here in the north, contemporary Vietnam has the volume turned down a bit as the traditional love of literature, art, and music maintains a toehold against the modern diversions of television, karaoke, and cellular phones. ❑

PRECEDING PAGES: former Viet Cong soldiers now guard bicycles in Hanoi.
LEFT: the sunset's molten glow on Vinh Ha Long, on the coast east of Hanoi.

142

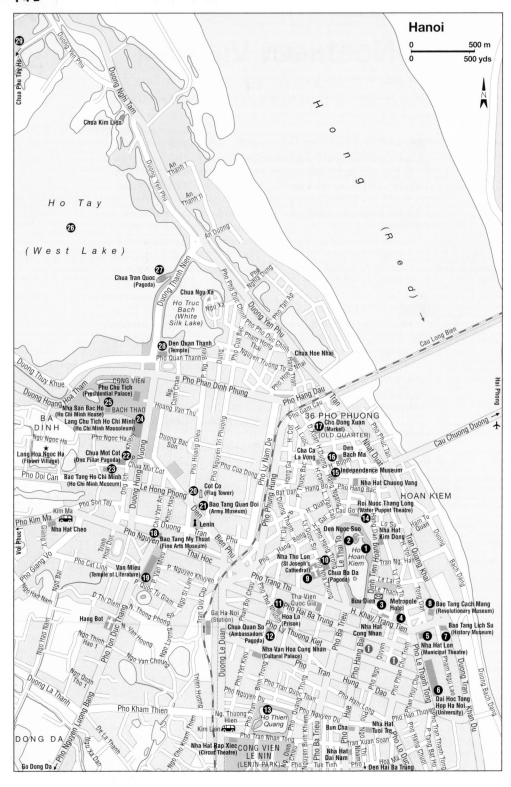

HANOI

*Few cities anywhere in Asia can wink seductively at a traveller
as can Hanoi, with its worn but experienced French charm and a
history that extends back to the rise of an ancient dragon*

Map
on page
142

Hanoi

Hồ Chí Minh

anoi is written as two words in Vietnamese: Ha Noi – *ha* meaning the
river, in reference to **Song Hong**, or the **Red River**, and *noi*, meaning
inside. The city's rich and complex history dates back to the Neolithic
era, when the ancient Viet people settled in the Bach Hac and Viet Tri regions
– in present-day Vinh Phu Province – at the confluence of the Red and Lo
rivers. Today, Hanoi is a decidedly cosmopolitan city with an uncanny
European embellishment. Indeed, it is ironic that this capital city of fiercely
independent people, who have battled for generations against foreign invaders,
possesses a decidedly European air. While people in Hanoi love to brag about
their beautiful city, they don't often admit that much of what makes it beautiful
is the French legacy.

Over the decades, the face of Hanoi increasingly reflected a harmony between
progress and tradition, although this harmony did not extend to the relations
between the Vietnamese and their French overseers. In the wake of new roads
and buildings, tradition suffered. As was the case with many old structures, the
Ba Tien Pagoda was knocked down to make way for a cathedral, and the Bao
An Pagoda was replaced by a post office; today, all that remains of that pagoda
is a small shrine beside Hoan Kiem Lake.

The French architectural legacy, and an abundance
of trees and lakes around the city, give Hanoi a
romantic air unusual for an Asian city. Still, aside
from being spruced up and illuminated in the past
decade, the city centre has evolved little since 1955 –
there are the same pagodas and temples, colonial
architecture, tree-lined streets, and lakes. The soul of
the ancient city rests in the Old Quarter, an area of
artisans and craftsmen dating from the 15th century.

The construction of luxury hotels and gleaming
office towers, which boomed in the mid-1990s when
it seemed that Vietnam was jumping into capitalism
with both feet, has ground to a halt while foreign
investors and companies have second thoughts. But
smaller, crumbling buildings are getting knocked
down or, more commonly, receiving new facades. The
new exteriors aren't usually all that charming but are,
rather, the standard glass-and-chrome front with large,
brightly lit signs.

Hanoi's history

In the third century, after a bloody, decade-long war
against Chinese invaders, King Thuc Phan descended
from the 100 Viet Principalities (a region of 100
separate states encompassing all of southern China)
and founded Au Lac. He installed his capital at Ke
Chu, the site of the vast spiral citadel of Co Loa (Old
Conch). After regaining independence, Vietnam's

BELOW: veterans
having a trim.

Ngo, Dinh, and Le dynasties – of the middle of the 10th to the beginning of the 11th century – installed their capitals at Hoa Lu, 100 km (60 miles) south of Hanoi. There it remained, until Ly Thai To arrived in Dai La – an ancient city along the Song Hong (Red River) – in the early 11th century.

According to legend, Ly Thai To saw an enormous golden dragon emerge from the lake and soar into the sky above the site. On the strength of this omen, he moved the capital from Hoa Lu to Dai La, which he then renamed as Thang Long, or Ascending Dragon.

He found the surrounding countryside at the new site too flat for defensive purposes, so he ordered that dikes and artificial hills be built. Even today, it is still possible to make out the contours of these ancient earthworks in the area.

The royal capital grew from a small lake-side village built on stilts into a town. The area between the West Lake and the citadel became the administrative city *(kinh thanh)*, where the mandarins, officers, soldiers, and general public lived. In the heart of this was the royal city *(hoang thanh)* and behind its high walls was the forbidden city *(cam thanh)*, where the king, queens, and concubines lived in seclusion. In 1010, the centre of the royal city contained eight palaces and three pavilions. Eight new palaces were built during 1029, and further additions were made in 1203. The Temple of Literature, the One Pillar Pagoda, and the Tran Quoc Pagoda were built during this time. In 1400, the capital was transferred to Thanh Hoa by the usurper Ho Qui Ly, who took over from the Tran dynasty. His capital, Tay Kinh (lit. Capital of the West), lasted until the Le dynasty restored the capital to Hanoi in 1428.

BELOW: near the old Opera House on Trang Tien, 1905.

From the 16th century onward, few new buildings were constructed in Hanoi. King Gia Long built a smaller Vauban-style citadel, but the French colonialists

Map
on page
142

tore down the walls and gates, and all that remains today is the flag tower. The royal city was destroyed twice in less than 50 years: first in 1786, when King Le Chieu Thong ordered the destruction of the Trinh Palace, then in 1820 by Gia Long's son, Minh Mang, in his fury at the Chinese emperor's recognition of Thang Long – and not Hue – as the capital. In 1848, Tu Duc had most of the remaining palace destroyed and its valuable contents moved to Hue, the 19th-century capital of the Nguyen emperors.

The dawn of the 17th century marked the arrival of Dutch, Portuguese, and French traders. Hot on their heels came Christian missionaries. The great influx of newcomers and diverse ideas from Europe brought many changes to the capital of Thang Long. The French presence and influence grew, eventually changing the course of Vietnamese history. When Hanoi fell into the hands of the French in 1882, the city underwent transformation and modernisation.

In the heart of the city

In the very heart of the old town of Hanoi lies **Ho Hoan Kiem ❶**, or Lake of the Restored Sword. Early-rising travellers can catch locals seriously pursuing their morning exercises of *taiqi quan*, calisthenics, badminton, or running before going off to work. In the evening, especially on holidays, the lake is ringed by a carnival atmosphere as vendors sell balloons and toys, with little girls dressed up in frilly dresses and music blaring from loudspeakers. Several outdoor cafes sell ice cream, coffee, and beer while looking out onto the water.

A legend that sounds like a Vietnamese version of Excalibur tells of how King Le Thai To received a magic sword that he used during his 10-year resistance against the Chinese Ming court in the early 1400s. After liberating the

One of Hanoi's early names, Dong Kinh, or Capital of the East, became Tunquin when Vietnamese became romanised. Tunquin, in turn, begot Tonkin, which is what France called the northern "protectorate" of Vietnam.

BELOW: couple at Ho Hoan Kiem.

Thap Rua reflected in Ho Hoan Kiem.

country, the king took a boat to the centre of the lake to return the magic sword given to him by the Divine Tortoise. The tortoise is said to have snatched the sword from his hand and disappeared into the lake. That, apparently, is how the lake acquired its name.

Near the middle of the lake stands the small, 18th-century tower, **Thap Rua**, or Tortoise Tower. A large tortoise is said to still live in the lake and on certain days of the year – usually when the seasons change – people claim to see the tortoise emerge from the water. Perched on a tiny islet in the lake not far from the tower is the **Den Ngoc Son ❷** (Temple of the Jade Mound). The temple is reached from the shore via the brightly painted red, arched bridge known as The Huc, or Sunbeam Bridge. On the small hillock at the end of the bridge stands a stone column in the form of a brush next to an ink well and inscribed with three Chinese characters, *ta tien qing*, meaning "written on the blue sky". Also on the islet are the remains of a small communal house.

The city's main post office is on Dinh Tien Hoang, on the southeast side of the lake. One block north of the **Buu Dien ❸** (Central Post Office) there is a small park where sweethearts hold late-night trysts and where during the day young men and boys play soccer. Opposite the park's eastern border, on Pho Ly Thai To, is the great Art Deco-style State Bank. Across from the park's southeastern corner is the arresting **State Guest House**. Yellow-coloured with green trim and protected by a wrought-iron fence, the building began in 1918 as the palace of the French governor of Tonkin.

Southwards, straddling Ly Thai To and Ngo Quyen, is the white **Sofitel Metropole Hotel ❹**, the only international-class hotel in French days and a rat-ridden firetrap by the 1980s. Thoroughly gutted by new French management in

BELOW: State Guest House.

the 1990s, it is purportedly the most expensive hotel in town. It's then only a short walk down Ly Thai To to the columned **Nha Hat Lon** ❺ (Municipal Theatre, often called the Opera House). After years of renovation, this renewed beauty has begun hosting performances by foreign orchestras and other high-culture events. A few days after the Japanese surrender in World War II, Viet Minh cadres rushed into the city. On 19 August 1945, they declared the establishment of an independent democratic republic from the theatre's balcony and unfurled their banners. Tens of thousands of peasants armed with machetes and bamboo spears were joined by tens of thousands of city residents. A few days previously, few of the latter had heard of the Viet Minh, but now they were caught up in patriotic euphoria and obeyed orders to seize important buildings from the Japanese and their Vietnamese collaborators.

Skirting the southern tip of the lake, Trang Tien, which terminates in front of the Municipal Theatre, was once the high shopping street of the French Quarter. When communists closed private enterprises, Trang Tien was one of the few areas retaining any commercial air. The communist whiff is still unmistakable in the drab, state-run art galleries, bookstores, and a "department store". In the blocks to the south and west, on quiet tree-lined streets, the colonialists' old villas now house many embassies and diplomatic residences.

The road southeast of the theatre, Pho Le Thanh Tong, runs by the **University of Hanoi** ❻ with its dilapidated colonial-era buildings. Indeed, some of the structures and plumbing appear not to have been touched since the French evacuated in the 1950s. Founded in the 1920s as the University of Indochina, it offered vocational and agricultural courses. In the 1930s, schools of law, medicine, science, and arts were added. The Indochinese students that studied

Map on page 142

BELOW: rainbow over the renovated Municipal Theatre.

Offerings at a Hanoi antique shop.

here, including the future Gen. Vo Nguyen Giap, truly were an intellectual (and probably financial) elite, given that the French commitment to lower education and literacy was always trifling. In 1937, the student body here numbered 631 and included French students. It was the only genuine university in all of Indochina, which then had a population of about 25 million.

Behind the Municipal Theatre, with a cupola resembling a pagoda, is **Bao Tang Lich Su** ❼ (History Museum; open Tues–Sun, 8am–4pm; admission fee). It occupies the old archaeological research institution of the French School of the Far East, which opened in 1910 and was substantially renovated in the 1920s. High on content and low on propaganda, this is perhaps the best museum in town. The excellent archaeological collection includes relics from the Hung era and Neolithic graves, Bronze Age implements, bronze drums from Ngoc Lu and Mieu Mon, Cham relics, stelae, statues, ceramics, and an eerie sculpture of the goddess of mercy, Quan Am, with her 1,000 eyes and arms. An ornate throne, clothes, and artefacts belonging to the 13 Nguyen-dynasty kings are displayed. Nearby, **Bao Tang Cach Mang** ❽ (Revolutionary Museum; open Tues–Sun, 8am–4pm, Sat to 11.30am; admission fee) on Tong Dan offers a carefully edited version of the struggles of the Vietnamese people from ancient times up until 1975. Displayed are the long, wooden stakes that crippled the Mongol fleet in Ha Long Bay, during one of three invasion attempts in the 13th century, and a bronze drum from 2,400 BC.

Southwest of Ho Tay

BELOW: strealside flower vendor.

Where Pho Nha Chung joins Ly Quoc Su is the oldest church in the city, **Nha Tho Lon** ❾ (St Joseph's Cathedral; the Vietnamese call it the "big church").

Simplified Gothic in style, it was consecrated on Christmas night in 1886. Some of the stained-glass windows date from then. The cathedral was built on the site of the Bao Thien Pagoda, which was razed to build the cathedral. Celebration of the Mass resumed here only in 1990. After more than 30 years of repression, faith proved to be remarkably resilient after reopening its doors; on Sundays, services are absolutely packed. Several shops in this area sell tribal clothing, handicrafts, water puppets, and painstakingly painted copies of famous Western art.

A narrow passageway next to 5 Nha Tho, the street facing the cathedral, leads to **Chua Ba Da ⑩**, between the cathedral and Ho Hoan Kiem. This charming pagoda was built in the 15th century after the discovery of a stone statue of a woman during the construction of the Thang Long citadel to the west. The statue, which was thought to have magic powers, disappeared and has since been replaced by a wooden replica. The pagoda's modest exterior belies its exquisite interior and atmosphere. An impressive line-up of gilt Buddha statues forms the central altar.

On Ly Quoc Su, to the north of the cathedral, is the small **Chua Ly Trieu Quoc Su**, a pagoda also known as Chua Kong, the Pagoda of Confucius. It was founded under the Ly dynasty in the 11th century and later restored in 1855. The pagoda contains some attractive lacquered wooden statues and carved roof beams, all overseen by an elderly bonze who is said to have lived there for over 60 years, and without ever leaving the building.

South about three blocks is the site of the infamous prison of **Hoa Lo ⑪**, known as the Hanoi Hilton to both American prisoners-of-war incarcerated and tortured here and to present-day cyclo and taxi drivers. The prisoners included the US ambassador to Vietnam in the late 1990s, Pete Peterson. It is of importance to Vietnamese for other reasons: the French imprisoned, tortured, and guillotined countless revolutionaries within the walled compound that until recently occupied an entire block. In 1932, 10,000 political prisoners were incarcerated in this and other prisons altogether.

In 1994, the prison was almost totally demolished to make way for an enormous foreign-financed, curtain-glass office tower and hotel complex. Topped with barbed and electric wire, the yellow concrete main gate and a few cells of Hoa Lo have been preserved as a museum, with exhibits of stocks and a guillotine. The vintage government propaganda found here is increasingly out of style elsewhere in Vietnam. Across the street from the prison is the Hanoi People's Court.

Several blocks away, the **Chua Quan Su ⑫** (Ambassadors' Pagoda), located on 73 Pho Quan Su, is perhaps the busiest pagoda in town. On the 1st and 15th days of the lunar month, throngs gather to make offerings. In the 17th century the site was a guesthouse for envoys from other Buddhist countries, hence its name. Rare for a Vietnamese pagoda, one is likely to catch sight of monks here. In the long, low buildings surrounding the temples are schoolrooms for novice monks and a small library of parchment and texts in Vietnamese and Chinese; this is a centre

Map on page 142

BELOW: studying the life of Buddha at Chua Quan Su.

American-style lighters for sale to tourists recall the Vietnam War.

for Buddhist research. Quan Su Street dead ends at a bare stone plaza to the south and the forbidding Soviet-style **Nha Van Hoa Cong Nhan** (Cultural Palace), sometimes used for sporting events and trade shows.

To the south of Quan Su pagoda about 500 metres (1,600 ft) is a lovely small lake, **Ho Thien Quang ⑬**, where visitors can rent paddle boats. Just south across the street is an entrance to **Cong Vien Le Nin** (Lenin Park) and, to the west, Hanoi's circus. Facing Pho Tran Nhan Tong, the park is said to have been built by local volunteer workers on marshy land once used as a rubbish dump. This attractive, well-maintained park is designed around the large **Ho Bay Mau** (Bay Mau Lake). A small train for children runs through the park.

The Old Quarter

Northward of Ho Hoan Kiem (Hoan Kiem Lake), many streets lead to a favourite haunt of travellers, the area known as **36 Pho Phuong** (36 Streets or the **Old Quarter**). The charm of the Old Quarter's narrow lanes lies in a 600-year history as an artisans' district, with crafts and trades concentrated in a single area on 36 lanes. Silverworkers were found on Pho Hang Bac (Silver Merchandise Street), bamboo basketmakers on Hang Bo (Bamboo Basket Merchandise), and so on. The present-day commercial frenzy (not to mention intense motorbike and bicycle traffic) has evolved from virtually nothing in less than a decade. It's all the more amazing considering that, with very few exceptions, the communists prohibited private trade for more than 40 years.

BELOW: hot evening at an outdoor *pho* restaurant.

The new tradesmen still tend to concentrate by speciality, but the speciality doesn't necessarily match the street name any longer. Silver jewellery, as well as gravestones, can still be found on Hang Bac, but the future of this street

clearly rests on travel agencies and tourist cafes. The street of Hang Gai (Hemp) specialises in silk, clothing, and embroidered articles. Hang Dau (Cooking Oil) is full of shoe shops. However, Hang Chieu (Mat) is still the place to find mats and Hang Ma (Paper Votive Objects) features stationery shops.

Each of the 36 craft guilds once had its own *dinh* (communal house). But like most of the quarter's pagodas and temples, they were shut down during the communist takeover and transformed into schools or housing. Similarly, the narrow storefronts, some less than 3 metres (10 ft) wide, once fronted single-family dwellings; these "tubehouses" still extend far back, punctuated by courtyards, but were re-apportioned among many families.

By examining the roof lines, one can sometimes discern an old temple. For example, at 120 Hang Bong (Cotton), a yellowing pagoda arch crowns a barber stall and a banner shop. A side alley affords entry to a tiny courtyard and a single remaining hall that still draws worshippers and seekers of good luck. The Hoa Loc Dinh, at 90 Hang Dao (Peach), was once a communal house for people from the village of Hai Duong. It is now a shop selling blue jeans. According to records discovered on a stele, these villagers settled here towards the end of the Tang-dynasty era and founded the artisan district of Thai Cuc, which became the street of Hang Dao.

There is a delightful nightly performance of water puppets, accompanied by traditional music, on the northeast corner of the lake at the **Roi Nuoc Thang Long** ⓮ (Thang Long Water Puppet Theatre) on the corner of Dinh Tien Hoang. In a small house on Hang Ngang is the **Independence Museum** ⓯. Here, Ho Chi Minh wrote Vietnam's declaration of independence, which borrows considerably from America's own declaration.

Map on page 142

BELOW: Old Quarter bicycle shop.

The 1,682-metre-long (5,520-ft) Long Bien Bridge, once known as the Doumer Bridge, dates from 1902. The bridge suffered damage from American bombing but was continually repaired. Until 1983, all northbound road and rail traffic passed over it. These days, it is reserved for cyclists, trains, and pedestrians.

Den Bach Ma ⑯ (White Horse Temple) on Hang Buom (Sails Street) is dedicated to the deity Bach Ma. Besides the giant wooden horse statue inside, a palanquin is adorned with carvings of phoenixes, cranes, and turtles. Originally built during the 9th century, it was reconstructed in the 18th and 19th centuries. In regular use, it remains in a good state of repair. This street runs into a little street called Ma May, which has a good selection of crumbling colonial facades fronting more ancient tubehouses.

The area around the **Cho Dong Xuan** ⑰, the large market at the end of Hang Dao in the northern part of the Old Quarter, is an interesting place to explore. The old colonial-era market, destroyed by fire in 1994, has been replaced with an already grimy four-storey building; its escalator, perhaps the city's first, is permanently frozen. This is the wholesale source for many dry goods. The counterfeit Calvin Klein T-shirts and other low-quality apparel seem intended for the Vietnamese customer, but it's a good place to shop for cooking utensils and kitchenware. In the streets around the market, farmers squat on the pavement selling their produce directly to passers-by. Keep an eye out for caviar, French wine, champagne, and Russian vodka, as they are surprisingly cheap in Hanoi and definitely the genuine article. Florists add a welcome splash of colour with their fragrant blooms. Nearby, a traditional medicine shop sells all manner of cures, including snake wine and lizards preserved in alcohol. Do not be put off by appearances; the gecko elixir is excellent. Other vendors sell live snakes, birds, and monkeys.

Near here, at the end of Hang Chieu and close to Tran Nhat Duat, is the crumbling brick gate of **Quan Chuong**, the last remnant of a wall that once encircled the Old Quarter.

BELOW: Long Bien Bridge.

Western Hanoi

At the **Bao Tang My Thuat** ⑱ (Fine Arts Museum; Tues–Sun, 8am–4pm; admission fee), on Pho Nguyen Thai Hoc, exhibits include displays on minority folk art and history and Dong Son bronze drums, Dong Noi stone carvings, Cham statues and carvings, communal house decorations dating from the 16th century, and 18th-century wood Buddha statues in some surprisingly undignified poses. There is information, too, on the evolution since the 17th-century Le dynasty of a Vietnamese speciality – lacquer painting on wood. Note the rare examples of lacquer painting on paper. In the 20th century, Vietnamese artists quickly adopted perspective and the use of oil paint and later were inspired by impressionism, post-impressionism, and the modernism of Picasso and Dali – right up until the present day. Some visitors are disappointed that most of the Social Realist and war-time propaganda paintings have been removed, but for content, this and the History Museum are the best in town.

Nearby, across the street just to the south, is the **Van Mieu** ⑲ (Temple of Literature). Built in 1070 under the reign of King Ly Thai Tong, the temple is dedicated to Confucius. In 1076, the temple was adjoined by the Quoc Tu Giam, School of the Elite of the Nation, Vietnam's first university. Under the Tran dynasty, the school was renamed the Quoc Hoc Vien, or the National College, in 1235. After passing exams at the local levels, scholars aspiring to become senior mandarins came here to study for rigorous triennial examinations. The subjects of study were literature, philosophy, and ancient Chinese and Vietnamese history, which Confucians believed provided the ideal training for government administrators. The Van Mieu became known as the Temple of Literature when the capital was transferred to Hue at the beginning of the 18th

Map on page 142

Sculpture at the Fine Arts Museum.

BELOW: breakfast of *pho* at street stand.

century. Above the main entrance gate is an inscription requesting visitors to dismount from horses before entering.

The large temple enclosure is divided into five walled courtyards. After passing through the Van Mieu Mon and the first two courtyards past this gate, one arrives at the Khue Van Cac (Pleiade Pavilion), where the men of letters used to recite their poems. Through the Dai Thanh Mon (Great Wall Gate), an open courtyard surrounds a large, central pool known as the Thien Quang Tinh (Well of Heavenly Clarity). Now regrouped and sheltered under a roof, the 82 stone stelae, survivors of an original 117, rest on the backs of stone tortoises. Until a few years ago, they were exposed to the elements under the trees on either side of the courtyard. (American Express funded the preservation effort, as they did with Beijing's Imperial Palace.) The stelae are inscribed with the names, works, and academic records of 1,306 scholars who succeeded in the 82 examination sessions held between 1442 and 1779. The French halted examinations here in 1915 (and in Hue in 1918). By then, the importation of Chinese-language materials had been prohibited for seven years; the French set out to shut down all Sino-Vietnamese schools still operating in villages. Dai Thanh (Great Success Gate) leads to the temple itself.

Facing it is the Bai Duong (House of Ceremonies), where sacrifices were offered in honour of Confucius. Today, musicians perform traditional music and charge a small fee to those who choose to sit and listen. Behind are the Eastern Gate and the Great Success Sanctuary, which have been renovated. In the final overgrown courtyard are the ruins of the National Academy, destroyed by French aerial bombing in 1947. These were the academy buildings where the examinations were held.

BELOW: street-side baguette seller.

To the north on Duong Dien Bien Phu is one of the symbols of Hanoi, the flag tower of **Cot Co ⓴**. Built in 1812 under the Nguyen dynasty as part of the Hanoi citadel, the hexagonal 60-metre (200-ft) tower is more or less all that remains of the citadel, which was destroyed at the end of the 19th century. Next to it, the **Bao Tang Quan Doi ㉑** (Army Museum; open daily 8am–4.30pm, admission fee), renovated in the 1990s, chronicles Vietnam's battles for independence and unification against the French and American patrons of South Vietnam. The crumpled wreckage of a B-52 bomber sits in an outside courtyard. Inside are the uniforms of captured American pilots, photographs of Vietnamese war heroes and items belonging to the fallen leaders of what was South Vietnam.

South across the street is a small, triangular-shaped park with a bronze statue of Lenin, depicted striding forth in a business suit and larger than life. It must be one of the world's last extant monuments to the Russian revolutionary. Children play soccer on the plaza in front of the statue and in the pleasant park behind it.

Continuing northwest up Dien Bien Phu, a small road called Chua Mot Cot leads to the unique **Chua Mot Cot ㉒** (One Pillar Pagoda). Originally built in 1049 under the Ly dynasty, this wooden pagoda rests on a single concrete pillar rising out of a lotus pool. It was most recently reconstructed after departing

French soldiers blew it up in 1954. The banyan tree behind the pagoda was planted by Pres. Nehru of India in 1958 during an official visit to the young Vietnamese republic.

Map on page 142

Legend has it that in a dream King Ly Thai To saw the goddess Quan Am seated on a lotus leaf offering him a male child in her outstretched arms. Shortly after his dream, he married a young peasant girl who bore him the male heir of which he had dreamed. The king built the pagoda as a sign of his gratitude.

Behind the park with the pagodas rises a massive, angular Soviet-style structure, the **Bao Tang Ho Chi Minh** ㉓ (Ho Chi Minh Museum; open Tues–Sun, 8am–4pm; admission fee). Potential visitors should proceed even if the vast car park is empty; it is still probably open. The exhibits include many photos, documents, and personal effects (such as Ho's pencil) that celebrate Ho's revolutionary life. Note Ho's letter, in English, written from Thailand to the Comintern in the late 1920s reporting his disappointing efforts to organise Christian Vietnamese immigrants in Siam and Laos. But this museum's notoriety stems from the bizarreness of other features. There's the gigantic lopsided table with a giant bowl of artificial fruit, a reconstruction of *Guernica*, a Constructivist iron tower, a plaster volcano, unconvincing "image-complexes" (such as Ho's childhood hut) and, most telling, the Ho statue arranged to evoke a Buddhist altar. Old American pop tunes (including the Carpenters) supply the museum's background music and the souvenir shop sells "Good morning, Vietnam!" T-shirts. Few foreigners can refrain from remarking that "if Ho had a grave, would he be spinning in it?" Exiting down the stairs, visitors are swiftly ushered into a windowless side room, where a small orchestra conducts a brief performance of soothing traditional music, often for an audience of one.

Ho Chi Minh's house.

Immediately north looms the massive marble-and-granite **Lang Chu Tich Ho Chi Minh** ㉔ (Ho Chi Minh Mausoleum; open Tues–Thurs, Sat–Sun, 7.30–11am; admission fee), in **Ba Dinh Square** where Ho Chi Minh delivered Vietnam's declaration of independence in 1945. The embalmed corpse lies in a glass casket within this monumental tomb, contrary to Ho's wish to be cremated. In autumn, it is advisable to check beforehand whether he is in residence. Rumour has it that he is packed off to Russia for an embalming refresher, although some Vietnamese say he is repaired in a basement cold storage with the help of Russian experts. Dressed in uniform, the guarded body lies displayed on a platform in a cold room.

BELOW: queuing at the Ho Chi Minh mausoleum.

Visitors are ushered quickly past either side. No cameras or handbags may be taken inside. Foreigners are whisked to the front of the queues. He died in 1969 on the same date as his independence declaration. (It was officially reported as 3 September for years, so as not to dampen National Day celebrations.)

Behind the mausoleum to the west is the charming **Nha San Bac Ho** ㉕ (Ho Chi Minh House; open daily 7am–4pm), overlooking a carp pond in a quiet and shaded park. Built on stilts, tribal-style, the modest living quarters consist of two small rooms. Below is an open-air meeting room. Although there are no toilet, washing, cooking, or dining facilities,

New wealth on the shores of Ho Tay.

Ho allegedly lived here most of the time during the war against the United States, preferring it to the sumptuous colonial mansion on the same grounds, the former **Presidential Palace**.

Closed to the public, the palace was formerly the residence of the French governor-general. Behind the palace, but best reached from Hoang Hoa Tham, is a quiet public park with rolling hills, contemporary sculpture, and trees.

Around Ho Tay (West Lake)

From Ba Dinh Square, where the National Assembly building is located across from the mausoleum and where there is a war memorial, head north towards vast **Ho Tay** ㉖ (West Lake), formerly known as the Lake of Mists. This lake, the largest in Hanoi, lies in an ancient bed of the Song Hong (Red River). Royal and warlord palaces once graced its banks; these were destroyed in feudal battles. Since the 1990s, the lake has seen considerable building activity – large villas, hotels, and restaurants, mostly of dubious taste, have sprung up. Many foreigners and new Vietnamese millionaires live in this area. Legend says the lake was previously the site of a huge forest, the lair of a wicked fox with nine tails. The creature terrorised the neighbourhood until it was drowned by the Dragon King, who, in the process of unleashing the waters to get rid of the beast, created the lake.

No less fantastic is an alternative legend that tells the story of an 11th-century bonze and a golden buffalo. The bonze, Khong Lo, had an enormous bronze bell made. When its sound first reached the ears of the golden buffalo, the confused creature, believing that he had heard his mother's voice, rushed immediately towards the south and in his stampede transformed the site into a lake.

Map on page 142

During an uprising against the occupying Chinese in 545, the national hero Ly Bon built a wooden-and-bamboo citadel at the mouth of the Song To Lich, at the same time building Chua Khai Quoc (Foundation of the Country Pagoda) beside the Red River. In the 17th century, the pagoda was transferred to its present site on the tiny peninsula of the Ho Tay and renamed **Chua Tran Quoc ㉗**. The Tran Quoc is perhaps Vietnam's most ancient pagoda; its stele, dating from 1639, recounts the pagoda's long history.

Separated from the lake by Duong Thanh Nien is **Ho Truc Bach** (White Silk Lake). This was the ancient site of Lord Trinh's summer palace, which later became a harem where he detained his wayward concubines. The lake derives its name from the beautiful white silk these concubines were forced to weave for the princesses. Nearby, the ornate **Den Quan Thanh ㉘** beside the lake was originally built during the Ly dynasty (1010–1225). This temple houses a huge bronze bell and an enormous, four-ton bronze statue of Tran Vu, guardian deity of the north, to whom the temple is dedicated. It was Tran Vu who helped King An Duong dispose of the devils and ghosts that harassed and plagued the building of Vietnam's ancient capital at Co Loa.

Situated at the lake's centre, at the tip of a small peninsula, is **Chua Phu Tay Ho ㉙**, a popular destination for pilgrims and unmarried Vietnamese, particularly on the 15th day of the lunar month. The long lane from Yen Phu is lined with restaurants, shops, and karaoke bars. The hall on the right is especially garish and will appeal to children. The altars are crammed with statuettes of strange beasts, grottoes, and miniature sailing ships. Added daily by worshippers are heaps of fruit and packets of biscuits, amongst other things, brought to the pagoda as offerings.

West of Hanoi, hills extend up to the 1,200-metre (4,000 ft) summit of Mt Ba, 65 km (40 miles) from the city. In the northwest, the city is bordered by Ho Tay, or West Lake.

BELOW: cyclo drivers at Ho Tay.

Map on page 142

Outside the city centre

In the south of the city on Pho Tho Lao is **Den Hai Ba Trung** (Temple of the Two Sisters), also known as the Dong Nhan temple after the village that surrounded the site at the time of its construction in 1142. The temple is dedicated to the two Trung sisters who organised an uprising against the Chinese Han invaders in AD 40. Two unusually formed stone statues recovered from the Red River and said to represent the two sisters are kept in a small room. They are brought out annually for a February procession, dressed in new clothes.

A little further south on Bach Mai, **Chua Lien Phai** and the pagoda's Buddhist monastery, Lien Phai Tu, or Lieu Khai, are sheltered in an attractive garden. The temple was built under the Le dynasty and reconstructed by one of the Trinh lords in 1732. It has been restored at least twice since. Three statues, two representing good and evil, occupy the main room.

The Tay Dang *dinh*, or communal house, in Hanoi's Bay Vi suburb is worth visiting for its beautiful architectural structure and carving. The original construction date is unknown, but inscriptions on a beam reveal that it was extensively restored in the 16th century and that further repairs were carried out in 1808, 1926, and 1942. Built entirely of hardwood, it comprises five partitions and four roofs, whose curling tops are decorated with *tu linh* – dragons, unicorns, tortoises, and the phoenix, the four animals that according to folklore bring happiness. Many valuable woodcarvings grace the interior.

Behind Thu Le Park in the northwest of the city is the 11th-century **Voi Phuc** (Temple of the Kneeling Elephants), built by King Ly Thai To in honour of his son who distinguished himself during the war against Chinese Song-dynasty invaders by charging the enemy with his squadron of elephants. The simple lakeside temple houses statues of the prince and his generals. In front of the temple are stone statues of kneeling elephants.

Southwest of the city, in Dong Da district, is the **Go Dong Da** (Mound of the Multitudes) on Tay Son, next to number 356. Legend says that Go Dong Da was formed by the bodies of Chinese soldiers killed after Quang Trung's victory. Very little remains of the temple that was constructed on the site, but dozens of steps lead to the top of the mound. Beyond the mound is a large statue of Quang Trung, built in the Social Realist style.

Bao Tang Dan Toc Hoc Viet Nam (Vietnam Museum of Ethnology), on Van Huyen, is Hanoi's newest and superficially most modern museum. Few tourists come here, but it would especially appeal to children. For those heading out to the northwest part of Vietnam, this is a good introduction to tribal clothing and housing. There are audiotapes, videos, full-scale models, crafts, and musical instruments. However, at least so far, few of the 54 ethnic groups are represented. It's to be expected that there would be no mention of the communists' assimilation policies, now largely abandoned. But perhaps because the French funded the museum, there is also the curious omission of genocidal colonial practices, such as forced labour on plantations, that wiped out some tribes and permanently altered the cultures of the others. ❑

BELOW: offerings at a spice shop.

Co Loa

In the Dong Anh district of Hanoi's western suburbs lie the remains of the citadel fortress of Co Loa. Excavations in the area have uncovered ancient arms and many bronze arrowheads. Co Loa dates from 257 BC, when it served as the capital of the Thuc dynasty under King An Duong Vuong. Of the nine ramparts that covered an area of more than 5 sq. km (2 sq. miles), three are still visible. Architectural and sculptural works remain in the citadel's centre.

Within the citadel's gateway, an historical banyan tree shades the shrine dedicated to Princess My Chau. Inside is a rough stone statue of a headless woman thought to be the princess. Further on is the upper temple dedicated to King An Duong Vuong. People gather here on 6 January every year to celebrate the king's efforts against foreign invaders. The Vietnamese, with their irrepressible talent for blending history and legend, will tell you that King An Duong Vuong, of Tay Au, invaded Lac Viet after his request to marry the king of Vietnam's daughter was unceremoniously refused. He managed to annex the country of his coveted princess and amalgamated the territories of Tay Au and Lac Viet to form the kingdom of Au Lac.

Aware that this expansion would antagonise his great northern neighbour, China, An Duong Vuong wasted no time in building the walls of his new capital. But for some mysterious reason his efforts were frustrated and the walls repeatedly collapsed. The mystery was finally revealed when the golden tortoise, Kim Quy, appeared to the king in a dream and disclosed that occult forces were responsible. Aided by the tortoise, the king was able to defeat the evil forces and complete his indestructible fortress. China, however, wanted the fortress destroyed. Gen. Trieu Da was picked for the task. But the repeated attempts of his powerful forces proved futile.

The golden tortoise again appeared to the king and this time provided him with a magic crossbow. The following day the Chinese forces suffered heavy losses from the arrows of the crossbow. Seeing this, Trieu Da realised that all was not as it appeared and

so called for peace. He asked for, and was granted, the hand of the king's daughter, My Chau, for his son Trong Thuy. During the honeymoon, Trong Thuy asked his young wife to show him her father's crossbow. The unsuspecting My Chau obediently did so, but Trong Thuy took the magic crossbow and substituted another in its place. The king was so furious when he discovered this that he beheaded the princess. Her inconsolable husband is said to have drowned himself.

Co Loa was not only Vietnam's first capital but also something of an architectural marvel. Three earthen walls, 4 to 5 metres (13 to 16 ft) high and at certain strategic points 8 to 12 metres (26 to 39 ft) high, enclosed the capital. The 8-km-long (5-mile) outer wall was reinforced with thorny bamboo hedges and surrounded by a deep moat. Watch towers were built at the eight cardinal points of the citadel's ramparts. Guards held vigil throughout the night, kept awake by gongs that resounded every half hour until dawn. The citadel's spiral form amplified sound from within and carried it to nearby villages. ❑

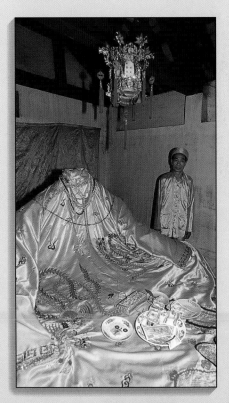

162

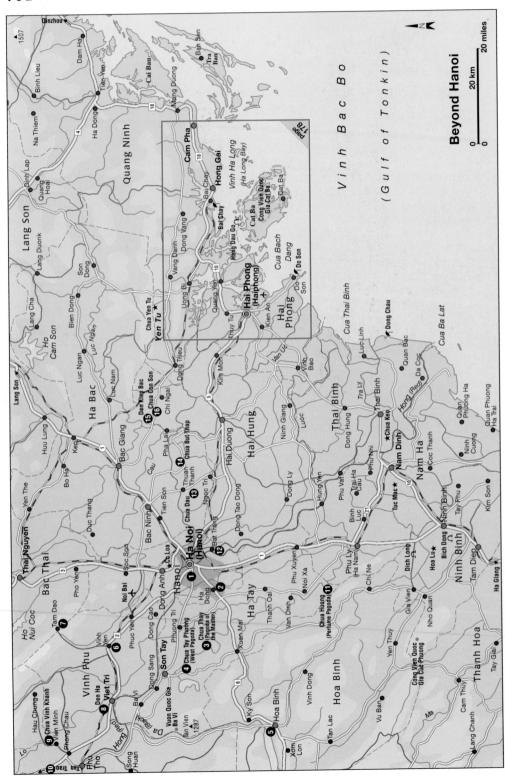

Beyond Hanoi

BEYOND HANOI

Map
on page
162

*Northern Vietnam is defined by the fecundity and moods of the
Song Hong, or Red River, whose delta makes the area
a lush rice-growing region and cradle of Vietnamese civilisation*

Excursions beyond **Hanoi ❶** add an element to the Vietnam experience
that makes the effort well worthwhile. Some of the trips can be booked with
tour agencies in Hanoi, others require use of local buses (slow and uncomfortable) or even trains (slow and uncomfortable). The area is agriculturally
rich and expansive, nurtured by the **Song Hong**, or **Red River**, which spreads
its alluvial deposits over much of northern Vietnam. Beyond the rice paddies,
several ancient pagodas are within reach in a day or two, as are some highland
escapes. Closer to Hanoi, craftsmen offer their efforts in shops.

The province neighbouring Hanoi to the northwest, Vinh Phu, is the cradle of
the pre-Vietnamese Hung Lac people and the ancestral land of the Viet, who first
settled here before moving into the Song Hong delta region. Bronze relics 4,000
years old have been discovered in the region. The area still bears the mark of the
early settlers' presence in the remains of the Hung temples. These were built by
the rulers of the Van Lang kingdom between the 7th and 3rd centuries BC, when
a line of 18 Hung kings graced the throne of Vang Lang.

PRECEDING PAGES:
terraced rice fields.
BELOW: a schoolgirl
cradles two goats.

West of Hanoi

Leaving Hanoi by the southwest, Highway 6 traverses a plateau. It takes about
an hour to negotiate the sprawl of vehicles and con-
struction around Hanoi, but then traffic thins
markedly. The two-lane paved road, flat and in good
condition, is well suited for touring by bicycle or
motorbike through the rice fields. Hills and cliffs gradually appear in the distance.

Highway 6 passes through **Ha Dong ❷**, a traditional silk-weaving village. It is sometimes a stop on
day-tours from Hanoi to Thay and Tay Phuong pagodas. Both are reached by a road that branches off to
the west at Ha Dong.

One of Vietnam's oldest pagodas, **Chua Thay ❸**
(Pagoda of the Master) nestles against the hillside in
Sai Son, about 40 km (25 miles) from Hanoi. (Its official name is Thien Phuc Tu.) Founded in 1132 by
King Ly Thai To, the pagoda has often been renovated. Its dedication is threefold: to Ly Than Tong,
king of the Ly dynasty from 1127 to 1138; to Sakyamuni, the historical Buddha, and his 18 *arhat*, or disciples; and to the venerable bonze Dao Hanh (the
Master). All are represented by many statues here,
some dating back to the 12th and 13th centuries.

Dao Hanh was a great herbalist who had been a
medical man in his native village before entering the
pagoda. He was also very fond of the choreographic
arts, particularly the traditional water-puppet theatre,
which was performed in the artificial lake in front of
the pagoda. During the annual Tet festival, Hanoi's

Rice is a mainstay of agriculture in the fertile delta of Song Hong, or Red River.

BELOW: a temple just outside of Hanoi for good luck in business.

premier Phu Da troupe stages shows in this authentic outdoor setting. Folk theatrical plays, chess games, a recital of Dao Hanh's feats, and a procession of tablets are also features of the festival, which draws participants from four villages. The two arched, covered bridges spanning the lake date from 1602. Within the pagoda is a large, white sandalwood statue of Dao Hanh, which can be moved like a puppet using cleverly intertwined strings. A climb up the hillside leads to two more small shrines and a superb view of the pagoda, lake, village, and surrounding countryside. This idyllic place is an excellent spot for a picnic. Several limestone grottoes in the vicinity are worth exploring, notably Hang Cac Co (The Mischievous).

Usually linked with Thay Pagoda on day-tours is **Chua Tay Phuong** ❹ in the picturesque village of **Thac Xa**. It perches on top of the 50-metre (160-ft) Tay Phuong hill. The pagoda dates from the 8th century and is famous for its 73 wooden lacquer statues, which are said to illustrate different stories from the Buddhist scriptures; their facial expressions reflect the varying attitudes and faces of human nature. The pagoda is reached by climbing 262 laterite steps, where incense and fan sellers will be hot on your ascending trail hoping to be rewarded for their efforts, if not on the way up, then while you're catching your breath at the top. Built of ironwood with bare brick walls, the pagoda with its round windows comprises Bai Duong (Prostration Hall), Chinh Dien (Central Hall), and Hau Cung (Back Hall). Together they form the Tam Bao (Three Gems). The overlapping roofing of the halls is richly decorated with engravings and terracotta figures of dragons and animals. Perhaps the best examples of 18th-century sculpture are here, including beautiful wooden statues of the *arhat*, Buddha's disciples. Day-tours to Thay and Tay Phoung also sometimes stop at

the village of **So,** where the age-old occupation is the production of noodles from the flour of yams and manioc.

Highway 6 continues on into the outer limits of the Song Hong delta and the culture of irrigated-rice cultivation. The area was once inhabited by the prehistoric Lac Viet people, and many relics from the Hoa Binh culture of the Lac Viet have been recovered in the area. Ethnic groups – including Muong, Hmong, Tai, Tay, and Dao (pronounced *zao*) – make up the local population.

Constructed by the French with forced labour, by the early 1950s the unpaved "Road Number 6" hadn't been repaired in more than a decade and had been bombed by French and Viet Minh alike during the war against the French. There were many French fortifications along this 75-km (45-mile) route between Hanoi and **Hoa Binh** ❺, but the thick roadside underbrush was perfect camouflage for Viet Minh. The guerrillas regularly attacked forts and convoys and then melted back into the distant cliffs and hills.

For the French in the early 1950s, this road became especially treacherous after crossing the Song Day (Day River). Song Day marked the western boundary of the so-called de Lattre line, a defensive perimeter intended to protect French-controlled Hanoi and the Song Hong delta, although throughout the war it always enclosed about 30,000 regular and irregular Viet Minh troops. Beginning in November 1951, a famous set-piece battle – the Hell of Hoa Binh or the Hell of Road Number 6 – raged for two months in this vicinity. In the previous year, the French had lost all their positions north of the Song Hong (Red River) to the Chinese border. On 14 November French paratroops easily recaptured the Viet Minh-held town of Hoa Binh. The rationale was that Hoa Binh would underpin the communication routes to Hanoi via Road No. 6. Hoa Binh was also

Map on page 162

BELOW: soldiers at a military academy outside of Hanoi.

the de facto capital of the Muong people, who were allied with the French; two Muong battalions were among the French-led troops. A victory here would be a psychological boost for the Muong and for the Tai armies loyal to the French in the northwestern mountains. In the beginning, the Western press hailed the operation as "a pistol pointed at the heart of the enemy".

The Viet Minh infantry employed human-wave attacks that left barbed wire entanglements covered with carpets of their bodies. The French troops – which included Muong, Vietnamese, Moroccan, and Algerian units, in addition to Foreign Legionnaires – fought the Viet Minh hand-to-hand. Some of the bloodiest battles were on the Song Da (Black River) around the so-called Notre Dame Rock. No longer a ragtag collection of guerrillas, by now the Viet Minh were armed with tanks, mortars, automatic weapons, and howitzers of both Chinese and American make. The latter were captured by the communist Chinese in Korea and transferred to the Viet Minh. At the end of February, the French painfully evacuated via the Song Da and Road 6. The war lasted two more years, but for the Viet Minh, Hoa Binh was a dress rehearsal for the showdown at Dien Bien Phu. Hoa Binh means "peace".

Today, Hoa Binh, the provincial capital, is a substantial industrial town. Five km (3 miles) away sits Southeast Asia's biggest hydroelectric project. Built with technical assistance and money from the former Soviet Union, construction of the dam took 10 years and displaced approximately 50,000 ethnic minority people from the Song Da (Black River) valley, which is now under a reservoir. However, running the facility now employs around 35,000 people. Electricity generated is the main source for a transmission line running north to south and supplying places as far away as the Mekong Delta.

BELOW: ferrying a load of shrimp nets.

It's not obvious that minority people are the majority in this area because few wear traditional clothing, but from Hoa Binh town, one can arrange tours and overnight stays to tribal villages. The town's markets and shops are good sources of tribal souvenirs. On the whole, though, foreign tourists have shunned Hoa Binh, stopping only briefly before heading for the more rural ambience of Mai Chau, a valley, 60 km (40 miles) further down the road.

North of Hanoi

From 1945 on, the wooded Tam Dao mountains were Viet Minh sanctuary. But the road leading here from Hanoi, now Highway 2, was within the French domain. Visitors today will notice that the road up to the Tam Dao resort branches north off Highway 2, about 16 km (10 miles) from Hanoi, at the industrial town of **Vinh Yen ❻**. In 1951, it was reduced to rubble and, for a short time, Vinh Yen seemed to augur the French path to victory.

Gathering 81 battalions, Gen. Vo Nguyen Giap believed the Viet Minh were ready to switch to counter-offensive battlefield warfare and push into Hanoi by the Tet New Year holiday. His well-armed troops began on 13 January by destroying small hill posts around the town. With the most intensive aerial bombardment of the entire French war, the French (including battalions of Senegalese, Moroccans, Algerians, and Vietnamese) emerged the victors as the Viet Minh retreated back into the mountains four days later. Six thousand Viet Minh were killed in three days and perhaps 8,000 were wounded. Several thousand were roasted to death by napalm.

To escape the heat and humidity prevalent through much of the year in the capital city, Hanoi residents flock to the mountain retreats and cooler tempera-

Map
on page
162

A Viet Minh officer described the terror in his diary: "Hell comes in the form of large, egg-shaped containers... sheets of flames, extending over hundreds of metres... napalm, the fire which falls from the skies".

BELOW: boys with good hands, and a music teacher.

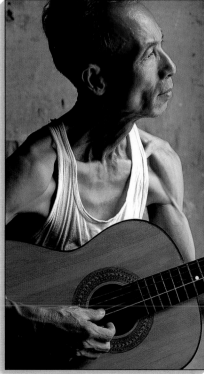

Established by the French as a cool retreat from Hanoi, the hills of Tam Dao were once peppered with French-style homes and buildings. After the French defeat of 1954 at Dien Bien Phu, most of the homes were destroyed by the French before the Viet Minh arrived.

tures at the **Tam Dao** ❼, established by the French in 1902 as a hill station. At an altitude of 880 metres (2,850 ft), Tam Dao sits on a large plateau within a valley about 90 km (50 miles) northwest of Hanoi in the Tam Dao mountain range. These mountains stretch from the northwest to the southeast, separating Vinh Phu Province from Bac Thai Province in the north.

Tam Dao means "three islands". The name derives from three mountains – Thien Thi, Thach Ban, and Phu Nghia, all at about 1,400 metres (4,500 ft) and which dominate the landscape – appearing from a distance like three islands jutting above a sea of clouds. Rare trees and plants cover the mountain slopes, while the forests harbour many species of animals, butterflies, birds, and flowers. It's chilly and very damp during most of the year, but it's a refreshing escape from Hanoi in the depths of summer, although facilities and accommodation are, for the most part, rundown and tired. Suoi Bac (Silvery Stream) meanders its way past the foot of Thien Thi, creating languid pools perfect for swimming. A waterfall cascades in three stages to form a lake; nearby are several pagodas.

For Vietnamese, Tam Dao also has melancholy revolutionary significance. After the disastrous Thai Nguyen mutiny and uprising in August 1917, 100 or so remnant survivors fled here to make a doomed 3-month last stand against the French army. Close to the end, one legendary leader, Sgt. Trinh Van Can, committed suicide. The French made a meticulous effort to track down and kill every rebel soldier and escaped political prisoner; in the end, the French claimed that only five eluded them.

There are three Hung temples on the slopes of Nghia Linh, 80 km (50 miles) northwest of Hanoi. The lowest temple, **Den Ha** ❽, is reached by climbing up

BELOW: Black Tai girls in the far northwest.

225 steps. Below the temple at the foot of the hill is an arched portal flanked by two huge stone columns engraved with two parallel sentences glorifying the origins of the Vietnamese people.

A further 168 steps lead up to the middle temple, **Den Hung**. Only 102 steps remain to reach the superior temple, **Den Thuong**. This temple is dedicated to the deities of heaven, earth and rice and to Than Giong, the infant hero who in the 3rd century BC is said to have chased out the Chinese Han invaders, assisted by a genie in the form of an iron horse. It was here that the last of the Hung kings transferred his power to the Thuc king at the end of the 3rd century. Vinh Phu's diverse scenic beauty is enhanced by a range of flora, extensive green-tea plantations, and, in winter, the beautiful white blooms of sasanca.

In Lap Thach district in the northwest, the **Binh Son Tower** of the **Chua Vinh Khanh** ❾ rises 16 metres (50 ft) into the sky. Built under the Tran dynasty in the 13th century, the 11-tiered, baked-clay tower of this pagoda is adorned with a wide variety of sculpture. Nearby is the Vinh Son snake farm, in Vinh Lac district. Established over a decade ago, it breeds snakes and produces snake wine and an ointment containing snake venom that is used to relieve muscle and joint inflammation.

In 1945, with the Japanese defeat by the Allies on the horizon, Ho Chi Minh came south and settled in **Tan Trao** ❿. This village is located high in the mountains east of Tuyen Quang, north of Vinh Phu. Here, Ho Chi Minh set up the Communist Party headquarters. A few days after the Japanese surrender on 10 August 1945, Ho organised the Viet Minh march into Hanoi and seized governmental power from the disordered Japanese rulers. Ho himself followed the Viet Minh on 26 August.

Map on page 162

BELOW: boats for the journey to Chua Huong, and fishing in flooded fields.

Standard day-tours to Chua Huong from Hanoi are by Highway 6, branching off to the southeast at Ha Dong and then to Du Khe, in Ha Son Binh Province. The fee includes the round-trip boat trip. It is possible to stay a few days and hire a boat to visit at least seven other pagodas that nestle in the hills along the Yen.

BELOW: boats to Chua Huong.

South of Hanoi

One makes a pilgrimage to the mountain cave of the **Chua Huong** ⑪ (Perfume Pagoda) for the journey as much as the sacred site itself. Almost 60 km (40 miles) southwest of Hanoi, it is best approached by rowboat on the wide, swiftly flowing Song Yen. Looming over the strangely quiet countryside are the jagged karst Hoang Son mountains.

This dreamy landscape has been compared to Guilin in China. Each of the flat-bottomed boats is propelled by a powerful oarswoman, who rows in an unusual and demanding fashion: facing the bow, she pushes the oars forward. Many women are even adept at rowing in this way with their feet. If a Vietnamese interpreter is along for the ride, the boatwoman can identify the shapes that identify such peaks as the Crouching Elephant, Nun, and Rice Tray.

After 4 km (2½ miles), the boats pull up to the riverside near a cluster of pavilions and market stalls. The most important pagoda is the 17th-century Thien Chu (Leading to Heaven). In front of it stands a 3-tiered bell tower. Pilgrims shouldn't dawdle, though. The winding, often slippery route up the crags of Huong Tich (Fragrant Traces) to Chua Huong is less than 4 km (2½ miles) long, but the hike is arduous even when there aren't hordes of tourists pressing ahead. The pagoda itself is inside a big cave. During festival time, the "perfume" from the incense offerings is so thick that it obscures the view of the Buddha images. Visiting during the annual 7-week festival, in March and April, is an incredible experience. From the racing boats, the passengers cry greetings of "A di da phat!" ("Praise to Amitabha Buddha!"). Yet it may be best to avoid this time because the crowds can be frustrating and even frightening, and the aggressive souvenir sellers turn out in greater intensity than usual.

East of Hanoi

In the village of **Bat Trang** ⓬ potters carry on a 500-year-old tradition. Rather incongruously, shiny showrooms with large glass windows dominate the main street, only 10 km (6 miles) southeast of Hanoi. The oldest part of town, near the river, is threaded with walled alleys. What look like cowpats stuck on the brick walls are blobs of coal, drying out for use as fuel. One steps down to enter homes or workrooms: the ground of alleyways is so high as a consequence of ashes piling up over the centuries. Inside are brick kilns and great vats of white, liquid clay fed by a network of troughs. Bat Trang artisans used to make bricks, but now they concentrate on glazed ceramics, which include teapots, dinnerware, and 3-metre-tall (12-ft) blue-and-white urns destined for temples and pagodas. Along the riverside is the village's communal house, dedicated to Bach Ma (White House), King Le Thanh Tong's guardian spirit, as well as five village heroes, including Hua Chi Cao, who introduced ceramics here. A wall plaque, villagers say, was a gift from Emperor Gia Long and honours Bat Trang for bricks used to construct the imperial city of Hue in the early 19th century.

The once infamous craft village of **Dong Ky**, 15 km (9 miles) from Hanoi, was the country's firecracker hub until 1995, when firecrackers were banned. The highlight of the year was once the January firecracker festival, when elderly competitors with pillar-sized firecrackers vied to produce the loudest bang. The festival no doubt evolved from ancient religious rites of begging for thunder, lightning, and rain. Firecrackers have now been banned throughout Vietnam (though at any festival in Vietnam, people are still exploding something) and Dong Ky villagers are alternatively engrossed in making carved hardwood furniture in both private and state workshops. In these dark brick buildings with

Map on page 162

Quality ceramics of Bat Trang.

BELOW: master potter in Bat Trang.

corrugated metal roofs, barefoot men and women labour away with chisels and hammers, earning US$35 a month, a decent wage by Vietnamese standards.

The final products and plenty of carved knick-knacks are for sale in show-rooms along the dusty main street. The evidence here is that rich Vietnamese have abandoned all pretensions to austerity. Heavy, black-wood settees with matching chairs seem constructed for giants and are riotously adorned with rococo carvings of dragons and snarling lions. With complementary armoires, side tables, and 10 or so other pieces, the entire set can be had for a mere US$30,000. Salespeople say buyers are overseas Vietnamese and newly wealthy domestic "millionaires". Fortunately, there are a few simpler designs and lighter finishes, with and without mother-of-pearl inlay. Pieces can also be made-to-order and sent abroad. *Caveat emptor.*

The return to Hanoi can be timed for a delicious snake dinner at **Le Mat**, only 7 km (4 miles) from Hanoi. Le Mat is in the business of hunting snakes, raising snakes, and serving snake cuisine. The cobra and buffalo snakes are cooked in many ways and served as soups, entrees, and appetisers. They all taste like chicken. One can observe the snake being captured from a cage, gutted, and its blood squeezed into a glass of rice alcohol. Bottles of this snake "elixir" with a cobra draped attractively inside make challenging souvenirs.

Le Mat is a legendary village apart from snakes. A daughter of the 11th-century king Ly Thai Tong was cruising on the Song Duong when a devil overturned the boat. A young Le Mat man dived in, killed the snake, and rescued the princess. The king offered a reward, but the young man instead requested that he and many poor people be allowed to reclaim land west of Hanoi. They were successful, established 13 settlements, and returned to Le Mat every year to

TIP

A word of warning: restaurant staff are very tourist-friendly, but visitors should ascertain the price before tasting even a crumb of fried snake-skin. Bargaining is advised. The less adventurous can partake of samples at street stalls.

BELOW: harvesting salt from ponds.

express their thanks at festival time. At this annual festival in March, a big pot is carried on a palanquin to a pond and solemnly filled with clean, filtered water. A carp from the pond is added to the palanquin and escorted into the communal house, where a ceremony of gratitude ensues. Of much more recent origin is a snake dance related to martial arts and performed by village youth.

Chua Dau ⓭, 30 km (20 miles) from Hanoi, dates from the 13th century. The pagoda is a bit off the beaten track but the trip is well worth it, for the route passes through picturesque countryside and affords a glimpse of traditional village life. The pagoda houses two lacquered statues that contain the mummified remains of two bonzes, the brothers Vu Khac Minh and Vu Khach Truong, who lived here three centuries ago. Not far away and also in Tien Son district, the village of **Lim** is the site of a popular festival held every year shortly after Tet. For 3 days, from the 13th to the 15th of the first lunar month, people from all over the region converge on the village for the competitions of popular *quan ho* folk songs, sung alternately by young men and women.

A visit to **Chua But Thap** ⓮, near Dinh To village in Ha Bac Province, makes a pleasant day-trip. The style of this pagoda, originally built in the 13th century, is very Chinese. In this quiet site by a canal there is also an unusual 4-storey stone stupa, Bao Nghiem. Among the many stone statues is one that depicts the goddess of mercy, Quan Yin, the Buddhist manifestation of ancient India's *bodhisattva* Avalokitesvara, with her thousand eyes and arms. Those who worship her believe that her many eyes and arms have supernatural power, the eyes to see and the hands to help those in need. Martial arts and other competitions that mark But Thap's annual festival, falling on the 23rd day of the third lunar month, are of very ancient origin.

Map on page 162

BELOW: ploughing a field with hand-plough and buffalo.

Map on page 162

The traditional theatre at the communal house in Dinh Bang is something of an architectural marvel on stilts. Built of ironwood in 1736, the building is one of the largest of its kind in Vietnam.

BELOW: a durable truck carries the load.
RIGHT: tending to the rice.

Heading towards the east, on the way to Hai Phong and the coast, the road passes through the relatively flat province of Hai Hung, famous for its beautiful orchards. Fruit from Hai Hung, especially longan and lychee, is reputedly the best in northern Vietnam, supplying the Vietnamese royal court in earlier centuries. Today, Hai Hung is known for its porcelain; the largest factory of porcelain in northern Vietnam, built with the assistance of China, is located here. A food known as *banh cuon*, which is a rice pancake wrapped around minced pork, originates from Hai Hung.

In Hung Dao commune, **Den Kiep Bac** ⑮, 60 km (40 miles) from Hanoi, dates from the 13th century. It is a temple dedicated to the national hero Tran Hung Dao, who vanquished the Mongols in the 13th century and was made a saint by the people. His army encamped here in the Kiep Bac Valley. His statue – plus those of Gen. Pham Ngu Lao and the genies of the Northern Star and Southern Cross, not to mention his two daughters – are venerated in this temple. The temple festival falls on the 20th day of the eighth lunar month. This site is shared by an old garden of medicinal plants, formerly used in the army's medical service.

Nearby, the pagoda of **Chua Con Son** ⑯ is the home of another national hero, Nguyen Trai (1380–1442), who helped King Le Loi chase out the Ming invaders from China and free the country from Chinese domination at the beginning of the 15th century. At the foot of the hill, the well-maintained Hung pagoda contains statues of Nguyen Trai, his maternal grandfather, and the three superior bonzes who founded the Truc Lam Buddhist sect. Some 600 stone steps lead up to the summit, where the energetic will find a superb view of the surrounding mountain ranges.

North to China

The northern circuit from Hanoi to the Chinese border begins in Ha Bac Province and its key region of Bac Ninh, then crosses the rice paddies of the Hong Song (Red River) delta before entering the mountainous regions near the Chinese border, the site of several skirmishes between the Chinese and Vietnamese armies since the late 1970s.

Ha Bac Province is full of historical, cultural, and religious vestiges, and the area around **Bac Ninh**, the largest city, is home to more cultural and religious festivals than any other area in Vietnam. Among the architectural remains are the ancient Luy Lau citadel, and the temple and mausoleum of Si Nhiep, the governor of ancient Giao Chi. The pagoda of **Phat Tich** (Relic of Buddha), on a hill in Phuong Hoang village, was built in the 11th century under the Ly dynasty. It has been badly damaged by the ravages of time and war, but a 40-metre (120-ft) stone statue of Amitabha Buddha dating from the 11th century remains intact.

Dong Ho, in Bach Ninh, is a village famous for its communal production of woodcut prints. The prints depict traditional themes and their preparation is as historic in nature as the prints themselves. The various stages of production – carving the wood block, preparing the paper, obtaining natural colours from plants and minerals – are tasks shared by the family. ❑

HAI PHONG AND HA LONG

Northern Vietnam's most important port, Hai Phong, gladly yields to what's beyond: Vinh Ha Long, the most wondrous of bays sculpted when an ancient dragon swished its immense tail

Map on page 178

Heading east from Hanoi eventually leads to white-sand beaches washed by **Bien Dong**, or the **South China Sea** (which remains a constant source of contention between Vietnam and China, as both claim rights to the sea and to the archipelago offshore, possibly rich in oil reserves). Even more enticing to travellers are the limestone islands of Vinh Ha Long, or Ha Long Bay.

The 120-km (75-mile) road from Hanoi to **Hai Phong ❶** winds ever deeper into the densely populated **Song Hong** (Red River) valley. In the late 1940s and early 1950s, this road, Highway 5, was lined with garrisons, watchtowers, and "Beau Geste" forts surrounded by barbed wire fences, trenches, and mine-fields. The larger ones had airfields. At the small end of the scale were hundreds of isolated, 10-man, reinforced-concrete bunkers (by the end of the French period, there were 2,200 such bunkers throughout the delta). Vehicles ventured along this road only in convoys and during daylight hours. At night, the road was officially closed – though not to the elusive Viet Minh guerrillas.

Today the road is jammed with trucks carrying goods to and from the port and bicycles and motorbikes laden with chickens, bags of rice, and pigs on their way to market. The city's industrial area sprang up after the French departure. Today, many industrial plants, engineering factories, glass, brick and cement works, and lime kilns are evident from the main road into Hai Phong. More recently, local industry has grown to meet the demands of construction in the area. In the early 1990s the government hoped to build an industrial zone along this route, but with the flight of foreign investors by the end of the 20th century, that doesn't seem likely anytime soon.

Hai Phong, the country's third-largest city and the north's most important port, is in the northeast of the Bac Bo delta. It occupies the right bank of the busy Cua Cam, 20 km (13 miles) and many sand banks from the open sea. A small port town at the time of the French conquest of Tonkin in 1883, Hai Phong quickly became a city as the colonialists drained swamps and threw up monumental buildings. Since the city is crossed by 16 rivers, setting the founda-tions in the soggy soil was no simple task.

The most famous of these rivers is the Bach Dang, where in 938 the national hero Ngo Quyen defeated the large southern Chinese fleet. The Song invaders suffered a bitter defeat here in 981 and the Mongols suffered the same fate in 1288. The first of the French warships arrived in Hai Phong in 1872. The lure was access, via the Song Hong, to China's Yunnan region. The last units of the French expeditionary forces also exited the same way in 1955.

Hai Phong was also where, in late 1946, a skirmish between French and Viet Minh militia – occupying

LEFT: unloading rice in Hai Phong from the Mekong region. **BELOW:** keeping cool in the heat.

Near Hai Phong is Bao Ha, known for its high-quality woodcarving since its founding by a master craftsman in the late 1600s. The fragrant jackwood is preferred by the craftsmen, who value its beauty, lightness, and softness. This is also a good place to buy water puppets.

different zones of the city – erupted following a dispute over which had the authority to collect customs duties. Anxious to forestall similar incidents throughout the country, the French fleet shelled the city and aircraft bombers demolished residential neighbourhoods. French and Viet Minh soldiers fought house to house. With the help of artillery, the French quelled the uprising in a few days. The much-disputed death toll was perhaps 6,000. During the war with the United States, Hai Phong was sporadically bombed from air and sea between 1965 and 1972. In 1972, the US President, Richard Nixon, ordered the mining of the harbour to stem the influx of Soviet military supplies.

Hai Phong's troubles didn't end with peace in 1975. For more than a decade, the harbour was the most popular departure point for northern "boat people" fleeing economic and political hardship. Hai Phong's fishing fleet was decimated. Persecuted during the 1979 war with China and always suspected as "commercial opportunists", most members of the city's large ethnic Chinese community joined the exodus, if they hadn't already fled to China.

Rambling through Hai Phong

Hai Phong doesn't attract many tourists. Even by Vietnamese standards, Hai Phong is notorious for official corruption, individual avarice, and quick tempers. Most of the tourism trade for Ha Long has therefore shifted to Bai Chay *(see page 182)*. This is perhaps unfortunate because Hai Phong is, for Vietnam, an attractive city. There are wide shady streets, well-tended spots of greenery, and a surprising number of colonial-era administrative buildings and wooden shophouses. The great waves of bicycle and motorbike traffic, however, can reach truly Chinese proportions. It is not a city for faint-of-heart pedestrians.

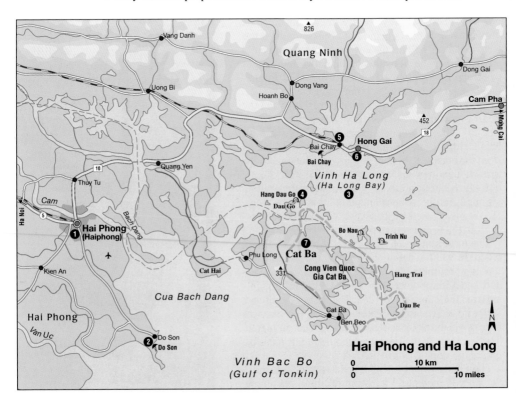

Hai Phong and Ha Long

The city centre curves around the Song Tam Bac. In the city centre are several impressive colonial-era hotels, administrative buildings, and the mysterious red-sandstone city museum. While a few very odd opening hours are posted, it's unlikely to be open even at those times. Beyond the Catholic cathedral is a square overlooked by the pink, neo-colonial municipal theatre, also known as the Opera House. During the first days of the 1946 French attack, actors with antique muskets held off French troops here.

Like every city in Vietnam, Hai Phong has its temples. The pagoda of **Du Hang** in the south of the city was built three centuries ago, but it has been restored often since. It is dedicated to Le Chan, the valiant woman warrior who aided the Trung sisters in the uprising against the Chinese in AD 39. The long, low wooden building with a swooping roof is reached by passing through a triple-tiered bell tower and a covered courtyard. Inside, an enormous palanquin is decorated with carvings of dragons. Behind the carved offering table is a baby Buddha protected by nine dragons. Visitors are warned not to confuse – as many locals and even cyclo drivers do – the pagoda of Du Hang with the nearby **Hang Kenh** *dinh*, or communal house. The communal house – well worth a visit – is off Nguyen Cong Tru and fronted by a neglected lotus pond. Beyond the spacious courtyard is the long and low wooden building with a curling, tiled roof. Within the dim interior, 32 ironwood pillars support the roof. The beams of the ceiling are adorned with hundreds of relief sculptures of contorted dragons. Once upon a time, every village had a dinh. Where they still exist, dinh are often shut up and many of the centuries-old decorations have been destroyed.

About 20 km (12 miles) southeast of Hai Phong, at the tip of a peninsula, is **Do Son ❷**, home of Vietnam's only legitimate gambling casino.

BELOW: placid canal of Hai Phong.

GAMBLE IN ISOLATION

At the very end of the peninsula southeast of Hai Phong and housed in a renovated 1930s hotel is Do Son Casino, Vietnam's only legal gambling den. With little islets sprouting off the peninsula, it would have the best view in town if it had any windows. In the heady days of 1994, Stanley Ho, Macao's casino impresario, made a very risky bet that a casino could succeed here. It was the country's first since South Vietnamese Pres. Ngo Dinh Diem closed the last legal one in the 1950s. Still, Ho lost big time. Not that Vietnamese don't love gambling. Before the communist takeover in the 1950s, people of all ages and classes were chronic gamblers.

Under the terms of Ho's joint casino venture with the Vietnamese government, Vietnamese are forbidden to enter it. Instead, the casino was supposed to draw gamblers from Hong Kong and other overseas Chinese business people who were working in Vietnam. Of course, well-connected Vietnamese do sneak in occasionally. Chances are, though, that foreigners will have the entire place to themselves. For those who don't mind solitude, it's nowhere near as seedy as any of the Macao joints. Slot machines, roulette and card games are on offer.

Ha Long vegetation.

Vinh Ha Long

No trip to northern Vietnam could be complete without visiting Quang Ninh Province. This province shares a common border with China in the north and harbours one of the wonders of the world, **Vinh Ha Long ❸** (Ha Long Bay), with probably the most stunning scenery in Vietnam. The bay's tranquil beauty encompasses 4,000 sq. km (1,500 sq. miles) dotted with well over 1,600 limestone islands and islets, many of them without names. Bizarre rock sculptures jutting dramatically from the sea and numerous grottoes have created an enchanted, timeless world. The sails of the junks and sampans gliding on the bay add further to the beauty of the scene. The bay was recently declared one of UNESCO's World Heritage Sites.

Ha Long means "dragon descending" and the name originates in local legend. A celestial dragon and her offspring were ordered by the Jade Emperor to halt an invasion from the sea. The creative dragons spewed out bits of jade that turned into wondrous islands and karst formations, thereby scuppering the enemy ships. According to other versions, the jewels were pearls and the bay was created when the dragon flung herself into the sea; on the way, her swishing tail dug deep valleys and crevices in the mainland, which were subsequently filled by the sea. Regardless, the dragon, was so pleased with her creations that she settled amongst them. She is said to live under the bay to this day. All of the well-known caves have their own legends. Even humble limestone piles are known to local fishermen by fanciful nicknames. They say that the Dog or Turtle or Toad is derived from the dolomite rock's uncanny resemblance to the animal's shape.

No typical one-day tour can take in more than a few caves. Those with enough

time and specific sites to visit in mind could spend days cruising. Boats are hired by bargaining with the eager captains at the piers in the town of Bai Chay *(see page 182)*, the usual jumping-off point. Tours can be negotiated for a few nights, overnight, or an entire week.

An alternative is to base oneself on Cat Ba *(see page 184)*, the bay's largest island and a national park. Not only is it more rustic, clean, and quiet, it's closer to many of the most dramatic grottos. The boatmen here are just as eager to be tour guides, although Bai Chay skippers generally speak more English. Whichever you choose, bring along a swimsuit so the boatman can drop you within swimming distance of an uninhabited island with a pristine beach.

Folklore claims that **Trinh Nu** (Virgin) cave was named after a young girl whose parents were poor and could not afford to own a boat. They had to rent one from a rich man, but when they could not pay what they owed him, the rich man demanded their beautiful daughter in lieu of their debt, and so forced her to marry him. The poor girl refused all his advances. He had her beaten but still she would not submit to him; he finally exiled her to a grotto, where she starved to death. She was immortalised in stone by a rock resembling her figure that emerged from her burial site.

The most spectacular of the bay's grottoes is the beautiful cave of **Hang Dau Go ❹**, with its stalactites and stalagmites resembling beasts, birds, and human forms. It was christened the Grotte des Merveilles (Wonder Grotto) by the first French tourists who visited it in the late 19th century.

Ha Long has been the setting of many historic battles against invasions from the north. It is believed that the sharp bamboo stakes that Gen. Tran Hung Dao planted in the Song Bach Dang to destroy Kublai Khan's invasion

Map on page 178

BELOW: boats set out at dawn.

Altar detail of a fisherman's temple in a grotto of Ha Long.

fleet were stored in caves here. **Hang Hanh** is a tunnel cave that extends for 2 km (1¼ miles). Access by sampan is strictly regulated by the tides. A visit to the lagoon on Dau Bo also must be carefully timed, since it can only be reached from the sea by navigating through three low tunnels at low tide.

Hang Thien Cung encloses a chamber worthy of royalty (as its name claims) or giants and is adorned with stalagmites and stalactites. Its decaying villas now sinking back into the forest, the island of **Tuan Chau** once served as a most exclusive retreat for the colonial elite. Ho Chi Minh used to summer here and his house, of course, has been preserved as a memorial. In such a place it comes as no surprise to hear that some people claim to have seen the Vietnamese equivalent of the Loch Ness monster. It is said to be a black creature resembling a snake about 30 metres (100 ft) long, which supposedly inhabits the bay. (Maybe it's the ancient dragon?)

Created only in 1994, the town of **Ha Long** actually comprises two towns, Bai Chay and Hon Gai, as well as surrounding districts. Locals, as well as transport companies, still treat them as distinct entities. **Bai Chay ❺** is the quintessential tourist trap, devoid of character or attraction. Shops specialise in key chains and other bric-a-brac fashioned from precious coral and limestone formations. There are about a half-dozen new or renovated luxury hotels, all nearly vacant, and scores of new but rickety mini-hotels. On summer weekends, the latter are filled with Vietnamese tourists and their overseas relatives, apparently drawn by the karaoke facilities. Outside the summer months, Bai Chay is nearly deserted, save for the persistent postcard hawkers.

BELOW: fisherman at a grotto altar praying for a good catch.

At least there is plenty of fresh, well-prepared seafood. Most popular are the umbrella-draped, open-air restaurants lining the main avenue, which runs along

the waterfront. A short walk further along this avenue reveals two swimming beaches. Both are rocky and uninviting and few Westerners care to test them out. Conditions might improve in a few years, though, because the World Bank has launched a wastewater clean-up project. There are rumours that real sand might be dumped on the beaches, too. (In fact, many of the area's beaches are less than appealing to overseas visitors.

Grimy and industrial, **Hon Gai ❻** is nevertheless more interesting than Bai Chay. The ferry from Bai Chay takes only takes a few minutes. Hon Gai appropriately enough means "coal mine" in Vietnamese. When the French colonisers launched their final successful onslaught of the north, they seized Hon Gai in 1883 to safeguard the coal mines. Today, open-pit mining continues in the surrounding hills; sooty warehouses hunker near the docks. The full range of Soviet architecture – shabby, decaying, or collapsing – is dispiriting as well.

Visitors are advised to soldier on to the knobby hill called Nui Bai Tho. At its base, close to the long-distance (Hai Phong and Cat Ba) ferry pier, are a market, food stalls, and fishing village.

The gaudy pagoda of Long Tien, guarded by statues of fierce armoured soldiers, is reputed to be 500 years old and dedicated to the ever-popular general Tran Hung Dao, who beat back Mongol invaders in 1284. Along the path around the hill and through the fishing village are inscriptions carved into the rock face. These are poems in praise of Ha Long's loveliness and date back hundreds of years. (Nearby is a museum that contains bones, fossils, ornaments, and other artefacts discovered on the nearby islands. It is only open by appointment, which should be arranged through a government tourism agency well before visiting.)

Map on page 178

BELOW: cuisine of Vinh Ha Long.

UNDERWAY ON ORANGE SAILS

The most picturesque way to circumnavigate Cat Ba island – docking at villages along the way – would be aboard one of the low-riding, two-masted, family-sized junks, which are often constructed from planks or plaited reeds. Powered with the bay's distinctive orange sails, they usually rely on outboard motor power as well. They may appear fragile, but it's common to come upon a lone fisherman in such a sailing vessel.

Smallest of all are the rowboats, their rounded hulls constructed from plaited reeds sealed with tar, that function as taxis in Cat Ba's harbour. Hire one of the "drivers" who are always lingering near the waterfront and catch a closer look at the motley flotilla and a very unusual way of life. The boat people live on board all day, all year-round, heading out to sea at night on their fishing runs. Therefore, all the scenes of daily life – cooking and laundering, toothbrushes dangling from the masts, and babies crawling precariously – are open to view. A few of the inhabitants are picking up English, but most are illiterate in Vietnamese and few children attend school.

Cat Ba is served by twice-daily ferries from Hai Phong. It's also a regular stop for cruise ships and the standard overnight tours out of Bai Chay.

Map on page 178

Deer antlers are harvested in the Cat Ba archipelago for their medicinal qualities.

BELOW: hotel in Ha Long Bay.

Cat Ba archipelago

The Cat Ba archipelago consists of 366 islets and islands that cover some 20,000 hectares (50,000 acres), peppered with beautiful beaches and grottoes. Twenty km (12 miles) from Hai Phong, with the Gulf of Tonkin to the west and Vinh Ha Long to the east, the island of **Cat Ba** ❼ covers 190 sq. km (75 sq. miles). Its beautiful landscape features forested hills, coastal mangrove and freshwater swamps, lakes, and waterfalls.

Much of the island is covered in forest. Half of the island and 90 sq. km (35 sq. miles) of surrounding waters are part of a national park. The park's rich diversity of flora and fauna includes 21 species of birds – among these the hornbill – reptiles, and 28 species of mammals, including wild cats, boar, porcupines, monkeys, deer, and gibbons. Wherever you hike, don't count on glimpsing any of the fabled wildlife, though a lucky few report butterfly sightings. The park has severe poaching problems. Human remains and stone tools from the Neolithic era have been discovered in some of the island's caves. Submerged vegetation, hot springs, and limestone lakes add to the attractions.

The island's population is less than 15,000, perhaps not even half the number of 20 years ago. With its remote harbours, Cat Ba's fishing fleet was ideally situated to serve the needs of fleeing "boat people" throughout the north in the late 1970s. Endemic poverty combined with communist economic policies might have been sufficient incentives to set out for the high seas and new homelands, but there was yet another incentive: the majority of islanders were also ethnic Chinese. When Vietnam launched persecutions of its Chinese minority shortly before its war with China in 1979, Cat Ba islanders joined the flood in earnest. As a consequence, many of those left behind now have relatives in the United States, Canada, and Australia.

Gifts and loans from overseas relatives helped to build the line-up of narrow mini-hotels in the village of Cat Ba. Overlooking the Gulf of Tonkin, it is the island's main settlement and port. There are two scraps of clean beaches within walking distance (admission charged even if foreigners only want to look at them).

For those who want to explore the interior, a bus regularly travels from the waterfront, passing though lychee orchards and abandoned farms before reaching the park entrance about 18 km (11 miles) later. The easiest hike is only a few kilometres, straight uphill. As long as it's not muddy, the climb isn't difficult, but it's a good idea to take a guide. Any of the little girls toting bags full of canned soft drinks will do fine; they're going up to sell you drinks anyway. The reward at the top of the mountain is a magnificent vista of rugged, forested mountains framed by the sea.

The more adventurous can take the 18-km (11-mile) hike across the island, which involves up to six hours of strenuous climbing but includes stops at caves. It ends up at the far-flung coastal village of **Viet Hai**. Arrange beforehand to have a Cat Ba boatman pick you up here. The boatmen in Cat Ba harbour are eager to provide other excursions. At the large end, the creaky wooden trawlers are suitable for journeys out to the islands and grottoes of Ha Long. ❑

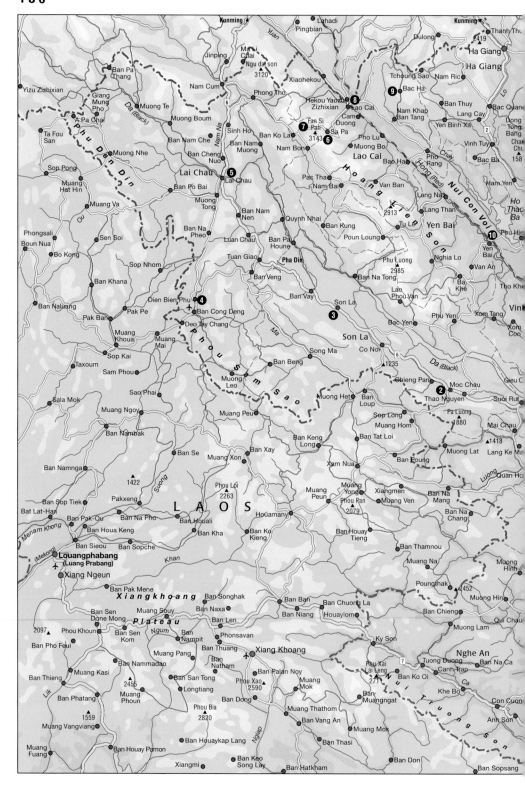

Northern Vietnam

0   50 km

0   50 miles

THE FAR NORTH

Dismal roads embedded with memories of the French and Viet Minh at war lead to Sa Pa's ethnic minorities in the northern reaches along the Lao and Chinese frontiers

Map on pages 186–7

To the north and northwest of Hanoi, the flat rice-growing delta of the **Song Hong** (Red River) quickly gives way to craggy mountain peaks inhabited by ethnic minority tribes and draped by winter's cold. This region has long and often violent borders with Laos and China, where today minority tribal people farm in the shadow of modern hydroelectric dams supplying power for much of the country. Ancient kings, warriors, and rebellions are honoured throughout the northern mountains. The Vietnamese defeat of the French colonial rule happened in a remote and mountainous valley known as Dien Bien Phu. For all the allure of its tribal peoples and historical footnotes, travel in most of the far north is anything but convenient and predictable. Roads can be rendered impassable after heavy rains and travellers can become stranded. This place is for the traveller with time, patience, and an appreciation of adventure and roughing it.

PRECEDING PAGES: Black Tai girls. **LEFT:** Hmong farmer. **BELOW:** Black Tai village.

West of Hanoi

The Moc Chau district west of Hanoi and **Hoa Binh** ❶ is a stunningly beautiful highland valley surrounded by low mountains. The valley is sprinkled with the prosperous villages of Muong and White Tai and is laced with a vast irrigation network. The canals extend not only through the fields of wet-rice and manioc but throughout the villages of high-stilted houses; many houses have their own fish ponds. Yet Moc Chau's wealth probably stems from gold. The valley's dirt roads are ideal for strollers (and water buffalo); one may stumble on villagers in a shallow stream using a primitive pump to suck the mud and then sifting for grains of gold.

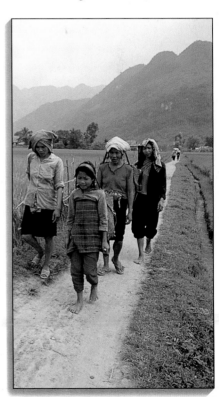

The Muong people are among Vietnam's oldest inhabitants, perhaps even predating the Viets. Relative newcomers, the Tai peoples began migrating from southern China over 2,000 years ago. It's possible, though, that the ancestors of the White Tai in Moc Chau arrived much more recently from China or Laos; the Lao province of Sam Neua (famed for its government re-education camps) is less than 30 km (20 miles) south of the valley, over mountainous terrain. Despite the long distance, travellers speaking Lao or Thai will recognise many words of the White Tai dialect (there are actually several local Tai sub-dialects; this is Tai Khao). As examples, *ban* is still village and *muang* is district.

Muong and White Tai are first languages, but there is some intermarriage and much intermingling of cultures. Both peoples, for example, live in wooden houses perched on high, thick stilts, with springy bamboo floors, wooden shutters, and overhanging thatched or tiled roofs that are often compared to a turtle's shell. Indoors is a single and enormous, high-ceiling room. An ancestral altar near the front is a hint that this is a Muong household. This room is where foreign visitors sleep on mats – sheltered in individual mosquito nets – if they wish to stay overnight. Both Muong and White Tai women embroider, but the White Tai, like Black Tai, are the master weavers. Beneath each of their stilt houses is a loom or two, and sometimes a display of fine shawls and scarves for the tourist trade.

Moc Chau is the gateway to the valley of Mai Chau, dotted with villages of minority groups, especially White and Black Tai.

Neither people ordinarily wear traditional dress in Moc Chau, but performers do when they provide visitors with an evening of traditional songs and dance. Women of both groups wear tight blouses held together in front by a row of silver clasps; their sarong-type skirts are usually dark-coloured with thin plain or warp *ikat* horizontal stripes and sometimes embroidered hems. The supplementary warp waistbands are peculiar to Moc Chau. The musicians play reed pipes, clappers, drums and cymbals, and the less traditional accordion. The evening is topped off with a tasting of manioc alcohol, sipped through reed straws from a communal bowl.

About 150 km (90 miles), or less than four hours' driving time from Hanoi, **Moc Chau ❷** and the valley of **Mai Chau** makes an ideal overnight outing. You will know you are approaching the sprawling 1,500-metre (5,000-ft) market town of Moc Chau by the black-and-white cows wandering across the road. Thanks to Australian aid, much of the area is devoted to dairy farming. It's also a base for treks to highland villages. The people of Moc Chau are willing guides, but since few speak English, a Vietnamese interpreter is also necessary. Moc Chau is also the first (or last) stop for those on the way to Dien Bien Phu and other points on the northwest loop. Beyond Moc Chau, a Russian jeep or

BELOW: dusk over flooded rice fields.

Map on pages 186–7

other four-wheel-drive vehicle is necessary. The roads, virtually all unpaved, are never good, but in the summer months from May to September there is more rain and therefore a risk of wash-outs – and passengers therefore might be stranded for weeks. Traffic is very thin in the northwest. During the coldest months, January and February, the temperature can fall to –3°C (27°F). Central heating is unknown anywhere here.

As Highway 6 from Moc Chau climbs to the west, the hills are cultivated with tea, cotton, and fruit trees, including mulberry, whose leaves feed silkworms. Highway 6 winds through the mountainous far-western province of Son La, which borders Laos on the south. The region is home to many ethnic minorities, including Hmong, M'nong, Muong, Mun, Kho Mu, Dao, Tay, White and Black Tai, Xinh Mun, and Chinese.

From Moc Chau to **Son La** ❸, 100 km (60 miles) to the northwest, and indeed further northwest, the scenery is much the same. Where the mountains aren't barren, the bushes and trees are young enough to indicate recent deforestation. Some of the devastation is due to logging, which continues apace despite being outlawed. Much has also been caused by the inhabitants of this hostile terrain. Mostly tribal people, they have plundered the forests for firewood and house construction and, at least traditionally, the Hmong and other highlanders practised slash-and-burn cultivation. From here on as well, one will often see Black Tai people plodding along the roadside. The women are identified by the colourful and elaborately embroidered folded cloths that they balance precariously on their heads

Son La, which is also the capital of Son La Province, sits on the southern bank of the Song Nam La. It is the familiar, faceless provincial town of dusty

BELOW: tobacco plants, and grave of a Meo girl.

roads, crumbling concrete, tin-roofed shacks, and very few creature comforts. In early morning, however, many traditionally garbed Hmong, Muong, Xinh Mun, and Black and White Tai come to trade in the town market. On **Khau Ca**, overlooking the town, are the brick ruins of **Bao Tang Son La** (Son La Prison; open Mon–Sat, 7am–5pm; admission fee), built in 1908 and once the residence of many a political prisoner. Most of the compound was blasted away during the war against the French.

In French times, Son La was so remote, inaccessible, and disease-ridden that being sent there was akin to a labour-camp sentence in Siberia or Qinghai. As the prison superintendent promised a superior in a 1932 letter, "If they stay in Son La for six months, malaria will weaken and subdue them".

In the old warden's building is a small ethnographic museum that displays crafts, jewellery, and clothing of tribal people. A few watchtowers and cells have been reconstructed and there are displays of shackles, weapons, possessions of well-known political inmates, and contemporary black-and-white photos. Among the prison guests were future Communist Party secretary-generals, including Le Duan and Truong Chinh. Communist prisoners here were renowned for teaching fellow inmates to read and write *quoc ngu,* and for circulating clandestine newspapers. Today at the site there is also a rare mention of a Tai chieftain, Bac Cam Chau, who was beheaded at Son La after leading a major Black Tai insurrection from 1915 to 1916. The Tai insurgents began by storming the prison and killing the French warden.

After the bleakness of the town, Son La's environs are refreshingly verdant and lush, laced with rice fields and fruit orchards. **Ban Mong**, a Black Tai village outside of Son La and about 6 km (4 miles) south of the prison, has hot

BELOW: mother and daughter.

springs. The caves of **Tam Ta Toong**, northwest of town, aren't worth the effort nor the admission prices.

End of a colonial era: Dien Bien Phu

Continuing west from Son La for a bumpy three hours (75 km/50 miles) brings you to the small town of **Tuan Giao**. The road intersecting to the west is Highway 42, the route to **Dien Bien Phu ❹** (Chief Frontier Post), which is 80 km (50 miles) and at least another three hours away.

Called Muong Thanh by its Tai rice farmers, the heart-shaped, pancake-flat valley of Dien Bien Phu is 29 km (11 miles) from north to south and 8 km (5 miles) wide. The valley was the site of a 57-day siege and the ignominious end to French colonialism in Asia. It is encircled by steep, green hills from which tens of thousands of Viet Minh troops launched their assault on the French. To the south and west, it is less than 20 km (12 miles) to the Lao border.

The town of Dien Bien Phu sits on the east bank of the Song Nam Rom near the northern half of the valley. Today it is another blocky concrete provincial town in the throes of construction. The construction boom isn't due to tourism, but smuggling. Only about 600 tourists, mostly French, visit here each year, despite twice-weekly flights. But with the planned inundation by a reservoir of former provincial capital Lai Chau, to the north, Dien Bien Phu was made the capital of Lai Chau Province in 1993 and provincial buildings are under construction. For the moment, tribal people slightly outnumber Vietnamese. For the French, subduing the wild northwest was a 40-year process. To occupy the Dien Bien Phu Valley in 1889 they evicted Siamese soldiers. Long before, the area had been the domain of Tai kingdoms, Vietnamese, and Chinese warlords.

Map on pages 186–7

TIP

Although Dien Bien Phu is known for its history, it's not known for its choice of accommodation, which is minimal and often noisy. The fact that it's a somewhat arduous land journey to the area might account for this.

BELOW: Gen. Giap in Dien Bien Phu on the 40th anniversary of the French defeat.

In 1953, Gen. Vo Nguyen Giap launched excursions into northern Laos, reaching the outskirts of the royal city of Luang Prabang before withdrawing with the onset of summer rains. The French therefore believed Dien Bien Phu was key to preventing a Communist takeover of Laos, and French paratroopers easily recaptured it from the Viet Minh in late 1953. Dien Bien Phu was an old but ramshackle trading village where Hmong came down from hills to sell their opium to Tai brokers. The valley had strategic significance as the intersection of three supply routes. The road north to Lai Chau linked to China. The road northeast to Tuan Giao was the gateway east to central Vietnam. And just across the hills was the Lao province of Phong Saly.

Viet Minh dead and wounded totalled about 23,000. On the French side, about 11,000 survived to walk into captivity; not even half of these survived the 800-km (500-mile) death march and the appalling conditions of the northern prisoner-of-war camps.

French politicians were already resigned to the loss of Vietnam; more than 90,000 troops under the French flag had been killed or wounded. For the major powers, the recent armistice in Korea foreordained a settlement in Indochina. The momentum towards talks was accelerating as additional French troops were airlifted into the basin and Giap's army grouped in the surrounding hills. French forces numbered about 16,500 and the Viet Minh regulars at least 50,000, with well-maintained supply lines.

Apparently both sides believed that any victory on the battlefield would strengthen positions at the conference table. The French built fortified bases and two airstrips.

Beginning on 13 March, human-wave assaults quickly toppled three French bases. The French vastly underestimated Viet Minh strength and were astonished by the anti-aircraft guns and heavy artillery supplied by the Chinese and laboriously pulled over mountainous roads. The Viet Minh then spent weeks digging tunnels and trenches that encircled the valley. The final Viet Minh

BELOW: war veterans at Dien Bien Phu.

assaults were launched on 1 May. One by one the French outposts were overrun or abandoned when the French ran out of ammunition. On 7 May, Viet Minh troops planted a Viet Minh flag on the command bunker. Today, travellers can visit a reconstruction of the French command bunker, set amid a litter of rusty tanks and artillery. On the edge of modern-day downtown Dien Bien Phu, the site of the **Army Museum** (open 8am–4pm; admission fee) was once a battleground. On display are black-and-white battle photos, a model of the battle, and a selection of weapons. Across the street is a Viet Minh cemetery.

Map on pages 186–7

North from Dien Bien Phu

Running straight north of Dien Bien Phu, Highway 12 connects with the historic Tai town of **Lai Chau** ❺, 100 km (60 miles) away. While no roads in the northwest are good, this stretch can be particularly bad if it hasn't yet been repaired since the rainy season. If local people advise against it, it's better – and faster – to retrace one's route to Tuan Giao and then take Highway 6A to Lai Chau. The **Song Da**, or Black River, cuts through a deep mountain valley around which Lai Chau, once the provincial capital, is situated.

The market, a few stalls and small shops with corrugated roofs, occupies a lonely strip on the floodplain. If the shops look new and temporary, they are. In 1991 and 1996, the Da overflowed, causing fatal floods. Most housing is now far up on the grassy hillsides.

The plan is to construct a dam and permanently flood the entire valley. Since Lai Chau will disappear, the provincial capital has already been transferred to Dien Bien Phu. Besides visiting the market, which is frequented by tribal buyers and sellers, travellers may climb up the hillside near the People's Committee

BELOW: young men near Lai Chau.

VIETNAMESE ZODIAC

The Vietnamese calendar, like elsewhere in Asia, is based on the lunar cycle. Referenced to the solar calendar, the lunar new year changes annually. Each year in the 12-year lunar cycle is represent by an animal: rat, ox, tiger, cat, dragon, snake, horse, ram, monkey, rooster, dog, and pig. The dragon, for example, rules every 12 years – in 2000 and then in 2012. Rats are charming, active, and fussy; oxen are patient and industrious. Tigers are flexible but indecisive and volatile, while cats are ambitious and with supple mind. The dragon is strong and sincere. Snakes are wise, quiet, and determined, while the horse is generous and popular, but stubborn. The ram is calm, unassertive, and helpful. Monkeys are erratic and inventive, and the rooster is busy, smart, and a thinker. Dogs are vigilant, pigs honest, impulsive, and gallant.

The Vietnamese calendar has a repeating cycle of 60 years, similar in importance to the Western century of 100 years. In addition to the 12 zodiac signs, there are 10 celestial signs called "stems". The 60-year cycle starts when the first of 12 signs is matched with the first of the 10 celestial stems. When each of the 10 stems is attached to a zodiacal animal, 60 different sets result. Each stem has a modifying influence on the zodiacal animal.

Guesthouse. Here there are vestiges of the French garrison – a cluster of dilapidated buildings in peeling ochre plaster.

With the disappearance of Lai Chau, so will go a symbol of an illustrious history. A Tai people, the Lu, first immigrated from southern China in the 3rd or 4th century BC and settled in the Dien Bien Phu Valley, from which a Lu kingdom reigned for three centuries. Black and White Tai came later, perhaps in the 11th century. Today there are few Lu in Vietnam (though many in Laos).

During France's last war in Vietnam, the town of Lai Chau was one of the few French strongholds in the entire northwest. From a Lai Chau airstrip, long since erased, French planes dropped French-tribal guerrilla bands into remoter pockets of the northwest. After the July 1954 ceasefire, hundreds were stranded behind Viet Minh lines. The last were not captured or killed until the end of the 1950s.

Lai Chau Province shares a border with China in the north and Laos in the west. Among the ethnic groups here are Tai (or Thai), Hmong, Xa, and Ha Nhi. Much of the land – about 75 percent – is covered in forest containing valuable timber and animals, some of them rare, including tigers, bears, bison, and pheasants. Vietnam's most sparsely populated province, Lai Chau probably numbers around 30 people per square km. Yet it is 30 percent larger than the entire Song Hong (Red River) Delta, where average population density exceeds 1,000 people per square km.

The 200-km (125-mile) stretch from Lai Chau to Sa Pa – Highway 32 – runs north and then east. The mountains become higher and craggier and are more thickly forested. This is the Hoang Lien range. Along the way, the nondescript towns of Phong Tho and Tam Duong are little more than fuel stops, but the Monday market day at **Phong Tho** attracts a panoply of tribes. No doubt the

BELOW: harvesting near Sa Pa.

road carved into the steep mountainsides is subject to fierce landslides because this mixture of dirt, laterite, and gravel is perpetually undergoing back-breaking repair without the use of machinery. In the baking sun, small clusters of men break up rock with sledgehammers. Some, in striped pyjamas, appear to be prison inmates. Female workers, hauling big wooden baskets filled with gravel, patch up holes and depressions.

Map on pages 186–7

Sa Pa and hill tribes

Travellers will know they are approaching **Sa Pa** ❻, the northwest's tourism capital, from a few Dao shacks by the roadside shortly before the village of Binh Lu. For the first time, tribal people are neither shy nor indifferent to tourists or their cameras. On the contrary, they take off their metal jewellery and headpieces and proffer them for sale. Unlike the Dao villages closer to Sa Pa, these women have very close-cropped hair, usually hidden under a black turban, which holds the headpiece, a sort of metal cap with a small box-like crown.

Sa Pa was founded by the French as a hill station, and it's obvious why Sa Pa was rediscovered by backpackers in the mid-1990s and is now thriving on a burgeoning tourist trade. The blue peaks in the distance are a study in shifting mists and clouds. The lower hillsides are ripples of terraced rice fields. It's the Swiss Alps crossed with Nepal. Best of all, it doesn't take more than 10 minutes to stroll outside the still-small frontier town and be traipsing on a path through the countryside.

And for the truly adventurous or foolhardy, there is **Fan Si Pan** ❼, Vietnam's highest peak at 3,143 metres (10,311 ft) and directly west of Sa Pa. A guide is mandatory, although there is a trail blazed by immigrants from China. Sa Pa's

BELOW: northern waterfalls abound.

Guesthouses run tours with English-speaking guides for day treks to nearby Hmong, Dao (pronounced *zao*), and Giay (pronounced *zay*) villages. Also on offer are two- to five-day treks to more remote villages.

BELOW: in the town of Sa Pa.

guesthouses provide guides, porters, tents, and camping equipment. Located in the nature reserve of **Hoang Lien Son**, Fan Si Pan is good territory for sighting birds and rhododendrons. While it is not technically demanding, the excursion takes at least four days and often more if rain or mist is thick. December is perhaps the best time to visit, though cold.

With temperatures dropping below freezing, along with frequent winds and the occasional snow flurry, Sa Pa itself can be very uncomfortable in the winter, especially in January and February. (Yet visitors should not be tempted to use the charcoal burners in guesthouse rooms; the carbon monoxide fumes can be deadly.) The heaviest tourist season is summer, when both Vietnamese and Chinese flee here to escape the heat, yet rain can be quite common then.

Year-round, Sa Pa experiences a tourist surge on Fridays and Saturdays. Apparently travel agencies in Hanoi have ridiculously hyped the weekend as a "love market" to visitors from the big city. No doubt local youth come to town in the hope of meeting the opposite sex from other villages, but they are wise enough to avoid the gawking tourists and their cameras. What foreigners will see is the weekly rendezvous when villagers come to town to buy, sell, and socialise. It's all the more picturesque, since Sa Pa's market spans several levels connected by stairways.

Both Hmong men and women in this area wear dark-blue, almost black clothing. It's been dyed with indigo and there are always indigo fields near Hmong villages. The women and girls wear indigo turbans, skirts, vests, leggings, and many big silver hoop earrings. Men wear baggy shirts and trousers and a long vest, as well as silver and bronze necklaces. Although their

Map on pages 186–7

embroidered decorations are minimal, the motifs are unmistakably those that the Hmong use in Thailand and Laos. Hmong babies here too wear colourful little tasselled caps. Dao dress, like Dao culture and architecture, varies a lot in Vietnam. Here Dao men's attire is similar to the Hmong, but the little patches of embroidered decoration instantly identify them. Like that of their counterparts in Laos and Thailand, Dao embroidery is incredibly dense and colourful. Like their relatives in Thailand and Laos too, Dao women wear loose trousers that stop below the knee. Unlike them, however, Dao women here wear a jacket with a very long back panel. Some of these back panels are works of art, almost completely covered with dense embroidered designs. Both Dao men and women carry tasselled shoulder bags.

All of these items, some quite old, are sold – after fierce bargaining – by tribal vendors in Sa Pa. There is no need to worry about missing market day. Throughout the week, Hmong and Dao women wander about town aggressively touting their clothing and jewellery. If tourists have even once glanced at her wares, the vendor will pursue them for days, even ambushing them in guesthouses and restaurants. Perhaps the best course for visitors is not to contemplate shopping until their last day in Sa Pa.

In various stages of decay, a few villas, with balconies and cupolas, linger from Sa Pa's days as a hill station, but the future holds more karaoke bars, more nouveau Chinese claptrap architecture, and perhaps paved roads. Many of the old buildings were destroyed during the Chinese occupation of 1979. The charred appearance of the granite Catholic church is due to Chinese shelling at that time. Sa Pa's Catholics still suffer. Attending daily services here is a moving experience. In the early morning and early evening, the tiny practising

Sometime during Mass, a few scruffy young men who are obviously police or informers make a surveillance of the Sa Pa church. Perhaps they do so only when foreigners are in attendance.

BELOW: White Tai woman.

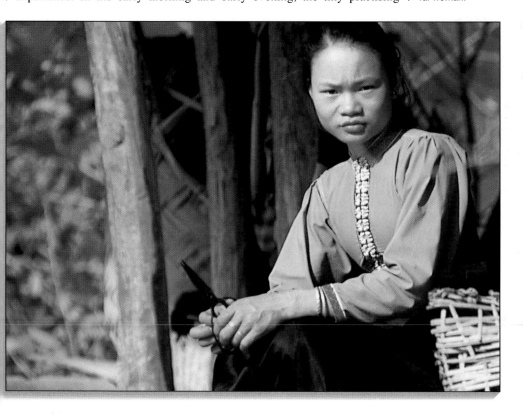

*Warm northern
Vietnamese dish.*

congregation gathers to recite Mass – from memory, without a priest. The church has not had a priest for many years and seldom does the government grant permission for the bishop to visit.

On the border

The town of **Lao Cai** ❽ on the Chinese border should be rushed through as quickly as possible. The 35-km (22-mile) descent from Sa Pa, however, has spectacular views, and the road, finally, is sealed. In the French days, the colonial elite were carried up and down this route on sedan chairs. Unless tensions crank up again between China and Vietnam, it's perfectly legal to enter and exit China by walking across Lao Cai's narrow railway bridge during daylight hours. Beyond is the Chinese border town of Hekou and the train to Kunming. Travellers must have a Chinese visa in hand; Vietnamese visas must specify Lao Cai as an exit or entry point. Often, Vietnamese immigration police demand a gratuity of a few dollars, no matter how legal the visa.

Lao Cai is partly such an ugly, sterile city because it was flattened when China invaded in 1979. It was not the first time the city had been occupied by Chinese. Ironically, the Vietnamese have rebuilt it to resemble just another communist Chinese city, with lots of grim, oversized cement boxes, wide streets, and very little in the way of attractive greenery. But the Chinese aren't solely to blame. In early 1951, still testing out his new heavy artillery and the practise of offensive warfare, Giap pinpointed Lao Cai. With Viet Minh troops outnumbering French 5 to 1, he took the city within a few days.

Twenty-seven km (17 miles) to the east of Lao Cai, little **Bac Ha** ❾ may give Sa Pa a run for the tourist money. It's smaller, usually warmer, and has more of

BELOW: moving goods near the Chinese border.

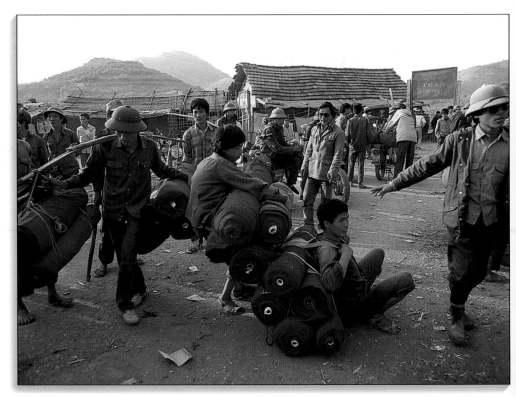

a frontier feel, probably due to the pony traffic. The appeal stems from the sheer variety of minorities represented, especially at the weekend markets. Most people in this area belong to one of the Hmong groups, but there are also Dao, Giay, Laichi, Lolo, Nhang, Nung, Phulao, Tai, Thulao, Chinese, and Vietnamese. There are several villages within walking distance of Bac Ha. Further afield are two photogenic markets, in addition to Bac Ha's on Sunday. The Can Cau market, in a village 18 km (11 miles) north of Bac Ha, runs on Saturday and features livestock sales.

As for the unusual two-storey house on the edge of town, now sheltering several families, townsfolk say it was the residence of their last "king", or chieftain, who now lives in France.

Back towards Hanoi

The 340-km (210-mile) road journey from Lao Cai to Hanoi is slow and tedious. The train is definitely preferable. Most likely only history buffs would bother stopping two-thirds of the way at the substantial concrete provincial town of **Yen Bai** ⑩, which also has a railway stop and is famous for its rubies. Yen Bai was the scene of several battles during the First Indochina War, but it is most famous for the "Yen Bai Uprising" of 1930.

Although communist annals would have it differently, it was actually the plan of another nationalist group, the Vietnamese National Party (better known by its Vietnamese acronym, VNQDD) to oust the French by military uprising. Only the Vietnamese troops at the Yen Bai garrison, however, proceeded with mutiny by killing their French officers. French troops quelled the mutiny within a day. It was the first time that aerial bombardment and napalm had been

Map on pages 186–7

TIP

There are twice-daily trains from Lao Cai to Hanoi. The journey, hugging the Red River all the way, takes about 10 hours, the same as by road. But the train is the more comfortable and preferred option.

BELOW: cycling canines en route.

THE HMONG IN VIETNAM

Most of the tribal people in this area are Hmong or Dao. Both have settled in Vietnam quite recently, having migrated from China in the past 150 years. The Hmong, numbering about 600,000 and comprising five subgroups and dialects in Vietnam, are sometimes known as Meo. The Dao number about 500,000 and are known as Mien or Yao in China, Laos, and Thailand. The irresistible garments of the Hmong girls and women alone draw many travellers. Their pleated indigo skirts with a batik effect are similar to that of many Hmong elsewhere in Southeast Asia, but the others don't decorate themselves with so much embroidery and applique, or express such devotion to pink and red.

In the 20th century, opium has often been the most profitable crop grown by the Hmong. Not surprisingly, then, Hmong in this area fought with their French patrons against the Viet Minh.

Living in the inhospitable uplands of China, Laos, Thailand, and Vietnam, the Hmong traditionally have relied upon environmentally damaging slash-and-burn farming. However, since the late 1980s there has been considerable success in shifting the Hmong farmers in the Bac Ha area to the cultivation of plum orchards.

employed in Vietnam. Hundreds of Vietnamese soldiers and 12 VNQDD leaders were summarily guillotined. It was perhaps coincidental and simply a response to hunger and heavy taxes, but following the Yen Bai uprising, the country was racked for a year with anti-colonialist strikes, riots, and even the creation of two "soviets" at Nghe-Tinh in Annam. Repression was so harsh that for the next 10 years, at least in the north, both the VNQDD and the Communist Party were broken.

Northward from Hanoi

Due north of Hanoi, **Thai Nguyen** ⓫ is a grimy industrial city and home of Southeast Asia's first steel mill, built with Chinese aid in the 1950s. It's worth a brief stop for Thai Nguyen's excellent museum of ethnic minorities, which has many handsome ethnographic displays. Although they can't be recognised by their dress, many of the factory workers in this area are in fact tribal people. Eighty km (50 miles) from Hanoi, Thai Nguyen claims a landmark in revolutionary history. In 1917, Luong Ngoc Quyen, a nationalist student, was imprisoned here after the French had him arrested in Hong Kong by the authorities there. His torture triggered the indigenous garrison to mutiny and seize the town.

The soldiers were supported by peasants and miners under the banner of the League for the Restoration of Vietnam. French troops from Hanoi suppressed the rebellion within a few days and Luong Ngoc Quyen was killed. Remnants of the group who fled westward were ultimately slaughtered in Tam Dao in 1918. During the First Indochina War, Thai Nguyen, like Yen Bai, had considerable strategic importance as the key Viet Minh depot for supplies from China in the fight against the French.

BELOW: coal-field workers in Quang Ninh Province.

Potentially, Cao Bang Province's greatest attraction for visitors is **Cong Vien Quoc Gia Ba Be** ⑫ (Ba Be National Park), due north of Thai Nguyen and Hanoi. Located on a modest mountain top in the southwest, **Ho Ba Be** (Ba Be Lake, or Three Seas Lake) is the largest natural lake in the country. Over a kilometre wide and 9 km (5 miles) long, it reaches a depth of 30 metres (100 ft) and offers an opportunity for a spot of sailing. The lake is surrounded by limestone cliffs and lush forests. In the summer, the height of the Vietnamese tourist season, there are many tour boats for hire for visits to surrounding caves and minority villages.

The national park is inhabited by many animals, including bears, tigers, macaques, pheasants – supposedly well over 200 animal species. A few colonies of the indigenous Tonkin snub-nosed monkey, recently suspected of being extinct, have been found here. Like Vietnamese, foreigners may stay overnight in a Tay village within the park.

The obstacle to enjoyment of the region, as so often is the case in Vietnam, is rapacious civil servants. Only since the mid-1990s have foreigners been allowed to travel in the Cao Bang area without first having to gain special permits. Unfortunately when the ban was lifted, park or provincial officials – or both – immediately began demanding sizeable visitors' fees and insisting that foreigners stay in the park guesthouse or in Cho Ra, a village 18 km (11 miles) from the lake. With overall tourist numbers to Vietnam falling, there are rumours that the forestry ministry has been concerned with rectifying the corruption.

The park's southern border straddles Bac Thai Province, a region intimately linked with anti-colonial resistance, particularly useful as its mountainous terrain rendered the region virtually inaccessible to French troops. The climate here is

Map on pages 186–7

BELOW: country road in Bac Thai.

both tropical and subtropical, with an average temperature of 28°C (82°F) during the hottest month and 14°C (56°F) during the coldest. Lush and tall palms brandishing wonderful, fan-shaped leaves and numerous varieties of bamboo abound throughout most of the province.

Beautiful Cao Bang Province is to the northeast and has only opened its borders to foreigners in the past decade. Highway 4 runs through ravines and mountain passes almost parallel to the Chinese border from the coast to the west. It was the site of numerous clashes in the late 1940s between French colonial troops and the Viet Minh guerrillas. Protected by a thin string of French forts, which were constantly under attack, Highway 4 was dubbed "Street Without Joy" by French-speaking soldiers, but the name soon came to apply to a wider geographical area.

With the 1949 communist victory in China, the Viet Minh not only benefited from a good supply of heavy weapons and Chinese advisors but also from training camps in China. In 1950, Giap switched from guerrilla attacks on isolated forts to full-scale attacks on the sizeable garrisons of Dong Khe and Cao Bang. As the Cao Bang defenders fled south to Lang Son on Highway 4, Giap ambushed them. Panicked, the French forces, which included many Vietnamese and North African soldiers, withdrew from Lang Son shortly after. The colonial side had lost almost the entire critical Chinese frontier. And the border town of Lao Cai to the west was soon to follow. Thus the Viet Minh had an assured line of supplies and support. And some would say that the French had already lost the war.

The province's capital and principal town is also called **Cao Bang** ⑬. Shelled by the Chinese in 1979, Cao Bang itself has little tourist appeal, aside from the

TIP

One only needs to watch other tourists around hill-tribe people to recognise the truth: foreign tourists can be insensitive and intrusive – and often obnoxious – with their cameras.

BELOW: fake money at a temple for bringing good luck.

ALLURE OF THE AO DAI

The national dress of Vietnamese women is the *ao dai*, alluring, beautiful, and provocative yet discreet *(see photo on pages 66–67).* Before the 18th century, women wore long skirts (still found in northern villages) but never the trousers of the *ao dai* (lit. long gown). In 1744, the Nguyen dynasty, ruling central and southern Vietnam, dictated a change in dress towards the lines of the Chinese style. Buttoned coats and trousers replaced skirts and split coats tied in front. Emperor Minh Mang imposed the wearing of trousers on all women. Colour and design were dictated and regulated by ceremonial requirements, social class, and professional hierarchy.

In the 1930s, an artist from a liberal reform group attempted to modernise the Vietnamese woman's dress through diversity in colour and designs. His new creation of a longer coat used different materials and could even be bare-shouldered. His innovations, gradually tempered with modifications, evolved to become today's *ao dai.* After the end of the Vietnam War in 1975 and the subsequent reunification of north and south, a period of severe austerity forced the *ao dai* into temporary retirement. In the late 1980s, however, the *ao dai* began to return to daily life, especially in the south.

Map
on pages
186–7

early morning market, which is thronged with tribal people and where Vietnamese are outnumbered by Tay, Hmong, Nung, Dao, and Lolo. The town is, however, the customary launching point for visits to the glorious mountainous surroundings and the Chinese border.

Cao Bang Province shares a long border with China. Forest covers 90 percent of the province, and the climate is cool, particularly in winter when snow caps the high peaks. The multicultural province has a population of about 500,000, covering an area of 8,450 sq. km (5,400 sq. miles), but the harsh terrain makes it a hard scrabble to survive from farming. The province's economic value lies in its rivers, which have been harnessed by 30 hydroelectric stations.

Along with Lang Son, Cao Bang Province is the home for almost all of the Nung minority, which totals about 700,000. They farm at both valley floors and high altitudes, such as the 1,000-metre-high (3,300-ft) Dong May plateau. They are fine weavers and makers of bamboo furniture and baskets. The women traditionally wear long indigo dresses and headscarves. Linguistically and culturally, the Nung share much with their neighbours, the Tay (or Tho), who number over 1 million. Their shared language is clearly Tai, but because both the Nung and Tay have been in Vietnam for nearly 2,000 years and have been isolated from most other Tai, their cultural practices seem closer to the Vietnamese than to the Tai of Vietnam or anywhere else. Notable, for example, are their ancestral worship practices, which appear to have Confucian origins. They also have many Buddhist practices.

In 1941, when Vietnam was occupied by the Japanese but still administered by the Vichy French, Vo Nguyen Giap and other party cadres began from here to build an organisation of scattered agents and guerrilla units, omitting the usual messages of propaganda about class struggle and emphasising instead resistance to foreign aggression and "national salvation".

Encouraged by Ho Chi Minh, the Viet Minh made assiduous efforts to recruit members of various ethnic minorities, most of whom were hardly predisposed to fight for a sovereign Vietnamese state. The Vietnamese *(kinh)*, after all, were a distinct minority and a historical enemy in the northern provinces, but now they shared a hatred of the French. And the kinh promised an autonomous tribal state after victory.

Tay and Nung cadres rose to high positions in the Communist Party hierarchy. One of the original Tay leaders of the aforementioned Bac Son units, Chu Van Tan, was defence minister in Ho Chi Minh's August 1945 cabinet. After the final defeat of the French, a Tay-Nung autonomous region was created in the late 1950s. Schools were allowed to teach native languages and the region did have some self-governing functions, but this and a Tai region in the northwest were abolished in 1980.

From 1943, the Viet Minh received weapons and funds from US intelligence groups. In return, they provided intelligence on the Japanese and rescued downed Allied pilots. By early 1945, the Viet Minh controlled large parts of four northern provinces, but it wasn't until then that Giap organised here the first regular troops: 34 men with 31 rifles.

BELOW: tribal woman and smile.

Hmong children outside of Sa Pa.

A good 2-hour drive north of Cao Bang, the cave at **Pac Bo** is yet another stop on the Ho Chi Minh pilgrimage trail. Just a kilometre from the Chinese border, this is near the spot where the man then known as Nguyen Ai Quoc crossed into his homeland for the first time in 30 years, in 1941. Later taking the name Ho Chi Minh, he only lived in the cave near the Nung village of Pac Bo for a few months, in early 1941, leaving the area in August 1942 and returning to China for two years. Nonetheless, there's a museum, Ho artefacts, a replica of his simple bed, and tourist trinkets. Ho named the stream flowing in front of the cave "Lenin Stream".

Also very close to the Chinese border, the waterfall at **Ban Doc** – perhaps the country's largest – is very popular with Vietnamese and Chinese tourists. Nearby is Nguom Ngao Cave. The picturesque falls of **An Giac**, in Trung Khanh district, are formed by a stretch of the Song Quy Xuan falling from a height of 30 metres (100 ft). Many wild orchids grow in the region. Limestone mountains and forests surround another of the province's beauty spots, Thang Hen, one of seven lakes in the area.

To the northeast

Ho Cam Son ⓮ (Cam Son Lake), in the district of Luc Ngan, is surrounded by limestone mountains. This tranquil, picturesque setting offers accommodation, with rest houses on some of the small islands in the lake.

The road north begins to climb into the higher elevations as it leaves Ha Bac Province and enters Lang Son Province. The ascent into the mountains presents stunning scenery. Lang Son Province shares a common border with China's Guangxi Province. Mountains and forests cover 80 percent of the province's

BELOW: northern minority women.

land area, and tigers, panthers, bears, deer, pangolin, chamois, and monitor lizards are among the animals found here.

Provincial specialities include forest products such as fragrant mushrooms, anise, and a fine-flavoured tobacco. Tay, Nung, Hmong, Dao, Nghia, and Chinese are among the ethnic minorities living in the province. The Song Ky Cung that flows through the province is unique in that it flows northward to China. The other rivers in the region all flow south.

The narrow gorge at **Chi Lang**, a series of passes connected by tortuous tracks forged between high mountains south of the Chinese-Vietnamese border, is a battleground where the Vietnamese have fought many major battles against Chinese invaders throughout history. In 1076, the Vietnamese defeated 300,000 Chinese Song-dynasty troops here, and in 1427, nearly 100,000 Ming-dynasty troops received the same treatment. The gorge's northern entrance is known as **Quy Quan Mon** (Barbarian Invaders Gate) and the southern exit is called **Ngo The** (Swearing Path). The almost incessant fighting on this northern border has forged the temperament and galvanised the resilient character of the northern Vietnamese people.

Highway 1 runs right through the provincial capital of **Lang Son** ⓯, about 150 km (100 miles) northeast of Hanoi. Unsightly new buildings are fast replacing the bombed-out old ones. When 85,000 Chinese troops invaded Vietnam in February 1979, Lang Son was a prime target. By the time the Chinese occupied the Vietnamese city 16 days later, 80 percent of the buildings were rubble. Almost immediately, they began to withdraw. The town was reviving on smuggled Chinese goods even before trade was legalised in 1993. Today all manner of capitalism – legal and illegal – flourishes.

Map on pages 186–7

Long a smuggling post, Lang Son is now a legitimate trade centre. It is just 18 km (11 miles) from the Chinese border. With proper visas, foreign travellers may cross into China from here.

BELOW: Black Tai.

Map on pages 186–7

TIP

The train between Vietnam and China crosses the border near Dong Dang. But it's not possible to board the train here for the trip into China. Foreigners must board it in Hanoi for the border crossing.

BELOW: festival crowd at temple.
RIGHT: market talk in Sa Pa.

The **Ky Lua** market, held in a village a few kilometres away, is a popular gathering place for members of the region's many minority groups. The town is also the transit point for trains from Hanoi. In early 1996, the line reopened to cross the Vietnam-China border. Only a few kilometres west of town is **Nhi Tam Thanh**, an area that includes numerous caves and grottoes, many of which are used for worship of spirits.

Overlooking the site is Waiting Woman Mountain. Legend says an outcrop of rock is a woman who waited so long for her husband that she turned into stone. In the area are also ruins of forts and walls built to keep the Chinese at bay.

In the mountains just west of Lang Son is a highland valley called **Bac Son**, inhabited by Tay (Tho) people. Briefly allied and supplied by the newly arrived Japanese, Tay guerrilla bands attacked isolated French military posts and retreating French soldiers in 1940. While the Japanese soon reconciled with the Vichy French, the guerrilla insurgency already had momentum. Communist Party cadres took over coordination and near the end of 1940 staged a general uprising in Bac Son and eight southern provinces – collectively known as the Bac Son Uprisings. The French quickly stamped out the rebellion and executed 100 cadres. The repercussions were especially devastating and long term for the Communist Party in the south. But it meant that Bac Son in particular and the far north in general became the base from which the Party would rebuild from virtually nothing.

A half hour's drive northwest is **Dong Dang** ⓰, a town right on the fortified border. Flattened during the 1979 invasion, the town has arisen anew on cross-border trade. The crossing here is known as the Friendship Gate, optimistically named given the sporadic exchanges of gunfire between Vietnam and China until 1992. For foreigners, this is probably the most popular exit to China. Once called Porte de Chine, it was through here that Japanese troops entered Vietnam in 1940 before attacking Lang Son.

Along the northeastern coast

Southeast from Lang Son along Highway 4 is **Mong Cai** ⓱, situated along the coastline on Vietnam's northeastern border with China and a busy town growing fat on trade in low-quality Chinese consumer goods, much of it illegal. The town was destroyed by retreating Chinese troops in 1979 and reconstruction began only when the border was reopened in 1991. This is one of three land-border gates to China open to foreigners, but it must be the least popular for non-Chinese; visas must specify Mong Cai as the exit point from Vietnam.

A few kilometres to the east, on an island separated from the mainland by a narrow sea channel, is Tra Co, which many say is the north's most attractive beach. It probably is the longest, and its numerous guesthouses do attract many foreigners in the summer months. However, the foreigners are all Chinese, as many Westerners object to the black sand and mud flats. At the southern end of the island is Mui Ngoc, a haven for local smugglers. Southwest (240 km/150 miles) are Hai Phong and Vinh Ha Long (*see Hai Phong/Ha Long chapter, page 177*). ❑

ETHNIC MINORITY CULTURE AND CLOTHING

Vietnam's ethnic minorities live mostly in isolated upland areas but in recent years outside contact has changed their traditional culture

There are two types of ethnic minority in Vietnam, each with its own distinct origins, cultural practices, and reactions to change.

In the northern highlands, groups of Tai, Dao, Hmong, Tay, and Nung people are "recent" settlers, having migrated from southern China over the past 500 years. The landscape here is rugged and isolated, and most of these groups have maintained their traditional way of life. They live in houses on stilts, wear decorative home-spun costumes on a daily basis, and sustain some of the best-preserved traditional upland cultures in Southeast Asia.

In the central highlands, by contrast, the Bahnar, Ra De (E De), Jarai and Sedang are indigenous to the region. But the rolling hills are suitable for coffee and have recently been settled by large numbers of Vietnamese who make money from cash crops.

Many minorities have adapted, building houses on the ground and abandoning their loincloth for clothes. Traditional costumes are used only on festival days and for ceremonies. Some of them, wishing to maintain their traditional lifestyle, move deep into the remaining forest to live in isolation and sustain themselves through slash-and-burn agriculture. They can be seen in urban centres on occasional market days trading their produce.

▷ **TAI HEADSCARVES**
Tai women in the northwest still wear the *khan pieu*, or headscarf. Men traditionally give young women a khan pieu in declaration of their love.

△ **THRESHING RICE**
Many agricultural tasks are done by women. This Tai woman in the Son La province typically wears her khan pieu even while threshing rice.

△ **HMONG TEXTILES**
Hmong people wear their home-spun clothes on their way to sell produce in Sa Pa market, Lao Cai Province.

▷ **EMBROIDERY**
Embroidery is thriving as minorities find a market among visitors and in Hanoi.

▷ **SILVER NECKLACES**
Apart from its decorative value, Hmong and Dao women believe silver jewellery has the ability to heal and prevent disease.

HILL-TRIBE TEXTILES

All the hill tribes of the northern highlands have retained their own textile industries, and these are enjoying a revival as the number of overseas tourists and Vietnamese visitors increases.

Tai people in Mai Chau valley (Hoa Binh Province) use home looms to weave long cotton scarves, which are then dyed in brightly coloured stripes using traditional vegetable dyes and tied at the ends into elaborate tassels. In the Sa Pa region, Hmong women (above) carry their embroidery with them to the terraced rice fields. Pausing from agricultural work, they make use of the rest time to decorate bags and hats, which they sell at Sa Pa market to supplement their income. Unfortunately, large numbers of imitation embroidered items, mass produced in the plains and transported up to Sa Pa, are now sold at the market. Visitors are urged to make their purchases with caution if they are after the genuine article.

▷ **SA PA MARKET**
Hmong people use home-grown linen and indigo to make clothes and exchange these goods for modern conveniences such as umbrellas and radios.

▽ **HILL-TRIBE CHILDREN**
Children in this central highland village traditionally went semi-naked. It's more common now to see them in imported shirts and dresses.

▷ **INNOVATIONS**
This E De woman illustrates the response of many central highlands people to change. Her clothes look traditional but are in fact an innovation.

THE TONKIN COAST

Northern Vietnam was called Tonkin by the French, and the French colonial charm is often encountered along the coast of the Gulf of Tonkin

Map on pages 186–7

Hanoi

Ho Chi Minh

Highway 1 stretches the length of the eastern coast for more than 2,000 km (1,200 miles), from Dong Dang at the Chinese border to Ha Tien in the Gulf of Thailand. Known in pre-colonial times as the Mandarin Way, the northern stretches are in poor repair compared to those in the southern half of Vietnam. Traffic is heavy and moves slowly. All along the way, depending on the season and the soil, there's produce drying on the dusty edge of the road – rice, straw, corn, chilli peppers, peanuts, potatoes. Heading south out of Hanoi, Highway 1 passes through the varied landscape of several provinces that contain every terrain imaginable – mountains, limestone hills, low-lying plains, inland waterways, rice paddies, and long stretches of sand along the **Vinh Bac Bo**, or **Gulf of Tonkin**.

The area surrounding **Nam Dinh** ⓲, on Highway 21 about 30 km (20 miles) from Highway 1 and the capital of Nam Ha Province, remains a Catholic stronghold, although many from here were among the 500,000 Vietnamese that fled south after the Communist takeover. Their ancestors were converted to Catholicism by Portuguese, Spanish and French missionaries in the 16th or 17th century, long before the French conquest. According to Vietnamese records, one of the first friars preached in this province in 1533.

This large industrial city lies 90 km (60 miles) from Hanoi on the southwest bank of the Song Nam Dinh (Nam Dinh River). Under the French, Nam Dinh became a centre for the domestic textile industry, which still flourishes today as the largest in the country. In the early 19th century, Nam Dinh was surrounded by a large citadel. The French dismantled it after occupying the area in 1882, but a single look-out tower still survives. The city was also heavily damaged during a 1947 Viet Minh siege and by US aerial bombing in the 1960s. The most interesting part of the city is by the riverside, where artisans and merchants still concentrate in the manner of Hanoi's Old Quarter.

Just to the north of Nam Dinh is the village of **Mac** and the ancient Tran ruins of **Thang Vang** (Golden City). These ruins are all that remain of the palaces built by the kings of the Tran dynasty, who defeated the Mongol Yuan-dynasty invaders from China three times in the 13th century. Tran Bich San, founder of the Tran dynasty, was born nearby. Among the ruins are the Thien Truong temples, which were dedicated to the 14 Tran kings, and the temple of Co Trach, which was dedicated to Tran Hung Dao. The only buildings left intact are the beautiful **Pho Minh** pagoda and a 13-storey tower, built in 1305 and which contains the remains of King Tran Nhan Tong.

East of Nam Dinh, on the road to Thai Binh and

PRECEDING PAGES: train between Hanoi and Ho Chi Minh. **LEFT:** making baskets. **BELOW:** Catholic church, Nam Dinh.

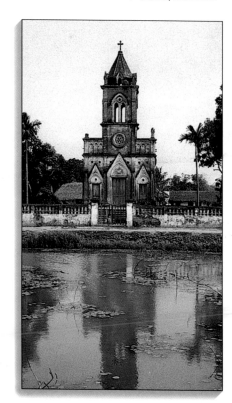

Hai Phong, is the site of 11th-century **Chua Keo** ⑲. Since the 17th century it has undergone much reconstruction, but it retains the spirit of the original design. It is considered one of the finer examples of traditional Vietnamese architecture in the northern delta, dedicated to Buddha, his disciples, and the bonze superior, the 11th-century Minh Khong. No metal nails were used in the construction of this impressive wooden pagoda and its three-storey bell tower, which contains bronze bells cast in the 17th and 18th centuries. Many traditional rituals and diverse forms of entertainment are performed here – some of them centuries old – particularly during the Tet holidays.

Ancient New Year wrestling festivals are justly famed in Nam Ha's Thanh Lien district. At **Cua**, folk games as well as contests in martial arts and wrestling honour a village son who helped 10th-century King Dinh Tien Hoang quell a rebellion of 12 vassals. This festival falls every year on the fourth day of the first lunar month. The more spectacular, 5-day Lieu Doi wrestling festival starts the next day in nearby **Liem Tuc**. The tale giving rise to the festival lacks not a single element of a Vietnamese legend...

A young village man of extraordinary strength, skilled in the martial arts and swordsmanship, volunteered to fight the foreign invaders. Prior to a glorious battlefield death, he had fallen in love with a female soldier. When she came to visit his hometown grave – after the victory, naturally – she was so distraught that she dropped dead.

The village subsequently built two temples honouring the star-crossed couple, now metamorphosed into a Thanh Ong (Male God) and a Tien Ba (Female God). The festival is launched with a procession carrying the Thanh Ong statue on a palanquin from temple to wrestling place. The matches include face-offs

BELOW: guitar teacher.

between new male infants (whose fathers actually wrestle on their behalf), native villagers, and wrestlers representing surrounding villages.

To the east of Nam Dinh, small Thai Binh Province has the highest population density in the Song Hong (Red River) Delta and in the country as a whole – well over 1,200 people per square kilometre. Salt fields cover extensive areas on the coastal shores. Under the French, all the salt had to be produced under the aegis of the government's salt monopoly. With the monopoly also on opium sales, the government reaped great revenues but at tremendous cost to peasants and fishermen, who were crippled (and sometimes inspired to revolt) by prices that continued to rise regardless of demand. Private production of salt was severely punished. In addition to rice, today jute, rushes, mulberry, sugar cane, and ground nut are also cultivated. Among the crafts found in Thai Binh, carpet making, silk weaving, wickerwork, and embroidery are common.

Back on Highway 1, about 30 km (20 miles) from Nam Dinh and 100 km (60 miles) south of Hanoi, the dusty town of **Ninh Binh** ❷⓪ has few redeeming features. However, situated a bumpy two hours from Hanoi, it is a good base for explorations of the eminently redeeming features of Hoa Lu, Tam Coc, Kenh Ga, Cuc Phuong, and Phat Diem.

In addition to the blow-off from Highway 1, Ninh Binh is dusty because of a nearby rock quarry. Most inhabitants of the town seem employed in carting around large rocks or repairing motors. Pedestrians should arm themselves with a sturdy stick since the town is full of mean dogs. Down by the riverside is an open-air wet market.

Across the river rises up a very large, bare crag. In French days, a fort perched on top. In 1951 Viet Minh – temporarily – overran the French positions in and

Map
on pages
186–7

TIP

Police keep a very keen eye on foreigners in Ninh Binh, which may explain why the locals are afraid to talk to visitors. It should be assumed that anything left in a hotel will be searched, and possibly stolen, by police or informers.

BELOW: fisherman and stilt house.

As with so many damaged churches throughout Vietnam, the government has not permitted the Ninh Binh church to be rebuilt, preferring that it testify to US aggression.

around Ninh Binh. Eighty French soldiers holed up in the local Catholic church; 19 survived. In the eastern part of town, in front of the train station, stands the shell of the church with a broken spire. Supposedly, it was destroyed during US bombing raids.

It's obvious why Ninh Binh was an anchor in the so-called de Lattre line, the triangular cordon established in 1950 to protect Hanoi, Hai Phong, and the great rice-growing, coal-mining Song Hong (Red River) Delta from Viet Minh incursions. Ninh Binh straddles both Highway 1 and the Song Day (Day River). Immediately to the north of Ninh Binh, the Song Day runs parallel and just to the west of Highway 1, which in the early 1950s was lined with French fortifications. To the west of the river was solid Viet Minh territory.

Across Highway 1 and only 13 km (8 miles) northwest of Ninh Binh is **Hoa Lu**, the beguiling site of the 10th-century capital of a Vietnamese kingdom known as Dai Co Viet. It was a rather small feudal kingdom, covering an area of 300 hectares (740 acres) and reigned over by the Dinh and Le dynasties of the 10th century and by the early phases of the Ly dynasty in the 11th century. The kingdom was enclosed by a citadel, bordering the Song Hoang Long and running along the Yen Ngua limestone hills. It's instantly evident why this defensible site was selected. The enemy were the Chinese, who had been expelled in 939.

An inner citadel enclosed the royal court. There are some remains of the earthen citadels and of the valley's palaces, shrines, and temples, but they are in a state that only archaeologists would appreciate. An enormous stone column engraved with Buddhist sutras, dating from 988, was found here. What do survive are two 17th-century temples modelled on 11th-century originals.

BELOW: kids at Hoa Lu, the ancient city.

After the capital was transferred from Hoa Lu to Thang Long (now Hanoi), the two temples were built, one dedicated to the founder of the 12-year Dinh dynasty, Dinh Tien Hoang, who reigned in the late 10th century, and the other to his successor, Le Hoan. **Den Dinh Tien Hoang** was reconstructed in 1696. The temple now faces east, although the original faced north. It is entered by passing through two brick arches, the so-called Outer Triumphant Arch and the Inner Triumphant Arch. The 17th-century Dragon Bed, in an area once used for sacrifices, lies in the centre of the courtyard in front of the main building. It was carved out of a single rock. Lightly carved on the surface is a very strange dragon floating in a mass of clouds: it has a long beard, the head and ears of a buffalo, paws resembling human hands, and fish-like scaly skin. Surrounding carvings depict a carp, shrimp, phoenix, and mouse. Gifts and food offerings are placed on the slab during festivals.

Statues of mythical animals – part dog, part lion – guard the brick pathway to the small temple. A huge drum in the forecourt was used by peasants to get the attention of mandarins. Inside the temple, King Dinh Tien Hoang, also known as Dinh Bo Linh, is worshipped at a central altar. The large characters written in ancient Vietnamese script translate as, "From this day onwards we have our independence". On one pillar is written "Dai Co Viet", the name Dinh Tien Hoang gave Vietnam. On the other, the script reads "Hoa Lu is prosperous as the capital". Behind the altar, passing by heavy carved beams, is a windowless back room with a 19th-century wooden statue of a paunchy Dinh Tien Hoang, framed by statues of his three sons. The single statue next to the king, on the viewer's right, depicts his eldest son, Dinh Quoc Lien. While Dinh Quoc Lien was the eldest, he was not chosen as heir apparent by his father, so he

Map on pages 186–7

BELOW: Hoa Lu.

masterminded the assassination of the anointed brother, Dinh Hang Lan, in 979. The next year, a palace official assassinated both the king and Dinh Quoc Lien. The six-year-old youngest son (whose statue does not appear childlike), Dinh Toan, became king but only ruled for six months. Gen. Le Hoan somehow eliminated him and founded the 29-year-long Le, or "Earlier Le", dynasty and defeated the Chinese at the gate.

A narrow dirt road, site of an annual 3-day festival, connects to the **Den Le Hoan**, a miniature of the Dinh Hoang temple and close to the present-day village of Truong Yen Ha. The 17th-century carvings around the entrance door and on roof beams portray playful animals. The temple has a series of three chambers: Hall of Worship, Hall of Heavenly Fragrance, and the Inner Shrine. In this last, a dim back room, are statues of Le Hoan, his queen, Duong Van Nga (supposedly the widow of Dinh Tien Hoang), and his sons, Le Long Dinh and Le Long Viet. These sons also quarrelled over succession after Le Hoan's death in 1005. The dynasty was finished in 1010, only 30 years after it began.

Near the entrance to this temple is a steep hill. Those who can climb 200 stone steps (and withstand aggressive hawkers flogging souvenirs and waving fans in the hope of tips) will be rewarded with a shrine to Confucius and a panoramic view of the ancient kingdom. The atmosphere within the temple grounds is blessedly peaceful because souvenir-selling pests are barred from them. However, it's a gauntlet to pass between the two temples.

Another scenic pagoda worth visiting in Hoa Lu district is **Chua Bich**, in the mountains. Built in 1428, the pagoda is renowned for its beautiful bronze and marble statues and for its huge bronze bell.

BELOW: eating *pho.*

The enchanting inland waterworld of **Tam Coc** (Three Caves) can be entered from the Van Lam village docks, only 9 km (6 miles) southwest of Ninh Binh. Here, travellers hire a flat-bottomed boat and a pair of helmspersons (rower and poler). In the initial segment of the 2- to 3-hour journey, the lazy Ngo Dong River blends with flooded rice fields. But soon the waterway is wending through three tunnel caves *(tam coc)* that have bored through the limestone hills. Through the lowest, passengers must duck to avoid scraping the roof. The largest has stalactites and stalagmites. In between are clear, shallow, glass-smooth lagoons encircled by green-furred limestone cliffs, where butterflies flutter and women in small boats claw through the vegetation for edible morsels. Birdwatchers might catch sight of herons and kingfishers.

Tam Coc has been called an inland Ha Long Bay, but the utter quiet and tranquillity are nothing like being near the sea. In the final lagoon, a lonely goatherd mills around a ruined pagoda on a small spit of land. An initial tributary reaches Den Thai Vi, a temple where a 13th-century king, Tran Nhan Tong, retired after his abdication.

The only disturbance to the tranquillity is the oarswoman, who continually nags passengers to buy embroidered T-shirts. Be warned that a purchase to stop the sales pitch only stimulates more intensive pestering. The best strategy is not even to glance at the articles.

Close to the boat dock and the stalls of T-shirt sellers is **Van Lan**, a village where shirts and table linen are embroidered. This is where most of the items sold in Hanoi's Old Quarter originate. Perhaps bargains can be had here, but no foreign traveller in years has been known to investigate. Fending off the vendors close at hand is so exhausting that it kills even a shopaholic's urges. Tam Coc is usually linked with Hoa Lu on day-tours from Hanoi.

Fortunately, there is a charming, and for the moment, pest-free alternative. The fishing village of **Kenh Ga** clings to karst cliffs – that is, the portion of the village that doesn't live on boats and return to the cove after a day of fishing. Kenh Ga can only be reached by boat, preferably a silent rowboat, though groups might like the larger, chugging ones. The journey begins by canal but then enters the Song Hoang Long, which is plied by loaded and slow barges.

The simple houses are constructed of stone, cement, and plaster; all the materials must have been hauled in. While the ground space is restricted, kids do learn from an early age to scoot around by boat. The villagers are pleased but puzzled when foreigners come to Kenh Ga.

Their pride and joy is the rustic Catholic church with ancient wooden shutters. Inside there are heavy wooden beams and pillars with interesting carvings. Donations are much appreciated and could conceivably prevent the entire population from becoming rapacious T-shirt hawkers. Lucky visitors will be at Kenh Ga at Saturday sunset as a fleet of small boats converge on the church, conveying ladies in their best sarongs.

To reach Kenh Ga, take the road jutting west off Highway 1 about 11 km (7 miles) north of Ninh Binh. A similar distance brings the desolate boat dock, but a caretaker can rustle up transportation to Kenh Ga.

Map on pages 186–7

karst (kärst): a limestone region marked by sinks, abrupt ridges, irregular protuberant rocks, caverns, and underground streams.

— MERRIAM WEBSTER
DICTIONARY

BELOW: babysitting the water buffalo.

Quiet walking trail in Cuc Phuong.

Cuc Phuong National Park

By continuing west 24 km (15 miles) along on the same semi-paved road that runs by the Kenh Ga boat pier, one arrives at the entrance to the 25,000-hectare (61,000-acre) **Cong Vien Quoc Gia Cuc Phuong** ㉑ (Cuc Phuong National Park). If visitors can only visit one national park in northern Vietnam, this should be it because the biodiversity here is the most compelling. The park shelters 250 bird and 64 mammal species, including tigers, leopards, bats, boars, civet cats, flying squirrels, and the endangered Delacour langur primate. As is true with other Vietnamese national parks, there is little likelihood of glimpsing an animal, least of all a dangerous one, because poaching is so extensive. But unlike other parks, the staff here genuinely do seem to have an interest in wildlife and environmental protection, as indicated by their spotted deer research centre near the park's entrance.

And visitors can get a sense of the great diversity of insects and flora within the park. Some large trees (*Parashorea stellata and Terminalia myriocarpa*), which reach about 50 metres (165 ft) in height, are estimated to be over 1,000 years old. Close to 500 medicinal plants and herbs, of both native and foreign origin, have been discovered growing in the park. Some of the park's many caves and grottoes are also easily accessible within two mountain ranges that enclose a valley, with a micro-climate quite different from that of the surrounding region. Three tombs, excavated in one of the grottoes in 1966, contained shells, animal teeth, rudimentary stone tools, and prehistoric human remains. For a therapeutic warm dip, try the park's thermal springs. These remain at a constant temperature of 37°C (99°F) and contain more than 20 chemical elements believed to have assorted healing properties.

BELOW: wilderness hikers.

Since the entrance is located 45 km (30 miles) from Ninh Binh and 140 km (80 miles) from Hanoi, Cuc Phuong can be visited on a day trip, but that may not leave time for more than the 7-km (4-mile) tourist trail. Visitors can take longer hikes, for which they must hire a park guide, if they stay overnight in one of the Muong villages within the park.

The bishopric of Phat Diem is eventually reached by a sealed road that runs southeast from Ninh Binh for 30 straight and flat kilometres (20 miles) to the small town of Kim Son. While the road is a bit bumpy, traffic is thin, making it well suited for motorbikes or bicycles. Unquestionably, this is Catholic country. Alexandre de Rhodes, the indefatigable Jesuit, won converts here in the early 17th century. The road is lined with Catholic cemeteries, their white coffin-shaped tombs sinking in the marshy land, and at least 10 well-maintained churches. More spires can be seen in the distance. Most are granite, in simplified gothic style with Vietnamese touches.

Notable is the one at **Phuoc Nhia**, set behind a pond about 20 km (12 miles) from Ninh Binh. Four-storey towers flank the Gothic doors. Behind is a bell tower with a pagoda roof and, behind it, a rare Buddhist pagoda, Thanh Anton. On the sides of the main church are two more chapels. Behind the northwestern wall is a Catholic school.

Once thinly lined with French forts (there are no obvious remnants), the western side of the road was Viet Minh territory, the eastern held by the French. Catholics here were in a bind. Few were pro-French; after all, most were poor peasants. In fact, throughout the 20th century many Catholics had been active in anti-colonialist movements. But by the late 1940s, the communists had killed off or out-organised rival nationalist groups and Catholics (like other Christians

Map on pages 186–7

BELOW: strolling in a fruit orchard.

TIP

Kim Son has a simple hotel quite near the Phat Diem Cathedral, but whether foreigners are allowed to stay depends upon the political temperature of the moment.

and the Buddhist clergy) were anti-communist. During the battles around this road in the early 1950s, locally organised militias, supplied by the French, successfully fought off the Viet Minh attacks.

The towering **Phat Diem Cathedral** is located in the friendly little town of **Kim Son** ㉒. Built in 1891, the Sino-Vietnamese-style cathedral has stone walls and towers, extends for 74 metres (240 ft), and is fringed with boxy cupolas with upturned tiled roofs. It was designed by a Vietnamese priest, Father Six (Tran Luc), who demanded that stone be towed from hundreds of kilometres away. Not counting the bishop's quarters behind a rear wall, there are a half-dozen other structures in the complex, including a cool, tomb-like stone chapel; a two-storey church with Romanesque arches, gargoyles, and a vaulted apse; and an 1890 stone bell tower.

Mounting the internal staircases of the bell tower, visitors eventually reach the enormous bronze bell protected by a Vietnamese-style tiled roof. The bell itself, capable of sheltering several good-sized people, represents an engineering feat as it was hauled up here on a ramp of earth.

The top of the bell tower offers a sweeping view of the cathedral complex and the town. The complex is fronted by an island in the middle of a large pond. On the island a white stone statue of Jesus triumphant in resplendent attire rises above the tree-tops. Although Mass is celebrated at least once daily (at 5am), during most of the day all the buildings are locked. Phat Diem is a popular destination for Vietnamese tourists, however, and tour group leaders are likely to have a key for at least the bell tower.

As for Kim Son itself, on the road back to Ninh Binh there is a 19th-century wooden covered bridge, arching across the Song Day.

BELOW: riding the train from Ho Chi Minh to Hanoi.

Annam and Thanh Hoa

Leaving behind Ninh Binh Province, one enters Annam, the central region, and the beautiful but impoverished province of Thanh Hoa. It is the first in an almost unbroken succession of seven coastal provinces hemmed between the South China Sea and the Indochinese mountain range.

From Thanh Hoa down to the former Demilitarised Zone (DMZ) – that is, through Thanh Hoa, Nghe An, Ha Tinh and Quanh Binh provinces – Highway 1 is especially bad, potholed, and corrugated. Provincial governments are charged with road maintenance, so the state of the road reflects a province's poverty. The sandy soil has never made for good harvests. Only able to grow one rice crop a year, peasant families scrape by on manioc and peanuts. But with seed money from Britain, many farmers in Thanh Hoa since the 1980s have become successful apiarists and honey producers.

Thanh Hoa, the cradle of the Dong Son culture, harbours a great many historical sites and is an important settlement area for the Muong minority. At the beginning of the 20th century, archaeologists discovered many relics of the Dong Son civilisation dispersed along the length of the Song Ma (Ma River) valley: bronze drums, musical instruments, statues, jewellery, various tools, and domestic objects. Some of these are now displayed at the Fine Arts Museum in Hanoi. The Muong still adhere to their ancient language, similar to Vietnamese, and use the bronze drums inherent to their unique culture and festivals. Although there has been much intermarriage and cultural melding over the centuries, the Muong probably predated the Viets in Vietnam.

As the Vietnamese grew in strength, however, they pushed the Muong further and further from the Song Hong (Red River) valley. Trieu's invasion in 208

Map on pages 186–7

BELOW: the north-south train.

BC was responsible for the Viet southward migration, and these first emigrants settled in the Phu Ly and Dong Son regions.

Before reaching Thanh Hoa, in Nam Ha Province, Phu Ly is where the first bronze drum was discovered in 1902. Other similar drums were acquired from the Long Doi Son Monastery and the village of Ngoc Lu. The figurative and stylised designs on the drums depict birds, animals, and scenes from everyday life. The Ngoc Lu bronze drum, 80 centimetres (30 in) in diameter, is decorated with an image of the sun. Its many rays are surrounded by 16 concentric circles of various designs depicting deer, aquatic birds, people, and vignettes of daily life. The drum's surface is engraved with pairs of animals and birds heading east towards the sun. In 1924, a member of the Ecole Francaise d'Extreme Orient unearthed several bronze drums and other bronze objects at Dong Son.

Mieu Than Dong Co (Temple of the Spirit of the Drum) is found in the village of Dan Ne, on the hill of Tam Diep. The temple contains a bronze drum 2 metres (6 ft) in diameter, which, according to popular belief, is said to have belonged to one of the Hung kings. The drum's face is decorated with nine concentric circles engraved with ancient characters.

The megalithic-style Ho Citadel in **Tay Giai** ㉓ was built in 1397 under the orders of the usurper king, Ho Qui Li. He named the new citadel Tay Kinh (Capital of the West). It was more or less a replica of the citadel of Dong Kinh (Capital of the East). But unlike the other citadels of Hoa Lu and Co Loa, whose walls were built of earth, the Ho citadel's huge walls, 5 metres (16 ft) high and 3 metres (10 ft) thick, were made of stone. Some blocks weigh an estimated 16 tons and show a high degree of quarrying and stone-carving skill.

BELOW: vendors of fowl at market.

The Muong minority village of **Lam Son** ㉔, in the Thanh Hoa highlands,

was the native village of Vietnam's national hero, Le Loi, who became King Le Thai To. It was from here that Le Loi launched a decade-long uprising against the Chinese Ming-dynasty occupiers of Vietnam. The struggle, waged from 1418 to 1428 in this mountainous region, finally ended in complete victory for Le Loi and his troops.

The temple here is dedicated to Le Loi and contains his bronze likeness, cast in 1532. Nguyen Trai, Le Loi's advisor, penned the epitaph on the large Vinh Lang stele dedicated to the life and works of Le Loi, in 1433.

Other memorials document the 12 reigns of the Le family. Remains of the royal palace's ancient citadel of **Lam Kinh** are still visible. A mausoleum at the foot of Tung Son in Phu Dien is the final resting place of the national heroine Trieu Thi Trinh, who led an uprising against the Chinese in 247, aided by her elder brother Trieu Quoc Dat. The attempt failed and Trieu, rather than have her fate decided by the victorious Ngo rulers, committed suicide. A temple was built in her memory, and today a festival is celebrated here in her honour on the 24th day of the second lunar month every year.

Sixteen km (10 miles) southeast from the provincial capital of Thanh Hoa, the white sands of **Sam Son** ㉕ stretch for 3 km (2 miles) along the coast, from the Song Lac Hoi to the heights of Truong Le. Superb scenery surrounds the clear waters of Sam Son, named after the coastal mountains. Accommodation still tends to be high-rise, state-run, Eastern-bloc. The resort is packed in the summer months, deserted the rest of the year.

The temple of **The Doc Cuoc**, half-way up the slopes of Truong Le, is dedicated to a one-legged deity said to have divided himself in two and who is believed to have supernatural powers that protect and save swimmers and

Map on pages 186–7

In 1964, attacks by North Vietnamese patrol boats on the USS Maddox (and a disputed attack two days later on another US ship) in the Gulf of Tonkin led to a US Congressional resolution that authorised American military escalation in Vietnam.

BELOW: moving the harvest by boat.

Map on pages 186–7

"Rich in good looks" appears to mean poor luck and tears of woe, Which may sound strange, I know, But is not really so, I swear, Since Heaven every- where seems jealous of the fair of face.

— THE TALE OF KIEU

BELOW: holding up a successful catch. **RIGHT:** ancient tree at Cuc Phuong.

navigators in distress. It is also said to guarantee the fishermen a good catch, although the local fishermen may have a different story. At the end of the range is another temple, Co Tien, or Fairy Temple.

Numerous Muong villages lie scattered throughout the highlands of Thanh Hoa. Although the lowland Vietnamese, the Kinh, lost their original written script after 1,000 years of Chinese domination, the Muong have nonetheless retained theirs. Known as *khoa dau van*, it is similar to Thai and Lao, which have Sanskrit origins. Muong has an alphabet of 30 basic consonant signs.

Nghe An

South of Thanh Hoa Province lies Nghe An Province. With a long history of peasant uprisings, it is also the birthplace of several revolutionaries, including Phan Boi Chau and Nguyen Ai Quoc (more famously known as Ho Chi Minh), along with the national poet Nguyen Du (1765–1820), author of *The Tale of Kieu*, Vietnam's poetic epic *(see page 108)*. The findings of archaeologists revealed the existence of both a stone-age and a bronze-age culture in the province.

In Nghe An Province and its neighbour to the south, Ha Tinh, mountains and midlands give way to coastal plains along a 230-km (140-mile) coastline, and forests cover three-quarters of the land. The harsh climate often causes rain storms and flash flooding. More than 100 rivers and streams, the longest of which is the Song Lam Dong, feed the two provinces. The Lam Dong is a busy waterway plied by numerous boats, sampans, and rafts carrying bamboo and timber. Deer, raised for their antlers that are used for medicinal purposes, are a common sight grazing amongst the orange orchards.

In 1959, the inhabitants of **Hoang Tru** ㉖, 11 km (7 miles) northwest of **Vinh**, recreated the humble three-room house, with bamboo walls and a palm-leaf roof, where Ho Chi Minh was born as Nguyen Sinh Cung in 1890. Ho's family moved from here to Hue when he was five.

His father, a mandarin and minor official in the Hue court, became disillusioned by the French rulers and was eventually dismissed and returned to this area in 1901. He settled close to Hoang Tru, in **Kim Lien** (sometimes called Lang Sen), where he and Ho Chi Minh's grandfather taught. Young Ho Chi Minh spent a few years here before he and his father returned to Hue.

Kim Lien villagers constructed a replica of the second house, also in 1959, and turned it into yet another Ho Chi Minh shrine. It is very similar to the one in Hoang Tru. Nearby is Ho's three-room museum displaying memorabilia, old photographs, Ho's poems, and some actual shirts he wore.

It's easy to confuse these two Ho Chi Minh houses. Since there is very little in the way of English ex-planation at either, it is also not obvious that these are in fact replicas of the original homes or that Ho spent little of his life in either place. During his 30-year odyssey, Ho rarely contacted his family in the area, and he returned to his childhood homes just once in his life, in 1961. ❑

Central Vietnam

0   50 km
0   50 miles

BIEN DONG

(SOUTH CHINA SEA)

H a i n a n

CHINA

L A O S

CAMBODIA

CENTRAL VIETNAM

*The central, slender stretch of Vietnam offers some of the
country's more arresting sites, including Hue and Hoi An*

Along string of coastal provinces, linking the vast rice-growing
regions of the Song Hong (Red River) Delta in the north and
the delta of the Mekong in the south, forms the narrow neck of
central Vietnam. At the heart of Vietnam's centre lies Hue, the imperial city of the Nguyen kings. It is a magnificent city despite the
damage of war, with a majestic citadel, fortifications, and imperial
mausoleums. Threading through its centre is the River of Perfume –
Song Huong – a name that teases with its promise. Centuries ago,
after the Champa kingdoms fell to the invading Viets from the north,
Hue was called Thuan Hoa: *thuan*, meaning allegiance or submis-
sion, and *hoa,* meaning transformation. The name Hue is believed to
have come about through the common mispronunciation of hoa.

Outside of Hue to the north, the narrow, central coastal provinces
of Quang Tri and Dong Ha suffered mightily during the Vietnam
War, as they were directly south of the DMZ, or demilitarised zone.

South of Hue, Deo Hai Van funnels into Da Nang, an active port
city and Vietnam's fourth-largest urban centre, with energetic commerce within and lovely beaches nearby. Da Nang is the gateway to
Quang Nam Da Nang Province and the ancient kingdom of Champa.
The distinctive red-brick Cham towers and sacred sites, built between
the 8th and 12th centuries, stand as silent testimony to the kingdom
that flourished here before its absorption by the Vietnamese descending from the north.

Nearby is the charming, though increasingly touristic, 15th-century
town of Hoi An, which was the biggest seaport and most important
centre of trade in the country during the 17th and 18th centuries,
when it was known to Europeans as Faifo. Its beautifully preserved
communal houses, pagodas, and other places of worship reflect the
presence and influences of the Chinese, Japanese, and Westerners
who later settled in the region. ❑

PRECEDING PAGES: descendants of the royal family, Hue.

HUE

A dynastic citadel stands in Hue, despite destruction inflicted by the Viet Cong and the Americans. Nearby, along the seductively named Perfume River, are the ancient tombs of the Nguyen emperors

Map on page 234

The ancient imperial city of the Nguyen kings, **Hue ❶** is located 12 km (7 miles) from the coast on a narrow stretch of land in Thua Thien Hue Province, which borders Laos in the west. It is approximately midway between Hanoi to the north and Ho Chi Minh to the south. Always an important cultural, intellectual, and historical city, Hue remains one of Vietnam's main attractions. The charm of this timeless old city lies not only in its historical and architectural value, but also in the natural beauty of its location along the banks of **Song Huong**, or the fabled Perfume River. On the river's north bank is the ancient citadel and mostly residential areas, while on the south bank are the city's commercial area and the old French quarter. Further south are the Nguyen tombs. There is a quiet grace to the city.

The first noble to reach Hue was Nguyen Hoang, in the spring of 1601. He found a particularly good location to build a capital and erected the citadel of Phu Xuan. The Nguyen lords administered the whole region with the agreement of the often-rival Trinh lords. This arrangement operated smoothly at first, but the rivalry flared up as the territory was extended southwards. Bloody battles broke out between the two rival families. Each side was fiercely determined to consolidate and assert its own sovereignty, but eventually the Nguyen lords gained the upper hand. As a result, Hue became a new kingdom under the reign of Vu Vuong in the mid-1700s, independent of the north. Nguyen Hoang was the first in an uninterrupted succession of 10 feudal lords to rule over the area of Hue until 1802. That year, after quelling the Tay Son uprising, the 10th Nguyen lord proclaimed himself Emperor Gia Long and founded the Nguyen dynasty, which would last for 143 years, until 1945. But just 33 years into the dynasty's reign, the French invaded Hue.

A quick succession of emperors graced the throne. The anti-French demonstrations and strikes of the colonial era were followed by the Japanese occupation in 1945 and the abdication of Bao Dai, the last of the Nguyen emperors, in the same year.

The relative peace that reigned after 1954, when Hue became part of South Vietnam following the country's division into two parts by the United Nations, was shattered under Ngo Dinh Diem's regime. Repressive anti-Buddhist propaganda sparked off a series of demonstrations and protest suicides by Buddhist monks in 1963. Hue's imperial city suffered extensive damage during the Tet Offensive of 1968, in which the Viet Cong held out in the fortified ancient citadel against American attack for nearly two months. Although many priceless historical monuments and relics were destroyed in the battle, amazingly many survived.

LEFT: the pagoda of Thien Mu.
BELOW: Thien Mu.

Girl in costume for traditional festival.

BELOW: south gate of the Imperial City.

Dai Noi: The Imperial City

Three walled enclosures make up Hue's **Dai Noi** Ⓐ (Great Palace or Imperial City; open daily 7am–5.30pm; admission fee): Hoang Thanh (Yellow Enclosure) and Tu Cam Thanh (Forbidden Purple City) are enclosed within the all-encompassing Kinh Thanh (the exterior enclosure). Stone, bricks and earth were used for the exterior wall, which measured 8 metres (26 ft) high and 20 metres (65 ft) thick and was built during the reign of Gia Long. Later, 10 large and fortified gates, each topped with watch-towers, were built at points along the wall. Most of what visitors see today is found within the Hoang Thanh, or Yellow Enclosure; other areas were destroyed during the Tet Offensive of 1968.

Hoang Thanh (Yellow Enclosure) is the middle wall enclosing the imperial city and its palaces, temples and flower gardens. Four richly decorated gates provided access: Ngo Mon (the southern gate, or Noon Gate), Hoa Binh (northern gate), Hien Nhan (eastern gate), and Chuong Duc (western gate). Ngo Mon, first built of granite in 1834 during the reign of Minh Mang, was repaired in 1921. The gate is topped by the Lau Ngu Phung, the Five Phoenix Watch Tower, with its roofs brightly tiled in yellow over the middle section and green on either side. From here, the emperor used to preside over formal ceremonies and rites. Through the Ngo Mon, walk across the Golden Water Bridge, which at one time was reserved for the emperor. It leads to **Dien Thai Hoa** (Thai Hoa Palace, or Palace of Supreme Peace), the most important place in the imperial city. Here, the emperor received the high dignitaries of the land and foreign diplomats. The royal court organised important ceremonies here, as well. Built in 1805 during Gia Long's reign, the palace was renovated first by Minh Mang in 1834 and later by Khai Dinh in 1924. Today, it stands in excellent

condition, its ceilings and beams decorated in red lacquer and gold inlay. The emperor used to rest in Truong Sanh (Palace of Longevity) and read the classics in the palace or the garden.

Map on page 241

The temples within the enclosure are dedicated to various lords: the temple of Trieu Mieu to Nguyen Kim, the Thai Mieu to Nguyen Hoang and his successors, the Phung Tien temple to the emperors of the reigning dynasty, and the Hung Mieu to Nguyen Phuc Lan, emperor Gia Long's father. The well-preserved The Mieu, dedicated to the sovereigns of the Nguyen dynasty, houses the shrines of seven Nguyen emperors plus monuments to the revolutionary emperors Ham Nghi, Thanh Thai, and Duy Tan, which were added in 1959.

In front of the temple, completely undamaged, stands the magnificent **Hien Lam Cac** (Pavilion of Splendour), with the nine dynastic urns known as **Cuu Dinh** lined up before it. The urns, cast in 1822 during Minh Mang's reign, are decorated with motifs of the sun, moon, clouds, birds, animals, dragons, mountains, rivers, historic events, and scenes from everyday life. Hundreds of artisans from all over the country were involved in their casting. Each urn represents an emperor of the Nguyen dynasty and weighs up to 2,500 kg (5,600 lbs). **Dien Tho**, a palace built by Gia Long in 1804, served as the Queen Mother's residence. In the first enclosure of the royal city, towards the Chuong Duc gate, are Sung Than Cong, or the Nine Deities' Cannons. Five on one side represent the primary elements – metal, water, wood, fire, earth – and the other four represent the seasons. Each cannon weighs 12 tons.

Beyond Dien Thai Hoa, **Tu Cam Thanh** (Forbidden Purple City) was reserved solely for the emperor and the royal family, who resided here behind a brick wall 4 metres (13 ft) thick. Each of seven gates set into the wall had a

BELOW: Cuu Dinh, the dynastic urns.

Flower vendor at Hue's market.

special function and name glorifying the ancestral virtues. This area was extensively damaged during the Tet Offensive of 1968 – the Viet Cong used the citadel as a bunker – but it is undergoing continuing renovation.

The main building in the enclosure is **Can Thanh**, or Palace of Celestial Perfection. The other once-grand palace, Can Chanh, now sadly in ruins, was used by the emperor to receive dignitaries and settle the affairs of the kingdom. Its remaining walls, riddled with shell and bullet holes, stand as a crumbling reminder of the weapons that wrought such destruction to this once-splendid complex. Beyond lies an empty stretch of ground where the royal apartments once stood. The most modern palace in the enclosure was the palace of Kien Than that Khai Dinh had built in the 1920s, complete with all the Western comforts. Unfortunately, this too was a casualty of the Vietnam War, and the palace still awaits reconstruction.

Beyond the citadel walls

Another world lies beyond the walls of the citadel, which is surrounded in the south and east by Hue's commercial area. This is confined mainly to the area around the arched **Cau Trang Tien** ❸ (Trang Tien Bridge), which spans the Song Huong (Perfume River), and **Cau Gia Hoi**. Both bridges lend their names to the areas surrounding them.

Near the east gate of the citadel, the **Museum of Royal Fine Arts** ❹ (open daily 7.30am–4pm; admission fee), built in 1845 under Thieu Tri, houses treasures bequeathed by the royal family and nobility. (It has been under renovation and some parts of it are closed to the public.) Sadly, many objects have disappeared without a trace since 1946 during revolution and war.

BELOW: moat of the old imperial city.

Map
on page
241

Across the street, the **Bao Tang Thuan Thien-Hue** (Hue Provincial Museum; open daily, 7am–5pm; admission fee) was opened in 1975 and is one of the finer collections related to the Vietnam War; another part of the museum covers natural history. The displays, photographs and maps must be viewed with a jaundiced eye, however, for they read as propaganda. However, the English translations are superior to those of other museums around the country, and the setting is brightly lit, air-conditioned, and clean. The guides are helpful, as well. There is a large topographical map with lights showing the movements of the American troops, South Vietnamese military, and Viet Cong during the Tet Offensive of 1968. Outside, in a yard overgrown with weeds, are pieces of military hardware.

Located in the neighbourhood of Phu Cat, northeast of the citadel and with its mainly Chinese and Minh Huong (Vietnamese-Chinese) population, is the lively **Cho Dong Ba **, a market (*cho*) that has been around since the beginning of the 20th century and offers a great variety of local products and gastronomic delights. The district of Vi Da, on the other side of the river, is renowned as a popular refuge for artists, poets, scholars, and assorted mandarins. Of an entirely different character is the district of Phu Cam, best known for its cathedral and the fervour of its predominantly Catholic community.

Some 3 km (2 miles) to the west of the citadel, situated on a hill, is **Chua Thien Mu ❺** (Celestial Lady Pagoda). Built by Nguyen Hoang in 1601, it remains intact on the north bank of the Song Huong. The seven tiers of the temple's octagonal tower – **Phuoc Duyen** – each represent a different reincarnation of Buddha. Six statues of deities guard the Buddhist pagoda, which contains a gilt statue of the laughing Buddha, happy in prosperity, and

TIP

It would be foolish to visit Hue and not take a boat journey on the river to Chua Thien Mu, Hon Chen, and the tombs of Tu Duc, Khai Dinh, and Minh Mang. For extra mobility, ask if you can take a bicycle with you.

BELOW: tower at Thien Mu.

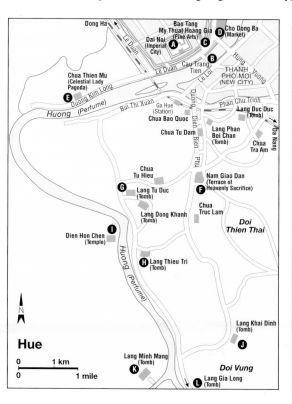

three superb, glass-enclosed statues of Buddha. Many generations have heard the tolling of the pagoda's enormous 2,000-kilogram (4,600-lb), 2-metre-high (6-ft) bell since it was cast in 1701. It is such a fine bell that it can be heard nearly 16 km (10 miles) away.

The main temple, Dai Hung, is found in an attractive garden of ornamental shrubs and trees. A statue of Maitraya Buddha presides over the first room. Behind this temple is the Quan Vo (God of War Temple), and behind that another, Quan Am, a temple dedicated to the goddess of mercy, Quan Am.

Tombs of the Nguyen dynasty

Unlike the other dynasties, the Nguyen dynasty did not bury its members in their native village, Gia Mieu, to the north in Thanh Hoa Province. Instead, their imperial tombs lie scattered on the hillsides on either side of the Song Huong, to the west and south of Hue. Although the dynasty had 13 kings, only seven of them reigned until their deaths, and only they are laid to rest in this valley of kings: Gia Long, Minh Mang, Thieu Tri, Tu Duc, Kien Phuc, Dong Khanh, and Kai Dinh.

To reach the tombs from Hue, head south, first stopping at **Nam Giao Dan** 🅕 (Terrace of Heavenly Sacrifice), an esplanade surrounded by a park of pines and conifers 2 km (1¼ miles) south of Hue's commercial centre. Built by Gia Long in 1802, in its day it was considered the most sacred and solemn place. Composed of three terraces – two square and one circular – the esplanade represents as a whole the sky and the earth. From here, the emperor paid homage to heaven in his capacity as the privileged mandatory on earth.

Every three years the Nam Giao (Festival of Sacrifice) took place at the

Emperor Minh Mang.

BELOW: the Song Huong, or Perfume River, located near Thien Mu.

Map on page 241

centre of the circular esplanade. A buffalo would be sacrificed to the god of the sky, who is believed to govern the destiny of the world. A communist war memorial that briefly dominated the Nam Giao has now been removed.

The Nguyen tomb sites themselves are spread out and one could easily budget two full days visiting them. Each has a large brick-paved courtyard *(bia dinh)* containing stone figures of elephants, saddled horses, soldiers, and civil and military mandarins. In front of this stands the stelae pavilion, containing the tall marble or stone stele engraved with the biography of the deceased king written by his successor (except in the case of Tu Duc, who wrote his own). Beyond this is the temple *(tam dien)* where the deceased king and queen are worshipped and their royal belongings displayed. The king's widows would keep incense and aloe wood perpetually burning before the altar until their own deaths. Behind and on either side of the temple are the houses built for the king's concubines, servants, and the soldiers who guarded the royal tomb. The emperor's body is laid in a concealed place *(bao thanh)*, enclosed by high walls behind well-locked bronze doors.

When setting foot in any of the tombs, one feels a sense of admiration for the noble grandeur and elegant style of the architecture. This sense of awe is described by one of Vietnam's celebrated writers, Pham Quynh, a former minister of national education: "This tomb is the general blending of all the colours of the firmament and of all the tints of water; it is an amalgamation of high mountains, of thick forests, of wind blowing through foliage. This tomb is a spectacle of nature, a marvel of great beauty, added to another sight, created by the hand of man, of a beauty no less marvellous. It is the patient and inspired work of the artist whose intention was to colour the countryside to awaken the

BELOW: guardian image at pagoda.

RULE OF THE NGUYEN DYNASTY

The Nguyen dynasty ruled from 1802 until 1945. Three centuries earlier, the Nguyen family had ingratiated itself with the ruling Le dynasty, becoming northern lords for the weak Le rulers. By the mid-1500s, the Trinh family usurped this power, pushing the Nguyens to the south. The rivalry between the Nguyen and Trinh escalated into warfare in 1620, which lasted for half a century before both families agreed to a de facto division of the empire. The Nguyen family ruled over southern Vietnam, extending settlement – mostly by Chinese refugees escaping the collapsing Ming dynasty – into Cham and Cambodian lands. The 1771 Tay Son uprising threatened Nguyen power in southern Vietnam; a young prince, later to become Emperor Gia Long, led the recovery of Nguyen territory. Gia Long would rule over the whole of Vietnam from 1802, the beginning of the Nguyen dynasty.

Nguyen dynasty policy often thwarted foreign interference. In response, the French invaded Vietnam in 1858. The French dominated all of Vietnam after invasions in 1883–85, although they retained the Nguyen dynasty with nominal governance over central Vietnam (called Annam by the French) and northern Vietnam (called Tonkin). In 1945, the last Nguyen emperor, Bao Dai, abdicated.

awaiting soul, soaring in the silence of this mournful place or whispering in the top of the lone pine tree. There are not the words to express the bizarre sensation, both gentle and of tender exhilaration, which grips one with an eagerness for poetry in this scenery charged with depth and mystery".

The **tomb of Tu Duc** 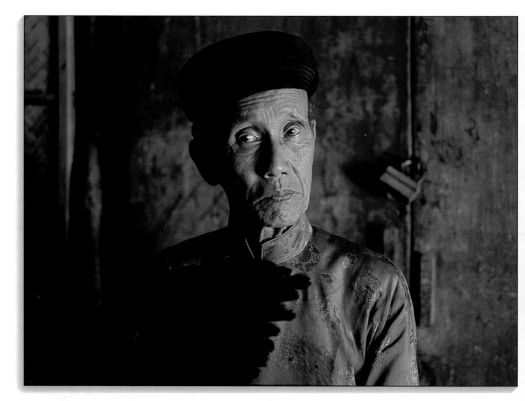, just a bit southwest of Hue, can be reached by a very pleasant cycle ride through pine forests and lush hills. The mausoleum construction, begun in 1864, took three years to complete. The result resembles a royal palace in miniature and harmonises beautifully with the natural surroundings. A work force of 3,000 men was used in its construction. Tu Duc, the son of Thieu Tri and the Nguyen dynasty's fourth king, reigned for 36 years, the longest reign of any of the Nguyen kings.

He spent his leisure hours in the two pavilions beside the lake, Luu Khiem. Here he wrote poetry, no doubt inspired by the beauty of his surroundings, fished, and enjoyed the fragrance of the lotus. The more popular of the two lakeside pagodas is Xung Khiem, a pavilion that dates from 1865. A staircase leads to the Luong Khiem mausoleum, which contains a collection of furniture, vases, and jewellery boxes. Further on is the terrace leading to the tomb, with its stone elephants, horses, and mandarins. The tomb itself, ritually inaccessible, is covered by dense pine forest. The tombs of Tu Duc's adopted son, Kien Phu and Queen Le Thien An, lie beside the lake.

The tomb of **Thieu Tri** ⓗ is located nearby. Thieu Tri, Minh Mang's son, was the third Nguyen emperor and reigned from 1841 to 1847. His tomb was built between 1947 and 1948, in the same elegant architectural style as his father's but on a much smaller scale.

On the western bank of the Song Huong, on the opposite side of the river

BELOW: a relative of Bao Dai, the last emperor of Vietnam.

from the tombs of Thieu Tri and Tu Duc, is the temple known as both **Hon Chen ❶** and Ngoc Tran Dien, where the goddess Po Nagar, protector of the Champa Kingdom, is worshipped. Po Nagar, greatly venerated by the Chams in the past, is also to a lesser extent worshipped today by the Vietnamese, who supplanted them in the narrow stretch of land that was once the Kingdom of Champa. A festival takes place here on the 15th day of the seventh lunar month every year, when worshippers march in a long procession, accompanied by ceremonial music and a heavy cloud of incense.

Completely different from any of the other Nguyen tombs, the tomb of **Khai Dinh ❶** resembles, if anything, a European castle, its architecture a blend of the oriental and occidental. Made of reinforced concrete, it took 11 years to complete and was finally finished in 1931. Khai Dinh, Bao Dai's adopted father, ruled for nine years during the colonial era. A grandiose dragon staircase leads up to the first courtyard, from where further stairs lead to a courtyard lined with stone statues of elephants, horses, and civil and military mandarins. In the centre of the courtyard stands the stele inscribed with Chinese characters composed by Bao Dai in memory of his father. The exterior lacks the tranquil charm and beauty of Minh Mang's or Tu Duc's mausoleum, and the giant dragons flanking the staircase appear rather menacing.

Once inside, however, the contrast is striking. Coloured tiles pave the floor, a huge "dragon in the clouds" mural, painted by artists using their feet, adorns the ceiling of the middle chamber. Jade green antechambers lead off to the left and right. Bright frescoes composed of many thousands of inlaid ceramic and glass fragments depict various themes. Animals, trees, and flowers provide a visual feast after the less-inspiring blackened exterior of the mausoleum. A

Map on page 241

Tomb guardian.

BELOW: tomb of Khai Dinh.

Map
on page
241

life-size bronze statue of Khai Dinh, made in France in 1922, rests on a dais on top of the tomb.

The tomb of **Minh Mang** ⓚ can be reached by hiring a small motorboat from any of the local owners opposite the Perfume River Hotel. Alternatively, take a car to the village of Ban Viet and from there take a boat across the Song Huong. Minh Mang was Gia Long's fourth son and the Nguyen dynasty's second king. He built the Imperial City and was highly respected for his reforms in the areas of customs, traditions, and agriculture. His mausoleum is located where the Ta Trach and Huu Trach tributaries of the Song Huong meet. Its construction was begun a year before his death, in 1840, and was finished by his successor Thieu Tri in 1843. The setting blends the beauty of nature with the majestic architecture and superb stone sculpture created by its many anonymous craftsmen. The setting is at its best in mid-March, when the Trung Minh and Tan Nguyet lakes bloom with a mass of beautiful lotus flowers.

The tomb of **Gia Long** ⓛ, 16 km (10 miles) southwards from Hue and on a hillside, is somewhat inaccessible by road; a more pleasant way to reach it is by boat on the river. The tomb, begun in 1814, was completed a year after Gia Long's death in 1820. Unfortunately, the site was in the middle of a guerrilla zone during the Vietnam War and the tomb was considerably damaged by bombs. It has since become rather neglected, but the wild beauty of the site itself, with its mountainous backdrop, makes the effort to get there well worth the time.

The nearby temple, **Minh Thanh**, also in very bad shape, is dedicated to Gia Long's first wife, Queen Thua Thien Co. On the left is Gia Long's sepulchre, where he and his first wife are buried side by side. ❑

BELOW: tomb of
Minh Mang.
RIGHT: royal
guardians.

FADING DMZ BLUES

The so-called Demilitarised Zone, or DMZ, is where some of the bloodiest fighting of the Vietnam War took place. The DMZ stretched for 8 km (5 miles) on either side of the Song Ben Hai, 100 km (60 miles) north of Hue. It was the line of demarcation between North Vietnam and South Vietnam, established at the Geneva Conference in 1954 after the end of the war against the French. Following the 17th parallel, the border was supposed to be temporary, until elections could be held in 1956. The elections never were held and Vietnam remained divided along this line until the two countries were officially reunified in 1976, following the collapse of South Vietnam.

Today, there are still desolate stretches of scorched earth. Just south of the Ben Hai, Highway 9, which runs west towards Laos, passes sites of famous Vietnam War battles and old US military bases like Con Thien and Khe Sanh. North of the DMZ , in Vinh Muoc, a series of tunnels are where an entire village camped out for several years to escape the constant bombings. Most of the people had evacuated to other parts of the country, but some stayed. For five years, from 1966 to 1971, some 300 people lived in the 2,000-metre-long (6,500-ft) network of tunnels. Seventeen babies were born in the subterranean home.

Rush to Preserve

For a country with a long and rich history, Vietnam boasts relatively few architectural landmarks. Those that have survived the centuries of invasions, war, typhoons, and harsh climate have suffered from human neglect. Historical preservation, after all, is something of a luxury for a country preoccupied with fending off invaders and, later, grappling with poverty.

Today, however, Vietnam has begun to show an interest in saving its historical sites. Some of this has to do with the gradually improving economy, in part due to tourism.

In part, too, this movement to preserve is a facet of the government's emphasis on nationalism – in politics, culture, and entertainment. (Recently, for example, a karaoke contest had one rule: the contestants had to sing a patriotic song.) Restoring architectural ruins is one way to develop national pride.

More importantly, however, restoration is commercially viable. All government officials needed to do was look at tourists climbing about China's Great Wall or Cambodia's Angkor Wat to figure out there is money in a pile of old rocks. If the rocks are well maintained, that is. And until now, Vietnam's architectural gems have lacked historical lustre.

The citadel and tombs of Hue, however, recently grabbed international attention when they were included on a list of endangered sites. "This will make Vietnamese feel they have more responsibility in preserving the site", said one hopeful historian in Hanoi.

The government has pledged to spend at least US$1 million a year on the Hue conservation effort. Foreign organisations, both from Japan and also UNESCO, have also contributed funds. Vietnam does not have many trained restoration workers, but it is attempting to use native crafts people – stone cutters, wood carvers, pottery makers – to learn advanced skills from overseas experts.

Right now, conservationists have their work cut out for them. Many of the stone pillars and statues have crumbled; the wood structures have been badly damaged by termites and water. Damage from the Vietnam War was severe. There are bullet-ridden stone walls visible on the grounds of the Citadel.

Many statues and artefacts were destroyed. There are still standing reminders, however, that look as if the fighting ended just last week, such as a broken mirror in a house behind the Thai Hoa Palace.

Hue is not the only place in Vietnam drawing the interest of historic preservationists. Others include Hoi An, the 18th-century port, with Chinese and Japanese architecture; the Cham towers along the south-central coast, near Nha Trang; pagodas throughout the country; and the monuments of My Son.

Historians also are keen to preserve the cultural traditions that are threatened with extinction because older practitioners have either died or have not passed down their knowledge. So there are efforts to research and preserve traditional music, festivals, handicrafts, and even royal cuisine. Much of this tradition, of course, is linked to Vietnam's old dynasties, a royalist tradition fought against by the Communists. But reviving traditions doesn't seem to faze the government. "This is our history", said one official. "We must not lose it". ❑

THE IMPERIAL CITADEL AT HUE

The citadel's history reflects that of Vietnam. Built by Confucian kings, it was occupied by the French, damaged in war, and is now under restoration

The imperial citadel was built by the early 19th-century Nguyen kings. It was fortified in the style of the French military engineer Vauban, but its internal arrangement reflects Chinese architectural principles. The interior comprised three concentric walled cities: the Kinh Thanh (Capital), Hoang Thanh (Imperial) and Can Thanh (Forbidden). The entrance to the Imperial City was the Ngo Mon (South Gate, 1833), which gave access to the Thai Hoa (Palace of Supreme Peace, 1805) and the Can Chanh (Palace of Heavenly Law, 1811), where foreign visitors were received. The structured hierarchy of this Confucian monarchy was thus abundantly expressed in the citadel's architecture. Symbolically, it took a major blow in 1884 with the entry of the first Frenchman into the Forbidden City. After the abdication of the last king, Bao Dai, in 1945, the citadel suffered the ravages of weather and war. Today, however, some beautifully restored buildings can be visited among the remains of other palaces, pagodas and gardens.

▷ **THE CITADEL**
Construction of the citadel was started by Gia Long (1802–20), the first of the Nguyen dynasty kings, who made Hue the country's capital.

△ **WAR DAMAGE**
The Forbidden City did not escape damage during the 1968 Tet Offensive, although restoration work has been underway for some years.

◁ **THIEN MU PAGODA**
West of the citadel, Thien Mu pagoda's famous Tower of Confucius, erected in 1661, was built with bricks of Cham origin.

▽ **NGO MON**
The central gateway of Ngo Mon, which gives access to the Imperial City, was reserved for the king. Others used the side gates.

TOMBS OF THE NGUYEN KINGS

The tombs were constructed on the banks of the Perfume River several miles upstream from the citadel. Each tomb reflected in its architecture the monarch's politics and personality. Minh Mang (1820–41), who was fascinated by Confucian administrative methods, had his tomb built in an elaborately Chinese style. Tu Duc (1848–83), whose tomb is the most aesthetically unusual, was renowned for his poetic and artistic temperament – unfortunate qualities, perhaps, at a time of invasion. The tomb of Khai Dinh (1916–25) contains numerous motifs drawn from Western influences, at a time when the king was a mere figurehead in the French colony. The kings were not buried under the granite tablets erected to proclaim their titles and exploits. To prevent exhumation by usurping dynasties, the actual burial places were kept secret and remain unknown to this day.

▷ **THE IMPERIAL TEMPLE**
Temple paraphernalia, including Confucian altars and ceremonial umbrellas, reflect the strong influence of China on Nguyen dynasty.

▽ **KHAI DINH'S TOMB**
The tomb of Khai Dinh (1916–25) reflects an eccentric mix of French and Vietnamese architectural styles.

▷ **IMPERIAL DRAGONS**
The *long nhan* (imperial dragon) symbolises mastery over land and water, and hence the king himself. It is distinguished from ordinary four-clawed dragons by its possession of five *long ngu chim* or claws.

Map
on page
234

DA NANG AND HOI AN

Anchoring Vietnam's centre, Da Nang was a strategic pivot in the wars of the 20th century. Nearby Hoi An, once an important port, retains enough atmosphere to make it a traveller's draw

Q uang Nam Da Nang Province lies about 800 km (500 miles) between Hanoi and Ho Chi Minh City, separated from Laos by the western Truong Son mountains. Forests of valuable timber – rosewood, ironwood, and ebony – cover more than 60 percent of the land. The drive from Hue to Da Nang is one of the most spectacular in Vietnam, as Highway 1 follows a vertiginous route up, down, and around mountains that hug the coastline.

The climate becomes noticeably warmer and more humid after descending the 1,200-metre (4,000-ft) summit of **Deo Hai Van** ❷ (Hai Van Pass), which adjoins another mountain, Bach Ma (White Horse), and descends to the scenic coastal region. To the north of Da Nang and east of Hai Van Pass on the road to Hue, the palm-shaded peninsula of **Lang Co** ❸ rates as one of the most superb spots in the country. To one side lies a stunningly clear lagoon and on the other, miles of unspoiled beach washed by the South China Sea. The town, dependent on fishing, is heavily Catholic.

The provincial capital, **Da Nang** ❹, located on the west bank of the Song Han (Han River), has grown from a fishing village into an important port and the country's fourth-largest city with 400,000 people. While it is not quite as hectic as the capital, Hanoi, or the southern commercial hub, Ho Chi Minh, Da Nang is rapidly becoming a thriving city. Officials here are banking on tourism to revive the economy, and limited international flights in and out of Da Nang's airport are available. Right now, there is not much in the way of high-class accommodation, however. Overseas developers have been planning for years to build resorts along the coastline south of Da Nang, particularly in an area known to American GIs from the Vietnam War as China Beach.

Those plans, however, have faced a myriad of obstacles; actual construction and opening of hotels, golf courses, and condominiums probably won't be completed for years. That may be a good thing for visitors who wish to avoid huge crowds; for now, Da Nang is a rather sleepy destination.

People here are generally quite friendly, and many speak English because of Da Nang's development as an American military town during the Vietnam War. Don't be surprised to meet middle-aged men and women who worked for the Americans as interpreters, mechanics, bartenders, or in the many businesses that sprung up to offer all kinds of services to soldiers – everything from laundries to bars.

Among the specialities produced in the province are cinnamon from Tra, pepper from Tien Phuoc, tobacco from Cam Le, silk from Hoa Vang, saffron from Tam Ky, and sea swallow nests from the islands off the coast. The *nuoc mam* (fish sauce) produced in

PRECEDING PAGES: Hoi An canal. **LEFT:** clam digging near Da Nang. **BELOW:** guard at Deo Hai Van.

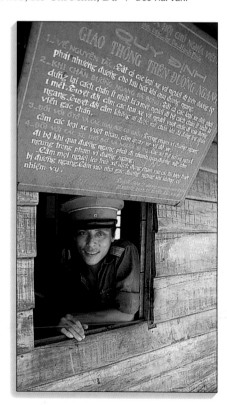

Da Nang transport.

the fishing village of Nam O, about 15 km (9 miles) from the city towards Hai Van Pass, is reputedly the best in Vietnam. (But then, too, is the nuoc mam from Phan Thiet and from the island of Phu Quoc.)

Divided and difficult history

Because of its location in the centre of the country, Da Nang found itself a city divided during the Vietnam War. Many people in the area supported the South Vietnamese regime, but others quietly (until after 1975) worked for the Viet Cong. Sometimes families themselves had split allegiances; it's not uncommon that brothers fought against each other. There are a few relics of the war era still standing. North of town, along the shoreline, are the rusted shells of an old air base, now used by the Vietnamese military for training. The Da Nang airport runway is lined with revetments. The old American consulate is on Bach Dang, parallel to the Song Han.

Known as Tourane under the French, Da Nang is perhaps best remembered abroad from the role it played at the beginning and end of the Vietnam War. The first 3,500 US Marines came ashore here in 1965. Ten years later, communist troops rolled into town facing little resistance as South Vietnamese soldiers shed their uniforms along the side of the road and fled. Two American 727 jets evacuated refugees, most of them soldiers, in a scene of panic broadcast around the world. So many people tried to climb onto the planes that, as one of them took off, people clinging to the wheels fell into the South China Sea.

Other foreigners came here long before the Americans, however. In the 17th and 18th centuries, the first Spanish and French landings were made here. Subsequently, Da Nang became the scene of battles between the Vietnamese

BELOW: avoiding the rainy season.

Map on page 234

who fought first the Spanish and later the French. In the course of the 19th century, it had superseded Faifo (present-day Hoi An) as the most important port and commercial centre in the central region.

The ancient kingdom of Champa once stretched all the way from Phong Nha, in northcentral Vietnam, to Vung Tau in the south. The kingdom incorporated the five provinces of Indrapura, Amaravati, Vijaya, Kauthara and Panduranga. The Quang Nam Da Nang area was the centre of the Cham civilisation for many centuries. The most ancient capital, Singhapura (Lion City) at **Tra Kieu**, 40 km (25 miles) southwest of Da Nang, was built during the course of the 4th century. Early in the 8th century, the capital was moved south to Panduranga. In the late 8th century, it was transferred back to Quang Nam Da Nang and renamed Indrapura (City of the God of Thunder). Indrapura lasted until the early 11th century.

The ancient site of Singhapura – with its dozens of monuments, hundreds of statues, and bas reliefs – attests to the rich culture that once flourished here. A stele, erected by the eighth Champa king to the memory of Hindu poet Valmiki, author of the *Ramayana*, stands intact. The sacred Buddhist-inspired site of Indrapura, now known as **Dong Duong**, lies 60 km (40 miles) from Da Nang. The site's scattered monuments – some of them Buddhist and others Brahman-inspired – are engraved with texts about a line of nine kings and their deeds. Archaeologists have discovered many artefacts at the site, including the 2nd-century bronze Dong Duong Buddha that now resides in the National Museum, in Ho Chi Minh City. A large Buddhist monastery and many holy shrines also are located here.

The valley of **My Son ❺**, southwest of Da Nang, was chosen as a religious sanctuary by King Bhadravarman I, and from the 4th century on, many temples and

Cham, Mnong, Hoa, Ka Tu, Sedang and Co are among the ethnic minority groups found in the region.

BELOW: Cham sculpture.

THE RISE AND FALL OF CHAMPA

Champa was a kingdom established by the Cham, of Malayo-Polynesian heritage and Hinduised culture. It extended over the central and southern coastal region of Vietnam. Champa was founded in AD 192 when the Chinese official in charge of central Vietnam (the Han dynasty in China was collapsing) formed his own empire in central Vietnam. Absorbing Indian cultural influence, Champa maintained a powerful coastal fleet used for commerce – and piracy of the Chinese coast.

In 446, the Chinese invaded Champa and brought the area under their control. In the 6th century, Champa shed Chinese control to start a period of independence, prosperity and aesthetic excellence. In the late 8th century Champa was attacked by Java, unsuccessfully. A century later, the Chams were pushing into Cambodia.

In 1145 the Khmers conquered Champa. Two years later a new Cham king pushed out the Khmers; his successor attacked Angkor, the Cambodian capital. In the 13th century the Chams were fighting the Khmers, Vietnamese, and Mongols from China.

By the late 15th century, the Champa kingdom was crumbling, to be completely absorbed by the Vietnamese in the 17th century.

More than 70 architectural sites once stood in My Son. Today, less than 20 remain, as My Son fell in a free-fire zone for B52 bombers during the Vietnam War. There are still unexploded mines in the area.

BELOW: Museum of Cham Sculpture.

towers *(kalan)* were built in the area. Most were dedicated to kings and Brahman divinities, including the god Shiva, who was considered the creator, founder, and defender of the Champa kingdom and the Cham royal dynasties. Some 12th-century stelae discovered here attest to a unified religious belief practised in the sanctuary's first temple, which was erected for the worship of Shiva-Bhadresvara.

The Cham towers were ingeniously constructed of dried bricks and placed together with resin from the *cau day* tree. Once the tower was completed, it was encircled by fires kept well stoked for several days. The intense heat fired the whole structure, completely melding and sealing the bricks and tree resin together to form a structure able to withstand the combined onslaught of time and the elements – but not, unfortunately, 20th-century bombs. Indeed, tourists should not explore off the beaten track, as there are still several unexploded mines in the area. Keep to the main temples and marked paths.

The Chams were divided into two groups: the Dua, who inhabited the provinces of Amarvati and Vijaya, and the Cau, from the provinces of Kauthara and Pandaranga. The two clans differed in their customs and habits, and conflicting interests led to many clashes and even war. But they usually managed to settle disagreements through intermarriage. The influences that shaped the culture and history of the Cham people are revealed through their various sculpture and carvings.

An insight into the Cham people is provided at the excellent **Museum of Cham Sculpture** (open daily, 7am–6pm; admission fee), in Da Nang. Established in 1936 by the Ecole Francaise d'Extreme Orient, its extensive collection is displayed in rooms featuring four different periods according to their origins: My Son, Tra Kieu, Dong Duong, and Thap Mam.

Map on page 234

From Da Nang to Hoi An

South of Da Nang, towards the coast, stand five large hills: **Ngu Hanh Son** (Marble Mountains), the Mountains of the Five Elements: Kim Son (metal), Thuy Son (water), Moc Son (wood), Hoa Son (fire), and Tho Son (earth). These mountains were once a group of five offshore islets, but because of silting over the years they became part of the mainland. Mysterious caves within the mountains shelter altars dedicated to Buddha, *bodhisattvas* and the different deities created in stories of the area's inhabitants. The most famous of these is Thuy Son. Used by the Cham for their sacred rituals, these caves today still serve as religious sanctuaries. One can visit several temples, including **Tam Thi**, built in 1852, and **Linh Ung**.

Children in the area descend upon visitors who come to climb Thuy Son and its caves. While they appear to be pests, they can actually be quite helpful and entertaining, shouting out a funny assortment of English-language words: "Awesome", "Don't worry be happy", "I'm cool", and the ubiquitous "America number one". They will direct travellers in and out of a maze of steps and hidden caves and up a final ascent that provides a good view of the area. Of course, at the end of the hike, the children expect you to buy something.

The mountains are also a valuable source of red, white, and blue-green marble. At the foot of the mountains, skilful marble carvers chisel out a great variety of objets d'art. Alongside the mountains is a long stretch of beautiful, quiet beach. To the south is **Bai Bien Non Nuoc ❻**, known to many foreigners as China Beach, near the village of Non Nuoc. China Beach was a place American GIs went for rest and recreation during the war. However, some people contend the real China Beach is to the north, at My Khe.

Stay on marked paths at My Son, as there are several unexploded land-mines among the tombs and temples

BELOW: bicycles on China Beach.

Old French print of the harbour of Faifo, or today's Hoi An.

Hoi An

About 25 km (15 miles) southeast of Da Nang and near the coast, the ancient town of **Hoi An** ❼ nestles on the banks of the Song Thu Bon (Thu Bon River), a few kilometres inland from the coast. This charming old town was once a flourishing port and meeting place of East and West, in what was central Dai Viet under the Nguyen lords. Hoi An appeared in western travelogues in the 17th and 18th centuries as Faifo or Hai Po. Originally a sea port in the Champa kingdom and known as Dai Chien, by the 15th century it had become a coastal Vietnamese town under the Tran dynasty.

At the beginning of the 16th century, the Portuguese came to explore the coast of Hoi An. Then came the Chinese, Japanese, Dutch, British and French. With them came the first missionaries – Italian, Portuguese, French, Spanish. Among them was Alexander of Rhodes, who adopted the Roman alphabet for the Vietnamese language.

For several centuries, Hoi An was one of the most important trading ports in Southeast Asia and an important centre of cultural exchange between East and West. By the beginning of the 19th century, Hoi An's social and physical environment had changed drastically. The conflict between the Trinh and Nguyen lords and the Tay Son caused Hoi An considerable damage. Moreover, rivers changed course as the mouth of the Thu Bon silted up and prevented the flow of sea traffic. Another port was built at the mouth of the Song Han – Da Nang, replacing Hoi An as the centre of trade.

Today, Hoi An is a quiet town of about 75,000 people – 12,000 of them living in the old quarter that has been restored and renovated as something of a historical showpiece for tourists. Many of the older homes, built with wood

BELOW: old doors.

beams, carved doors and airy, open rooms, have been turned into souvenir shops fronting as museums.

In the early 1980s, UNESCO and the Polish government took the initiative and funded a restoration programme to classify and safeguard Hoi An's ancient quarters and historic monuments. The town faces yearly floods as water spills over the river banks and submerges some streets in two to three metres of water. That, of course, damages the timber construction of the houses. Rains and the resulting floods in 1998 nearly threatened landmarks like the Japanese Bridge.

Hoi An has become a popular tourist spot, so popular that it can seem to be crawling with foreigners at times. In fact, older residents worry that the very thing that makes Hoi An attractive – its quiet charm – is being ruined. People will kindly invite visitors into their homes to look at the architecture, but then some locals demand a donation. But for better or worse, Hoi An is stuck with the tourists. Today, in the old part of town, nearly 80 percent of the people derive their income from tourism. The rest of the residents work primarily as fishermen.

Walkabout

The oldest part of town is in the southern section, bordering the **Song Thu Bon**. Running perpendicular to the river, Le Loi was the first street to be built, four centuries ago. The Japanese quarter, with its covered bridge and Japanese-style shops and houses, followed half a century later on the west side of town, followed by the Cantonese quarter 50 years later. Hoi An's past is superbly preserved in its architecture. The old quarter is a fascinating blend of temples, pagodas, community houses, shrines, clan houses, shop houses, and homes.

Map on page 234

BELOW: one of many Chinese temples in Hoi An.

Map
on page
260

As in many towns, **Cho Hoi An Ⓐ**, the central market, is a good place to start a proper ramble. Some pagodas and 20 clan houses stand in the centre of the old town. Most of these temples and houses were built by the Chinese migrant community over a span of 40 years, between 1845 and 1885. On Tran Phu at the corner of the market, the **Mieu Quan Cong Ⓑ**, built in 1904 and also known as Chua Ong, is dedicated to Quang Cong, a talented general of the chaotic Three Kingdoms period in Chinese history, which lasted from AD 221 until 265. Adjacent is the **Hoi An Historical and Cultural Museum Ⓒ**, which is located in a former pagoda.

In fall of 1998, rising river water from heavy rains nearly destroyed Hoi An's Japanese covered bridge.

The temple of **Phuoc Kien Ⓓ**, on Tran Phu and built in 1792, has been the meeting place of many generations of the same clan, who arrived from Fujian, along the coast in southern China. Here, they remember their origins and worship their ancestors. The temple, once a pagoda, is dedicated to the cult of Lady Thien Hau and contains many exquisite woodcarvings.

Although many of the old homes and monuments have been restored over the years, they retain their original wooden framework, carved doors and windows and sculpted stuccos, as well as very rare and ancient furniture from Vietnam, China, Japan, and the West.

The most characteristic examples of Hoi An's architecture are the old houses along Nguyen Thai Hoc and parallelling the river, particularly the **Tan Ky House Ⓔ**. These elongated houses front onto one street and back onto the street behind. All the houses are built of precious wood in a very refined, two-storey style. The front facade serves as a boutique, and the area behind is generally used as storage space. The interior is terraced for living, and an inner courtyard is open to the sky with a veranda linking several living quarters.

Right: fishing
on China Beach.

One of the most remarkable features of these old homes is the diversity in their architectural structure. This varies greatly from one house to another in terms of space distribution, sculptural art, decoration and inner courtyard gardens. Space is creatively utilised. The unique crab-shell roof style extensively used is typical of Hoi An.

Walking in the streets of this lovely and charming town, observe the influence of the architecture, sculpture, and decorative styles of China and Japan, along with the skill of the Vietnamese architects who have absorbed these outside influences and created something similar yet somehow different.

One of the most remarkable historical architectural examples is **Cau Nhat Ban Ⓕ** (also, **Lai Vien Kieu** or the **Japanese Covered Bridge**). Built by the Japanese community in the 17th century, it links the districts of Cam Pho and Minh Huong. The bridge's curved shape and undulating green-and-yellow tiled roof give the impression of moving water. In the middle of the bridge is a square pagoda dedicated to Dac De and Tran Vu, two legendary figures.

Many of the temples in Hoi An venerate Buddha, along with Confucianism, Daoism, and a diversity of other animist gods and beliefs. The 15th-century **Phuc Thanh**, a pagoda on the outskirts of Hoi An, contains many beautiful statues and is one of the oldest to be found in the region. ❑

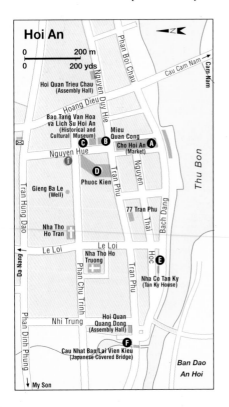

Hoi An

0   200 m
0   200 yds

Hoi Quan Trieu Chau
(Assembly Hall)

Phan Boi Chau

Cau Cam Nam

Cam Nam

Nguyen Duy Hieu

Hoang Dieu

Bao Tang Van Hoa
va Lich Su Hoi An
(Historical and
Cultural Museum)
Ⓒ

Mieu
Quan Cong
Ⓑ

Cho Hoi An Ⓐ
(Market)

Nguyen Hue

Ⓓ

Phuoc Kien

Tran Phu

Nguyen

Thu Bon

Gieng Ba Le
(Well)

Tran Hung Dao

77 Tran Phu

Bach Dang

Nha Tho
Ho Tran

Le Loi

Da Nang

Le Loi

Nha Tho Ho
Truong

Phan Chu Trinh

Tran Phu

Hoc

Ⓔ

Nha Co Tan Ky
(Tan Ky House)

Phan Dinh Phung

Nhi Trung

Hoi Quan
Quang Dong
(Assembly Hall)

Ⓕ

Cau Nhat Ban/Lai Vien Kieu
(Japanese Covered Bridge)

Ban Dao
An Hoi

My Son

SOUTHERN VIETNAM

Entrepreneurial in mind and tropical in ambience, the south is heady and hot and defined by the delta of the Mekong

Far removed from the more traditional north and centre, southern Vietnam has a character all of its own. Saigon, the former capital of South Vietnam until it collapsed in 1975, now bears the name of Thanh Pho Ho Chi Minh, or Ho Chi Minh City, a change that many of its residents (and foreigners) still resist three decades later. Traditions and habits die hard.

But whatever one calls it, this furiously active and commercial city is definitely going somewhere. The streets are filled with new motorbikes and new taxis, and construction is adding a glittering shimmer to the downtown boulevards.

It's always been an entrepreneurial centre, and for decades people from all over the country have flocked here to make their fortunes. This is Vietnam's city of dreams – and sometimes, nightmares. Many become disillusioned and they may be seen on the streets, looking for a job or a place to sleep. But the effort and luck needed to find fortune has done little to deter the flow of hopefuls. Indeed, their spirit gives the city an optimistic edge. Southern Vietnam, especially Ho Chi Minh, has always been noted for its business acumen. Cho Lon, the city's long-established and thriving Chinese community, never seems to sleep.

An increasingly important facet of Vietnam's economic growth, however, can be found some 125 km (70 miles) to the east, in Vung Tau, the centre of the country's growing oil industry. One of the country's major ports, Vung Tau bathes in a mild climate and is a popular weekend seaside resort lined with decent beaches.

Although oil may portend a prosperous future for Vietnam, for the moment its export powerhouse is the rice-growing delta of the Mekong River – the River of Nine Dragons, or Cuu Long. The vast delta stretches from the eastern coast to the western border with Cambodia and as far south as Ca Mau, the southernmost tip of the country. An extensive network of waterways, irrigation canals and rivers laces the region, which is plied by ferries and every type of sailing vessel imaginable, linking the various towns and provinces to Ho Chi Minh City.

Rice fields stretch as far as the eye can see, creating a many-hued and textured patchwork. It is a quiet, isolated life, one that apparently makes many a person restless and thus drawn to the bright lights of Ho Chi Minh – or Saigon, if one prefers. ❏

PRECEDING PAGES: overseas Vietnamese buying fowl in Ho Chi Minh.
LEFT: high monsoon waters in the Mekong Delta.

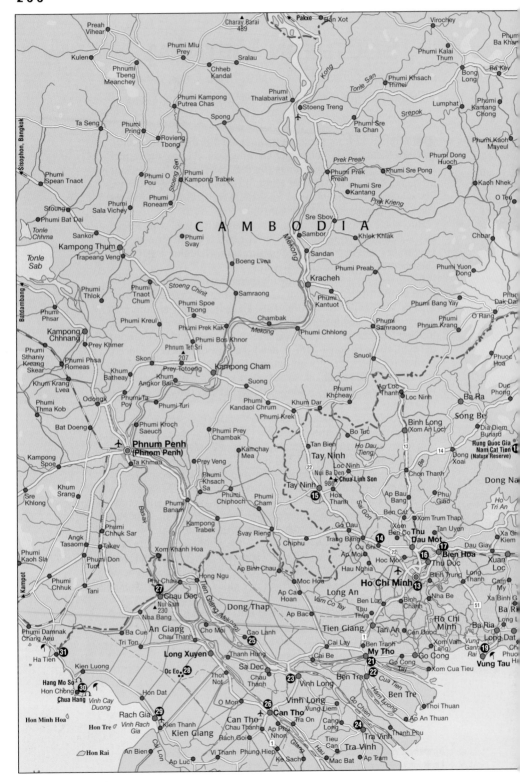

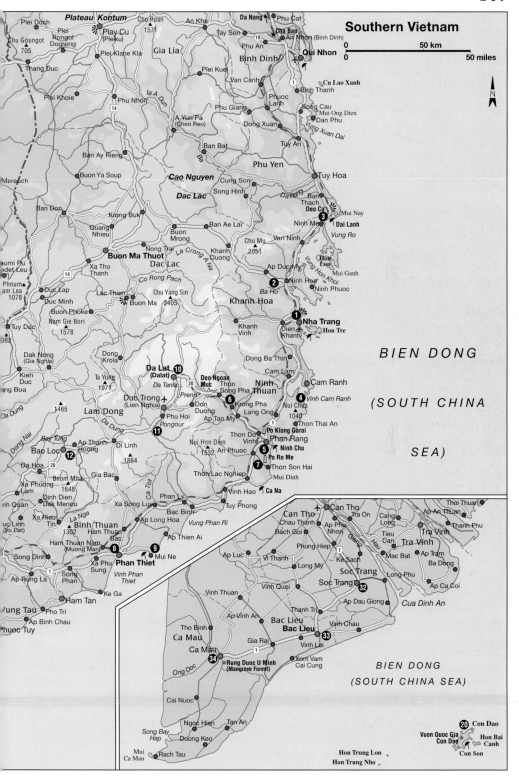

Southern Vietnam

0   50 km

0   50 miles

BIEN DONG

(SOUTH CHINA

SEA)

BIEN DONG
(SOUTH CHINA SEA)

NHA TRANG

*If the charm of rustic travel is wearing somewhat thin,
consider Nha Trang's rather fine beaches and unfettered life.
What's more, there are the evocative ruins of old Champa to explore*

Map
on page
266

Along the south-central coast, travellers can glimpse two sides of life in Vietnam: the relaxed beach life of the picturesque Nha Trang and then the hard scrabble existence of the desolate areas around Phan Rang and Phan Thiet. The drive along the Pacific coast, from Da Nang to Nha Trang, provides spectacular vistas of beaches, coves, cliffs and mountains jutting out into the sea, with long stretches of rice paddies bordered on one side by blue-tinted mountain sides and on the other by the sea, even more blue.

Vietnam's most picturesque coastal town and beach resort, **Nha Trang ❶**, is the ideal place to break a journey, relax and soak up the sun. With its population of 300,000, it is now the provincial capital of Khanh Hoa Province, which lies to the east of the Central Highlands. According to popular belief, the town derives its name from the Cham word *yakram* (lit. bamboo river).

Nha Trang is a good place to idle. The beaches are relatively clean and quiet, although the crowds can become frustrating, especially during local school holidays, and vendors are becoming increasingly aggressive – as elsewhere in Vietnam. In recent years, there has been a considerable amount of construction, mainly hotels, along Tran Phu, a street that runs parallel to the shoreline. But the beach itself, especially the southern end, has been left reasonably undisturbed, and most of the hotels are smallish family-run operations, although eventually large hotels will change the small-town feel of Nha Trang's beach.

PRECEDING PAGES:
family on the train.
OPPOSITE: beach
at Nha Trang.

A small amusement park, with a Ferris wheel and a fun house, fronts the shore. There are several good restaurants right on the beach, serving everything from pizza baked in a brick oven to the expected fresh seafood; the large shrimp is especially good.

The attitude here is generally more relaxed and carefree than elsewhere in Vietnam. Visitors will find pick-up soccer games on the beach, the sky filled with colourful kites, and vendors peddling juicy fruit, steamed corn, delicious crabs, tacky T-shirts, relaxing massages, and even manicures on the beach. It's possible to sell and trade books not only in English, but also in French and German. Besides risking a sunburn, reading a book, and napping – in other words, doing not much of anything – there are plenty of things to see in and around Nha Trang.

Just east of the Nha Trang railway

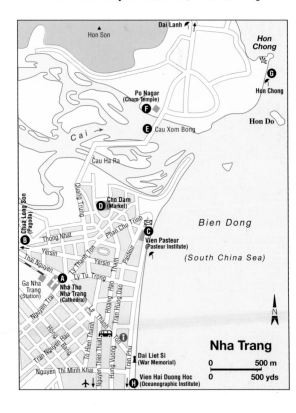

Nha Trang

0   500 m
0   500 yds

Pool is popular.

station stands the large **Nha Tho Nha Trang** (Nha Trang Cathedral). Built in a gothic style, the cathedral is the home of Nha Trang's Catholic bishop. A white, 19-metre-high (62-ft) Buddha statue commands an excellent view from his seat at the top of the hill behind **Chua Long Son** . The pagoda was built in 1886 and has been reconstructed several times since. Glass and ceramic mosaics depicting dragons adorn the main entrance and roofs.

The Buddha statue was erected in 1963 to commemorate the Buddhist struggle against the repressive South Vietnamese regime of Ngo Dinh Diem, who was overthrown that same year. Images of the Buddhist nuns and monks who laid down their lives as a final protest are at the base of the statue. The most famous of them, Thich Quang Duc, was a bonze from Van Gia, a town a little over 70 km (40 miles) north of Nha Trang. He made headlines when he immolated himself in the centre of Saigon in 1963.

The **Pasteur Institute** (open Mon–Sat, 1.30–4.30pm; admission fee), on Nha Trang's seafront, was founded in 1895 by Dr Alexandre Yersin, a French microbiologist, military doctor, and overall Renaissance man who had worked as an assistant to Dr Pasteur in Paris. He arrived in Vietnam in 1891 and was among those Europeans who first appreciated Da Lat. Yersin was also responsible for introducing and establishing Brazilian rubber trees and *quinquina* plantations – quinine-producing trees – in the region of Suoi Dau, about 25 km (15 miles) southwest of Nha Trang. He is buried here among his rubber trees, according to his wishes.

A new museum has been built at the Institute that displays many of Dr Yersin's personal effects, documents and laboratory equipment. Many of his books are kept in the library opposite the museum, a library he himself

BELOW: Nha Trang harbour.

designed. Today, the Institute still produces vaccines and carries out research, though with a very limited budget.

Map on page 271

During the day, one can catch the interesting sights and smells of Nha Trang's main market, **Cho Dam** ⓓ, which was built in 1972. Goods include everything from fruit and vegetables to clothing, hardware and electronic goods.

A guaranteed sight is the return of the local fishing fleet to shore in the early morning. One place to watch is from the **Xom Bong** ⓔ, a bridge located at the base of the knoll on which the Cham towers rest. The bridge spans the **Song Cai**, which joins several waterways from the western forests and flows to the Song Nha Trang mouth. The province's largest river, the 300-km-long (180-mile) **Song Da Rang**, is also the longest in central Vietnam. Canals branch off, carrying water to the vast fields of rice, maize and beans.

On a hill at the town's northern entrance stand the majestic towers of the famous Brahman sanctuary and temple, **Nha Trang Huu Duc**, or **Po Nagar** ⓕ. The main tower is dedicated to the Cham goddess Po Ino Nagar, the Lady Mother of the Kingdom and reputedly Shiva's female form. Today, she is still worshipped, adopted by Vietnamese Buddhists who refer to her as Thien Y-ana. Her statue resides in the main temple, but it was decapitated during French rule, and the original head now resides in the Guimet Museum, in Paris. Only four of the sanctuary's original eight temples, all of which face east, remain standing. These date from between the 6th and 11th centuries. The remaining pillars and crumbling steep steps leading up to the towers hint at the majesty of the original temple. At the end of the 1990s, the towers were restored, though this did not deter tourists and vendors who continue to flock here.

Along the banks of the Cai near the bridge, the village of **Xom Bong** is

BELOW: Nha Trang fishing boats.

known for producing many of the dancers at the Po Nagar festivals. From the top of **Hon Son** (Son Hill), behind the ancient Cham towers, a superb panorama looks out over Nha Trang.

Not far from here, the jagged rocks of **Hon Chong** ⑥ jut out into the clear aquamarine waters of the South China Sea. The beach here is relatively small and quite dirty. Northwest of here is **Tien Co** (Fairy Mountain), as its three summits are thought to resemble a fairy lying on her back.

The **Oceanographic Institute** ⑪ (open 7am–5pm; admission fee) is located south of the town in the fishing village of **Cau Da**. The Institute was founded in 1927 on the initiative of a biologist, Armand Krempf. It houses aquatic flora and fauna. Its aquariums – rows of small fish tanks lined up along the walls and a few specimens preserved in jars – and open-air pool are home to many different species of fish and other marine life.

From the Nha Trang harbour located here at Cau Da, visitors can take a 20-minute boat ride to neighbouring **Hon Mieu** (Mieu Island) where the larger **Tri Nguyen Aquarium** is located. Cau Da does a brisk business in shells, coral and tortoise-shell items – necklaces, bracelets, and the like – at reasonable prices. The ever-present Vietnamese condiment, *nuoc mam* or fermented fish sauce, is produced here in large quantities.

Just north of Cau Da, Emperor Bao Dai's five villas are set amongst well-manicured trees and shrubs on three hills. The villas were built in the 1920s, their location obviously chosen for the superb views over the sea, the bay and the port. Three cycles of Vietnamese leadership have used the site for rest and relaxation. Bao Dai and his family came here until the royalty was ousted. From the mid-1950s until 1975, high-ranking officials of the South Vietnamese

BELOW: beach near Nha Trang.

government enjoyed staying at the villas. After 1975, they were supplanted by Communist leaders from Hanoi. Today, the villas have been restored and given over to the provincial tourism authorities who are using them as a hotel. With rooms for rent and a restaurant that's open to the public, the *hoi polloi* can now enjoy the site too.

Palm trees line the dazzling sands and clear waters of Nha Trang's gently curving bay. Idyllic islands, easily accessible by boat, lie just off the coast to the west. One of the more popular things to do in Nha Trang is to take a boat excursion to visit the islands and coral reefs, where snorkelling is excellent. Deep-sea fishing is also possible. **Hon Tre** (Bamboo Island) is the largest of the islands, while **Hon Lao** (Monkey Island) to the north is home to more than 300 monkeys.

North of Nha Trang

About 30 km (20 miles) north of Nha Trang, near the village of Phu Huu, is a quiet, isolated park with a stream and waterfalls called **Ba Ho ❷**. The scenery is varied and quite magnificent. Here, amid lush green forests are three pools in ascending height, formed by water cascading over large boulders. Enterprising youngsters will follow you the entire way, offering helping hands and liquid refreshments, all of which become greatly appreciated as the climb grows increasingly steep and slippery. Of course they expect to be rewarded at the end of the trek. Northeast of here on its own peninsula is the lovely and secluded beach at **Doc Let**, which looks out over the South China Sea. In the west, the famous Mother and Child Mountain reaches a height of 2,000 metres (6,600 ft). From a distance its silhouette resembles a woman carrying a child.

Maps
Area 266
City 271

Many islands, such as Hon Yen, are home to sea swallows, whose famous nests, gathered in vast quantities, are a source of nutrition and income. Nests are collected in spring and autumn. Most rare are the orange and red nests, believed to be therapeutic.

BELOW: road traffic outside Nha Trang.

Cham temple detail near Nha Trang.

Further north, National Highway 1 traverses the plain of Minh Hoa before climbing the sinuous **Deo Ca ❸** (Ca Pass) over the mountain of Dai Lanh. Here, in 1470, King Le Thanh Tong and his troops stopped and erected a stele to mark the boundary between Dai Viet and the Kingdom of Champa. Today, this spot marks the boundary between Phu Yen and Khanh Hoa provinces. Forests in the northern part of the region produce many kinds of wood, including sandalwood, aloe wood, eagle wood, barian kingwood, rosewood, and ebony.

Southward from Nha Trang

Leaving Nha Trang to the south, the coastal road passes **Vinh Cam Ranh ❹** (Cam Ranh Bay), the deep-water bay used as a naval base, first by the Americans and later by the Soviets. Today the base is occupied by the Vietnamese army and remains off-limits to the public. Absolutely no photography is permitted. The sand from the bay is of a quality much sought-after for manufacturing lenses and high-quality crystal. Before the Vietnam War, enormous quantities of sand were exported to Japan, Europe, and America.

The area of Cam Ranh alone has more than 300 hectares (750 acres) of salt marsh that yield around half a million tons of salt per year. Immense sugar cane plantations cover certain areas of the province.

South of Cam Ranh, the road enters Ninh Thuan Province. The coastal road passes through a rather monotonous, sand-covered landscape. Mountains and forest cover two-thirds of Ninh Thuan and Binh Thuan to the south. They are one of the country's poorest areas, due to the lack of agricultural resources.

BELOW: Cham tower near Phan Rang.

The town of **Phan Rang ❺**, capital of Ninh Thuan, is an ancient Cham

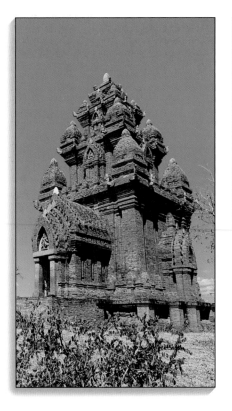

CHAM MUSICAL INFLUENCES

Like the music of Korea and Japan, Vietnamese music is derived from Chinese musical tradition. Still, some of its musical elements are local or absorbed from elsewhere in Southeast Asia. Some of it is also derived from Champa, the old Hinduised kingdom of central Vietnam. Most famous, of course, are the kettle drums of Dong Son *(see picture, page 26)*. Archaeological research in Dong Son village uncovered ancient kettle gongs, mouth organs, percussive clappers made of wood, and the conch-shell trumpet or horn. Between the 10th and 15th centuries, both Indian and Chinese influences melded together in Vietnamese music. For example, at least two traditional Chinese musical ensembles and theatrical art were introduced to the Champa repertoire.

By the 1700s, Chinese influence was considerable. Vietnamese court music *(nha nhac)* was performed by two orchestras: one with a 12-stone chime, 12 bells, 25-string and 7-string zithers, flutes, double-headed drum, and mouth organ. The second orchestra offered 16 iron chimes, 20-string harp, lute, double flute, double-headed drum, and mouth organ. The royal ceremonial music, no longer found or heard in Vietnam, was derived from traditional court music.

principality on the **Song Chai**. The town lies in an extremely arid landscape dotted with menacing-looking cacti and poinciana trees. From here, the scenic Highway 20 leads to the central highlands resort of Da Lat *(see chapter on Da Lat, page 278)*. About 7 km (4 miles) down this road, four 13th-century Cham towers known as **Po Klong Garai** stand on an arid hill. These brick towers were built under the reign of the Cham King Jaya Simhavarman III to worship King Po Klong Garai, who had constructed a much-needed local irrigation system. The entrance to the largest tower is graced with a dancing, six-armed Shiva, and inside a statue of a bull known as Nandin is the recipient of offerings brought by farmers to ensure a good harvest. Under a wooden pyramid is a linga painted with a human face. A rock on a nearby hill bears inscriptions commemorating the construction of a linga by a Cham prince in 1050.

Further up the road, 40 km (25 miles) before Da Lat, is **Krong Pha ❻**, with the crumbling remains of two old Cham towers. Even more interesting are the colourful, traditionally clad Cham people who live in the foothills around this extremely poor area. This region is also renowned for its grape production.

About 15 km (10 miles) south of Phan Rang is a Cham tower, **Po Ro Me ❼**, named after the last King of Champa, Po Ro Me, who ruled from 1629 to 1651 and died a prisoner of the Vietnamese. The lovely white-sand beaches and turquoise waters of the beach at **Ca Na**, roughly 30 km (20 miles) south of Phan Rang, is an excellent place to break a journey.

Phan Thiet ❽, the provincial capital of Binh Thuan, has a population of 170,000. Fishing is the mainstay of Phan Thiet and the province as a whole. A great many different varieties of fish are caught in the region. Visit the fishing harbour early in the morning, when the fishermen are unloading their catch, and you'll be treated to an unusual – and quite spectacular – sight. Along the southern coast, another common sight is that of fishermen transporting themselves in large, round baskets known as *thung chai* (pitch baskets). Made of woven bamboo strips and sealed with pitch, these 2-metre-wide boats are paddled standing up. As in many other towns along the coast, the pungent odour of *nuoc mam* hovers over the town. Among the other products of the region are mineral water from a spring called Vinh Hao, cashew nuts, grapes and cuttlefish.

Twenty-two km (13 miles) east of Phan Thiet along the coast and located on its own peninsula is the small fishing village of **Mui Ne ❾**. With lovely beaches and offshore islands a short boat ride away for the exploring, this is a delightful place to drop out for a while. The stretch of lonely coast leading to Front Beach is bordered on one side by the blue ocean and on the other by the beautiful, stark, salmon-coloured sand dunes for which the village is famous. Visitors can hike and even stay overnight amidst these graceful, sculpted forms. Anticipating that this area will be the next hot vacation spot, developers have rushed in to build resort hotels, especially along the road between Phan Thiet and Mui Ne, often before roads and other infrastructure are in place to cater to travellers. For now, Mui Ne is still off the beaten path and so remains quiet and unspoiled. ❑

Map on page 266

BELOW: beach lined with palms.

Maps
on page
266–7

Hanoi

Da Lat

Ho Chí Minh

BELOW: the subtle
Da Lat skyline.

DA LAT AND BEYOND

*An old colonial hill retreat, Da Lat is but a few hours from Ho Chi
Minh. A favourite of the last emperor, even dour communist cadres
have found Da Lat to be a salve for the Party life*

A cool, tranquil, and lush retreat from Vietnam's large cities, **Da Lat** ⑩
was first developed as a highland getaway by the French. Located in Lam
Dong Province, Da Lat, the city of Eternal Spring, is today Vietnam's
most popular mountain resort and escape. Although accessible by several inland
routes from the coastal provinces of Khanh Hoa and Ninh Thuan, the most
used route is the 300 km- (180 mile-) long route via Bien Hoa from Ho Chi
Minh, about a 5-hour trip on Highway 1 then northeast on Highway 20. Another
route, on Highway 11 from Nha Trang, passes areas with the residue of Cham
ruins. Da Lat is nestled among mountains, pine-covered hillsides, lakes and
forests on the Lam Viet plateau, beside the **Song Cam Ly** (Cam Ly River). Da
Lat's name comes from two words: *da*, meaning river or source, in reference to
the Cam Ly, and *lat*, the name of an ethnic minority living here.

With a population of about 150,000, the city's economy is based on
agriculture and tourism. The average annual temperature of about 17°C (63°F),
fresh mountain air, and tranquil beauty first attracted the French, who developed
the resort and built holiday villas on the hillsides.

Da Lat has long been a favourite destination for lovers and honeymooners.
Many natural beauty spots await visitors in and around this charming old town,

COFFEE-CAT COFFEE

O ne of the world's largest coffee exporters, Vietnam is
also home to a rather discriminating connoisseur
of the bean: the civet cat, a relative of the mongoose
that looks a little like a fox. Said to choose only the best
beans from the coffee plant (introduced in the central
highlands by the French about a century ago), the cat's
discriminating choice of beans usually make it through
the complete digestive system of the cat. Later, after the
cat has returned to its traditional forest habitat, human
connoisseurs of coffee retrieve the undigested beans at
the base of forest trees for recycling into what is said to
be amongst the world's best cups of coffee: *caphe cut
chon*, or fox-dung coffee.

Recipes abound. One is to dry the reclaimed beans
in the sun for months. After the outer skin peels off, the
beans are mixed with salt, butter, perhaps some sugar,
and a glug of French red wine. Then the beans are
roasted. However, as the civet cat's habitat of forests is
disappearing – often for new coffee plantations – the
cats themselves are increasingly scarce. This has led to
an industry in counterfeit beans. One restaurateur in Ho
Chi Minh claims that Viet Cong soldiers drank caphe cut
chon for a caffeine-induced fighting edge in battle.

whose colonial-era villas and buildings are decorated with attractive gardens of roses, poppies, sunflowers and gladioli.

Da Lat was at one time projected to become the capital of the French colonial Indochinese State Federation. In the late 19th century, the French governor of Cochin China sent a delegation to explore the region. On the strength of their findings, the governor established a meteorological and agricultural research centre here. There is still something of a French colonial air about the place. The grand Dalat Palace Hotel commands a prime location in town, above a vast green lawn (perhaps the only such piece of grass anywhere in Vietnam) overlooking the central lake, Xuan Huong. The hotel, built by the French in 1922, was renovated in 1995 and reopened by the French Sofitel chain. Whether staying or not, it is worth a visit for its architecture.

On Tran Hung Dao, more than two dozen villas built by the French in all manner of European styles stand under tall trees, looking out over the valley and the mountains surrounding it. Villas built as summer residences for Vietnam's last emperor, Bao Dai, and one for the French governor-general are nestled among the pine trees. Small houses are cosily perched, side by side, on the town's hilly terrain.

The beauty and serenity have made Da Lat a popular retreat. But its appeal has a downside. All around town, especially at many of the parks, lakes and villas, the tacky side of tourism has sprung up: photographers with hill-tribe costumes for visitors to don while posing for a picture by a lake; young men dressed as American cowboys leading children on pony rides; souvenir stands selling all manner of kitsch. The risk, of course, is that the sideshow of tat will upstage Da Lat's main attraction: its natural landscape, beauty and quiet.

TIP

Nothing is free in Da Lat, including a visit to a hill-tribe village. Visitors need a permit, not free, to visit most villages. Once there, travellers are always surrounded by villagers selling their goods and they can be persistent, if not a complete nuisance.

BELOW: vegetable farms near Da Lat.

Market in Da Lat.

BELOW: garden of Chua Linh Son.

Central Da Lat

Da Lat's hilly terrain means many of its sights are scattered all over town. The old French quarter, near the bridge spanning the Song Cam Ly, has managed to retain much of its old charm. From a distance, this area of town looks like a village plucked from the French Alps.

The colourful **Cho Da Lat** Ⓐ (Central Market) in the heart of Da Lat is an ideal place to encounter some of the ethnic minorities, distinctive in their traditional dress, who come from the surrounding villages to sell their produce. Here also are the great diversity of fruit, flowers and vegetables produced in the region. Da Lat's strawberries – and the jam made from them – are famous throughout the country. Avocados, artichokes, mushrooms, tomatoes, asparagus – just about any fruit, flower and vegetable found in Europe or America can be bought here. Flowers from Da Lat are sent to all parts of Vietnam. A wide range of handicraft items find their way to the market from various parts of the country, including bamboo handbags, rattan boxes, pressed flowers and fur hats. Just to the market's west is Hoa Binh Square.

Ho Xuan Huong Ⓑ (Xuan Huong Lake), formerly part of the town's golf course during the colonial era, lies in the heart of the town. The surrounding low hills, villas, and pine forests provide a lovely backdrop, although the water itself is muddy with red clay most of the year, as the surrounding hillsides, bare of trees, are eroding. Drivers offer rides in horse-drawn carts from the edge of the park. On the north side of the lake, a golf course originally built for the last emperor Bao Dai has been renovated and expanded, supplanting what had been a public park. Near the golf course is the small campus of Da Lat University. Not too far away, the well-manicured **Flower Gardens** Ⓒ offer a

quiet retreat. Established in 1966, a walkway winds through the gardens and around a small pond.

To the south of the market is a large, pink Catholic cathedral, or **Nha Tho Con Ga D**, built in 1931 and with stained-glass windows made by Louis Balmet, in Grenoble, France. In what is perhaps an ominous sign of things to come, however, in 1997 the government erected a new telecommunications tower resembling the Eiffel Tower across from the cathedral. No doubt built in an attempt to emulate *Le Petit Paris* – what Da Lat was called during its French heyday, this hunk of steel has now become, together with the old villas and churches, an indelible part of the landscape.

North of the central market area is **Chua Linh Son E**, an active pagoda and Da Lat's centre of Buddhism. Not far away is a pink evangelical church, on Nguyen Van Troi, built in 1940. Since 1975, Vietnam's Protestants have suffered persecution, and even today the government restricts the activities of this church, whose congregation is composed mostly of converted hill-tribe people. Also pink, the quiet and peaceful Domaine de Marie convent, built between 1940 and 1942, perches on a hilltop on Ngo Quyen. There were 35 nuns in residence before 1975, but only less than a dozen remain today. They operate a school for novices and sell handmade crafts and embroidery.

Bao Dai, Vietnam's last emperor.

Da Lat's **Ethnic Minority Museum** usually exhibits traditional costumes, ornaments, jewellery, baskets, hunting implements, and musical instruments. The museum's archaeological display features a statue of the Hindu goddess Uma, 12th- and 14th-century Cham pottery vases, rice-wine jars more than 200 years old, an unusual stone xylophone and tools used in the province more than 1,500 years ago. In 1999, however, the museum was closed; it is now searching for new premises, as the old site was reclaimed by its owner.

Da Lat environs

Tucked away under pine trees a few kilometres southwest of the centre of town, **Biet Dien Quoc Truong F** was the **Summer Residence** of Vietnam's last emperor, Bao Dai. Construction was begun in 1933 and finished five years later. Inside, there is a room with photographs of Bao Dai, his wife and children along with a desk with two telephones, one supposedly used by Bao Dai and the other by a former president of South Vietnam, Nguyen Van Thieu. (South Vietnamese leaders used the villa after Bao Dai left Vietnam; communist government officials have used it since 1975.) Today, visitors can rent rooms here. Among the items on display are a large map of Vietnam, a grand piano and frayed furniture covered in red velvet. Although guides will say that the furnishings were used by Bao Dai, in fact many of his belongings have been carted away over the years.

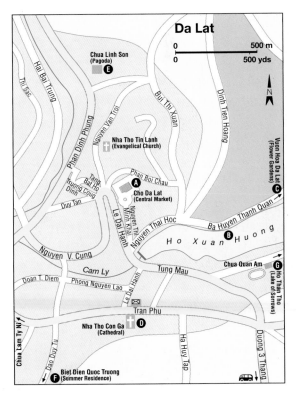

Not far from the summer residence, on Thien My to the north and due west of downtown, is **Chua Lam Ty Ni**, founded in 1961. The pagoda's flower beds and garden, and much of its wooden furniture, are the handiwork of the pagoda's founder and sole monk, Vien Thuc, who also has several thousand of his Zen paintings he will happily sell visitors. Vien Thuc is something of a character around Da Lat and not always an endearing one. While many tourists have found this hermit monk who writes *haiku* poems, speaks several languages, and has been exhibited in Europe to be delightful and profound, a number of locals consider him to be a hypocrite and fraud.

Several waterfalls liberally sprinkle the landscape in and around Da Lat. (Note that most of them charge fees to visitors.) The falls at **Cam Ly**, just to the north of Lam Ty Ni, are best visited during the rainy season, if at all; at other times the dry bed emits a foul odour.

The French governor-general's palace, similar to Bao Dai's summer palace, is on Tran Hung Dao, southeast of the centre of town. Local lore has it that there was an escape tunnel built in the basement. Rooms can be rented here as well, although as at Bao Dai's villa, there are daily pilgrimages of tourists tramping in and around the villa.

Not far from here down Khe Sanh is **Chua Thien Vuong** or **Chua Dao** (Chinese Pagoda), as it is known to the many domestic visitors who throng the site. Built in 1958, the pagoda houses in its main sanctuary a statue of the Thich Ca Buddha flanked by the goddesses of mercy and power. At 4 metres (13 ft) high and weighing 1,500 kg (3,300 lbs) each, these gilded sandalwood statues were brought from Hong Kong. On a hillside behind the temple is a giant, white statue of Buddha.

BELOW: produce market, Da Lat.

Map
on page
281

That tacky commercialism has infected even a hallowed pagoda is evident in the handful of young people dressed in animal costumes skulking about the temple, offering themselves as photo opportunities. (In many ways, the Vietnamese do little to make travelling an authentic cultural experience.)

Much quieter and nicer is the **Thien Vien Truc Lam** (Bamboo Forest Meditation Centre), located 5 km (3 miles) south of the centre of town. Built in 1993, this Zen Buddhist monastery sits atop a hill overlooking a tranquil Paradise Lake. A large hall contains a statue of Buddha holding a lotus flower. There are 120 monks and nuns in residence here as well as several lay students.

About 6 km (4 miles) north of town is **Thung Lung Tinh Yeu** (Valley of Love), so named for the courting couples from nearby Da Lat University who frequent the park. One can wander in the forest where Bao Dai used to hunt. Sailboats can be rented on the nearby artificial lake, **Ho Da Thien**, formed during flooding in 1972. Visitors must pass through a sometimes tedious gauntlet of souvenir stands, however, which has led locals to dub the place "Valley of Shops".

Ho Than Tho ❻ (Lake of Sorrows, or Sighs) lies 5 km (3 miles) northeast of Da Lat. It derives its name from the patriotism of a young couple, Hang Tung and Mai Nuong. When Hang joined Quang Trung's resistance forces against the Tsin invaders, Mai, believing Hang would be better able to serve his country unencumbered, drowned herself in the lake. Since then, the lake has been known by its present name, sometimes translated to mean Lake of Sighs – which is what visitors might do when they see the scum-filled lake and tacky gift stands that have sprouted on the lake's edge, not to mention wooden cutouts of a heart where couples can pose for a photo.

BELOW: bananas are available.

Map on pages 266–7

Ankroet waterfall.

BELOW: mask for Tet.
RIGHT: fast meal in Da Lat.

Visits can be arranged to hillside minority villages and hamlets, where villagers make a meagre living from the rice, corn, pumpkins, squash, tobacco, and, sometimes, cotton that they grow on hillsides. They also work in tea and coffee plantations. Located about 12 km (7 miles) to the north of Da Lat at the foot of the mountain Lang Bian, the village of **Lat** consists of several hamlets occupied by different ethnic groups. The Ma minority women are excellent weavers and dye their cloth using natural bark extracts. The men use simple traps and spears to hunt and fish. A toxic substance extracted from leaves is sometimes used in fishing. This stuns the fish but is apparently harmless to humans. Other minority groups around Lat are the Lat, Chill and Koho tribes.

Highlands to the north

Far north of Da Lat, the area known as the Central Highlands is often a tempting lure for the adventurous traveller. In the western part of the highlands, the main towns of **Buon Ma Thuot**, **Pleiku** and **Kontum** remain off the beaten path for many travellers, not only because there is comparatively little of interest here, except for visits to different ethnic minority villages and the occasional war-era prison, but much of the road network serving this part of the country is in very poor shape and travel is often a nightmare for anyone on any sort of schedule. Perhaps equally confounding is that local tourist authorities have a monopoly on hotels and tourist facilities, making travel expensive and a hassle.

South towards Ho Chi Minh

The area around Da Lat offers a number of fine waterfalls. Be warned, however, that commercialism increasingly threatens what would otherwise be pleasant and refreshing settings. Beyond Da Lat and to the south, the pleasant **Da Tanla** waterfalls cascade into a pool enclosed by high rock walls and surrounded by luxuriant greenery, tree houses and delicate bamboo bridges. Enclosed within the pine-covered hills 9 km (6 miles) south of Da Lat, the falls of **Prenn**, also known as **Thien Sa**, descend 15 metres (50 ft) across the mouth of a cave, entered from behind the falls via a small bridge.

Water from the **Ankroet**, or Golden Stream Falls, drops from a height of 15 metres (50 ft). Some 30 km (20 miles) south of town are the falls of **Lien Khuong**, and 8 km (5 miles) further on, the silvery waters of the **Gougah**, or Pot Hole Falls, drop from a height of 20 metres (60 ft), creating rainbows on sunny days. Most impressive of the waterfalls is **Pongour ⓫**, 55 km (35 miles) south of Da Lat and deep within thick primeval forest. The sound of the waters falling from a height of 30 metres (98 ft) can be heard even from several kilometres away during the rainy season. South of Da Lat, Highway 20 passes through coffee, tea and pineapple plantations. In **Bao Loc ⓬**, 100 km (60 miles) southwest of Da Lat, is a silkworm farm with immense mulberry orchards, one of the largest in the world. New silkworm hybrids, bred to survive the cooler highland climate, are raised year-round. Special permission must be obtained from the authorities before a visit can be arranged. ❑

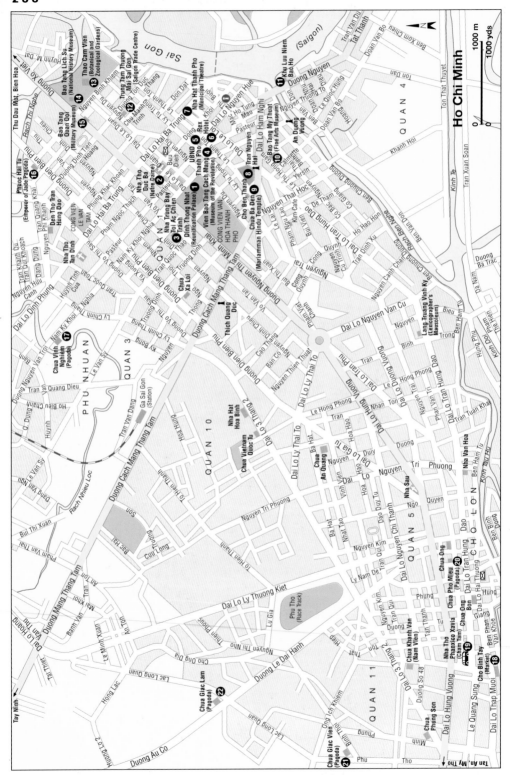

Ho Chi Minh

1000 m
1000 yds

QUAN 4

Sai Gon (Saigon)

QUAN 1

QUAN 3

PHU NHUAN

QUAN 10

QUAN 5

CHO LON

QUAN 11

Tay Ninh

1 Dinh Thong Nhat (Reunification Palace)
2 Nha Tho Duc Ba (Notre Dame)
3 Toi Ac Chien Tranh
4 Vien Bao Tang Cach Mang (Museum of the Revolution)
5 Thanh Pho
6 Rex Hotel
7 Nha Hat Thanh Pho (Municipal Theatre)
8 Chua Ba Den
9 Chua Ba Den (Mariamman Hindu Temple)
10 Bao Tang My Thuat (Fine Arts Museum)
11 Khu Luu Niem, Bac Ho
12 Trung Tam Thuong Mai Sai Gon (Saigon Trade Centre)
13 Thao Cam Vien (Botanical and Zoological Gardens)
14 Bao Tang Lich Su (National History Museum)
15 Bao Tang Quan Doi (Military Museum)
16 Den Tho Tran Bien Hoa (Emperor of Jade Pagoda)
17 Chua Vinh Nghiem (Pagoda)
18 Cho Binh Tay (Market)
19 Nha Tho Phanxico Xavia (Cham Tam)
20 Chua Pho Mieu (Pagoda)
21 Chua Giac Vien (Pagoda)
22 Chua Giac Lam (Pagoda)

UBND
Thanh Pho

CONG VIEN
LE VAN
TAM

CONG VIEN
HOA THANH
PHO

Ga Sai Gon (Station)

Nha Hat Hoa Binh

Chua Vietnam Quoc Tu

Chua An Quang

Nha Sau

Chua Ong

Chua Khanh Van (Nam Vien)

Chua Phung Son

Phu Tho (Race Track)

Tan An, My Tho

HO CHI MINH

If coming from relatively sedate and proper Hanoi, prepare yourself for Vietnam's entrepreneurial tempest, where even a Marxist renaming of Saigon failed to quench pursuit of capitalism

Map on page 288

Built on the site of an ancient Khmer city, **Thanh Pho Ho Chi Minh** (Ho Chi Minh City) was a thinly populated area of forests, swamps and lakes until the 17th century. In 1698, Saigon – as Ho Chi Minh was called before the communists changed the name – was established as a territory of the Gia Dinh Prefecture. By the end of the 18th century, Saigon had been linked with Ben Nghe (present-day Cho Lon), and the area became an important trading centre within the region. In 1998, Saigon celebrated its 300th anniversary.

Different theories expound on the origins of the city's original name of Saigon, still used by many people, even in official capacities: the river coursing through the city remains the **Song Sai Gon** (**Saigon River**), for example, and the state-owned tour company is Saigon Tourism.

Some say the name derives from the former name Sai Con, a transcription of the Khmer words *prei kor* (lit. kapok-tree forest) or *prei nokor* (forest of the kingdom), in reference to the Cambodian viceroy's residence that was located in the region of present-day Cho Lon.

In the 19th century, southern Vietnam, particularly Saigon, prospered despite the incessant fighting between the Vietnamese and Cambodians, and between the Vietnamese themselves, who were divided in their support of either the Nguyen lords from Hue, on the central coast to the north, or the Tay Son insurgents from Binh Dinh.

In 1859, French and Spanish ships landed in southern Vietnam. The French unloaded troops and weapons and embarked upon their conquest of the country. Saigon itself was captured later the same year and became the capital of the French colony of Cochin China. Modernisation of Saigon accompanied colonisation, and the French filled in the ancient canals, drained marshlands, built roads, laid out streets and quarters, and planted many trees. The city developed rapidly, acquiring something of the character of a French provincial town and served by two steam-powered trams. After the division of the country in 1954 by the United Nations, Saigon became the capital of the Republic of South Vietnam until the republic fell to the communists in 1975. The revolutionary authorities renamed it Thanh Pho Ho Chi Minh, after the founder of the modern Vietnamese state, who was, of course, anathema to supporters of the southern regime that lost the war. To many of its 6 million inhabitants, the city remains Saigon.

Today, Ho Chi Minh, 80 km (50 miles) inland from the coast and Vietnam's largest city and river port, sprawls across an area of 2,000 sq. km (760 sq. miles) on the banks of the Song Sai Gon. The city is divided into 17 urban and five rural districts.

This is a city on the move, although it is disorderly

PRECEDING PAGES: talk in the slow lane. **BELOW:** south along the Saigon River.

TIP

In the Mekong Delta region, including Ho Chi Minh City, the dry season lasts from November to April, while the rainy season usually endures for the rest of the year.

movement bordering on chaos. While the building boom of the late 1990s led to a glut of hotel rooms and empty offices in the city's centre, not to mention the abandonment of several new hotels under construction by international hotel chains, construction nevertheless continues everywhere. The streets and sidewalks overflow with the business of commerce, something that has always come quite naturally to the Saigonese. In the space of a block it is not unusual to see locals slurping *pho* (noodle soup) at Lilliputian sidewalk tables and chairs, a cyclo driver wooing a potential fare, shopkeepers peddling their wares, and young Saigonese transacting business on their mobile phones. After a decade or so of having their entrepreneurial talents suppressed by a socialist system, the business tycoons are out in full force. Much of this comes from the city's large ethnic Chinese community, centred in the Cho Lon district in the western part of the city but branching throughout to other parts of the city.

Called *viet kieu*, Vietnamese who now live in the United States, Australia, France and other countries have had much to do with fuelling the economic boom here, as well, but on a smaller scale than the overseas Chinese. On many streets and in many neighbourhoods, it is easy to pick out the families with relatives overseas – they have newer houses, nicer clothes and more amenities, and often they are the ones who have opened new shops and restaurants. The city is quickly taking on the air of a modern, yet still developing, Asian city as old houses and muddy swamps give way to modern high-rises, shopping complexes and highways. Throughout the city there are new restaurants, bars, cafes and the ubiquitous karaoke lounges catering to the naturally sociable Saigonese, who stay up until late at night socialising, in contrast to early-to-bed Hanoi.

But, in fact, the traditionally darker side of Saigon life – prostitution, drugs,

BELOW: Diep Minh Chao, Ho Chi Minh's personal sculptor.

and drinking – has begun to emerge again in Ho Chi Minh. There are massage parlours and drinking clubs with private rooms, and prostitutes advertise themselves on some street corners. Petty crime is up.

Although not to the degree that one finds in Hanoi, the French presence still remains in this southern city, lingering not only in the minds of the older generation but physically in the legacy of colonial architecture and the long, tree-lined avenues and streets they left behind. But the French era is quickly being overwhelmed by today's rush to open a business, make money, get rich. English, not French, has once again become the foreign language to practise on foreigners. Although visitors may encounter disgruntled soldiers who fought on the losing side of the war, in fact, most people long ago stopped living the war years of the 1940s, 1950s, 1960s and early 1970s and are consumed with the task of making a life. Most people are no fans of the communist government, but they nonetheless appreciate recent economic reforms and have learned to simply ignore the government, with the hope that the government will ignore them and that the momentum of capitalism will force the old men at the top to yield. But now, they say, is not the time to talk of politics.

Yet politics still looms within Vietnam's public buildings and museums. While some of the anti-American rhetoric has been toned down, there are still reminders of the war that divided the country for so many years.

Central Ho Chi Minh

Prominently located in the city's Quan 1 (District 1) is a building that symbolises, to the communists, the decadence of the Saigon regime. The former Presidential Palace of South Vietnam is today called **Dinh Thong Nhat** ❶

Map on page 288

Interior of one of the city's renovated colonial-era hotels.

BELOW: Western companies are making inroads.

(Reunification Palace; open daily, 7.30am–4pm; admission fee). Nowadays, it is occasionally used as a setting for parties and receptions for foreign companies introducing their products to Vietnam. Surrounded by large gardens, this large modern edifice rests on the site of the former French governor's residence, the Norodom Palace, which dated back to 1868. After the Geneva Agreement put an end to French occupation, the new president of South Vietnam, Ngo Dinh Diem, installed himself in the palace.

In 1962, the palace was bombed by a South Vietnamese air force officer, and a new building known as the Independence Palace was erected to replace the damaged structure. The present structure was designed by Ngo Viet Thu, a Paris-trained Vietnamese architect, and completed in 1966. The left wing of the palace was damaged by another renegade pilot in early 1975, and on 30 April 1975 communist tanks crashed through the palace's front wrought-iron gates and overthrew the South Vietnamese government.

Today, the former palace is a museum, with everything left much as it was on that fateful day. The basement houses the combat strategy room, communications room, map room, and the all-important presidential bomb-shelter. The ground floor includes the banquet room; state chamber, from where the South Vietnamese government surrendered; and the cabinet room, which was used for the daily military briefings during the period leading up to the overthrow of the South Vietnamese government.

BELOW: garden of Reunification Palace, and an interior staircase.

On the first floor is the president's reception and residential domain, complete with a Catholic chapel, dining room and bedroom. The second floor hosts the reception rooms of the president's wife. A private theatre and a helipad are found on the third floor, which commands an excellent view over Dai Lo Le

Duan (Le Duan Boulevard), which runs northeast to the zoo and botanical gardens. Behind the palace is **Cong Vien Van Hoa**, a nice and shady green park complete with a small topiary and carnival rides, which attracts flocks of school-children and families, especially on weekends. In front of the palace, Le Duan is bordered by a large park shaded with trees, where street vendors gather to sell their wares.

Just northeast of the Reunification Palace, on Duong Dong Khoi (Dong Khoi Street) is Saigon's largest church, **Nha Tho Duc Ba ❷** (Notre Dame or Cathedral of Our Lady), with two bell towers, which stands in the square next to Buu Dien (Central Post Office), an attractive colonial-style building. Construction of the cathedral began in 1877. A statue of the Virgin Mary stands in front of the cathedral, looking down Duong Dong Khoi.

A busy shopping street that was called Tu Do before 1975 (and rue Catinat before 1954), Dong Khoi has evolved from a seedy strip of hustlers, bars and two-bit souvenir stands into a glitzy parade of art galleries, antique shops and shops selling designer clothes, watches and perfume.

Further up Le Duan about 4 blocks, a new American consulate has been built on the site of the former US embassy, where in 1975 the American ambassador and last US troops escaped from the rooftop by helicopter just as Communist troops were advancing towards Saigon. Earlier, in the Tet Offensive of 1968, an event that marked a turning point of the war, Viet Cong guerrillas attacked southern cities and assaulted the American embassy. Completion of the building is another step in eradicating the physical vestiges of a more turbulent time.

Nha Trung Bay Toi Ac Chien Tranh ❸ (War Remnants Museum; open daily, 7.30am–4.45pm; admission fee), occupies the former US Information

Map on page 288

BELOW: the Notre Dame Cathedral, and a store on famous Dong Khoi.

Nearly anything is available in southern Vietnamese markets.

Agency building on Duong Vo Van Tan, immediately west of the Reunification Palace. Among items on display here are American tanks, infantry weapons, photographs of war atrocities against the Vietnamese and the original French guillotine brought to Vietnam in the early 20th century. Graphic pictures of deformed children show the effects of chemical defoliants like Agent Orange. Although a visit here is likely to be distressing, it is a sobering reminder of the heavy toll of war and is a must-see for many visitors.

The **Vien Bao Tang Cach Mang ❹** (Museum of the Revolution; open Tues–Sun, 8am–4.30pm; admission fee), one block east from Reunification Palace on Duong Ly Tu Trong, is found in a white neoclassical structure once known as Gia Long Palace. Built in 1866 and renovated as recently as 1998, this grand colonial edifice contains pictures of the war and displays of the flat-bottomed boats in which Viet Cong soldiers used to hide guns.

A network of reinforced concrete bunkers stretching all the way to the Reunification Palace lies beneath the building. Within this underground network were living areas and a meeting hall. It was here that Pres. Diem and his brother hid just before they fled to a church in Cho Lon, where they were captured and subsequently shot.

Diagonally across from the Revolutionary Museum and next to the Reunification Palace on Duong Nam Ky Khoi Nghia is the **Toa An Nhan Dan** (People's Court). Though not a usual tourist stop, this sprawling yellow building is another example of colonial-style architecture, albeit in need of a renovation.

BELOW: People's Committee building, or City Hall.

If the Reunification Palace is a symbol of the former South Vietnam regime, then **UBND Thanh Pho ❺** (People's Committee/City Hall) is the symbol of the

French colonial era. Formerly the Hotel de Ville, it was decorated by Ruffier and finished in 1908 after almost 16 years of ferment over its style and situation. Its ornate interior, complete with crystal chandeliers and wall-size murals, is now the headquarters of the Ho Chi Minh City People's Committee. Unfortunately, visitors are prohibited and must content themselves watching the paint peel off its grand exterior instead. Illuminated at night, the building is a lure for insect-hungry geckos.

In front of City Hall, just to the southeast and at the intersection of Le Loi and Nguyen Hue, there is a plaza with a statue of Ho Chi Minh in his role as favourite uncle to all children. Near the **Rex Hotel ❻**, which sits on the corner in a rather ostentatious fashion and once played host to American servicemen during the war, the plaza is abuzz on many nights, but especially on weekends, with young people, parents with children, and hustlers trying to sell souvenirs or cyclo rides to tourists. Watch out for pickpockets here and for passing motorcyclists grabbing backpacks, purses and even eyeglasses.

At the corner of Le Loi there is another plaza with a fountain that is crowded with a carnival-like atmosphere late into the night as courting couples and families alike cruise by on their motorbikes. Extending southeast from the plaza, Dai Lo Nguyen Hue is being developed into a broad boulevard lined with fancy hotels, upscale restaurants and commercial high-rises. This area of town buzzes with energy, especially at night.

At the northeastern end of Le Loi is the **Nha Hat Thanh Pho ❼** (Municipal Theatre), which faces Dong Khoi between the Delta Caravelle and the Continental hotels. The theatre was originally built in 1899 for opera but was used as the fortress headquarters of the South Vietnam National Assembly. Given a

Map on page 288

Classic Rex Hotel.

BELOW: popular intersection, with Rex Hotel and the City Hall.

Exterior detail of the Continental Hotel.

face lift in the late 1990s, this pink, colonial-style building now serves its original purpose and presents different programmes ranging from traditional Vietnamese theatre to acrobatics, gymnastics and classical music.

At the junction of Ham Nghi, Le Loi and Tran Hung Dao boulevards, a few blocks southeast of Reunification Palace, is the busy **Cho Ben Thanh ❽**. This market covers over 11,000 sq. metres (118,400 sq. ft) and was opened in 1914. Here is an amazing collection of produce, meat, foods, CD players, televisions, cameras, refrigerators, fans, blue jeans, cosmetics, and leather bags, all imported from around the world. The smell of spices and dried seafood assails the nostrils, and the colour of the many varieties of fresh fruit and vegetables provides a veritable feast for the eyes. At the back of the market, small food stalls serve a wide variety of local dishes.

The **Mariamman Hindu Temple ❾**, at 45 Truong Dinh and three blocks from the Ben Thanh market, was built at the end of the 19th century and caters to the city's small population of Hindu Tamils, as well as to a number of ethnic Vietnamese. The influence of local customs and practices is apparent in the use of joss sticks in this Hindu temple.

Not far from the Ben Thanh market, down Duong Pho Duc Chinh, is the interesting **Bao Tang My Thuat ❿** (Fine Arts Museum; open Tues–Sun, 7.30am–4.30pm; free), housed in a grand colonial-era building built about a century ago by a wealthy Chinese merchant. Several art galleries occupy the basement. The first floor features changing exhibitions of contemporary Vietnamese art. On the second floor the rooms display what can be described as revolutionary – or war – art, such as a lacquer paintings depicting guerrillas in the jungle and a plaster sculpture of Ho Chi Minh with his future revolutionaries.

BELOW:
Ben Thanh market.

REUNIFICATION EXPRESS

Thong Nhat, or the Reunification Express, a misleading title in every sense, refers to the train that crawls along at an average speed of 30 km (20 miles) per hour during the 48- to 58-hour journey between Hanoi and Ho Chi Minh City for 2,000 km (1,243 miles). It's not that the ancient trains are slow, but rather that there is only one track in poor condition, damaged in the north by American bombing and in the south by Viet Cong sabotage. There are few places where trains in opposite directions can pass; if the northbound train is running hours late, so too will the southbound be late.

The Reunification Express first ran on 31 December 1976 after a massive reconstruction effort that repaired 1,334 bridges, 158 stations, and 27 tunnels. The trains on the Hanoi-Ho Chi Minh stretch, like throughout Vietnam, are old. Of the 4,000 train carriages that are in use, 600 date from the French colonial era.

Comfort is not a priority on Vietnam's trains, including Thong Nhat, or the Reunification Express. Seats are hard, sleepers are hard, compartments are crammed with food vendors squatting in the aisles and children slung in hammocks. Petty theft is a problem. Tireless vendors descend on the train at each and every stop.

On the third floor, labelled the contemporary wing, the art is much older: porcelain pots, statues of Buddha, and Cham, Thai and Khmer sculpture.

Near the museum, on Le Cong Kieu, is the city's antique street. Here, two dozen or so shops sell old clocks, silver, glass and ceramics: much of it once belonged to wealthy Saigonese who fled the country after 1975. There is quite a bit of junk for sale here, too, but also some valuable furnishings. Down Duong Nguyen Thai Binh, near the corner of Yersin Street, is the **Cho Dan Sinh**. In the back of this market, a few stalls sell "old" US Army jackets, combat boots, gas masks, and fake dog tags.

To the south on Duong Nguyen Tat Thanh, in Quan (District) 4 and near where the Kinh Ben Nghe, a tributary, enters Song Sai Gon, there is a salmon-coloured memorial to Ho Chi Minh, **Khu Luu Niem Bac Ho ⑪** (open daily, 7.30am–4.30pm; admission fee), also known as Nha Rong (Dragon House). Documents and pictures relating to Ho's life and revolutionary activities are displayed here. The house dates from 1862 and was originally used as the head office of a French shipping company. It was from this place that Ho Chi Minh, then going under his given name of Nguyen Tat Thanh, left Vietnam in 1911 as a cook on a French merchant ship.

Northeast of downtown

As another sign of Saigon's desire to reinvent and modernise itself, the newly erected **Saigon Trade Centre ⑫** – an office complex with the no-doubt-temporary honour of being the tallest building in Vietnam at 33 floors – stands just off Le Duan on Ton Duc Thang.

At the end of Le Duan is **Thao Cam Vien ⑬** (Botanical and Zoological

Map
on page
288

TIP

Visitors can opt to take a leisurely cruise up the Song Sai Gon to the Bin Quoi Tourist Village, in Binh Thanh district. Largely a tourist trap, it offers a dinner programme and songs and dances from a traditional wedding ceremony.

BELOW: city girls.

Gardens). The gardens were established in 1864 by two Frenchmen – one a botanist, the other a veterinarian – as one of the first projects the French embarked upon after they established their new colony. The somewhat run-down zoological section houses rather dejected-looking birds, tigers, camels, crocodiles, and dancing elephants. Even though the gardens constitute one of the more peaceful places in Ho Chi Minh City, the whole place has fallen into a state of woeful neglect.

Bao Tang Lich Su ⑭ (National History Museum; open Tues–Sun, 9am–4.30pm; admission fee), located just within the entrance of the botanical gardens, was built by the French in 1927. It documents the evolution of Vietnam's various cultures, from the Dong Son bronze-age civilisation through to the southern Chinese Funan civilisation, the Chams and the Khmers. Among its exhibits are many stone and bronze relics, stelae, bronze drums, Cham art and ceramics, and a display of the traditional costumes of ethnic minorities. Behind the building, on the third floor, is a research library that is closed to the general public except by special permission. It houses an interesting and quite extensive collection of French, English and Russian books from the colonial era. Just opposite the museum is the **Den Hung**, a temple dedicated to the ancestors of Hung Vuong, the founding king of Vietnam.

Across Nguyen Binh Khiem, outside the zoo, the tired and run-down **Bao Tang Quan Doi** ⑮ (Military Museum; irregular hours) displays American, Soviet and Chinese military hardware, including the tank that crashed through the gates of Reunification Palace in 1975. There is little of interest inside, actually, except perhaps some of the old photographs. The hardware outside is garnished with sprouting weeds.

BELOW: National History Museum.

Northern suburbs

The small Sino-Vietnamese **Phuoc Hai Tu**  (Tortoise Pagoda) or Chua Ngoc Hoang (Emperor of Jade Pagoda), at 73 Mai Thi Luu and on the northern extents of the central city, was built by Cantonese Buddhists in 1909 and is one of the city's most colourful pagodas. A haze of heady incense and candle smoke envelops a fascinating array of weird and wonderful wooden statues, some Buddhist, others Daoist-inspired. The elaborately robed Daoist Jade Emperor surveys the main sanctuary. Just to his right, the triple-headed, 18-armed statue of Phat Mau Chau De, mother of the Buddhas of the Middle, North, East, West, and South, looks out in three directions from her encasement.

A door off to the left of the Jade Emperor's chamber leads to the Hall of Ten Hells, where carved wooden panels portray, in no uncertain detail, the fate that awaits those sentenced to the diverse torments found in the 10 regions of hell. Next door is a small room containing figurines of 12 women, said to represent the range of human characteristics.

The more recent Buddhist pagoda of **Chua Vinh Nghiem**  on Nam Ky Khoi Nghia, Quan 3 and west of Phuoc Hai Tu, is the newest and largest of the pagodas in the city. Built with aid from the Japanese Friendship Association, this Japanese-style pagoda was begun in 1964 and finished in 1973. Each stage of its 7-storey tower contains a statue of Buddha. In the huge main hall stands a large statue of Buddha surrounded by his disciples. Behind are altars consecrated to the dead, where tablets and photographs of the deceased are placed for the first 100 days after their death. The temple's screen and large bell were made in Japan. The bell, a gift from Japanese Buddhists, was presented during the Vietnam War as the embodiment of a prayer for an early end to the conflict.

Map on page 288

Detail from Emperor of Jade Pagoda.

BELOW: altar of the Emperor of Jade pagoda.

Chinese sausages in Cho Lon.

The large 3-storey funeral tower behind the main temple holds ceramic burial urns containing the ashes of the dead. There are 45 monks in residence here and a Buddhist college for nuns. The pagoda becomes the scene of great vivacity and colour during the Buddhist Ram Thang Gieng festival, which takes place on the 15th day of the first lunar month.

Cho Lon

Ho Chi Minh City's Chinatown, **Cho Lon**, was formerly a separate sister city but is now in the city's Quan 5, thanks to the outward growth of the suburbs. As the name (lit. big market) indicates, Cho Lon remains a thriving commercial centre. With a population of around half a million Hoas – Vietnamese of Chinese origin – Cho Lon has come a long way since 1864 when it was home to just 6,000 Chinese (mostly shopkeepers or traders), 200 Indians, and 40,000 Vietnamese. Today, countless small family businesses operate in this area. Day and night, Cho Lon's streets, markets and restaurants are scenes of noisy animation and much activity. On Hau Giang, between Thap Muoi and Ben Phan, is Cho Lon's main market, the large **Cho Binh Tay** ⓲, offering the usual plethora of goods and fresh produce.

East of here, at the end of Dai Lo Tran Hung Dao, is **Nha Tho Phanxico Xavia** ⓳ (Cham Tam Church), where Pres. Ngo Dinh Diem was captured and shortly afterwards executed along with his brother in the November 1963 coup d'état. The church was built around the start of the 20th century.

One of the largest churches in the city is the **Cho Quan Church**, on Tran Binh Trong. Built in 1896 by the French, it has a belfry with an excellent view, although the climb up is hard work as the stairs are steep and have not been well-

BELOW: avenue in Cho Lon, and public transport in a downpour.

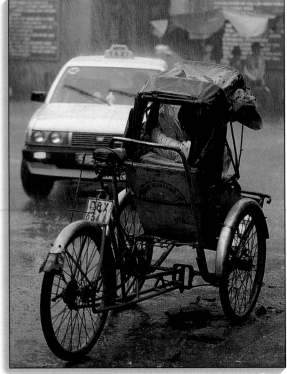

maintained. The neon halo that glows around the head of the statue of Jesus is glaringly late 20th-century.

As fast as the French, and later the Americans, were embedding their ways in Saigon, the Vietnamese were retaliating with the many pagodas, shrines and temples that sprung up all over the city – Buddhist, Indian, Muslim. The small **Cho Lon Mosque**, on Nguyen Trai, was built by Tamil Muslims. (The larger Indo Mosque on Dong Du in District One was built on the site of an older mosque by southern Indian Muslims in 1935. Only a handful of Indian Muslims remain, since most fled the country after 1975.)

The many richly decorated Chinese temples and pagodas found in Cho Lon are distinctly different from their Vietnamese counterparts, and they are best visited in the morning if you wish to see the faithful at their prayers. At number 710 Nguyen Trai is **Chua Pho Mieu** ⑳, the temple of Thien Hau, the Goddess Protector of Sailors and more commonly known as Chua Ba (Women's Pagoda). This Chinese temple was built by Cantonese Buddhists at the end of the 18th century in thanksgiving for having been safely delivered from their perilous sea journey from China.

The temple is frequented mostly by women, who bring their offerings to the altar of the Heavenly Lady with its three statues of Thien Hau located at the back of the temple. Votive paper offerings are burnt in the big furnace just inside the entrance. Large coils of slow-burning incense hang over the main sanctuary, creating a heady atmosphere. Among the other altars is one dedicated to the protection of women and newborn babies, and yet another to sterile women or mothers who have no sons.

Nearby is Chua Ba's counterpart, **Chua Ong**, the men's pagoda. (Its official

Map on page 288

Many Vietnamese and Chinese temples are not actually Buddhist, but instead are dedicated to the worship of certain legendary or national heroes from history.

BELOW: Binh Tay market, and betting at the races.

Map on page 288

name is Nghia An.) An intricately carved wooden boat hangs over the entrance. A statue of Quan Cong with red face, long black beard, and ornate regalia presides over the main altar. Today's worshippers come to pray, not surprisingly, for peace, happiness and prosperity in business.

North of Cho Lon

Northwest of Cho Lon in Quan 11, the smaller Buddhist **Chua Giac Vien ㉑**, on Lac Long Quan, was built in 1803. It was formerly known as Chua Ho Dat (Earth Pit Pagoda) due to the vast amounts of earth required to fill in the site before its construction. Some 153 beautifully carved wooden statues are housed within the pagoda. A statue of founder Hai Tinh Giac Vien stands near the rear of the temple's second chamber. Due to its remote location, few foreign travellers make it out here.

BELOW: an official of the former South Vietnam who was sent to the "re-education" camps.
RIGHT: urban boulevard.

Chua Giac Lam ㉒, in Tan Binh district and about 3 km (2 miles) north of Cho Lon, is a pagoda that dates from the end of the 17th century and is thought to be the oldest in the city. It is also an ancestral temple. Reconstruction work was last carried out on it from 1906 to 1909. Carved wooden pillars within the main building bear gilded inscriptions in Chinese characters. Portraits of monks of previous generations adorn the left wall. The main sanctuary houses many beautifully carved, gilded jackwood statues of Buddha, reincarnations of Buddha, judges and guardians of hell, and Quan Am, the goddess of mercy. As is typical in many Vietnamese pagodas, there is also an object resembling a Christmas tree, with 49 light bulbs symbolising the 49 days the Sakyamouni Buddha meditated under the bodhi tree to attain enlightenment. The pagoda has a 7-storey tower with an excellent view of sprawling Ho Chi Minh City. ❑

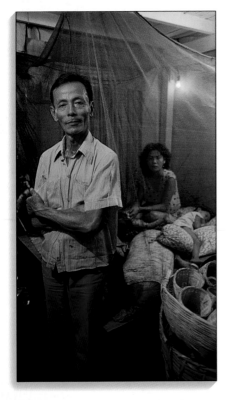

A FRENCH MAN'S CONQUEST

Charles Rigault de Genouilly was a naval officer who led the French invasion of Vietnam in 1858. Rigault de Genouilly entered the navy in 1827 and in 1847 he participated in an attack upon the port of Da Nang, ostensibly to protect the French Catholic mission there. Rigault de Genouilly later took command of French naval forces in China and Cochinchina.

The following year he attacked Da Nang under strict orders that there would be no negotiations with the Vietnamese. Following the fall of Da Nang, he started towards Hue but his armada was turned back by the shallow river. So he headed south instead and attacked Saigon in 1859 with the help of mercenary Spanish troops. But disease and the heat, combined with low supplies and no reinforcements, thwarted his efforts to consolidate his conquests or subjugate the Vietnamese. The following October he was relieved of his post at his request and he returned to France.

In 1867, after a stint as senator, he was named minister of the marine and of the overseas colonies. In the 1870 war between France and Germany, he refused his appointment as commander in chief of an expedition to the Baltic Sea and retired to Spain instead.

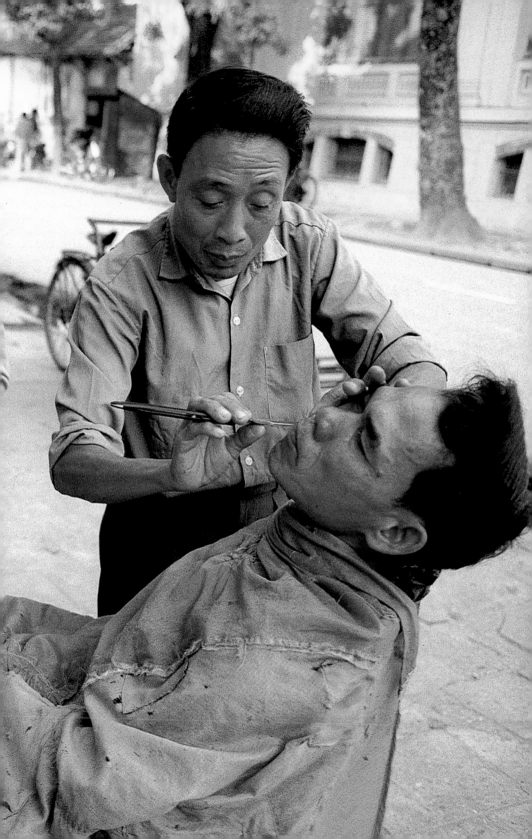

BEYOND HO CHI MINH

The highways leading out of Ho Chi Minh lead to some fascinating sites, including tunnels of the Viet Cong, the Cao Dai temple and some glorious tropical coastal beaches

Map on pages 266–7

To see the city of **Ho Chi Minh** 🔞 and the suburbs beyond from a different perspective, take a boat trip on the **Song Sai Gon** (Saigon River). From the river one sees a downtown skyline dominated by construction cranes and modern high-rises, many of them empty. At the same time, industrial development and overcrowding have forced an expansion into outlying areas. Just south of Ho Chi Minh City, plans are underway to build whole satellite cities complete with residential areas, parks, and universities on what was once swamp land. Less affected by urban renewal, some of the other suburbs make for fascinating side trips. Beyond are numerous options of interest and allure.

To the north of Ho Chi Minh

Located 65 km (40 miles) to the northwest of Ho Chi Minh is the town of **Cu Chi** 🔞, made famous during the Vietnam War for its extensive network of underground tunnels spanning almost 200 km (125 miles). The tunnels at Cu Chi, which ran three levels deep, were first used by the Viet Minh against the French in the 1940s, then later became hideouts for the Viet Cong, who at one point had even tunnelled under the Mekong Delta headquarters of the US Army's 25th Division. Guerrillas and villagers often lived for months underground, surviving on tapioca and breathing with the help of an ingenious and elaborate ventilation system. From these hiding places, Viet Cong were often able to spring surprise attacks on their enemies. In fact, by the mid-1960s, nearly 250 km (150 miles) of tunnels laced the region around Cu Chi.

The ground through which the tunnels burrowed is of red clay and above the water table, both factors advantageous for tunnel digging. But what to do with the removed earth without alerting the enemy? It was often used to fill in bomb craters or dumped into the Song Sai Gon (Saigon River). Visitors will note that the Cu Chi tunnels open to foreign tourists today have been enlarged for the Western frame. Some tunnels were just 80 cm (30 inches) in diameter. A tunnel complex could have up to four levels with elaborate ventilation, clinics, toilets and meeting rooms. Surgery was performed in the rustic medical clinics; blood was collected from the patient and pumped back into him with tubing and bicycle pumps. Needless to say, morale could be a problem under such conditions, and living conditions within the tunnels were almost unbearable.

The Americans often used trained dogs to sniff out the tunnels; the Viet Cong would deflect them with pepper at entrances and vents. It is said that the VC would even use the same soap as Americans so as to confuse the dogs. Numerous tactics were used by the

PRECEDING PAGES: street barber. **LEFT:** boatwoman on the Saigon River. **BELOW:** unloading a boat, Vinh Long.

Americans to eliminate the tunnels' effectiveness, but with little long-term effect until B52s began extensive carpet bombing.

Although the Americans eventually destroyed much of the subterranean network, it was a temporary and Pyrrhic victory. The tunnels had already fulfilled their function by giving the Viet Cong not only the advantage of surprise but also control of many villages. The Cu Chi tunnels are a vivid testament to the ingenuity and perseverance that eventually helped the Vietnamese win the war and are definitely worth a visit. Visitors can shudder at the specially designed booby traps used by the guerrillas as well as crawl through a small section of tunnel. Re-forested eucalyptus trees attest to the area's recovery from the ravages of chemical defoliants and large-scale carpet bombing.

Further to the northwest, Tay Ninh Province shares a border with Cambodia. The province's main river, Vam Co Dong, separates Vietnam from Cambodia. From the 7th to the 14th century, Tay Ninh belonged to the powerful Funan empire. Later, it became part of the Chen La kingdom, the forerunner of the Champa kingdom. In the early 18th century, the Nguyen lords defeated the last remnants of Champa and established the province of Gia Dinh, which integrated and administered Tay Ninh.

During the war against the French, Tay Ninh was a hot bed of anti-colonial resistance, and in the 1950s, bearing the standard of the Cao Dai religious sect, a hero of the armed resistance forces conducted his efforts against the central government in the Nui Ba Den (Black Lady Mountain) area.

Tay Ninh's greatest attraction is found approximately 100 km (60 miles) northwest of Ho Chi Minh City, in the township of **Tay Ninh** ⓕ itself. Here,

TIP

Photography was once restricted within the Cao Dai temple, but nowadays the taking of photographs is readily accepted, and flash can be used without problems.

BELOW: Cao Dai believer and the temple exterior.

resplendent in all its glory, stands the holy see of the Cao Dai religious sect. Founded in 1926 by Ngo Minh Chieu, the Cao Dai religion is an amalgamation of Buddhism, Daoism, Confucianism and Christianity, with a bit of Islam, animism, and ancestral worship melded in for diversity. Despite the competing influences in the religion, adherents believe in one ultimate deity and practise meditation and vegetarianism. (There are an estimated 2½ million Cao Dai followers in Vietnam.)

This surreal temple has to be seen to be believed. The best time to arrive is before the daily ceremony at noon, though there are also daily ceremonies at 6am, 6pm, and midnight. On the outside, a large eye symbolising the religion guards the entrance. The interior is like something out of fantasyland with a blue, star-studded vaulted ceiling and dragon-entwined pillars. Followers in their colourful ceremonial gowns of azure, yellow and white cut striking figures in their procession towards the altar.

The most outstanding natural feature in the province, **Nui Ba Den** – the Black Lady Mountain – overshadows the town of Tay Ninh. At 986 metres (2,900 ft) high, the mountain is dotted with many temples and pagodas, and it shelters a black stone statue of a Brahman goddess, the Bhagavati protectress of the region. More than 1,500 steps – almost a 400-metre (1,300-ft) climb – lead up to **Chua Linh Son** half way up the mountain, from where a splendid view takes in the region and the Mekong Delta beyond. For the less athletically inclined, an effortless cable car travels the same route. The Black Lady Mountain Festival takes place here during the spring months, from February through May. At the foot of the mountain is a monument to the soldiers killed in the fierce fighting in the province during the Vietnam War.

Map on pages 266–7

The single eye is the symbol of the Cao Dai religious sect.

BELOW: two field workers outside of Ho Chi Minh.

*Children are often
essential for the
harvest of crops.*

To the east

Leaving Ho Chi Minh City via the east-northeast exit, the road passes through **Ba Chieu**. The **Lang On Ba Chieu**, a temple dedicated to Le Van Duyet, the ancient viceroy of Cochin China under Gia Long's reign, is here. Quite a story surrounds this historical figure, who loomed even larger than life after his death. According to numerous records, this respected person is said to have manifested his presence throughout the Mekong Delta area after his death, performing miracles. This caused quite a stir, as might be expected, not only amongst the Vietnamese but also amongst the equally superstitious Chinese community, particularly in Ho Chi Minh's Cho Lon district. And anyone who perjured an oath that was made before the tomb of this revered individual could expect impending death.

The temple and Le Van Duyet's tomb are set in a park. Emperor Minh Mang destroyed the tomb after Le Van Duyet was posthumously tried and found guilty of treason. Later, Emperor Tu Duc repaired the injustice and restored the marshall's tomb and standing through a royal decree. The temple is easily recognised from a distance by its large triple entrance gate. Inside the temple are several altars dedicated to various cults. A portrait of Le Van Duyet in full court costume hangs over the central altar. During the Tet festivities, thousands of Vietnamese and Chinese pilgrims visit the temple for their horoscopes. The temple is most crowded on the anniversary of Le Van Duyet's death, which falls on the 30th day of the seventh lunar month.

BELOW: cycling schoolgirls.

From Ba Chieu, the road continues to the market town of **Thu Duc ⑯**, 20 km (12 miles) northeast of the city. Thu Duc is a rapidly growing suburb that is congested with truck traffic along the main road leading to Vung Tau. The area

was popular with South Vietnam's leaders; former Pres. Nguyen Van Thieu had a weekend retreat here that he reached by helicopter. Today's new elite – wealthy entrepreneurs – are turning the area into a haven for the rich, complete with a golf resort and the south's first water park.

Song Dong Nai (Dong Nai River) marks the boundary between Ho Chi Minh City and Dong Nai Province to its east. Originating in the Central Highlands far to the north, the river flows through the province for 290 km (120 miles). Once a rural area growing a variety of agricultural crops like sugar cane, maize, coconut palms and peanuts, Dong Nai Province is quickly transforming itself into a loud, boisterous, dusty industrial zone.

The highway leading through the province and the provincial capital, **Bien Hoa ⑰**, is lined with new factories. There is a large concentration of Catholics here, too, evidenced by the number of Catholic churches lining the highway. Many of the people originally migrated from Hanoi and elsewhere in the north in 1954 when Viet Minh forces defeated the French colonialists and the communists came to power. The province also had a large number of refugees who tried to flee as part of the "boat people" exodus to Hong Kong, Malaysia and elsewhere in Asia during the 1970s and 1980s.

The town of Bien Hoa is an important industrial centre 30 km (20 miles) from Ho Chi Minh City, on the banks of the Dong Nai. In the 17th century, Bien Hoa was a focal point for Chinese emigration. One of their leaders, Tran Thuong Xuyen, built a fort on **Cu Lao Pho**, an island in the Dong Nai, though nothing remains of the fort today. Trinh Hoai Duc – the minister that Emperor Gia Long sent to China to negotiate the country's change of name to Viet Nam – was buried on the island.

Map on pages 266–7

BELOW: Tet faces near Can Tho.

Markets ooze smiles and entrepreneurial energy in the south.

Towards the wharf, on the left bank of the river, stands a temple dedicated to Nguyen Huu Canh, who founded Saigon in 1698. In true Vietnamese fashion, this national hero, better known in southern Vietnam as Chuong Binh Le, has acquired the status of a saint and is venerated by the population as their protector. Several times a year, notably on the general's birthday, and during the spring and autumn seasons, festivities are held at the temple. During the Vietnam War, Bien Hoa and neighbouring Long Ben were the site of a large US army base. Nowadays, few tourists make it out here.

About 50 km (30 miles) to the northeast, the **Cat Tien** ⓭ nature reserve lies in an area adjacent to the three provinces of Dong Nai, Binh Phuoc and Lam Dong. This primeval forest, covering an area of roughly 10,000 hectares (25,000 acres), is the habitat of some rare and unusual creatures, including species of pythons and crocodiles, not to mention the nearly extinct Asian rhinoceros.

South to the coast and Vung Tau

Just before Bien Hoa, Highway 51 heads southeast into the coastal province of Ba Ria-Vung Tau. Before reaching the Vung Tau peninsula, a separate road leads east to **Long Hai**, a coastal district with beautiful scenery. With nice, as yet unspoiled beaches stretching for several kilometres, Long Hai is developing into a more attractive alternative to venerable Vung Tau.

Some ancient pagodas stand near the mount of Minh Dam, not far from the beach. **Dinh Co**, near a stretch of beach used by fishermen, is dedicated to a young lady who, as the story goes, was carrying a letter to Emperor Quang Trung when huge waves sank her boat. Local people reputedly built the temple in memory of this patriotic girl.

BELOW: Vung Tau, the Bay of Boats.

Map
on pages
266–7

The road between Long Hai and **Vung Tau** ⓭ (Bay of Boats) passes many salt fields and shrimp hatcheries. Vung Tau is located on a peninsula 125 km (80 miles) southeast of Ho Chi Minh City. In the 15th century, after Le Thanh Tong had conquered the kingdom of Champa, Portuguese merchant ships were already anchoring in the bay of Vung Tau. Known as Cap Saint Jacques under the French, this popular seaside resort has grown increasingly commercialised and has lost much of its old charm. This seaport and economic centre also has a thriving oil-and-gas industry. There is a small community of Russians here who arrived in the late 1970s to work in the oil industry.

Restaurants, colonial villas and cafes line the resort's largest beach, **Bai Sau**, also known as Thuy Van, which stretches for 7 km (4 miles) along the eastern coast. Here, for a small fee, relax on deck chairs under brightly coloured umbrellas. Thuy Van is very popular with the locals and becomes decidedly crowded on weekends. **Bai Dau**, or Mulberry Beach on the west coast, offers more privacy and better views, but the beach tends to be rocky. **Bai Truoc**, the beach opposite the hotel area, is full of silt. Although popular with Vietnamese, Vung Tau's beaches are unremarkable and by no means the nicest in Vietnam.

Aside from the beaches, Vung Tau has a number of Buddhist pagodas and temples. Typical of temples found in Vietnamese fishing villages, the **Lang Ca Ong**, or the Whale Temple, is dedicated to a whale cult. Built in 1911, the temple's most frequent visitors are fishermen who revere the whale as humanity's saviour from the perils of the high seas. Skeletons of whales that have been beached on the shores in the region are kept in huge cases, some of them 4 metres (13 ft) long and dating from 1868. The Vietnamese adopted the whale cult from the people of Champa, who worshipped the whale deity. Every

BELOW: coastline of Vung Tau.

Map on pages 266–7

year, on the 16th day of the eighth lunar month, fishermen gather at the temple to make offerings to the whales. Indeed, numerous anecdotes occur in Vietnamese folklore about whales as saviours.

To the northeast of the peninsula, a winding, bumpy road leads inland across **Nui Lon**, or Large Mountain, to **Thich Ca Phat Dai**, the Pagoda of the Buddha, a site popular with domestic tourists. Built in 1961 and inaugurated in 1963, the pagoda has an enormous white statue of the Grand Buddha sitting on a pedestal. Nearby is a bodhi tree, and further on there is a large stupa with four urns placed at its four corners. These are said to contain lumps of earth taken from the four places in India relating to Buddhism: Buddha's birthplace and his places of enlightenment, preaching, and attaining *nirvana*.

Set in lovely grounds of frangipani, bougainvillaea and rare trees on the Nui Lon hillside, **Villa Blanche** (White Villa) commands a superb view over Vung Tau. It was built by French Governor-General Paul Doumer as his summer residence, but he never spent a single day here because by the time the villa was completed, he had been dispatched back to France. Instead, King Thanh Thai was held here for a few years before he was packed off in exile to Reunion Island, where his son King Duy Tan was also sent in 1916. Later the villa became the seaside residence of two of South Vietnam's presidents, Diem and Thieu. As if giving a sermon on the mount, a 30-metre (100-ft) statue of Jesus with arms outstretched looks out across the South China Sea at the peninsula's southern point. The statue was erected by the Americans in 1971.

Inland from the beach at **Bai Dua** is the most celebrated of Vung Tau's pagodas, **Niet Ban Tinh Xa**. *Niet ban*, Vietnamese for nirvana, is symbolised in the pagoda's long, reclining Buddha, who, having attained *niet ban*, can lie back and enjoy it. The statue is made of concrete overlaid with marble. Each of the Buddha's 12 metres (40 ft) represents one of the 12 stages of re-incarnation, all of which are engraved on the Buddha's feet. The goddess Quan Am is also represented here. The statues standing at the entrance gate are those of Than Thien, the good deity, and Than Ac, the evil deity, both of whom are believed to guard the entrance to nirvana.

From Vung Tau, a 13-hour boat trip due south links the mainland with the **Con Dao** ⓴, an archipelago comprised of 14 islands that boast unspoiled beaches, coconut groves, corals and clear waters. Sea turtles laboriously make their way onto the beaches to lay their eggs. Between February and July they are captured for their shells.

Dense virgin forest, rich in precious woods, covers the islands' interiors. Today's image of unspoiled natural beauty is a far cry from that of the dreaded penitentiary of **Poulo Condore** (Devil's Island), run by the French on the main island of **Con Son** for almost a century and later by the South Vietnamese regime as a prison for communist sympathisers. Reminders of the island's less attractive past are present in the remains of the penal colony. The few residents on the island today raise peanuts and teakwood, amongst other crops, dive for pearls, or fish the local waters. ❑

BELOW: chairs for hire, Vung Tau.
RIGHT: interior of the White Villa.

MEKONG DELTA

Map on pages 266–7

Cuu Long, the river of nine dragons and known in the West as the Mekong, is one of the world's mightiest rivers. In the south, the river enriches and nourishes the land as it enters the ocean

The Mekong's Vietnamese name, **Cuu Long**, means Nine Dragons, as the river branches into nine mouths that empty into the sea. The vast delta of the Cuu Long (Mekong River) is formed by the alluvium deposited by the multiple arms and tributaries of the river. The river descends from its source high in the Tibetan plateau and follows a 4,500-km (2,800-mile) course through China, Burma (Myanmar), Laos, Thailand, Cambodia and southern Vietnam before emptying into the South China Sea.

The delta, an ancient Khmer territory, was an area of marshlands and forest before the first European colonisers arrived by sea in the 16th century. During the rule of the Nguyen lords (1802–1945), great expanses of marshlands were reclaimed and a network of small canals was built. By the end of the 18th century, two huge canals – the Thai Hoa, which linked Rach Gia and Long Xuyen, and the Vinh Te, linking Chau Doc and Ha Tien – were in use. The region is still populated by a large percentage of Khmer, Chinese and Chams, as well as Vietnamese. Among them are followers of diverse religions, including Buddhism, Catholicism, Islam and sects of Cao Dai and Hoa Hao.

The delta's 12 provinces – Long An, Dong Thap, An Giang, Kien Giang, Tien Giang, Ben Tre, Vinh Long, Tra Vinh, Can Tho, Soc Trang, Bac Lieu and Ca Mau – are served by more than 100 ferries and an adequate road network. The condition of the roads vary from paved highways serving the larger cities to pothole-riddled mud tracks in rural areas. The comprehensive waterway network carries a busy and greatly varied flow of traffic. Unless travelling by river, travel is slow and less than methodical. However, crossing the river at its main points can take hours, as there are no bridges and waiting for a ferry can be time-consuming.

The region has greatly recovered from the ravages of the chemical defoliants and bombs dropped on it during the 1960s. The markets in the region are abundantly supplied with fish and a variety of produce yielded by the delta's rich alluvial soil: rice, sesame, peanuts, cashews, pineapples, pumpkins, tangerines, melons, cabbages, dragon fruits and durians. (For fruit lovers, April is a good month to visit and sample the rich variety of fruits in season.) The area is known as Vietnam's bread basket, or more aptly, rice bowl, because the region produces much of the country's rice. In many places there are three full harvests during the year.

That increasing modernisation will change life in the delta is a fact. But visitors to the region will still find a way of life that is as closely tied to the laws and moods of nature, or in this case, of the Mekong, as it is to the region's rich if turbulent history.

PRECEDING PAGES: Can Tho floating market. **LEFT:** unloading boat at rice factory. **BELOW:** rice harvest.

Delta rice field.

Southward from Ho Chi Minh

The province of Long An, which stretches from the Cambodian border in the west straight across the country to the east coast, is more of historical than scenic significance. It was here, at **Nhat Tao** on the Song Vam Co Dong, that the French battleship *l'Espérance* was completely burnt by the Vietnamese, led by national hero Nguyen Trung Truc in 1861. This decisive battle cost the life of everyone on board and forced the French out of the south, at least temporarily.

The northern part of Long An is slightly hilly, although most of the province occupies a level plain a few metres above sea level. The Vam Co Dong, Vam Co Tay and Sai Gon rivers flow through the province, bringing rich alluvial silt to the extensive rice fields. Travellers may notice the occasional burial tomb in the rice fields. Many farmers believe that burying the dead on home soil helps discourage outsiders from buying their land. The town of **Go Den** in the southern part of the province is famous for producing the best rice wine in the Mekong Delta.

South from Ho Chi Minh on Highway 1, Tien Giang Province represents one of the country's main rice-growing areas. Land reclamation began in this extremely fertile region during the 17th century. This ancient Khmer territory was colonised by the Vietnamese towards the end of the 17th century, then taken over by the French in 1861. Major rivers such as the Tien, Go Cong, Ca Han and Bao Dinh flow through the province. Combined with the extensive canal network, these provide excellent waterway access to Ho Chi Minh and Phnom Penh. The sites of Rach Gam and Xaoi Mut, by the Song Tien, are where the peasant hero Nguyen Hue won his first victory in an historic river battle that claimed the lives of 40,000 Siamese troops in 1785.

BELOW: rambutan vendor, and floating market.

My Tho ㉑, the provincial capital with a population of 100,000, lies on the left bank of the **Song My Tho**, the northernmost branch of the Mekong. Founded in 1680 by political refugees from Taiwan, the city is easily reached from Ho Chi Minh, 70 km (40 miles) away, by a one-and-a-half-hour bus journey or six-hour trip by river ferry. The old Saigon–My Tho railway, the earliest built in Indochina in 1883, was last used in 1958, but the province has a more-than-adequate road network.

The busy central market is located on Trung Trac and Nguyen Hue streets and is closed to vehicles.The Catholic church here was built at the end of the 19th century, and there is still a large Catholic congregation numbering more than 7,000 followers. The **Vinh Trang**, the largest pagoda in the province, is an eclectic mix of French, Chinese, Vietnamese, and Khmer architectural styles. A dozen or so monks live here, performing charitable works in the area.

From My Tho, a boat can be taken to one of the nearby islands, an interesting and enjoyable excursion. **Con Phung**, or Phoenix Island, lies in the Song Tien Giang a few kilometres from My Tho and can be reached by hired boat. Other islands in the Tien Giang include Con Qui (Turtle Island), Con Lan (Unicorn Island), visited for its extensive fruit gardens, and Con Long (Dragon Island).

Con Phung was the home of the Coconut Monk, Ong Dao Dua, a charismatic character who founded a religion known as Tinh Do Cu Si, a synthesis of Buddhism and Christianity, with Jesus, Buddha and the Virgin Mary forming a challenging triumvirate. Born Nguyen Thanh Nam in 1909, the future Coconut Monk studied physics and chemistry in France between 1928 and 1935 before returning to Vietnam, where he married and had a daughter. In 1943, he left his family to live the life of a monk and for three years is said to have sat on a

Map on pages 266–7

BELOW: Vinh Trang pagoda, near Vinh Long.

Bonsai in Vinh Long.

BELOW: snakes in alcohol are said to assure virility.

stone slab beneath a flag pole meditating and eating only coconuts. His philosophy advocated peaceful means of reunifying his country.

This concept did not go down at all well with the South Vietnamese governments, in whose prisons he was a frequent guest. During the Vietnam War, the Coconut Monk gained many new followers, a number of whom were reportedly trying to avoid conscription. He died in 1990, a prisoner of the communist regime that arrested him for anti-government activities. After his arrest, his band of followers dispersed. The island boasts the remnants of a bizarre open-air sanctuary where the Coconut Monk addressed his following. Today, its faded dragon-entwined columns, multi-tiered tower with a great metal globe atop, and Apollo rocket set stand forlorn and neglected and are not worth the entrance fee required.

Twelve km (7 miles) to the west of My Tho is a snake farm at **Dong Tam**, where the snakes yield a variety of medical substances used in traditional medicines. Their flesh is believed to be an effective remedy against a number of ailments ranging from mental disorders to rheumatism and paralysis. Snake gall combined with other drugs is used to treat coughs and migraine. An excellent alcoholic tonic is obtained by steeping three special varieties of snake in alcohol. Some men also believe snake to be a virility enhancer.

Despite My Tho's attractions, it must be said that the Tien Giang People's Committee (the local communists) is reputedly one of the most corrupt in Vietnam, with a stranglehold on all things connected with tourism. The result is that travellers have to contend with high prices and poor facilities and service. Consequently, many tourists either avoid My Tho entirely or visit as part an organised day-tour from Ho Chi Minh.

To the south, Ben Tre Province lies between the My Tho and Co Chien rivers. More coconut palms are grown here than in any other province in the country, contending for agricultural space with the province's extensive rice fields. The provincial capital, **Ben Tre** ㉒, is located on the Ham Luong tributary. The temple of **Nguyen Dinh Chieu** here is dedicated to a poet of the 19th century who was born in nearby Ba Tri.

A boat trip along the Bai Lai–Ham Luong waterway provides an opportunity to become better acquainted with everyday life on the river. Smaller canals lead to bee farms and fruit orchards. Many species of birds can be seen in the bird sanctuary of **Cu Lao Dat**, which covers 30 hectares (74 acres) of forest in the small village of **An Hiep**. Off the main roads, quiet Ben Tre sees few visitors.

West of Ben Tre Province, Vinh Long Province is crisscrossed by canals and has an elevation of just 2 metres (6 ft 4ins) above sea level. Outside the provincial capital, also named **Vinh Long** ㉓, is an interesting pagoda, the Confucian **Van Thanh Mieu**. Boats leave from in front of the Cuu Long Hotel for the An Binh and Binh Hoa Phuoc islands, located in the middle of the Song Tien. The trip is a treat for fruit lovers, as it takes in villages whose gardens and orchards produce a great variety of seasonal fruit such as mangoes, mandarins, rambutans and longans. Visitors can also stroll through well-tended bonsai gardens or stay overnight with local families on the islands.

Southeast of Vinh Long, Tra Vinh Province is bordered by the Tien and Hau rivers. Off the beaten tourist path, Tra Vinh is home to about 300,000 ethnic Khmers. Mostly farmers, these Khmers speak both Khmer and Vietnamese. Top sights in and around the capital of **Tra Vinh** ㉔ include **Ho Ba Om** (Ba Om Lake), where a number of important Khmer festivals are celebrated, and **Chua**

Map on pages 266–7

"It became necessary to destroy the town in order to save it".
— U.S. OFFICER ABOUT THE U.S. BOMBING OF BEN TRE DURING THE TET OFFENSIVE, 1968

BELOW: flower seller in boat.

Co (Stork Pagoda), a Khmer pagoda that shelters hundreds of real storks.

Bordering Cambodia in the north, Dong Thap Province is one of the three provinces lying in the marshy area known as **Dong Thap Muoi**, or the Plain of Reeds. The province takes its name from the 10-storey Thap Muoi tower built long ago in the commune of An Phong. The tower, no longer standing, was used as a lookout by the resistance forces against the French.

The province was formerly inhabited by the ancient Phu Nam kingdom and later the Chan Lap civilisation, a people who in the 1700s exchanged the area of Sa Dec with Vietnam for military aid that restored order to the area. The Chan Lap were subsequently wiped out and assimilated by the Vietnamese, and today the area is populated primarily by people of Chinese, Khmer, Cham and Thai origin.

Interesting sights around the provincial capital **Cao Lanh** ㉕ include several bird sanctuaries and **Rung Tram**, a forest that harboured an underground Viet Cong camp, **Xeo Quit**, during the war. **Sa Dec**, the former provincial capital, is famous for its many nurseries and flower gardens that cultivate roses.

Can Tho ㉖, the capital of Can Tho Province, is the largest and most modern city in the Delta and the only one with a university. This important commercial centre and river port, with a population of 200,000, lies on the banks of the Song Hau. Can Tho's university, established in 1966, is involved in valuable agricultural research and development that has contributed substantially to improving production and pest control.

As the hub of the Mekong Delta, Can Tho is a booming city. While it has a friendly feel about it, there is not a great deal of sightseeing to be done here. The animated Can Tho market, which spreads out along Hai Ba Trung, with its

BELOW: village near Can Tho.

main building at the intersection of Hai Ba Trung and Nam Ky Khoi Nghia streets, boasts the largest fruit market in the Delta region. Several restaurants along the waterfront serve specialities of the region: frog, turtle, snake and fish.

Of greater interest are boat trips on the Song Hau. Off the main waterways, flimsy bamboo bridges stretch across the smaller canals. These were built for the lighter and more agile Vietnamese and are to be avoided or else negotiated with extreme care unless one wants to end up in the canal, an all-too-easy possibility. At the lively Cai Rang floating market, all manner of boats and sampans gather, their occupants busily engaged in buying or selling a wide variety of fruit, fish and vegetables.

To the west, An Giang Province borders the Cambodian province of Takeo. This border remains a somewhat politically sensitive area. Here, the Mekong enters the province and splits into two branches, forming the Tien and Hau rivers, which every year deposit millions of cubic metres of alluvium in the adjacent areas. This prosperous region, rich in natural resources and fertile land, produces many varieties of fruit trees and crops of soya bean, tobacco, groundnut and mulberry.

Long Xuyen, the provincial capital located in the east of the province, has a population of about 120,000 people. Its Catholic church, built between 1966 and 1973, can seat 1,000 and is the largest in the Delta. On the northern outskirts of town, an area famous for its incense production, clusters of fuchsia and saffron joss sticks line the roadside, drying in the sun. **Chau Doc** ㉗, not far from the Cambodian border, is situated on the right bank of the **Song Hau Giang**. Chau Doc has a population of 65,000. The **Dinh Than Chau Phu** in the township was built in 1926. In this temple, the locals worship Thai Ngoc Hau, the man

Map on pages 266–7

BELOW: floating market on the Han River, Can Tho.

At the water market.

responsible for the nearby Chau Doc canal, which opens the frontier between Cambodia and Vietnam. He held a high official rank under the Nguyen lords and then later during the Nguyen dynasty.

From the Chau Giang terminal, a ferry crosses the Hau. On the other side is the **Chau Giang Mosque**, which serves the district's Muslim Cham community. Numbering around 20,000 people in the Chau Doc area, many Chams live in stilt houses on the water and make their living from fishing and weaving. From here, travellers can pick up a lift to Tan Chau district, famous throughout southern Vietnam for its silk industry and prosperity. The market there offers many imported goods from Thailand, which are brought into the country through Cambodia.

Chau Doc is also renowned for its floating villages. Living in houses built on empty metal tanks or small boats, many villagers survive on and often prosper from fishing. Metal nets under the houses facilitate the capture of large quantities of fish. Although their living conditions may not reflect it, several fishing families in the area are reputed to be millionaires.

Some 4 km (2½ miles) from Chau Doc is **Nui Sam**, a mountain so named because the surrounding area was once the home to many king crabs, called *sam* in Vietnamese. At 230 metres (755 ft) high, this beautiful site has many Buddhist and Daoist shrines built into the hillside.

Climbing up the south side of the mountain, visitors will find spectacular views of the surrounding countryside greeting them at the summit. On a clear day, even Cambodia is visible. A military outpost at the summit still houses a few soldiers, more interested nowadays in their badminton games than in Khmer Rouge incursions, given that the Khmer Rouge army collapsed in the late 1990s.

BELOW: hill of Chau Doc, with Cambodia in the distance.

On festival days, vendors and fortune-tellers turn out in force to greet arriving worshippers. At the foot of the mountain, the tomb of Thoai Ngoc Hau holds his remains plus those of his two wives. Also buried here are some of the workers who died during the construction of the Chau Doc canal.

Map on pages 266–7

Sharing the base of the mountain are the Indian-style **Tay An**, a pagoda that dates from 1847 and is famous for its many finely carved religious figures, and **Mieu Ba Chua Xu** (Temple of Lady Chua Xu), where a granite statue of Lady Chua Xu is worshipped. Bales of colourful cloth donated by worshippers from Cho Lon are stored here.

This temple is reputed to be the richest temple in Vietnam – worshippers including many Chinese from Ho Chi Minh City, Hong Kong and Taiwan flock here bearing money and gifts. Every year on the 22nd day of the fourth lunar month, a large procession of religious followers begins a week-long series of festivities and ceremonies to celebrate their pilgrimage. One special ritual involves the washing of Lady Chua Xu's statue by three virgins. Thus made holy, the bath water is then dispensed to the waiting crowds.

Lady Chua Xu is in fact a statue of stone, reputedly discovered on the slopes of Nui Sam some time during the 19th century.

About 40 km (25 miles) west of Chau Doc lies Vietnam's killing fields, **Ba Chuc**. In April 1978, Khmer Rouge forces massacred 3,157 civilians in the commune of Ba Chuc. Many of the victims were tortured to death. A pagoda built in 1991 contains the skulls and bones of 1,155 victims, and on display in the temple are some graphic photos depicting the aftermath of the slaughter. Due to the poor condition of the roads, few visitors make it out here, even though a visit is well worthwhile, though not for the faint of heart.

Phu Tan, a village in the north of the province, is the birth place of Huynh Phu So, founder of the Hoa Hao religious sect. Its male followers are easily

BELOW: pagoda at Tay An.

identified by their long beards and equally long hair tied into a bun. Adhering to simplicity, Hoa Hao followers reject the need for altars, temples, or any other intermediaries between them and a supreme deity.

Ancient civilisation

Oc Eo, ringed by a protective moat, has been linked to the extensive trade that plied between Asia and Europe, as evidenced by the ancient Roman, Egyptian, Indian, Persian, and Chinese artefacts uncovered at the site.

Some 40 km (25 miles) southwest of Long Xuyen, in the hilly area of Ba The, are the ruins of **Oc Eo** ㉘, which was a major trading port during the first centuries AD. Oc Eo lay submerged for centuries until it was rediscovered in the 1940s. Remnants of architectural structures and other finds made by researchers here indicate that it was a city closely linked with the ancient Chinese kingdom of Phu Nam (Funan), which dates back to the 1st century AD and reached its peak in about the 5th century.

Most of what we know about this ancient civilisation – gleaned from excavations at Oc Eo – reveals evidence of contact with the Roman Empire, Persia, China, Thailand, Malaysia and Indonesia; in addition, there are the written accounts of Chinese travellers and emissaries referring to the site. Oc Eo's elaborate and intricate canal system was used not only for irrigation but also for transportation.

It is difficult but possible to visit the ruins themselves; however, during the rainy season the area tends to be flooded and is impossible to visit, as the roads, such as they are, are impassable.

Not far from here are the long irrigation canals of the district of Tri Ton, where a significant percentage of the population is now Khmer, including the thousands of refugees who poured into the area during the late 1970s as they fled Pol Pot's Khmer Rouge forces in Cambodia.

BELOW: Khmer Buddhist monk.

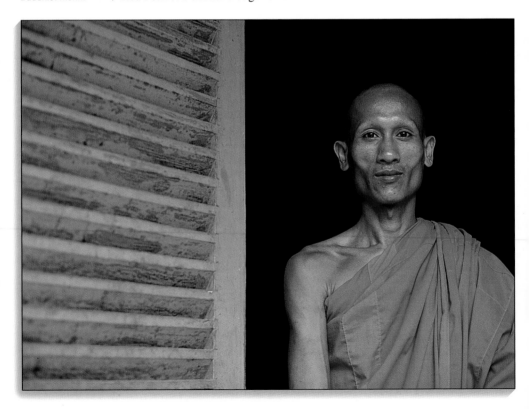

Into the deep south

Kien Giang Province, in the southwest of the Delta, shares a common border in the northwest with Cambodia and in the west is washed by waters from the Gulf of Thailand. Forests, plains, offshore islands and a 200 km- (125 mile-) long coastline contribute to Kien Giang's rich scenic diversity.

Map on pages 266–7

The journey up the coast begins in the provincial capital, **Rach Gia** ㉙, an active fishing port with a population of around 150,000. It is bordered by marshlands, much of which have been drained for rice cultivation.

The town has quite a number of interesting temples and pagodas. The large Khmer **Chua Phat Lon** (Big Buddha Pagoda) was established about two centuries ago. **Hoi Tuong Te Nguoi Hoa** (Ong Bac De), on Nguyen Du in the town centre, was built by the local Chinese community over a century ago. The central altar is occupied by a statue of Ong Bac De, the reincarnation of the Jade Emperor of Heaven. To his left is Ong Gon, the guardian spirit of happiness and virtue, and on his right is Quan Cong.

Nguyen Trung Truc, a temple at 18 Nguyen Cong Tru, is dedicated to Nguyen Trung Truc, who led the resistance campaign against the French during the 1860s, including the attack on the French ship *l'Espérance*. Although the French repeatedly tried to capture him, it wasn't until 1868 that they succeeded, after taking his mother and a number of civilians hostage. Truc eventually gave himself up and was executed by the French in the Rach Gia marketplace. Many Vietnamese consider this brave nationalist and pious son to be a deity, and worshippers from all over the Mekong Delta flock to this temple annually to observe the anniversary of his death in October.

Rach Gia is well known for its seafood, and it has a good selection of

BELOW: labourer in a Delta rice paddy.

restaurants serving both Chinese and Vietnamese food, as well as specialities such as eel, turtle, snake, frog legs, deer and cuttlefish.

The road from Rach Gia to the town of Ha Tien in the northwest corner of the province is rather rough, but it passes many small farms and villages and provides an interesting look at life on the canal. About 80 km (50 miles) from Rach Gia and 20 km (12 miles) from Ha Tien, a detour off the main road leads to the seaside town of **Hon Chong** ㉚. Unlike much of the pancake-flat Mekong Delta, this area is studded with impressive, towering limestone formations. Unfortunately, as a prime source of quality limestone for the cement factories near Hon Chong, increasingly these mountains are being blasted with dynamite and denuded, if not levelled entirely.

For now, however, Hon Chong remains relatively peaceful and beautiful. The best beach in the area is **Bai Duong**, which takes its name from the *duong* (casuarina) trees growing beside it. Its white, clear water and picturesque surroundings make it an ideal spot to break the journey with a swim. Looking out to sea, you will see the famous Father and Son Rocks, whose grottoes are a favourite haunt of sea swallows.

Right next to the beach is the **Chua Hang** (Grotto Pagoda). The grotto is entered from behind the altar of the pagoda, which is set back into the base of the hill. The grotto's thick stalactites are hollow and give off a bell-like resonance when tapped (lightly, please). Inside the grotto is a plaster statue of the goddess of mercy, Quan Am.

About 25 km (15 miles) from Ha Tien is the **Hang Tien** (Coin Grotto), which takes its name from the zinc coins found buried within it by Nguyen Anh – the future Emperor Gia Long – and his troops, who camped here while battling

BELOW: successful fisherman.

the Tay Son rebels. About 17 km (10 miles) from Ha Tien and 3 km (2 miles) from the main road is **Hang Mo So**. During the wet season, this grotto is accessible only by boat, but for the rest of the year it can be reached on foot. A torch and a local guide will come in handy when exploring the labyrinth of tunnels beyond the three main caverns.

A floating toll bridge completes the last watery stretch of the journey to **Ha Tien ㉛**. Nestling in a cove formed by the **Song Gian Thang**, Ha Tien has a population of 85,000 and is located only about 10 km (6 miles) from the Cambodian border. This charming town of Chinese origin was founded around 1670 by Mac Cuu, a Chinese immigrant from Guangzhou (Canton) who arrived here after the fall of the Ming dynasty in 1644. He refused to serve the Manchu rulers and instead explored the South Seas with his men. After procuring the agreement of the Cambodian kings and the Vietnamese Nguyen lords, he and his men installed themselves at Ha Tien, transforming it in no time into a prosperous principality equipped with a maritime port.

In 1714, Ha Tien was given to Nguyen Phuc Chu, a lord from Hue, who compensated Mac Cuu with the title *generalissimo* of Ha Tien. The principality prospered with the revenue accumulated from a gambling house and a tin mine. The governor used the tin to make coins for commercial exchanges. His only son, Mac Thien Tu, continued his father's work in improving administration and thus social and economic development. He organised an army equal to the task of repelling the Cambodian and Siamese invasions, and also founded an academy of arts, the Chieu Anh Cac (Pavilion of Quintessential Welcome).

Ha Tien's natural beauty attracts many visitors. To the east of Ha Tien, scenic **Ho Dong** (East Lake) greets the arriving visitor. The town has several temples

Map on pages 266–7

TIP

With its reasonably flat terrain, the countryside around Ha Tien lends itself nearly perfectly to bicycle touring. Several of the hotels in Ha Tien rent bicycles at modest rates by the day.

BELOW: beach at Binh An.

TIP

The best time to visit the delta is between January and March, when temperatures are from 22–34°C (72–93°F). From May onward, the rainfall and humidity increase. During the wettest months – July to October – some provinces are flooded and travel restricted.

dedicated to the Mac family and an even greater number of tombs that rest on the eastern flank of **Binh San**. These are built of bricks and contain the remains of both Mac Cuu and his relatives. His own tomb, built in 1809, is the largest and is decorated with finely carved figures of the traditional Blue Dragon and White Tiger.

Tam Bao, a pagoda at 328 Phuong Thanh, was founded by Mac Cuu in 1730. A statue of Quan Am atop a lotus stands in front of the pagoda. Nearby is the **Phu Dung**, a pagoda founded by Mac Cuu's second wife, Nguyen Thi Xuan, in 1750. Her tomb is built on the hillside behind the pagoda's main hall. The pagoda contains some interesting statues. In the centre of the main hall is one of the newborn Sakyamuni Buddha, in the embrace of nine dragons; on the main dais in a glass case is a bronze Chinese Buddha.

Ha Tien does a lively trade in items handcrafted from the shells of sea turtles. These creatures are domestically reared in pools along the coastline. It is also famous for its seafood and black pepper.

There are a number of beaches around Ha Tien that are popular with locals, such as Mui Nai, Bai No and Bai Bang. Don't expect pristine white sand or crystalline turquoise waters, however. The beaches are also full of pushy vendors, which hardly makes for a quiet, relaxing time.

One of the main attractions located a few kilometres from town on Mac Tu Hoang is **Thach Dong Thon Van**, the Grotto That Swallows the Clouds. The grotto shelters a Buddhist sanctuary and funerary tablets; altars to Quan Am and to Ngoc Hoang, the Jade Emperor of Heaven, are contained in several of its chambers. Exploring the grotto can yield breathtaking views of the surrounding rice fields and smaller offshore islands. Near the grotto is a mass grave where

BELOW: at Mac Cuu temple, Ha Tien.

130 people, victims of a massacre by Pol Pot's Khmer Rouge troops in 1978, are buried. To the left of the sanctuary's entrance is a stele known as Bia Cam Thu – the stele of hatred – that commemorates the victims.

The island of **Hon Giang** lies about 15 km (9 miles) off the coast of Ha Tien and can be reached by boat. It has a lovely and quite secluded beach.

A beautiful forested archipelago known as **Dao Phu Quoc** consists of 16 islands about 40 km (25 miles) west of Ha Tien. Phu Quoc, the largest island, is 50 km (30 miles) long, with a population of about 60,000 and covering an area of 1,300 sq. km (500 sq. miles).

The future Emperor Gia Long was sheltered here from the Tay Son rebels by the French missionary Pigneau de Behaine, who himself had used the island as a base between the 1760s and 1780s. The French later used the island as a prison. Today, Phu Quoc remains relatively undeveloped and is renowned for its bountiful fishing grounds, its black-pepper trees and its quality *nuoc mam* (fish sauce) production.

The deep south

About 35 km (20 miles) southeast of Can Tho is Soc Trang Province. About 300,000 Khmer people live here. Its capital **Soc Trang** ㉜ has a number of interesting Khmer temples and pagodas.

Of note is the striking **Kh'leng**. Originally built more than 400 years ago, this pagoda was rebuilt in 1907. Typical of Khmer pagodas, this one is richly decorated on the outside with carved griffins, snakes and statues of dancing maidens. Inside, a gilded bronze statue of Sakyamuni, flanked by marble statues of two of his first disciples, presides over the main altar. There are about two

Map on pages 266–7

BELOW: Grotto That Swallows the Clouds.

VIET CONG

A southern guerrilla force supported by Ha Noi that fought against the former South Vietnam and United States, the Viet Cong had its roots in 1950s-era opposition to the South Vietnam government of Pres. Ngo Dinh Diem. The name "Viet Cong" was derived from Viet Nam Cong San (Vietnamese Communists), perhaps first used by Diem as a slight to the rebels.

Initially a coalition of government opponents (including insurgent elements of the Cao Dai sect), anti-Diem opposition was later helped by members of the southern elements of the Viet Minh, a nationalist group from the north. The resulting Viet Cong became the military arm of the National Liberation Front (NLF) in 1960.

From the 1960s onward, most members of the Viet Cong were southern Vietnamese; training and support was provided by North Vietnamese Army soldiers from the north. The Viet Cong's military strength and efficacy faltered considerably from massive losses during the 1968 Tet Offensive. Afterwards, North Vietnamese troops supplanted the Viet Cong in military activity in the south.

Operating simply and in small units, for the most part the Viet Cong operated in rural areas, using the guerrilla techniques of ambush, sabotage, and terrorism.

Map on pages 266–7

dozen monks in residence and 170 monks attending the Buddhist college on the premises. Also here is a 25 metre- (80 ft-) long *ghe ngo*, or long-boat. During the Oc Om Boc Festival – on the 15th day of the 10th lunar month – the Khmer community turns out to watch long-boat races on the Soc Trang river. Opposite the pagoda is a Khmer museum.

Not far from here on 68 Mau Than is the fascinating **Chua Dat Set**, built in 1906. Made of clay, this Chinese pagoda houses statues and figurines that are also made of clay. An intricately sculpted Bao Thap tower is remarkable for having a little Buddha figurine on every lotus petal. Also here are six giant paraffin candles, two of which have been burning since 1970 when they were first made.

On the outskirts of town is **Chua Doi**, or the Bat Pagoda. Less ornate than the Kh'leng pagoda, this Khmer temple is more famous for the several thousand screeching fruit bats residing in its gardens. It is said that while these bats may attack the fruit trees in other orchards, they know not to eat from the trees that shelter them. Colourful murals depicting scenes from Buddha's life adorn the inside of the temple.

As the newest province in Vietnam, Bac Lieu was carved from the former Minh Hai Province in 1997. During French rule, the area saw a rise in the number of wealthy landlords. Much of the land was confiscated by the government after 1978, although it was eventually returned in the mid-1980s. Nevertheless, a majority of the population here is still landless and quite poor, and many of the locals make a living through fishing. **Bac Lieu** ㉝ today is mostly a rest-stop for travellers on their way to Ca Mau.

The southernmost province of Vietnam, the peninsula of Ca Mau is not best described as a tourist destination. **Ca Mau** ㉞, the largest town, lies 180 km (110 miles) south of Can Tho on the Song Gan Hao, in the heart of an immense, submerged plain covered in mangroves and rich in fishing.

Ca Mau marks the extreme southernmost tip of Vietnam. It is a shifting tip and peninsula, however, as the continual deposit of silt from the Mekong and its tributaries is actually extending the shoreline by up to 80 metres (260 ft) a year. Moreover, the average elevation of the Ca Mau peninsula is just 2 metres (6 ft 7 ins) above sea level.

Until World War II, most of the peninsula lacked any vehicular roads at all. During the French years following World War II, the peninsula was held by the Viet Minh, and during the Vietnam War with the Americans, it was a refuge and base of operations for the Viet Cong guerrillas.

The mangrove forest at **U Minh**, just outside of Ca Mau and the largest of its kind in the world outside of the Amazon Basin, was seriously damaged by defoliants dropped by the Americans during the Vietnam War. Still, the dense and swampy undergrowth is home to numerous varieties of venomous snakes, leeches, unidentifiable things and mosquitoes. Locals catch the snakes and breed them, selling them for pharmaceutical products and for food. Other local delicacies are rats and tortoises. ❑

BELOW: Muslim men of the south.
RIGHT: boats at Ben Tre.

INSIGHT GUIDES
Travel Tips

Insight FlexiMaps

Maps in Insight Guides are tailored to complement the text. But when you're on the road you sometimes need the big picture that only a large-scale map can provide. This new range of durable Insight Fleximaps has been designed to meet just that need.

Detailed, clear cartography
makes the comprehensive route and city maps easy to follow, highlights all the major tourist sites and provides valuable motoring information plus a full index.

Informative and easy to use
with additional text and photographs covering a destination's top 10 essential sites, plus useful addresses, facts about the destination and handy tips on getting around.

Laminated finish
allows you to mark your route on the map using a non-permanent marker pen, and wipe it off. It makes the maps more durable and easier to fold than traditional maps.

The world's most popular destinations
are covered by the 125 titles in the series – and new destinations are being added all the time. They include Alaska, Amsterdam, Bangkok, Barbados, Beijing, Brussels, Dallas/Fort Worth, Florence, Hong Kong, Ireland, Madrid, New York, Orlando, Peru, Prague, Rio, Rome, San Francisco, Sydney, Thailand, Turkey, Venice, and Vienna.

INSIGHT GUIDES
The world's largest collection of visual travel guides

CONTENTS

Getting Acquainted

Background 338
The Economy 338
Government 338

Planning the Trip

What to Wear 339
Electricity...........................339
What to Bring.....................339
Entry Regulations................339
Health 341
Money Matters....................341
Public Holidays 342

Practical Tips

Getting There 343
Business Hours 344
Postal Services 345
Telecommunications 345
Doing Business 345
Media 346
Emergencies......................346
Tourist Information 348
Airlines/Government Offices ..349
Embassies 350
Online in Hanoi...................350

Getting Around

Travel Options 351
Transport Hubs...................353

Where to Stay

Hotel Listings.....................355

Eating Out

General..............................362
Where to Eat......................363

Attractions

Museums...........................365

Festivals

Traditional & Religious
Festivals 367

Shopping

What to Buy........................368
Where to Buy 369

Language

General..............................370

Further Reading

General..............................371

Getting Acquainted

Background

Name: Socialist Republic of Vietnam.

Area: 329,556 square km (127,242 sq miles), half the size of Texas or slightly larger than Italy.

Situation: Vietnam forms the eastern edge – meeting the South China Sea – of the area formerly called Indochina. Due north is China. On the country's western border are Laos and Cambodia. Directly east, across the South China Sea, are the Philippines.

Population: Approaching 80 million.

Language: Although numerous hill-tribe languages pepper the country, Vietnamese is the national language. Amongst older people, French is sometimes spoken. In the south, especially, English is quite widely spoken.

Religion: Mahayana Buddhism predominates. Catholicism is common, along with elements of Daoism, Confucianism, Hinduism and Islam.

Time Zones: Vietnam, like Laos, Cambodia and Thailand, is +7 hours GMT. The sun sets relatively early, around 5.30pm in winter and 8pm in summer in the north.

Currency: Vietnamese *dong*.

Weights & Measures: Vietnam employs the metric system. One kilometre is equal to 0.6 miles; one metre is equal to 3.3 feet; one kilogram is equal to 2.2 pounds; one litre is equal to 0.3 US gallons or 0.2 imperial gallons. To convert Celsius to Fahrenheit, multiply by 1.8 and add 32; to convert Fahrenheit to Celsius, subtract 32 and multiply by 0.56.

Literacy: Estimated at 92 percent.

Life Expectancy: 65 years.

The Economy

Vietnam is essentially an agricultural country, with rice cultivation accounting for 45 percent of the GNP and employing 70 percent of the population. Other major crops include tea, coffee, maize, bananas, manioc, cotton, tobacco, coconut and rubber.

Industry represents over 30 percent of the country's GNP and 11 percent of the active population. Electricity, steel, cement, cotton fabrics, fish sauce, sea fish, wood, paper, and the growing petroleum exploration and production industry represent Vietnam's major areas of industrial production.

Ho Chi Minh City now boasts a small oil refinery and has become Vietnam's economic capital, accounting for 30 percent of national industrial production.

The country's standard of living ranks amongst the lowest in the world. Despite a protracted effort to revive the rural economy, disastrous economic policies, coupled with the drain of more than 50 percent of the country's budget on supporting its occupation forces in Cambodia and Laos, have had devastating effects on Vietnam's economy. In an effort to revive the ailing economy the country has recently opened its doors to encourage foreign investment and tourism, while further reform policies have been geared to re-establish a market economy and encourage production in the private sector, agriculture and light industry.

Recently there has been an infusion of consumer goods, many of them smuggled across the border from China.

In the cities, particularly Ho Chi Minh City and Hanoi, there is a burgeoning consumerism reflected in the number of motorcycles, electronics, Western clothes and music for sale. In the two cities, an estimated 95 percent of households now own TVs. Nationwide, about half the population regularly watches TV (although in the countryside most people cannot afford such a luxury).

Government

Vietnam is a socialist republic ruled by the Vietnamese Communist Party since the fall of Saigon in 1975, and the country's subsequent imposed reunification in 1976. Vietnam's domestic policy is shaped primarily by the party and its Secretary General. The Prime Minister presides over drafting of laws and day-to-day governing. The President oversees state policy, the military and internal police apparatus.

The government is nominated by the National Assembly, proposed by the party and theoretically elected by the people. Although the National Assembly has in the past been something of a rubber-stamp operation, recently it has become more aggressive in challenging government functions, implementing laws, debating policy, and holding government ministers accountable.

The republic is divided into 53 administrative areas: three cities – Hanoi, Ho Chi Minh City and Hai Phong – and 50 provinces. Traditionally provincial officials maintain some level of independence in implementing state policy. Ostensibly there are elections at the local level for provincial officials. However, the candidates are all screened and are members of the Communist Party. Vietnam has generally avoided major upheavals within its power structure. When high-level officials retire, they still maintain important advisory roles.

If there is any crisis in leadership in Vietnam today, it is that there does not appear to be a younger generation of leaders ready to step in and take the reins of power. Thus there is considerable speculation that the current leadership will most likely continue in their positions instead of retiring as was earlier expected.

Party leaders emphasise that there is no room for political pluralism at this point and that the Communist Party will maintain its hold on power.

Planning the Trip

What to Wear

The main thing to consider is the weather, as it can be freezing cold in the mountainous north and at the same time hot and humid on the central coast. If you are travelling in the north or the Central Highlands during the winter months definitely bring jeans and a warm coat or sweater. It seems that it is always raining somewhere in Vietnam, so lightweight rain gear is essential.

In the hot months, dress cool but conservative. Many Vietnamese cannot understand why foreigners insist on wearing shorts, tank tops and sleeveless T-shirts when they have the money to dress well. For the Vietnamese, appearance is very important, so if you are dealing with an official of any rank make sure you are dressed appropriately.

Electricity

The voltage in the cities and towns is generally 220V, 50 cycles, but sometimes 110V in the rural areas. Electric sockets are standard European or American. It is a good idea to bring adapter plugs in case your plugs do not fit the sockets, which are sometimes two round pins, other times three pins. If you do not have the correct size plug, however, it is easy to buy an adaptor.

If you bring a computer to Vietnam, you must use a surge suppressor to protect your circuits. Large Taiwanese voltage regulators can be bought at computer stores in Vietnam to give greater protection.

Entry Regulations

VISAS & PASSPORTS

It used to be incredibly difficult for independent travellers to gain entry to Vietnam. Today, it is fairly straightforward to get a visa. It is possible to get a tourist visa for about US$60 in five to ten working days from travel agents in Bangkok and Hong Kong. Bangkok is definitely the best place in Asia to pick up a visa and many travel agents offer attractive round-trip flight and visa packages.

Other types of visas available include business, press, family visit and official visit. To enter Vietnam on business, you must contact your Vietnamese sponsor, who will then submit an application and letter to the embassy you are applying to. This process can often take weeks, so make sure you get a head start.

It is also wise to obtain a visa well in advance because Vietnamese embassies in the past have abruptly suspended issuing visas for short periods of time due to domestic political reasons. The most recent instance was in the summer of 1998, when visas were suspended to halt foreigners from attending inaugural ceremonies marking year-long celebrations at the Catholic pilgrimage site, La Vang. Similar restrictions were expected for similar celebrations in the future.

Certain Vietnamese companies have the connections to have visas issued on arrival in Hanoi and Ho Chi Minh City for US$50. If you do enter Vietnam without a visa in hand, and there is a problem with immigration, remain calm. Usually the worst thing that will happen is you'll be put in the airport hotel for a night while your host hopefully secures your visa.

Without the right connections, it can be very difficult to get any type of visa issued for more than one month. Most visas must be used within one month of their issue. Note that the period of your visa begins on the date you specify – not on the date in which you actually enter the country; postponing your visit by two weeks means that your month-long visa will only be valid for two weeks.

It is currently fairly easy to extend a visa for one month; the government prefers that travel agencies handle tourist extensions, for which the total cost should be less than US$30. But the government has been known to change such policies with no notice. Foreigners who enter on tourist visas and conduct business or government activities can be deported when caught. They may also be fined.

Overseas Vietnamese may be granted extensions for as long as six months, but family reasons must be proven. Visa extensions may also be granted for foreigners working in joint-venture offices, foreign representative offices and who have proper visas.

You will be given a copy of your landing card on your arrival. This, along with your visa, must be kept with you at all times and handed back on your departure. Even with a proper visa in hand, you may encounter popular airport scams.

What to Bring

It is best to travel light in Vietnam. One medium-sized bag and a daypack will provide more than enough room to carry everything you'll need to survive and enough space for the things you'll buy in Vietnam. There is an extensive black market for smuggled consumer goods in both Hanoi and Ho Chi Minh City, so don't worry about running out of something important.

However, there are three things that are difficult to find in Vietnam: sunscreen, tampons, and earplugs. It is difficult to get access to news in Vietnam, so you may want to bring a small short-wave radio. Film is available in cities; check the expiry date.

FOREIGN REGISTRATION AND INTERNAL TRAVEL PERMITS

Internal travel permits are not required when visiting major tourist areas in Vietnam. In 1993, Hanoi eased its internal travel policies and opened all provinces to tourists. However, each province has its own regulations. Many tourists have reported being arrested by provincial police in the Central Highlands and Mekong Delta for travelling in restricted areas. Occasionally innocent tourists walk unknowingly into sensitive border areas and military installations unaware that they are breaking the law. In Vietnam, ignorance of the law is no excuse. Regulations change daily and some provinces completely ignore directives from Hanoi. The best advice is to play it safe in remote areas and always contact the police. It may end up costing a few dollars, but it beats spending your holiday under house arrest.

Tourists staying in hotels and guesthouses outside of Hanoi and Ho Chi Minh do not need to register with the police directly. When you check in at reception the staff will take your passport to the police for registration. They will return it to you in the morning. In Hanoi or Ho Chi Minh City, they may only require your blue landing card, from which they can fill in details in a book and then return it. In other places, the staff may insist on holding your passport for your entire stay. This is probably a sign that police keep a very close watch on foreign visitors.

Note that procedures and policies change constantly and often without warning.

If you must turn over your passport, make sure that the proper one – and the correct landing card – are returned to you. Hotel staff are often prone to misplacing passports; don't wait until a half-hour prior to departure to request the return of your passport.

If you plan on staying with family or friends you may want to visit the local police station to avoid any late night visits by the police, as nosey neighbours often report suspicious foreigners.

Although you may consider this a nuisance, you will be saving your hosts quite a bit of trouble from authorities. It is always important to consider what impact your visit and contact may have on your friends who will be living and working in Vietnam after you have gone home.

Big Brother

Visitors should keep in mind that their activities may be monitored by security police.

Some tour guides have been told to report the activities of their clients: where they go, whom they meet with. Some private tour companies, and certainly state-owned ones, have members of the country's internal security apparatus working for them. Phone conversations with new Vietnamese friends or with foreign residents should always be circumspect since their phones and faxes are frequently monitored.

To what extent the government can monitor or censor e-mail is a topic of debate.

Vietnamese enforcement of rules and laws is very erratic. At times, many foreigners on tourist visas have been teaching English or doing other work in the two major cities. It's probably advisable to obtain a student visa by enrolling in a language course, which is what many English teachers do. The laissez-faire policies can abruptly change and foreigners may nonetheless be fined or deported. Journalists who attempt to work on tourist visas may encounter problems.

While visitors will not notice a heavy police presence – in fact, quite the opposite – be assured that there are many ways for the security police to keep tabs on visitors. The vast majority of police are not in uniform. It soon becomes apparent, from the patterns of their questions, which tour guides and hotel staff are unsophisticated low-level informers. In a friendly manner, they will inquire about your next destination in Vietnam and how long you plan to stay there; a vague answer will spur them to return repeatedly to the questions in the ensuing days or hours. They will, however, display no interest in places you have already visited in Vietnam, your experiences there, other travels or customs in your country.

After a few weeks of this, many Westerners can't resist lying about their innocuous travel plans; there don't seem to be any repercussions. On the other hand, responding with vague replies is asking for trouble. Your luggage may be searched and letters or travel journals stolen – while more valuable items are untouched. The low-level informers seem too unsophisticated to ferret out any information about any new friends, Vietnamese or expatriate, that visitors may have acquired. Others are not.

Police stations

Hanoi Police Office for the Registration of Foreign Visitors, 63 Tran Hung Dao, Hanoi.
Ho Chi Minh City Police Station, 161 Nguyen Du, Dist 1. Tel: 829 9398, 829 7107. Open 8–11am and 1–4pm.
Nha Trang Police, 2 Hai Thuong Street. Tel: 821 079.
Vung Tau Immigration Police, 14 Le Loi Street.
Da Lat Police Office, 2 Hai Thuong Street. Tel: 822 098.

Immigration offices

Hanoi, 40A Hang Bai. Tel: 826 0921.
Ho Chi Minh City, 254 Nguyen Trai, Dist 1. Tel: 839 1701.
Hue, 43 Ben Nghe. Tel: 822 134.
Da Nang, 1 Nguyen Thi Minh Khai. Tel: 821 075.
Hai Phong, 2 Le Dai Hanh. Tel: 841 251.
Da Lat, 31A Tran Binh Trong. Tel: 822 460.

Vung Tau, 422 Truong Cong Dinh.
Tel: 852 423.

CUSTOMS

Visitors to Vietnam are required to fill in a detailed customs declaration in duplicate upon arrival. Customs may inspect your luggage to verify that you have made a correct declaration. Although it is unpleasant to say this, authorities seem to cause more problems for overseas Vietnamese than for other foreigners. At times this is probably justified, as many overseas Vietnamese return loaded down with boxes and bags. The volume of baggage, as much as the nationality, may account for the extra scrutiny.

Currency, as well as most electronics items – cameras, radios, computers, video cameras – must be declared. Books, reading material and videos are supposed to be declared, but it doesn't seem expected. Your items may be inspected to check for anything considered culturally or politically sensitive. Some travellers report having books and videos confiscated.

You must keep a copy of the customs declaration form to show customs officials upon leaving Vietnam. They may check to see if you are leaving with the items declared, such as computers and cameras.

Official authorisation from the Ministry of Culture is required to export or take out antiquities. Visitors are not allowed to take ancient artefacts, antiques, or items of value to Vietnamese culture. An antique is defined as anything more than 30 years old. Travellers have reported problems in trying to leave with items that appear to be antiques, even if they are reproductions. It is a good idea to take a detailed receipt from the shop with a description of the item. However, your goods still may be confiscated. Shop owners will always insist that their products can

be exported; don't believe them. If you have the time to receive official permission, it is best to do so. But it may take weeks to obtain such permission. In practice, most tourists take the risk and hope that they won't be apprehended.

On both arrival and departure luggage will be exposed to an X-ray examination. It is probably a good idea to keep film and software away from this.

When leaving Vietnam, you may be stopped to have film, video and reading materials inspected. Usually this is just an annoyance, but if you are a journalist, your film or tapes will be seized unless you have permission to take them out from the government's Foreign Affairs Press Department.

Drinking Water

Do not drink tap water unless it has been boiled properly and avoid ice in drinks, especially in the countryside. Imported bottled water is available in most cities, but beware of bottles that are refilled with tap water.

All hotels provide free Thermoses of boiled water (with Chinese or black tea).

Health

The only vaccination required is for yellow fever, for travellers coming from Africa. Immunization against hepatitis (A and B), Japanese encephalitis and tetanus are strongly urged.

It is a good idea to consult a physician a month to six weeks before departing to leave enough time to obtain the immunizations.

Malaria is widespread in Vietnam, especially in the Central Highlands and the Mekong Delta. The best protection is prevention. Always sleep under a mosquito net when visiting rural areas, use a high concentrate DEET repellent, and wear long sleeves and pants from dusk to dawn when malaria carrying mosquitoes are active.

Lastly, consult with a

knowledgeable doctor to determine what anti-malarial drugs are best suited for your travels. Opinion is divided about using prophylactics for malaria. Some doctors argue against taking the anti-malarial drugs because of the potential side effects, because the side effects can mask symptoms of other illnesses and because malarial strains have developed that are resistant to the drugs.

Caution should be taken when eating, because food is often prepared in insanitary conditions. Doctors advise abstaining from shellfish, especially shrimp. Fruit and vegetables should be peeled before eating. Cooking them is a better idea. Some doctors advise avoiding even raw vegetables like the herbs and lettuces served with *pho*, the noodle soup, and spring rolls. Eat in restaurants that are crowded. Because most places do not have refrigeration, food is thrown away at the end of the day. If a place is crowded, it is a good sign that the establishment is not serving spoiled food. Avoid the usual suspects: mayonnaise and eggs that have not been cooked thoroughly, for example.

Should you have an accident or an emergency health problem in Vietnam, you may want to consider evacuation to Singapore or Bangkok for treatment. Vietnam has no shortage of well-trained doctors, but hospital services and supplies are in very short supply.

Imported pharmaceutical drugs are widely available in Hanoi and Ho Chi Minh City, but it is best to bring a small supply of medicine to cope with diarrhoea, dysentery, eye infections, insect bites, fungal infections and the common cold.

Money Matters

Vietnam's unit of currency, the dong (pronounced *dome*), currently circulates in bank notes of 50,000, 20,000, 10,000, 5,000, 2,000, 1,000, 500, 200 and 100 denominations. The dong's value against the dollar has been fluctuating slightly in the past few

Public Holidays

The most important celebration of the year in Vietnam is Tet, or Lunar New Year, which falls either in late January or early February, on the day of the full moon between the winter solstice and the spring equinox.

The dates of nearly all festivals vary from year to year because they adhere to the lunar calendar. By counting the days from a new moon, it's fairly easy to determine when, say, "the third day of the second lunar month" falls on the familiar Gregorian calendar. It's easier to consult a Vietnamese calendar, which always come with both systems.

Official Public Holidays
1 January – New Year's Day
3 February – founding of the Communist Party of Vietnam
8 March – Women's Day
26 March – Youth Day
30 April – Liberation of Saigon
1 May – International Labour Day
7 May – Victory over France
19 May – Ho Chi Minh's birthday
1 June – Children's Day
27 July – Memorial Day
19 August – celebrating the August 1945 revolution
2 September – National Day
20 November – Teachers' Day
22 December – Army Day

years – usually somewhere between 10,000 and 15,000 dong per US$1. Care should be taken when exchanging money or receiving change. The 20,000 dong notes and the 5,000 notes – both widely used – are the same size and colour (blue) and easily confused.

Vietnam's black market for US dollars isn't what it used to be. The difference between the street rate and the bank rate is very small – if there is any difference at all.

Changing money on the street is a foolish proposition. Because the dong notes are the same size and same or similar colours, you can easily be given the wrong denomination. As the old saying goes, you get what you pay for. It's best to stick to a bank or currency exchange booth, of which there are many in all the major cities.

After banking hours, it is possible to change dollars at almost any jewellery or gold shop; sometimes the rate is slightly higher than the bank rate. These shops are called *hieu van* or *hieu kim hoan* and are easily identifiable because their signs usually have bright, gold-coloured letters. Hotels, travel agencies, restaurants and cafes catering to foreigners are also usually eager to exchange dollars and will do so at bank rates.

Be prepared to be offered two exchange rates: one for denominations of 50 and 100 US dollars, a lower rate for smaller denominations.

Some banks will also exchange Vietnamese dong for other currencies: French francs, German marks, Japanese yen, Australian dollars, for example. But gold shops will not. Better to bring US dollars. Travellers' cheques in US dollars are accepted in most banks and in major hotels, but not in shops and not in smaller hotels and restaurants. Travellers' cheques denominated in Canadian dollars are nearly impossible to cash. Major credit cards are becoming widely accepted. A fairly high commission – 4 percent is standard – is assessed when using credit cards, however.

Cash advances can be collected from major credit cards (again with the 4 percent commission) from major banks, including Vietcombank. Vietcombank will also provide cash dollars for US dollar travellers' cheques – for a 4 percent charge. All transactions are supposed to be conducted in Vietnamese dong; in practice, a dual-currency system is in effect. That is, most purchases can be made in US dollars, as well as Vietnamese dong. However, often shops, restaurants and taxi drivers insist on a lower conversion rate – such as 12,000 dong to US$1 – when using dollars. To avoid haggling, it is better to carry some Vietnamese dong. (Sometimes this can work to your advantage. For example, if a shop owner says a bicycle costs US$50 dollars, they will tell you it costs 500,000 Vietnamese dong: US$50 dollars should actually convert to about 550,000 dong.)

One other potential problem is the quality of the notes themselves. Although the Vietnamese dong notes are often ripped, faded and crumpled, Vietnamese are reluctant to accept US dollars that are not crisp and new. Before taking US dollars from a bank, you should inspect them to make sure they have no stray marks or tears, or appear old, as some people may refuse damaged notes.

When you arrive in Vietnam, the custom form requires you to note currency brought into the country if it is worth more than US$2,000 dollars. However, visitors no longer have to account for money exchanged or spent during trips.

Practical Tips

Getting There

BY AIR

The easiest way to get to Vietnam is by air. International flights are available to Hanoi and Ho Chi Minh City, and direct flights are now available to Da Nang.

Ho Chi Minh City

Tan Son Nhat Airport (Hoang Van Thu Street, Tan Binh District, Tel: 845 6321) is located 7km (4½ miles) from the centre of Saigon. After immigration and baggage claim, travellers have to hand in a copy of their Customs Declaration Form to officials before they can go through another security check that will allow them to exit the airport officially. Unfortunately, there are neither signs nor booths to locate these customs officials. Just look beyond the crowds blocking the security check for the few bored-looking officials collecting white pieces of paper.

A number of the major hotels offer shuttle service but this has to be arranged ahead of time. There is also a bus that runs between the airport and the Vietnam Airlines office downtown. A taxi into town should cost around US$7. Even in a metered taxi, agree on the price beforehand as taxi drivers have been known to take long circuitous routes through heavy traffic. Other alternatives into town include cyclos (about US$2) and motorbike taxis (US$2–3).

There are domestic flights on Vietnam Airlines or Pacific Airlines to the following destinations: Buon Ma Thuot, Da Lat, Da Nang, Dien Bien, Hai Phong, Hanoi, Hue, Nha Trang, Phu Quoc, Pleiku, Quy Nhon, Rach Gia, Tuy Hoa and Vinh. Though there is no air service to Can Tho as of printing, plans are underway to reopen Can Tho's airport to shuttle flights from Saigon. Domestic departure tax is 20,000 Vietnamese dong.

Ho Chi Minh City is connected via international flights to Bangkok, Dubai, Guangzhou, Hong Kong, Kaohsiung, Kuala Lumpur, Macau, Manila, Melbourne, Moscow, Osaka, Paris, Phnom Penh, Seoul, Singapore, Sydney, Taipei, Vienna, Vientiane (change of plane in Hanoi), and Zurich. International departure tax is US$10.

Hanoi

Noi Bai Airport is served by direct flights from Bangkok (Thai, Vietnam Airlines, Air France), Berlin (Vietnam Airlines), Dubai (Vietnam Airlines), Guangzhou (China Southern Airlines), Hong Kong (Cathay Pacific, Vietnam Airlines), Moscow (Aeroflot, Vietnam Airlines), Paris (Air France), Seoul (Vietnam Airlines), Singapore (Singapore Airlines), Taipei (China Airlines, Vietnam Airlines), and Vientiane (Lao Aviation, Vietnam Airlines).

There are bus and taxi services from the airport into central Hanoi. Vietnam Airlines operates a shuttle bus between its central Hanoi office and the airport for US$4 (US$2 for Vietnamese nationals), a bit more if you want to be dropped off at your hotel. An official Vietnam Airlines taxi costs US$20; tickets for a taxi and the shuttle can be purchased near the baggage claim area. Freelance taxi drivers will also swarm around visitors. They will try to charge as much as they can; a car in good condition with air conditioning should cost around US$15. For an older car without air conditioning, US$10. Drivers will grab your arm and try to pick up your bags; negotiate the fare before letting anyone lead you away. If a driver refuses to come down in price, walk away. There are more than enough drivers. They may also try to charge you for a road toll. You should not pay this. If a driver insists, demand that you pay for the toll and keep the receipt. Also try to steer the driver onto the new highway; it will save you about 20 minutes. (Say: *Di duong Bac Thang Long – Noi Bai* or simply *Cau Thang Long*.) There are also metered taxis, although they are difficult to find at the airport. The fare should be about US$25.

BY RAIL

Trains leave Ho Chi Minh City for the northern coastal towns from the Railway Station (Ga Saigon), which is located at 1 Nguyen Thong Street, Dist 3 (tel: 823 0106). The ticket office is open daily 7.15–11am and 1–3pm. Book at least 2–3 days in advance for sleepers. Alternatively, many travellers find it worthwhile to pay extra to have a travel agency purchase the tickets. The five classes of train travel in Vietnam are hard seat, soft seat, hard sleeper, soft sleeper, and soft sleeper with air-conditioning, this last available only on certain trains. Due to the existence of only one track along the coast, train travel in Vietnam is slow and subject to frequent delays. The fastest Reunification Express between Ho Chi Minh City and Hanoi takes 34 hours, the slowest, up to 48 hours.

BY SEA

Though Ho Chi Minh City has a bustling port, few visitors choose to arrive here by boat. While the occasional cruise ship may dock here for a short stay, there is no ongoing regular service. Visitors who do arrive on cruise ships often find themselves shunted off on strictly regimented tours, all organised by the government-run monopoly Vietnam Tourist.

BY ROAD

It is also possible to enter Vietnam from China (and vice versa) at the Lang Son and Lao Cai border crossings. Border tensions between the two countries routinely flare, so find out what the situation is when making your travel plans.

It is true that a few travellers have managed to get permission to travel overland from Laos to Vietnam via the Lao Bao border crossing in Central Vietnam, but it is definitely not common practice to do so. Travellers also can enter Vietnam by crossing the border with Cambodia at Moc Bai, which is only a few hours by road from Ho Chi Minh City.

When applying for a visa, you must specify where you intend to enter and exit Vietnam. If you do not do so the immigration police may turn you away from the border. Exit points can be changed by the immigration offices in Hanoi and Ho Chi Minh City.

Business Hours

Offices and public services generally open early from around 7.30am and close for lunch at around noon or 12.30pm, opening again around 1pm until 4.30pm Monday to Saturday. Banks are open from 8am to 3pm Monday to Friday and closed on Saturday afternoons and Sundays. Private shops are open from 8.30am until late in the evening. Shops are generally open seven days a week. Food markets generally close around 5pm.

Banks

There are several foreign banks now in operation in Hanoi and Ho Chi Minh City. It is possible to receive cash advances on a major credit card (usually with a commission of 4 percent) and to open bank accounts. Money can also be wired into bank accounts from overseas banks.

To exchange money or cash travellers' cheques, it is advisable to go to a Vietnamese bank rather than a branch of an international, as the Vietnamese government requires foreign banks to charge higher fees.

Ho Chi Minh City

Several banks are located on or near Chuong Duong Street, which runs parallel to the Saigon River.

Many of the larger hotels offer foreign exchange but often at lower rates. Though there are an increasing number of foreign banks in Ho Chi Minh City, you'd do well to check with the individual bank beforehand as to the exact services they offer. Many have ATMs. Some can only cash travellers' cheques issued by their bank. Others are not licensed to conduct foreign exchange. To cash travellers' cheques or to receive cash advances on a major credit card, it is best to stick to one of the government-run banks like Vietcombank or Sacombank.

ABN Amro, 162 Pasteur, Dist 1. Tel: 822 2992; Fax: 829 7204.
ANZ Bank, 11 Me Linh Square, Dist 1. Tel: 829 9319; Fax: 822 9316. Open Monday–Friday 8.30am–4pm, Saturday 8.30am–12pm.
Bangkok Bank, Harbour View Tower, 35 Nguyen Hue, Dist 1. Tel: 821 4402; Fax: 821 3772.
Banque National de Paris (BNP), 2 Thi Sach, Dist 1. Tel: 829 9527; Fax: 923 0490.
BFCE, 11 Me Linh Square, Dist 1. Tel: 829 6495; Fax: 829 9126. Open Monday–Friday 8.30am–4pm, Saturday 8.30am–12pm.
Citibank, 15th Floor, 115 Nguyen Hue, Dist 1. Tel: 824 2118; Fax: 824 2267. Cashes only Citibank travellers' cheques.
Credit Lyonnais, 17 Ton Duc Thang, Dist 1. Tel: 829 9226; Fax: 829 6465.
Dai-Ichi Kangyo Bank, 5B Ton Duc Thang, Dist 1. Tel: 822 8638; Fax: 822 8640.
Deutsche Bank AG, Saigon Centre, 14th Floor, 65 Le Loi, Dist 1. Tel: 829 9000; Fax: 822 2760.
First Vina Bank, 3–5 Ho Tung Mau, Dist 1. Tel: 829 1581; Fax: 829 1583.
General Bank, 16th Floor, #1605, 2A–4A Ton Duc Thang, Dist 1. Tel: 829 4503; Fax: 829 4505.
HSBC, 75 Pham Hong Thai, Dist 1. Tel: 829 2288; Fax: 823 0530.

Indovina Bank, 36 Ton That Dam, Dist 1. Tel: 822 4995; Fax: 823 0131.
Industrial and Commercial Bank, 46–48 Hoa Binh Square, Da Lat. Tel: 822 364. Open Monday–Friday 7–11.30am and 1–4.30pm; Saturday 7–11am.
Industrial and Commercial Bank of Vietnam, 79A Ham Nghi, Dist 1. Tel: 829 7266.
ING Bank, 136 Nam Ky Khoi Nghia, Dist 1. Tel: 824 1500; Fax: 824 1502.
International Commercial Bank of China, 5B Ton Duc Thang, Dist 1. Tel: 822 5697; Fax: 822 5698.
National Bank of Kuwait, 69 Vo Van Tan, Dist 3. Tel: 824 3944; Fax: 824 3945.
Sacombank, 211 Nguyen Thai Hoc, Dist 1. Tel: 836 8607. Open 7.30–11.30am and 1.30–4.30pm.
Standard Chartered Bank, 3rd Floor, #302, 203 Dong Khoi, Dist 1. Tel: 829 8335; Fax: 829 8426.
State Bank of India, 41 Nguyen Thi Minh Khai, Dist 1. Tel: 822 4205; Fax: 822 4202.
Thai Military Bank, 11 Ben Chuong Duong, Dist 1. Open Monday–Friday 8am–3.30pm.
The Bank of East Asia, Ltd, 15th Floor, 8 Nguyen Hue, Dist 1. Tel: 822 8256; Fax: 822 8258.
United Overseas Bank, 1st Floor, 17 Le Duan, Dist 1. Tel: 825 1424; Fax: 825 1423.
VID Public Bank, 15A Ben Chuong Duong, Dist 1. Tel: 822 3583; Fax: 822 3612. Open Monday–Friday 8.30am–3.30pm, Saturday 8.30am–12pm.
Vietcombank, 29 Ben Chuong Duong, Dist 1. Tel: 823 0310; Fax: 829 7228. Open Monday–Friday 7.30–11.30am and 1–4pm; Saturday 7.30am–3pm.
Vietcombank, 17 Quang Trung Street, Nha Trang. Tel: 821 054. Open Monday–Saturday 7–11am and 1.30–4pm.
Vietnam Bank for Agriculture, 50 Chuong Duong, Dist 1. Tel: 829 3516.
Vietnam Bank for Investment and Development, 134 Nguyen Cong Tru. Tel: 823 0125.

Hanoi

(Some foreign banks will provide services for account holders only.)

ANZ Bank, 14 Le Thai To.
Tel: 825 8190; Fax: 825 8188.
Bank of America, 27 Ly Thuong Kiet. Tel: 824 9316; Fax: 824 9322.
Chinfon Commercial Bank, 55 Quang Trung. Tel: 825 0555; Fax: 825 0566.
Citibank, 17 Ngo Quyen.
Tel: 825 1950; Fax: 824 3960.
Credit Lyonnais, 10 Trang Thi.
Tel: 825 8102; Fax: 826 0080.
Indovina Bank, 88 Hai Ba Trung.
Tel: 826 5516; Fax: 826 6320.
ING Bank, 17 Ngo Quyen. Tel: 824 6888; Fax: 826 9216.
Standard Chartered Bank, 27 Ly Thai To. Tel: 825 8970; Fax: 825 8880.
VID Public Bank, 194 Tran Quang Khai St, Tel: 826 8307; Fax: 826 6965.
Vietcombank, 47–49 Le Thai To.
Tel: 826 5501; Fax: 826 9067.
Vietnam Bank for Investment and Development, 194 Tran Quang Khai. Tel: 826 6963.

Industrial and Commercial Bank of Vietnam, 16 Phan Dinh Phung. Tel: 823 2008; Fax: 823 3452.
Vietnam Bank for Agriculture, 4 Pham Ngoc Thach, Dong Da. Tel: 852 5374.

Postal Services

Post offices are open every day from 7am to 8pm. Every city, town and village has a post office of some sort, and the service is remarkably reliable and fast. Within the country, mail reaches its destination within three days, sometimes faster. There is also an express mail service that promises overnight delivery for about US$10. Overseas mail delivery is neither reliable nor very fast. Stamps come in small denominations, which means mailing a postcard will leave little room for actually writing a message. However, many post offices now have meter machines so stamps are no longer necessary.

Telegram and telex services are available 24 hours a day in larger cities. Most post offices in major

Doing Business

A growing number of foreign banks and trading companies provide various services for business people and visitors alike.

Many of the trading companies are involved in tourist services such as tours to neighbouring countries like Cambodia and Laos, transport, visa services and forms, import-export services, hotel bookings, guides, rail, boat and even helicopter tours, foreign exchange and banking services and shipping.

Note that by the end of the 1990s, many businesses were losing their patience with the government corruption and bureaucracy, and so are leaving.

Ho Chi Minh City

Import Export Corporation of Ho Chi Minh City "IMEXCO", 45–47 Ben Chuong St., Dist 1. Tel: 829 5232, 829 5931. Fax: 829 5927.

OSC Tourism Transactions and Guide Office, 65 Nam Ky Khoi Nghia, Dist 1. Tel: 829 6658. Fax: 829 0195.
Ocean Transport Company, 23 Nguyen Hue, Dist 1.
Tel: 829 0197.
Vietnam Overseas Shipping Agent, 57 Nguyen Hue, Dist 1.
Tel: 829 7694, 829 0194.
OSC (Oil Services Company), Head Office, 02 Le Loi Street. Vung Tau. Tel: 897 562, Telex: OSC SGN 307.
Ocean Shipping Company, 142 Nguyen Tat Thanh, Dist 4.
Tel: 829 3124.
Transimex-Ministry of Foreign Economic Relations, 406 Nguyen That Thanh, Dist 4. Tel: 822 2415, 822 5663.

Hanoi

Hanoi Foreign Trade Company, 56 Ly Thai To

cities also have fax machines where messages can be sent or received.

Central post offices

Hanoi, 75 Dinh Tien Hoang. Tel: 825 3544.
Ho Chi Minh City, 2 Cong Xa Paris. Tel: 823 2541. Open daily 6am–9.30pm.
Hue, 8 Hoang Hoa Tham.
Da Nang, 45 Tran Phu.
Can Tho, Hoa Binh Street.
Nha Trang, 4 Le Loi. Tel: 828 000. Open daily 6.30am–10pm. Internet service available. There is a branch office on Le Thanh Ton Street just east of Tran Hung Dao Street. Tel: 823 866; Fax: 821 907. Open daily 6.30am–10pm.
Da Lat, 14–16 Tran Phu Street. Tel: 822 586, 821 003. Open daily 6.30am–9pm. In addition to the usual services, the post office offers Internet service.
Hai Phong, 5 Nguyen Tri Phuong.
Vung Tau, 4 Ha Long Street. Tel: 852 689.

COURIER SERVICES

Ho Chi Minh City

Airborne Express, 2E Tien Giang Street, Tan Binh District. Tel: 848 5368; Fax: 848 5372.
DHL, 4 Huynh Huu Bac Street.
Tel: 844 6203.
Federal Express, 26 Truong Son Street, Tan Binh District. Tel: 848 5888. 146 Pasteur St., Dist 1. Tel: 829 0995. Open Monday–Saturday 7am–8pm, Sunday 9am–5pm.

Telecommunications

Country code for Vietnam is 84. International telephone connections are quite clear from Vietnam. However, the cost of calling overseas ranks among the highest in the world. Direct calls can be placed from hotels, post offices and residences. Reverse charges are not allowed, however. Expect to pay from US$4 to $5 a minute to call the United States, Europe, or Australia. Hotels will add a surcharge that can make calls about US$7 a minute. Domestic calling is still haphazard. The circuits between Hanoi and Ho Chi Minh City tend to be quite busy, so calling from one city to another can take many minutes, or even hours.

Fax machines are available in post offices and hotels. Be warned that the cost is quite high. A one-page fax overseas costs about US$11. Hotels will charge even more. Both Hanoi and Ho Chi Minh City have mobile telephone services and paging services.

To call within the country, dial 01 followed by the area code followed by the number. Phone numbers are either five or six digits. Telephone calls made within Hanoi take seven digits. Dial an 8 first, followed by the remaining numbers.

The only major phone companies with access codes are Sprint: 1201 1111; and MCI: 1201 1022.

AREA CODES: CITIES

Buon Ma Thuot	50
Da Lat	63
Da Nang	51
Hai Phong	31
Hanoi	4
Ho Chi Minh City	8
Hue	54
Long Hai	64
My Tho	73
Nha Trang	58
Phan Thiet	62
Vinh	38

AREA CODES: PROVINCES

Ben Tre	75
Binh Dinh	56
Can Tho	71
Chau Doc	76
Ha Tien	77
Ha Tinh	39
Hoa Binh	18
Khanh Hoa	58
Lai Chau	23
Lao Cai	20
Quang Nam-Da Nang	51
Rach Gia	77
Soc Trang	79
Son La	22
Tay Ninh	66

Thai Binh	36
Thanh Hoa	37
Thua Thien-Hue	54
Tien Giang	73
Vinh Long	70
Vinh Phu	21
Yen Bai	29

Media

The weekly newspaper *Vietnam Investment Review* and the monthly magazine *Vietnam Economic Times* are both products of joint ventures between foreign companies and Vietnamese government entities; they carry eminently less propaganda than the wholly state-run periodicals, which are published in Vietnamese, English and French.

The Review and *The Times* publish supplements – the weekly *Timeout* and the monthly *Guide*, respectively; these are useful guides to entertainment and events in both Hanoi and Ho Chi Minh City.

Ho Chi Minh City

There is a newsstand called *Lao Dong* on Nguyen Hue Street in Ho Chi Minh City, across from the Rex Hotel near City Hall. In Ho Chi Minh City, though, one doesn't need to look far to find foreign-language newspapers and magazines; in heavily touristed areas, such as Pham Ngu Lao Street, vendors stroll through restaurants. If they don't have a title you want, ask – they will often be able to secure it within a few minutes.

Hanoi

In striking contrast with Ho Chi Minh City, finding decent reading material in Hanoi or anywhere else in Vietnam is difficult. A few pavement vendors on Trang Tien Street sell foreign newspapers and there is a bookstore, near the corner of Ngo Quyen, and sometimes a pavement newsstand, but your best bet is one of the big hotels for the *Asian Wall Street Journal*, *International Herald Tribune* and *Financial Times* as well as English-language newspapers from Bangkok, Hong Kong and Singapore. They arrive at least a day late. Most hotel shops also sell French newspapers and fashion

magazines and English-language news weeklies, such as *Time* and *Far Eastern Economic Review*.

RADIO & TELEVISION

The Voice of Vietnam, the official radio station, broadcasts twice a day. Two stations transmit worldwide from Hanoi and Ho Chi Minh City in 11 languages: English, French, Spanish, Russian, Mandarin/Cantonese, Indonesian, Japanese, Khmer, Lao and Thai.

International stations can be received on a shortwave receiver.

Many hotels, even smaller ones, now have satellite dishes that bring in the BBC and CNN. They also show Star TV, which broadcasts a healthy dose of old and new American TV shows, like *Baywatch*, *Santa Barbara* and *MASH*, and a sports channel that is heavy on cricket, auto racing, golf and rugby. Vietnam TV has nightly broadcasts in English and French.

Emergencies

CRIME

In general, Vietnam is a very safe country to travel in and violent crimes against foreigners are very rare. However, there are dangers. In Ho Chi Minh City, tourists are increasingly becoming the victims of pickpockets, snatch and grab thieves and hotel burglars. Always leave valuables in a hotel safe, and when you must carry cash, put it in a money belt inside your clothes. When walking or travelling in a cyclo, keep one hand firmly on handbags and cameras.

Daylight travel is pretty safe on Vietnam's highways and trains. There are isolated cases of highway robbery and hijacking, but foreigners are rarely the targets of these attacks. When travelling on buses or trains always stay with your bag. If you intend on taking the train, bring a cable lock to secure your bags to your bed frame when you are sleeping.

The Vietnamese are extremely

friendly and generous, but caution must be taken when making casual acquaintances. On Vietnamese buses and trains, foreigners have been poisoned by drugged food and drink offered to them by fellow passengers. Vietnam also has its fair share of con men, who hustle everything from Cambodian gems to "genuine" bones of missing American servicemen. If you are offered American remains or ID tags, simply ignore the offer – more often than not you are being offered a box of animal bones. Trafficking in fake American remains and dog tags is dwindling somewhat. But it is not unheard of for someone to approach a foreigner claiming to know the whereabouts of an American still being held prisoner. These claims should be viewed with scepticism.

Women should take extra precautions when travelling alone, as some Vietnamese men can be very aggressive. Their behaviour ranges from following you to your hotel room to being prodded by their friends to physically touch you. Vietnam can be a very difficult country for an Asian woman, or a woman of Asian descent, who travels with a white male companion. Assuming such women are Vietnamese and prostitutes, Vietnamese men are often verbally abusive. Women staying alone in lower-priced rooms may want to consider using an extra lock on the door at night. Women, especially, should be careful late at night. The streets tend to be deserted, giving a sense of false confidence to many travellers. In fact this situation is when a "cyclo" or xe om driver is more likely to hassle a woman. This is most likely in Ho Chi Minh City, Da Nang and Nha Trang. It is a good idea to travel in groups or to arrange transportation ahead of time. A good driver can steer you clear of trouble; paying a little extra to have a driver wait for you is better than having to find a way to get home late at night.

Be careful of pavement vendors selling maps, books and souvenirs or people begging for money, especially in Hanoi and Ho Chi Minh City. They can easily distract you while a friend slips a hand in your pocket, grabs your wallet and is gone before you realise what has happened. Watches are easy prey, too, and even glasses are ripped off by passing motorcyclists.

Annoyances

Bring earplugs. Vietnam is a noisy country and the noise starts when Vietnamese arise – usually by 5.30am.

Villages and small towns offer no respite because here tourists will be wakened by early-morning loudspeaker broadcasts of martial music, calisthenics, and economic victories. While these broadcasts sometimes start at 6am and only last half-an-hour, a 4.30am kickoff is not unknown and a two-hour blast, as in Sa Pa, is common.

The latest noise development is karaoke. Nearly every hotel has a karaoke lounge and many villages have a karaoke shack. Fortunately, performances are usually over by 10pm.

From big city streets to the northwest mountains to the rowboats of Tam Coc, Vietnam's souvenir peddlers are aggravating and relentless. Displaying initial interest – or worse, purchasing something – only stimulates further hounding. This harassment can continue for hours or days.

The best strategy is to refrain from showing the slightest interest in the first place. If all else fails, shouting "Di! Di! Di!" ("Go! Go! Go!") is effective. A normal tone of voice is ineffective. While shouting may offend your dignity, you will see Vietnamese resorting to harsher measures.

Pharmaceuticals

Hospitals and clinics have a supply of pharmaceuticals. Medicine of almost every kind can be bought on the street or at pharmacies – nha thuoc – but there is a problem of fake drugs being sold.

MEDICAL SERVICES

While Vietnam has ably trained medical care professionals, it lacks adequate equipment, medicine and facilities. The Ministry of Health has designated five hospitals to treat foreigners. However, in an emergency, any hospital is allowed to treat foreigners. Often foreigners report they are directed to the officially designated facilities.

Ho Chi Minh City
Emergency/Evacuation
AEA International, 65 Nguyen Du, Dist 1. Tel: 829 8520; Fax: 829 8551.
International SOS Assistance, 151 Bis Vo Thi Sau, Dist 3. Tel: 829 4386; Fax: 824-2862.

General
OSCAT/AEA International Clinic, 65 Nguyen Du, Dist 1. Tel: 829 8520; Fax: 829 8551.
Dr. P. Mike Vannoort, 243–243B Hoang Van Thu, Tan Binh District. Tel: 844 3441.

Dentists
Orthodontology Centre, 263 Tran Hung Dao, Dist 1. Tel: 835 7595.
OSCAT/AEA International Clinic, 65 Nguyen Du, Dist 1. Tel: 829 8520; Fax: 829 8551.

Hanoi:
All the facilities listed below have English-speaking physicians or staff.
AEA International, Central Building, 31 Hai Ba Trung. Tel: 934 0555. Mobile: 09090 1919. Fax: 934 0556. Clinic, 24-hour emergency service, medical evacuation.
Hanoi Family Medical Practise, Van Phuc Diplomatic Compound, Kim Ma Road. Tel: 843 0748. Fax: 846 1750. Run by Westerners, including physicians, nurses, dentist, psychologist. 24-hour emergency;

MEDEX evacuation. Staff speak many languages.

Institute of Acupuncture, H3 Vinh Ho, Thai Thinh. Tel: 853 3881.

Swedish Clinic, 2 Nui Truc. Tel: 845 2464.

Viet Duc Hospital (Benh Vien Viet Duc), 40 Tranh Thi. Tel: 825 3531.

Vietnam International Hospital, Phuong Mai. Tel: 574 0740.

Traditional Medicine

National Institute and Hospital of Traditional Medicine, 29 Nguyen Binh Khiem, Hanoi. Tel: 822 6775. Acupuncture and therapeutic, traditional massage.

Tourist Information

Vietnam's tourist industry is being developed along the organised tour line. It is administered by the National Office of Tourism, which carries with it a ministerial rank. Vietnam Tourism is the official representative, responsible for promoting the industry both within the country and abroad. Its network of representative offices throughout the country provides information and services such as transport hire, hotel reservations and at least 17 different organised tours. These range from between 3 to 21 days, with an option of trips into neighbouring Laos or Cambodia, at a price fixed more for the foreign wallet than the actual standard of the service. A little patience is needed to overcome the complications that can arise in the absence of sufficient guides and chauffeurs competent in foreign languages.

Vietnam for the most part is open to tourism, yet some areas in the country remain closed to tourists and even to the Vietnamese themselves. "No go" areas include the north's high plateau region, Cao Bang and Lang Son in the north on the Chinese border and Cam Ranh Bay in the centre. However it is not impossible to visit these areas "unofficially", although it's not advisable to tempt fate too far. Any area can suddenly become sensitive these days due to the growing discontent with the present system, and if your request to visit an area is stonewalled, this may be the reason.

INFORMATION CENTRES & TOUR OPERATORS

Some other state organisations offer much cheaper and more flexible tours than Vietnam Tourism. For example, Trung Tam Du Lich Thanh Nien Vietnam (Vietnam's Youth Tourism Centre), 31 Cao Thang, Dist 3, Ho Chi Minh City, tel: 829 0553, 829 4602, provides a very accommodating service and will tailor a guided tour to suit your requirements.

Ho Chi Minh & the south

Ann Tours, 58 Ton That Tung Street, Dist 1. Tel: 833 2564; Fax: 848 832 3866; anntours@yahoo.com. A classy professional outfit, Ann Tours is a private agency offering everything from ticket booking to organising tours throughout the country. Friendly, stellar service, expert guides and drivers, all at competitive prices. Highly recommended.

Hau Giang Tourist Office 27 Chau van Liem. Tel: 821 852, 821 854.

Exotissimo Travel, 2B Dinh Tien Hoang, Dist 1. Tel: 825 1723; Fax: 825 1684; info@exotissimo.com.

Global Holidays, 104–106 Nguyen Hue, Dist 1. Tel: 822 8453; Fax: 822 8454.

Khanh Hoa Tourism, 1 Tran Hung Dao, Nha Trang. Tel: 822 753; Fax: 824 206. Open daily 7–11.30am and 1.30–5pm.

Lamdong Tourist Company, 7 Duong 3 Thang 2 Street, Da Lat. Tel: 822 125, 821 731; Fax: 828 330.

Rach Gia, Tourist Office, 12 Ly Tu Trong. Tel: 2081.

Saigon Tourist, Main Office: 49 Le Thanh Ton, Dist 1. Tel: 829 8129; Fax: 822 4987; sgtvn@hcmc.netnam.vn; Budget Office: 187A Pham Ngu Lao, Dist 1. Tel: 836 8542. Other branches throughout the city. This government-run agency has a monopoly over many of the hotels, restaurants and tourist sights in and around Ho Chi Minh City.

Saigon Tourist Association, 112 Cach Mang Thang Tam. Tel: 823 8653. Telex: 811514 EPO-VT. Fax: 848 24744.

Sinh Cafe, 248 De Tham, Dist 1. Tel: 836 7338. Overwhelmingly popular among budget travellers, Sinh Cafe offers, in addition to the usual travel services and inexpensive guided tours to the Mekong Delta and the Cu Chi Tunnels, the popular option of an open ticket on their daily bus between Saigon and Hanoi with stops at Da Lat, Nha Trang, Hoi An and Hue, all for under US$50. Travellers have given the agency mixed reviews for uneven level of service.

Vietnam Tourism, 234 Nam Ky Khoi Ngia, Dist 3. Tel: 829 0776; Fax: 829 0775; vnthcm@hcm.vnn.vn.

Vung Tau, OSC (Oil Services Company), 2 Le Loi Street. Tel: 852 405. Fax: 852 834.

Hue & the centre

Hue – Thua Thien Tourism, 15 Le Loi, Hue. Tel: 822 369.

Binh Tri Thien Province Tourist Office, 15 Le Loi, Hue. Tel: 822 288, 822 369.

Quang Nam – Da Nang, 48 Bach Dang, Da Nang. Tel: 821 423, 822 213.

Binh Dinh – Quy Nhon, 4 Nguyen Hue, Quy Nhon. Tel: 822 524, 822 206.

Nghe Tinh, Truong Thi Square, Vinh. Tel: 692 VINH.

Hanoi & The North

Ann Tours, 18 Duong Thanh Street, Hoan Kiem District, Hanoi. Tel: 923 1366; Fax: 832 3866.

Hanoi Tourism, 18 Ly Thuong Kiet, Hanoi. Tel: 826 6714; Fax: 825 4209.

Green Bamboo Travel, 42 Nha Chung, Hanoi. Tel: 826 8752; Fax: 826 4949. bamboo@netnam.org.vn.

Love Planet, 25 Hang Bac, Hanoi. Tel: 828 4864; Fax: 828 0913. loveplanet@hn.vnn.vn.

Old Darling, 142 Hang Bac, Hanoi. Tel: 824 3024; Fax: 926 0102.

Fax: 844 8287.
redrivertours@netnam.org.vn.
TF Handspan, 116 Hang Bac,
Hanoi, Tel: 844 828 1996, 825
7171; Fax: 825 7171.
tfhandspn@hn.vnn.vn.
Hai Phong, 15 Le Dai Hanh. Tel:
842 957.
Hoa Binh, 24 Tran Hung Dao, Ha
Dong. Tel: 824 053, 824 309.
Ha Long, Bai Chay Street, Ha Long
City. Tel: 846 320. Fax: 846 318.
Ha Nam Dinh, 115 Nguyen Du. Tel:
849 362, 849 439.
Thanh Hoa, 25a Quang Trung. Tel:
852 298.
Thai Binh Tourist Agency, Ly Bon
Tel: 831 296.

Airlines

Ho Chi Minh City
Air France, 127 Tran Quoc Thao,
Dist 3. Tel: 829 0985; Fax: 829
0818.
Aeroflot, 4H Le Loi, Dist 1. Tel: 829
3489; Fax: 829 0076.
Asiana Airlines, 141–143 Ham
Nghi, Dist 1. Tel: 822 2663; Fax:
822 2710.
British Airways, 7th Floor, Jardine
House, 58 Dong Khoi, Dist 1. Tel:
829 1288; Fax: 823 0030.
Cathay Pacific Airways, 58 Dong
Khoi, Dist 1. Tel: 822 3203; Fax:
825 8276.
China Airlines, 132–134 Dong
Khoi, Dist 1. Tel: 825 1388/89;
Fax: 825 1390.
China Southern Airlines, 52B Pham
Hong Thai, Dist 1. Tel: 829 1172.
Eva Air, 32 Ngo Duc Ke, Dist 1. Tel:
822 4488; Fax: 822 3567.
Garuda Indonesia, 132/134 Dong
Khoi, Dist 1. Tel: 829 3644; Fax:
829 3688.
KLM Royal Dutch Airlines, 244
Pasteur. Tel: 823 1990; Fax: 823
1989.
Korean Airlines, Saigon Centre, 65
Le Loi, Dist 1. Tel: 824 2878; Fax:
824 2877.
Lauda Air, 9 Dong Khoi, Dist 1. Tel:
829 7117; Fax: 829 5832.
Lufthansa, 132–134 Dong Khoi,
Dist 1. Tel: 829 8529; Fax: 829
8537.
Malaysia Airlines, 116 Nguyen Hue,
Dist 1. Tel: 842 4950; Fax: 842 4738.

Qantas, 159 Calmette Street, Dist
1. Tel: 821 4660; Fax: 821 4669.
Royal Cambodia Airlines, 343 Le
Van Sy, Tan Binh Dist Tel: 844
0126; Fax: 842 1578.
Singapore Airlines, Suite 101,
Saigon Tower Building, 29 Le Duan,
Dist 1. Tel: 823 1583; Fax: 823
1554.
Swissair, 11th Floor, Saigon Centre,
65 Le Loi, Dist 1. Tel: 824 4000;
Fax: 823 6550.
Thai Airways, 65 Nguyen Du, Dist
1. Tel: 829 2810; Fax: 822 3465.
United Airlines, 58 Dong Khoi,
Dist 1. Tel: 823 4755; Fax: 823
0030.
Vietnam Airlines, 116 Nguyen Hue,
Dist 1. Tel: 829 2118; Fax: 823
0273. Open Monday–Saturday
7.30am–6pm, Sunday and holidays:
8.30am–12.30pm.

Tour Operators

Organised tours are available
through a growing number of
overseas agencies and both
official and unofficial agencies
within the country. You may feel
that you are not getting what you
paid for or have been misled, but
try to deal with any
misunderstandings that may
arise with as much tact and
patience as you can muster – it
will get you further in the long
run. Private companies are more
reliable than state-owned ones or
state-private joint ventures; note
"Toserco" refers to a state
tourism company. Many
operators advertise their
services, both within Vietnam
and elsewhere, particularly
Bangkok. It pays to shop around
as prices vary considerably.

Visas may be acquired more
easily, at a price, through a
specialist agent or tour operator,
who can arrange an all-inclusive
package of visa, flight and hotel
accommodation. Taking an all-
inclusive package outside
Vietnam is usually considerably
more expensive than if you make
your arrangements yourself once
you have arrived.

Ticket Changes

There are several agents of
Vietnam Airlines in Hanoi,
including one inside the
Metropole Hotel. They can
change departure dates on
existing tickets, but changes of
itinerary or the issue of new
tickets require a visit to the
Quang Trung office *(see below)*.

Hanoi
Vietnam Airlines, 1 Quang Trung.
Tel: 825 0888.
Air France, 1 Ba Trieu. Tel: 825
3484; Fax: 826 6694.
Cathay Pacific, 27 Ly Thuong Kiet.
Tel: 826 7298; Fax: 826 7709.
Thai Airways, 25 Ly Thuong Kiet.
Tel: 826 6893; Fax: 826 7934.
Singapore Airlines, 17 Ngo Quyen.
Tel: 826 8888; Fax: 826 8666.
Malaysian Air, 15 Ngo Quyen. Tel:
826 8820; Fax: 824 2388.

Government Offices

Ho Chi Minh City
Chamber of Commerce Industry,
171 Vo Thi Sau Street, Dist 3. Tel:
823 0339.
City Post Office, 125 Hai Ba Trung
Street, Dist 1. Tel: 829 6644.
Customs, 125 Ham Nghi. Tel: 829
0095, 829 0096.
Department of External Relations,
6 Thai Van Lung Street, Dist 1.
Tel: 822 4311.
**Department of Foreign Economic
Relations**, 1 Nam Ky Khoi Nghia,
Dist 1. Tel: 829 8116.
Foreign Investment Services Co.,
12 Nam Ky Khoi Nghia Street, Dist
1. Tel: 829 3616.
Import – Export, IMEXCO, 8 Nguyen
Hue. Tel: 829 7424.
International Booking Office, 116
Nguyen Hue. Tel: 829 2118, 822
3848.
**Office for the Control of Cultural
Item's Import and Export**, 178
Nam Ky Khoi Nghia.
Office of Foreign Registration,
161–163 Nguyen Du.
Saigon Port, Ho Chi Minh City. Tel:
829 1825.
Service of Foreign Affairs, 6 Thai

Van Lung. Tel: 822 4127.
Tan Son Nhat Airport, Tel: 824 3250, 824 2339.
The People's Committee, 86 Le Thanh Ton Street, Dist 1. Tel: 829 1054.
The Vietnamese Information Agency (VNA), 120 Xo Viet Nghe Tinh.
Trade Department, 45–47 Ben Choung Duong, Dist 1. Tel: 829 9876.

Hanoi
Chamber of Commerce and Industry, 33 Ba Trieu Street. Tel: 825 3961.
Entry-Exit Procedures Bureau, 89 Tran Hung Dao Street. Tel: 826 6472.
Expatriate Affairs Bureau, 79 Tran Hung Dao Street. Tel: 825 3076.
General Department of Customs, Chuong Duong Street. Tel: 826 3961.
Hanoi Customs, 159 Ba Trieu Street. Tel: 825 7224.
Ministry of Foreign Affairs, 1 Ton That Dam Street. Tel: 825 8201.
Office for Foreign Registration (Immigration Police), 63 Tran Hung Dao. Open Monday–Saturday 8–11am and 1–5pm.

Foreign Embassies and Consulates

Embassies in Hanoi
Australia, Dao Tan Street Tel: 831 7755; Fax: 831 7711.
Belgium, 9th Floor, 53 Quang Trung. Tel: 934 6179; Fax: 934 6183.
Burma (Myanmar), A-3 Van Phuc. Tel: 825 3369; Fax: 845 2404.

Cambodia, 71 Tran Hung Dao. Tel: 825 3788; Fax: 826 5225.
Canada, 31 Hung Vuong. Tel: 823 5500; Fax: 823 5333.
China (Peoples Republic), 46 Hoang Dieu. Tel: 845 3736; Fax: 823 2826.
Denmark, 19 Dien Bien Phu. Tel: 843 6243; Fax: 823 1999.
France, 57 Tran Hung Dao. Tel: 825 2719; Fax: 826 4236.
Germany, 29 Tran Phu. Tel: 845 3836; Fax: 845 3838.
Indonesia, 50 Ngo Quyen. Tel: 825 3353; Fax: 825 9274.
Israel, 68 Nguyen Thai Hoc. Tel: 843 3140.
Japan, 27 Lieu Giai. Tel: 846 3000; Fax: 846 3044.
Laos, 22 Tran Binh Trong. Tel: 825 4576; Fax: 822 8414.
Malaysia, 68 Lang Ha. Tel: 831 3400; Fax: 831 3402.
New Zealand, 32 Hang Bai. Tel: 824 1481; Fax: 824 1480.
Netherlands, Daeha Office Tower, 360 Kim Ma St., Tel: 831 5651; Fax: 831 5655.
Philippines, 27B Tran Hung Dao. Tel: 825 2111.
Singapore, 41–43 Tran Phu. Tel: 823 3965; Fax: 825 1600.
Sweden, 2 Road 358, Van Phuc. Tel: 845 4824; Fax: 823 2195.
Switzerland, 77B Kim Ma. Tel: 823 2019.
Thailand, 65 Hoang Dieu. Tel: 823 5092; Fax: 823 5088.
United Kingdom, 31 Hai Ba Trung. Tel: 825 2510; Fax: 826 5762.
United States, 7 Lang Ha. Tel: 843 1500; Fax: 835 0484.

Consulates in Ho Chi Minh City
Australia, 5-B Ton Duc Thang, Dist 1. Tel: 829 6035; Fax: 829 6031.

Belgium, 230G Pasteur, Dist 3. Tel: 824 3571; Fax: 829 4527.
Cambodia, 41 Phung Khac Khoan, Dist 1. Tel: 829 2751; Fax: 829 2744.
Canada, 235 Dong Khoi, Dist 1. Tel: 824 5025; Fax: 829 4528.
China (Peoples Republic), 39 Nguyen Thi Minh Khai, Dist 1. Tel: 829 2457; Fax: 829 5009.
Denmark, 20 Phung Khac Khoan, Dist 1. Tel: 822 8289; Fax: 822 4888.
France, 27 Nguyen Thi Minh Khai, Dist 1. Tel: 829 7231; Fax: 829 1675.
Germany, 126 Nguyen Dinh Chieu, Dist 3. Tel: 829 1967; Fax: 823 1919.
Indonesia, 18 Phung Khac Khoan, Dist 1. Tel: 822 3799; Fax: 829 9493.
Italy, 17 Le Duan, Dist 1. Tel: 829 8721; Fax: 829 8723.
Japan, 13–17 Nguyen Hue, Dist 1. Tel: 822 5314; Fax: 822 5316.
Laos, 93 Pasteur, Dist 1. Tel: 829 7667; Fax: 829 9272.
Malaysia, 53 Nguyen Dinh Chieu, Dist 3. Tel: 829 9023; Fax: 829 9027.
Netherlands, Saigon Tower, 29 Le Duan, Dist 1. Tel: 823 5932; Fax: 823 5934.
New Zealand, 41 Nguyen Thi Minh Khai, Dist 1. Tel: 822 6907; Fax: 822 6905.
Singapore, Saigon Centre, 65 Le Loi, Dist 1. Tel: 822 5173; Fax: 825 1600.
South Korea, 107 Nguyen Du, Dist 1. Tel: 822 5757; Fax: 822 5750.
Spain, Economic and Commercial Section, 25 Phung Khac Khoan, Dist 1. Tel: 825 0173; Fax: 825 0174.

Online in Hanoi

Most big hotels in both Hanoi and Ho Chi Minh provide Internet and e-mail services. Fees for use of the Internet at cafes and travel agencies listed below run around five US cents per minute. Use of a Vietnam-based e-mail service (and address) costs about half that rate, but service is less reliable.

Check the post offices for online access. Note that government policies change whimsically.
Emotion CyberNetCafe, 52 Ly Thuong Kiet. Tel: 934 1066. E-mail: emotion@hn.fpt.vn.
Green Bamboo Travel, 42 Nha Chung. Tel: 826 8752, 824 9179; Fax: 826 4949.

E-mail: bamboo@netnam.org.
Queen Cafe, 65 Hang Bac. Tel: 826 0860; Fax: 826 0300. E-mail: queenaz@yahoo.com. Website: www.queencafe.com.vn.
TF Handspan Travel Agent, 116 Hang Bac. Tel: 828 1996, 825 7171; Fax: 825 7171. E-mail: tfhandspn@hn.vnn.vn.

Taipei, Economic and Cultural Office, 117B Nguyen Dinh Chinh, Phu Nhuan Dist Tel: 845 8646; Fax: 845 8649.

Thailand, 77 Tran Quoc Thao, Dist 3. Tel: 822 2637; Fax: 829 1002.

United Kingdom, 25 Le Duan, Dist 1. Tel: 829 8433; Fax: 822 1971.

United States, 4 Le Duan, Dist 1. Tel: 822 9433; Fax: 822 9434.

Vietnamese overseas missions & trade representatives

Australia, Embassy of the SR Vietnam, 6 Timbarra Section, O'Malley, A.C.T. 2606. Tel: 866 059. Telex: 62756.

France, Ambassade de la SRVN, 62 rue Boileau, 75016 Paris. Tel: 4524 5063, 4527 6255.

Germany, Botschaft der Sozialistischen, Republik Vietnam, Konstantin Strasse 37, 5300 Bonn.

Hong Kong. The Representation of the National Export Import Corporations of the SRVN, 17th floor Golden Star Building, 20–24 Lockhart Rd. Tel: 5283 3613. Telex 63771 VNCOR. Cable: VINACOR.

Japan, Embassy of the SR Vietnam, 50–11 Motoyoyogi-cho Shibuya-ku, Tokyo 151. Tel: 466 3315. Telex: 32440 Vietnam. Cable: VIETRADE.

Laos, Embassy of the SR Vietnam, Route de That Luang, Vientiane. Tel: 5578, 2707.

Malaysia, 4 Persiaran Stonor, Kuala Lumpur 5040. Tel: (03) 248 4036.

Singapore, The Representation of the National Import Export Corporations of the SRVN, 10 Leedon Park. Tel: 468 3747. Telex 26936. Cable: VINATRADE.

Thailand, Embassy of the SR Vietnam, 83/1 Wireless Road, Bangkok. Tel: 252 6950, 251 7201.

United Kingdom, Embassy of the SR Vietnam, 12–14 Victoria Road, London W8. Tel: 7937 1912. Telex: 887 361.

United States, Embassy of the SR Vietnam, 1233 20th St. NW, Washington, D.C. 20036, Tel: (202) 861 0737.

Getting Around

Travel Options

With travel restrictions loosening up, it is now possible to visit most places in Vietnam. However, poor services and infrastructure can still make journeys difficult and time-consuming.

National Highway 1, which spans the length of Vietnam from the Chinese border to Ca Mau, is in a state of serious neglect. The 800 km (500 miles) between Hanoi and Hue are torn up so badly that most vehicles can only manage to travel at a kidney-jarring rate of 35 km (20 miles) per hour. South of Hue, the road is smooth compared to the northern stretch, but it is still slow and uncomfortable.

BY BUS

There are no tourist-class, long-distance buses in Vietnam. There is a national bus system, including a 48-hour express service from Ho Chi Minh City to Hanoi, but it is not a very safe or comfortable option. Vietnamese bus drivers are notorious for overloading their buses with people, livestock and produce. If your idea of fun is riding on a bus with your knees pressed against your chest sandwiched between two betel nut-chewing grandmothers for 12 hours, then the bus is for you. Although it is probably illegal, ticket sellers and conductors charge foreigners many times the Vietnamese fare. Receipts or tickets, if they are given at all, do not indicate the rake-off. Fortunately, there are other options.

Many comfortable private mini-buses, of Japanese or Korean makes, run daily between Ho Chi Minh City and Hue, with stops at the popular destinations in between. There are also daily runs between Hue and Hanoi. Private tour agencies sell tickets for these. Fares are very reasonable.

BY CAR, VAN OR MOTORCYCLE

In Hanoi and Ho Chi Minh City it is possible to hire good Japanese cars and minivans to go on day trips or week-long excursions. In Ho Chi Minh City you can even hire a convertible Mustang or Citroen to drive the scenic coastal road north to Hue. Hiring a driver and vehicle in Vietnam is good value if your travelling party is large enough to spread out the cost. Ask to go for a test ride before committing to a driver to see if the car is running properly. Expect to pay a minimum of US$40 a day for a comfortable car from a reputable tourist agency.

Sometimes drivers from one part of the country are reluctant to drive into another. Drivers from Ho Chi Minh City, for example, are hesitant to drive to Hanoi. Licence plates on cars denote what province the car is from, and drivers fear police will give cars from out of the region trouble. A driver in Ho Chi Minh City might agree to take you as far as Da Nang, for example, and then help you find another driver to take you further north. Car costs can be expensive, but it is always a good idea to negotiate. One way to keep the costs down is to look for a driver returning to his home base. For example, someone from Nha Trang might have driven a passenger one way to Ho Chi Minh City and is returning alone. Usually you can negotiate a very cheap fare.

A few adventurous souls have managed to see Vietnam with cars and motorcycles that they have unofficially purchased or rented in Hanoi and Ho Chi Minh City. Refurbished American Jeeps can be bought for US$3,000, and a brand new 350cc Czech motorcycle will set you back US$800. Second-hand motorcycles are slightly cheaper. In the north, the Belarus-made "Minsk" is best for tackling the mountainous areas.

The Vietnamese laws regarding foreigners driving are a little vague. Expatriates are allowed to own vehicles and many have been issued Vietnamese driving licences. The Vietnamese also recognise international driving permits issued by the Automobile Association. However, more than one foreigner has been arrested for driving without a licence. Also beware that there is no road insurance in Vietnam. If you hit someone or have an accident, the Vietnamese will hold you until you have reimbursed the other party – even if it wasn't your fault. It's quite acceptable for foreign tourists to rent motorcycles, but they are not supposed to buy them. The fact remains that they often do and sell them prior to departing Vietnam.

In spite of the risks, driving is a great way to see the country and come in contact with the Vietnamese.

BY TRAIN

Train travel in Vietnam is very slow. The fastest Hanoi–Ho Chi Minh City express train covers 1,730 km (1,073 miles) in 36 hours, so if you need to get somewhere fast you can forget about the train. However, if you want to leisurely soak up the

Vietnamese countryside the train has a lot to offer including mountain passes, ocean views, tunnels, French-era bridges and an opportunity to get to know the Vietnamese up close and personal.

Expect to pay at least US$100 for a berth in a four-person compartment on the express train from Hanoi to Ho Chi Minh City. There are two express trains every day and berths are reserved fast, so try to make reservations two days in advance. There is a kitchen car on most trains, and waitresses serve food, but it is of questionable quality. A better option is to buy snacks from the many vendors that enter the train at local stops.

There are also local train services on the Hanoi-Ho Chi Minh City line that serve coastal cities. Lines also run from Hanoi northwest to Lao Cai, east to Hai Phong, and north to Lang Son.

In the cities the best way to get around is by bicycle or cyclo (trishaw). Bicycles can be rented for as little as US$5 per day from tourist cafes in Hanoi and Ho Chi Minh City. If you plan on staying in one city for a month or two, you may wish to consider buying one, as prices are very reasonable. If you have a mechanical problem or a tyre puncture, don't worry: there are stands set up on practically every street corner where most repairs will cost a few thousand dong. Vietnamese models are cheap (less

than US$30) but of extremely poor quality; they often disintegrate within a single day. Pay a little more and get a Chinese one. However, pirate Chinese bikes are quite common. Most of the components may in fact be Vietnamese.

There are also automobile taxis in the major cities. They have new cars, with meters and air-conditioning and are reasonably priced.

BY AIR

Flying is by far the best way to travel if you intend to visit only a few cities in Vietnam. A Vietnam Airlines flight from Hanoi to Ho Chi Minh City costs under US$200, whereas the train for the same distance, including meals for two days, costs roughly the same. Vietnam Airlines also flies to places that are very time-consuming to get to by other means, like Phu Quoc Island and Pleiku. The major problem with flying is finding space. Popular flights fill up a few days before departure, so it is imperative to book flights early. It is very common for Vietnam Airlines to bump Vietnamese passengers off domestic flights when foreigners are on the waiting list, as foreign ticket prices are twice the Vietnamese price. You can use credit cards to buy airline tickets in Hanoi and Ho Chi Minh City, but in other cities you may be asked to pay cash.

Scheduled Vietnam Airlines

The Ubiquitous Cyclo

No trip to Vietnam is complete without a ride in a cyclo (three-wheeled rickshaw). Vietnam has thousands of waiting cyclo drivers who can be hired by the kilometre or the hour. Expect to pay at least 3,000 dong for a short ride or 10,000 dong for an hour. It is essential to bargain with cyclo drivers beforehand.

As a rule, halve their first offer and work up. Write the agreed-upon figure on a piece of paper and ensure that the driver agrees; this method can prevent

acrimonious arguments at the conclusion of the journey. Most cyclo drivers in the south are former ARVN soldiers and speak a little English. Cyclo drivers are indispensable as guides, sources of historical information, and as the procurers of hard-to-find items.

A faster way to get around town in Hanoi and Ho Chi Minh City is a motorcycle taxi, called a *xe om* (say ome) or *Honda om*, which literally means "hugging taxi" as passengers grab onto the driver's waist. You don't need to look for *xe*

om; they will find you. Fares actually are cheaper than on cycles, and of course the ride is quicker. Once again, write the agreed-upon figure on a piece of paper.

Some of the drivers navigate the roads badly, however, so be careful. If a driver seems unsafe, tell him to stop, get off, and pay him. Find another driver.

Some women travellers have reported problems with *xe om* drivers getting too friendly; be careful travelling late at night, in particular.

flights from Ho Chi Minh City serve Buon Me Thuot, Da Lat, Da Nang, Hai Phong, Hanoi, Hue, Nha Trang, Phu Quoc, Pleiku, Qui Nhon and Rach Gia.

Da Lat is serviced by Lien Khuong Airport, located in Duc Trong District, about 30 km (19 miles) southwest of Da Lat. Taxis into town cost around US$20, motorcycle taxis, about US$6. If you're staying at one of the major hotels, you can pre-arrange airport shuttle service for a small fee.

From Da Lat, Vietnam Airlines has non-stop flights to Da Nang and Ho Chi Minh City (daily), and connections to Hanoi, Phu Quoc, and Singapore. In Da Lat, tickets can be purchased from the Vietnam Airlines office at 40 Ho Tung Mau Street, tel: 822 895.

For travel to and from the Delta, Vietnam Airlines currently has air service only between Ho Chi Minh and Phu Quoc Island, and between Phu Quoc Island and Rach Gia. Can Tho's airport (Tra Noc Airport) is scheduled to start operations in November 2001 with Air Mekong flying between Ho Chi Minh City and Can Tho. Tra Noc Airport is located 6 km (4 miles) from town on the road to Binh Thuy.

From Hanoi there are scheduled regular flights to Da Nang, Ho Chi Minh City, Hue, Vinh and Nha Trang.

From Nha Trang, there are several daily non-stop flights to Ho Chi Minh City (1 hour), one daily non-stop to Hanoi (2½ hours), and several flights a week to Da Nang. Nha Trang Airport is located near the beach in the southern part of town. Unless you're staying outside Nha Trang, you can take a taxi, or better yet, a cyclo to your hotel, which is probably just up the beach anyway and shouldn't cost more than US$3. Alternatively, check with your hotel about airport transfers.

Hanoi

Hanoi Railway Station, Nam Bo Street (located at the far Western end of Tran Hung Dao Street), Hanoi. The ticket office is open daily from 7.30–11.30am and

1.30–3.30pm. Buy tickets one day in advance.

Hanoi Bus Station, Kim Lien Street, Hanoi. There are daily express buses at 5am to Buon Me Thuot, Da Nang, Pleiku, Ho Chi Minh City, Kontum, Nha Trang, Quang Ngai and Qui Nhon. Most express buses leave at 5am. Local (non-express buses) leave Kim Lien Station for Sam Son, Thanh Hoa and Vinh throughout the day.

Ho Chi Minh City

Buses

For visitors travelling overland between Cambodia and Vietnam, there are daily long-distance buses between Ho Chi Minh City and Phnom Penh. Buses depart Ho Chi Minh City from 145 Nguyen Du, District 1 in the wee hours of the morning and cost US$7 per person. Alternatively, you can take one of the many mini-buses bound for Tay Ninh from the Tay Ninh Bus Station (Tan Binh District) but get off at Go Dau where motorcycle taxis will vie to take you to the border crossing at Moc Bai. Many budget travel agencies offer 4-day overland trips to Cambodia. Finally, in the spirit of least hassle, you could always hire a travel agency to arrange a private car for you. In any case, be sure to have Moc Bai listed as the entry or exit point on your visa.

From Ho Chi Minh City, public buses serve all the major cities in the Mekong Delta:
My Tho (72 km/45 miles)
Can Tho (169 km/105 miles)
Ben Tre (86 km/53 miles)
Vinh Long (136 km/85 miles)
Soc Trang (231 km/144 miles)
Bac Lieu (276 km/172 miles)
Ca Mau (344 km/214 miles)
Tra Vinh (194 km/121 miles)
Long Xuyen (184 km/114 miles)
Rach Gia (280 km/174 miles)
Ha Tien (360 km/224 miles).
Both express and local buses, as well as mini-buses, leave from Mien Tay Station, which is at 137 Hung Vuong in Binh Chanh District, tel: 877 6593. In addition, there is an express bus service to My Tho that departs from the Cho Lon Bus

Station. Getting to many destinations in the Delta often requires a combination of bus journey and ferry crossings.

Hydrofoil

Daily hydrofoil service between Ho Chi Minh City and Can Tho has been reinstated after being temporarily discontinued due to several accidents, some of them fatal. If you are willing to chance that safety standards have improved, this is definitely a more comfortable and convenient way of reaching Can Tho since the trip takes only 2 hours. In Ho Chi Minh, Vina Express hydrofoil tickets can be purchased at the port (Ben Bach Dang) across from the Majestic Hotel. The hydrofoil arrives at Ninh Kieu Wharf located directly across from the Quoc Te (International) Hotel.

Boats

To reach the more remote areas in the Delta, local boats have to be hired. For points north and east, buses depart Mien Dong Station for Bien Hoa, Buon Me Thout, Da Lat, Da Nang, Hai Phong, Hanoi, Hue, Long Hai, Nam Dinh, Nha Trang, Pleiku, Quang Ngai, Quy Nhon, Tuy Hoa, Vinh and Vung Tau. Mien Dong Station is 5 km (3 miles) north of the centre of town on Highway 13 (the extension of Xo Viet Nghe Tinh Street). All long-distance buses depart between 5 and 5.30am.

Private Buses

Because a number of roads in Vietnam are practically unnavigable in some places, and public transport is always overcrowded and often decrepit, and because the infrastructure in this still-developing communist country is simply not geared towards independent travel, many travellers, especially those on a budget, opt to enter or leave Ho Chi Minh City on private buses reserved for foreigners. Mainly operated by the lower-end budget travellers' cafes, these buses make stops at major cities along the route. An "open ticket" allows you to get on or off with few restrictions. With a Ho Chi Minh City–Hanoi ticket costing less than $50, this is certainly one of the cheaper ways of getting around. That this mode of travel significantly reduces the opportunity to interact with locals or to get at all off the beaten path, even for a while, is unfortunately a price one does have to pay.

Buses to Cambodia leave from the Phnom Penh Garage at 155 Nguyen Hue Boulevard.

Long Hai is 112 km (70 miles) southeast of Ho Chi Minh City and can be reached by bus or car in about 2–3 hours. Buses from Ho Chi Minh City to Long Hai leave from Mien Dong Bus station though service is infrequent. Check beforehand.

Trains

Saigon Railway Station, 1 Nguyen Thong Street, District 3, (10 km/6 miles from city centre), Ho Chi Minh City. The ticket office is open daily from 7.15–11am and 1–3pm. There are express trains to Hanoi daily.

In general, airline, boat, train and bus ticket prices for foreigners are twice that for locals.

Nha Trang

Buses

The **Lien Tinh bus station**, Duong 23 Thang 10 Street, a little less than 2 km (1 mile) west of the centre of town. Buses depart Ho Chi Minh City for Nha Trang from Mien Dong Bus Station. The trip takes approximately 11 hours and it can be rough, as stretches of Highway 1 are always under repair. From Lien Tinh station, buses depart for Buon Ma Thuot, Da Lat, Da Nang, Di Linh, Ho Chi Minh City, Phan Rang, Pleiku, Quang Ngai and Quy Nhon.

A nicer alternative is the chartered mini-buses organised by tourists' cafes. Buses serve Ho Chi Minh City (9 hours), Da Lat (6 hours), and Hoi An (11 hours) and cost $12, $6 and $11 respectively. In Nha Trang, the Sinh Cafe bus arrives and departs from the My A Hotel at 9 Nguyen Thien Thuat Street.

Other

If it's within your budget, cars with drivers can be rented at any travel agency.

Nha Trang is served by daily express and local trains from Ho Chi Minh City and Hanoi. **Nha Trang Railway Station**, 19 Thai Nguyen Street next to the Nha Trang Cathedral. Its booking office is only open from 7am–2pm. Any of the larger hotels or travel agencies in town can purchase tickets for you for a small fee.

Nha Trang Harbour is located south of town in Cau Da. Occasionally, visitors do arrive in Nha Trang on cruise ships, though such travellers are invariably on organised tours with pre-planned itineraries.

Phan Thiet

Buses

Phan Thiet is almost 200 km (124 miles) east of Ho Chi Minh City, 250 km (155 miles) south of Nha Trang and 247 km (154 miles) southeast of Da Lat. Buses to Phan Thiet from Ho Chi Minh City depart from Mien Dong bus station. In Phan Thiet, the bus station is on Tu Van Tu Street at the northern edge of town. Motorcycle taxis will take you into town or to Mui Ne.

If you arrive by chartered mini-bus, you will be dropped in town. Motorcycle taxis can take you to Mui Ne or any of the resorts on the Phan Thiet–Mui Ne coastal road. The higher-end hotels here can also arrange private transport to and from Ho Chi Minh City, all at a higher price, of course. The journey takes 3–4 hours by car.

Trains

The railway station serving Phan Thiet is at Muong Man, located about 12 km (7 miles) west of Phan Thiet town. The Reunification Express between Ho Chi Minh City and Hanoi stops here as do local trains. It is often difficult to book tickets, especially for soft sleepers, originating from Muong Man because they're usually sold out at the previous major stops such as Ho Chi Minh City or Nha Trang.

Availability for other types of tickets is known only after the train has left the last major station.

Hue

Hue bus stations: An Cuu Bus Station for southbound buses, An Hoa to northward destinations and Dong Ba for short-haul destinations. Contact the bus station at Hung Vuong Street, Tel: 823 817, for further information.

Hue Railway Station, Le Loi Street. Ticket office opens between 6.30am and 5pm.

Da Lat

Da Lat Bus Station, Duong 3 Thang 4 Street, about 2 km (1 mile) south of the centre of town. There are buses to Ho Chi Minh City, Nha Trang, Phan Rang, Da Nang, Quang Nai and Cat Tien. Public buses from Ho Chi Minh City leave for Da Lat from Mien Dong Station. Few, if any, foreigners, however, choose this mode of travel.

Da Nang

Da Nang Railway Station, Hai Phong Street – about 1 km (half a mile) from the city centre. Bus tickets for express and some non-express services from Da Nang Intercity Bus Station can be bought from the ticket office at 200 Dien Bien Phu Street: open 7–11am and 1–5pm.

Express services run to Buon Me Thuot, Da Lat, Hai Phong, Hon Gai, Hanoi, Ho Chi Minh City, Gia Lai, Lang Son, Nam Dinh and Nha Trang, and non-express services to Kontum, Vinh and Sathay.

Other non-express services depart from **Da Nang Bus Station** to Dong Ha, Hoi An, Hue, Quang Hgai, Qui Nhon, Tra My and various other destinations.

Vung Tau

Buses

Vung Tau is about 130 km (80 miles) southeast of Ho Chi Minh City. Non-stop, air-conditioned buses depart for Ho Chi Minh City from Mien Dong bus station. The trip takes between 2–3 hours depending on road conditions and costs about $5 for foreigners. In Vung Tau, the bus station is at 50 Nam Ky Khoi Nghia Street.

Minibuses to Vung Tau leave from 39 Nguyen Hue Boulevard at 7am daily. Buy tickets one day in advance. These buses are miserably overcrowded, so you may want to consider buying an extra seat to give yourself more room.

Hydrofoil

The easiest and most convenient way to reach Vung Tau is by hydrofoil. A one-way ticket costs $10 and the trip takes just under 2 hours. In Ho Chi Minh City, travellers can purchase hydrofoil tickets at the port (Ben Bach Dang) located across from the Majestic Hotel. In Vung Tau, the ticket office for Vina Express is at 116 Le Hong Phong, tel: 856 530.

Where to Stay

The Western concept of tourism is something foreign to Vietnam and the country has a very long way to go before it can offer the standard of services and accommodation found in other more developed tourist destinations. Vietnam's hotel infrastructure, particularly in the north and centre, is far from international standard. Rooms are often under-equipped or equipped with fixtures and appliances that don't work, and power cuts are frequent. Room rates are quite high, often more than the standard of accommodation warrants, particularly in contrast with other poor Asian countries. This is partly because the government sets minimum rates and hotel owners must pay high taxes. With so many vacant rooms, it's always worth bargaining. Some very good hotels have been built recently in Ho Chi Minh City, Vung Tau, Nha Trang and Da Nang, and other existing hotels are being refurbished. The hotels built during the French and American eras in Ho Chi Minh City, Hanoi and Da Nang retain a certain faded charm and well-worn comfort.

On the plus side, hotel staff are friendly and try to be helpful. Unfortunately, some basic services,

Dong, Not Dollars?

Officially, hotels are now required to accept payment only in Vietnamese dong. However, many still accept US dollars. Small ones prefer US dollars and will always quote rates in dollars. Many establishments, large and small, will now take major credit cards. Often, they charge a commission.

Price Categories

Usually, higher-end hotels charge an additional tax of about 10 percent and a service charge of about 5 percent.
Below US$50: $
US$50 to US$100: $$
US$100 to US$200: $$$
More than US$200: $$$$

such as taking telephone messages, are not up to par. People visiting on business might find such lapses in service frustrating. Charges for international phone calls from hotels tend to be astronomical.

There was a hotel boom in the mid-1990s in Ho Chi Minh City and Hanoi. Now it is easy to find accommodation. Although a few years ago demand outstripped supply, today the reverse is true. It is always a good idea to ask for a "discount". Many new hotels have offered "soft opening" rates, discounts of up to 40 percent, which they have sometimes extended indefinitely. It is worth asking for that rate. Also, hotels offer better rates for corporate clients, repeat customers and people booked by a travel agent. Thus, all of the rates listed should only be taken as a guide.

The South

HO CHI MINH CITY (SAIGON)

Bong Sen Hotel, 117–123 Dong Khoi Street, Dist 1. Tel: 829 1516; Room Resv. Tel: 829 1721; Fax: 829 8076; bongsen@hcm.vnn.vn. Conveniently located in the middle of the Dong Khoi shopping district and in close proximity to a number of excellent Vietnamese and French restaurants, this is a reliable, unpretentious favourite with many guests. The Saigon Health Club is on the 6th floor. **$$–$$$**
Continental Hotel, 132–134 Dong Khoi Street, Dist 1. Tel: 829 9201; Fax: 824 1772. Built in 1880 and last renovated in 1989, this

legendary French Colonial-style hotel with Chinese-style furniture tries hard to evoke a bygone era when Graham Greene haunted its corridors in the 1950s, and journalists sipped beers on the terrace during the war. Though facing stiff competition from a spate of newer hotels, the Continental's pleasant frangipani garden and excellent Vietnamese, Chinese and Italian restaurants still make it one of the more popular hotels in town. **$$$**

Delta Caravelle Hotel, 19 Lam Son Square, Dist 1. Tel: 823 4999; Fax: 824 3999; caravellehotel@bdvn.vnd.net. With a prime city centre location, this one-time favourite with journalists has been thoroughly renovated and expanded into yet another modern high-rise. The roof of the Caravelle offers a great view of Central Saigon. With 335 rooms, including suites and service apartments as well as familiar joints like the Hard Rock Cafe, it's possible to believe you never left home. One of the most popular downtown hotels. **$$$–$$$$**

Embassy Hotel, 35–39 Nguyen Trung Truc Street, Dist 1. Tel: 823 1981; Fax: 823 1978. This mid-range, no-frills hotel is located near the Reunification Palace. The decor's not much to write home about but the rooms are adequate, and there's always karaoke available. Breakfast included. Restaurant, foreign exchange. **$–$$**

Giant Dragon Hotel, 173 Pham Ngu Lao Street, Dist 1. Tel: 836 9268; Fax: 836 7279. Located near the heart of backpackers' quarters, this mid-range hotel offers 34 rooms with air-conditioning, phones and satellite TV. Restaurant on premises serves Western and Asian cuisine. Friendly staff. Easy access to travellers' cafes. **$–$$**

Hotel Equatorial, 242 Tran Binh Trong, Dist 5. Tel: 839 0000; Fax: 839 0011. Located in Cho Lon, this luxurious hotel attracts many business travellers and offers special packages for long-term guests and business executives. It is, however, located outside the city

centre. Health club, conference rooms, bakery, Western, Japanese, and one of the best Chinese restaurants in town, the Golden Phoenix. **$$$–$$$$**

Hotel Sofitel Plaza Saigon, 17 Le Duan Blvd, Dist 1. Tel: 824 1555; Fax: 824 1666; E-mail: salessaigon@accor-hotel-vietnam.com. The only 5-star hotel in the city, this posh new joint venture with Hong Kong and Singapore, which opened in September 1998, has friendly staff, tasteful rooms, full facilities including Western and Asian restaurants serving 7 different Asian cuisines, and a rooftop pool offering great city views. **$$$$**

Majestic Hotel, 1 Dong Khoi Street, Dist 1. Tel: 829 5514; Fax: 829 5510; majestic.s.hotel@bdvn.vnd.net. Originally built in 1925, this old classic has since undergone numerous renovations, the last in 1995. Overlooking the Saigon River, the hotel offers majestic suites and the usual full facilities, as well as an *ao dai* fashion show every Saturday night. **$$$–$$$$**

New World Hotel, 76 Le Lai, Dist 1. Tel: 822 8888; Fax: 823 0710; E-mail: nwhs@hcm.vnn.vn. One of the largest hotels in town, the New World is of late looking a little lacklustre on the outside. It offers the usual modern conveniences, five restaurants and full facilities including an outdoor pool, tennis courts and a golf driving range. Caters to many business travellers and Japanese tour groups. **$$$–$$$$**

Norfolk Hotel, 117 Le Thanh Ton, Dist 1. Tel: 829 5368; Fax: 829 3415; norfolk@mailser.ut-hcmc.edu.vn. This pleasant 3-star hotel is located near the business and shopping districts and offers comfortable rooms. A monthly "Second Friday" social allows business people to exchange ideas. The hotel caters to business people and journalists. Health club and business centre. **$$$**

Omni Saigon, 251 Nguyen Van Troi Street, Phu Nhuan District. Tel: 844 9222/9333; Fax: 844 9200;

omnisgn@saigon.teltic.com.vn. Located 10 minutes from the airport, this elegant 4-star hotel offers class, luxury, the usual amenities and free shuttle service to the city centre 15 minutes' away. Western, Chinese and Japanese restaurants up to international standards and prices. **$$$–$$$$**

Oscar Saigon Hotel, 68A Nguyen Hue Blvd., Dist 1. Tel: 829 2959; Fax: 829 2732. Formerly the Century Saigon Hotel, this Hong Kong joint venture is located in the central business district. The hotel has a rather bland air about it, with 109 adequate but unspectacular rooms. Health club, conference rooms, business centre, and the requisite disco and karaoke rooms. **$$–$$$**

Palace Hotel, 56–64 Nguyen Hue Boulevard. Tel: 84-8 829 2860; Fax: 824 4230; Telex: 811 208 HOTHN-VT; palace@hcm.vnn.vn. Restaurant, bars, disco, video, swimming pool, souvenir shop, money changing facilities and laundry. **$$**

Pham Ngu Lao

Together with Bui Vien and De Tham streets, this area, 1 km (half a mile) west of downtown Saigon, marks the main area for budget accommodation. Mini-hotels and guesthouses abound here, as do travellers' cafes with Internet access.

Dai Hoang Kim Hotel, 196 Bui Vien Street, Dist 1. Tel: 836 8691; Fax: 837 0914. Small but clean rooms with hot water, air-conditioning, fan, fridge, phone and satellite TV. **$**

Que Huong – Liberty 2 Hotel, 129–133 Ham Nghi Blvd. Dist 1. Tel: 822 4922; Fax: 823 0776. The second in a string of four Liberty Hotels, this one is centrally located near the Ben Thanh Market. Rooms are basic. Breakfast is included. A restaurant on the 10th floor affords a panoramic view of the city. **$$**

Rex Hotel, 141 Nguyen Hue Blvd., Dist 1. Tel: 829 2185; Fax: 829 3115; rexhotel@hcm.vnn.vn. That this hotel is still a popular choice has less to do with its garish mix of

Eastern and Western decorative styles than with its colourful history of having once housed US military officers. Great location with full facilities. The popular rooftop garden with bonsais and singing birds provides 24-hour dining as well as excellent views of bustling downtown Saigon. **$$–$$$$**

Riverside Hotel, 18 Ton Duc Thang Street, Dist 1. Tel: 822 4038; Fax: 825 1417. Dark and unimpressive on the inside, this old colonial building could use an exterior facelift too. Located very near the Saigon River, the hotel offers 77 rooms, a business centre, an international restaurant and karaoke rooms with a view. **$$–$$$**

Saigon Prince Hotel, 63 Nguyen Hue Blvd, Dist 1. Tel: 822 2999; Fax: 824 1888; Reservations: 822 5666; saigon-princehtl@hcm.vnn.vn. This modern, spacious hotel complete with fountains and wide, curving staircases right in the heart of downtown attracts mostly business executives and tour groups. Serves Vietnamese, Singaporean, Japanese and Western cuisines. **$$$–$$$$**

Windsor Saigon Hotel, 193 Tran Hung Dao Street, Dist 1. Tel: 836 7848; Fax: 836 7889. Located less than a kilometre from downtown Saigon, this boutique hotel with balconies and wide arched windows has 64 spacious rooms and caters to many Europeans as well as long-term business travellers. Pleasant ambience, full facilities, excellent restaurant and bakery. **$$$**

OUTSIDE HO CHI MINH

Long Hai

Anoasis Beach Resort, Domain Ky Van, Long Hai, Baria-Vung Tau. Tel: 868 227; Fax: 868 229. This is so far the nicest resort in still-developing Long Hai. Set around 32 acres of tropical parkland and overlooking the ocean with a private beach, this secluded hotel offers accommodation in thatched cottage bungalows. Facilities and services include a business centre, conference rooms, a swimming

pool, beach sports, and even helicopter service. **$$$–$$$$**

Thuy Duong Hotel, Phuoc Hai Village, Long Dat District, Baria-Vung Tau. Tel: 886 215; Fax: 886 180. This modest resort nestled between the hills and the beach offers accommodation in a variety of bungalows and cottages. In addition to the usual resort amenities, a swimming pool, tennis courts, Jacuzzi, sauna, karaoke and billiards can be found here. **$**

Vung Tau

Cap Saint Jacques Hotel, 2 Thuy Van Street. Tel: 807 068; Fax: 859 519. Formerly the Phuong Dong Hotel, this modern complex on Back Beach boasts 109 comfortable rooms, some with great sea views. Facilities include 2 restaurants serving Western and Asian cuisines, a swimming pool, tennis court, gymnasium, nightclub and karaoke. **$–$$**

Grand Hotel, 26 Quang Trung Street. Tel: 856 469; Fax: 856 164. Right on Front Beach, this ugly low-rise offers two separate wings, 70 rooms, and all the entertainment facilities you could want. **$**

Hai Yen Hotel (formerly The International Hotel), 8 Le Loi Street. Tel: 852 571; Fax: 852 858. With 25 rooms. **$**

Nha Nghi 72, Back Beach. Rooms with fan. **$**

Pacific Hotel, 4 Le Loi Street. Tel: 856 740; Fax: 852 391. Famous for its Czech restaurant. **$**

Palace Hotel, 11 Nguyen Trai Street. Tel: 856 411; Fax: 856 878. Located a block from Front Beach, this hotel with 120 rooms appears to be popular with Western and Asian tour groups. Rooms are somewhat tacky but the staff is friendly. In addition to the usual facilities and services, the hotel also offers a traditional folk show. **$**

Rex Hotel, 1 Duy Tan Street. Tel: 852 135; Fax: 859 862. Centrally located on Front Beach, this 8-storey hotel has 75 somewhat ugly rooms, 3 restaurants serving Asian, European and seafood specialities, health club, sauna, karaoke, souvenir shops and a very nice

pool. Bears no relation to the Rex Hotel in Ho Chi Minh City. **$–$$**

Royal Hotel (formerly Canadian Hotel), 48 Quang Trung Street. Tel: 859 852; Fax: 859 851. The Royal Hotel overlooks Front Beach. All 53 guest rooms are equipped with IDD telephone, satellite TV, mini-bar and safe deposit box. Full business and entertainment facilities. **$$**

Sammy Hotel, 18 Thuy Van Street. Tel: 854 755; Fax: 854 762. Located on Back Beach with both mountain and ocean views, this joint venture with Hong Kong has all the conveniences but also the blandness of a large modern hotel. Facilities include business centre, a Chinese restaurant, Western cafe, sauna, massage, and the usual entertainment outlets. **$$**

Sea Breeze Hotel, 11 Nguyen Trai Street. Tel: 856 392; Fax: 856 856. A comfortable modern hotel. **$$**

Vietnamese Youth Tourist Centre, 46A Thuy Van. Bungalows. **$**

Villa Nha Rong Bimexco, Thuy Van Street, Back Beach, Ward 8. Tel: 859 916; Fax: 853 470. Accommodation is in somewhat run-down bungalows on a dirty stretch of beach. Rooms with air-conditioning and hot water are US$25, those with air-conditioning and cold water are $14 and rooms with fans run $10 to 17.

The Delta

Can Tho

Hau Giang Hotel, 34 Nam Ky Khoi Nghia. Tel: 835 537, 825 181, 821 851. A very friendly hotel, excellent food, video room. **$**

Hoang Cung Hotel, 55 Phan Dinh Phung Street. Tel: 835 401, 825 831. Singles/doubles with air-conditioning and private bath. **$**

Huy Hoang Hotel, 35 Ngo Duc Ke Street. Tel: 825 833. Standard budget accommodation. **$**

Price Categories

Below US$50:	$
US$50 to US$100:	$$
US$100 to US$200:	$$$
More than US$200:	$$$$

Ninh Kieu Hotel, 2 Hai Ba Trung.
Tel: 821 171; Fax: 821 104.
Located at the end of Hai Ba Trung
in its own compound, this relatively
quiet hotel has large, clean rooms
and friendly staff. A riverfront
restaurant serves both Asian and
Western cuisine. **$**
Quoc Te Hotel, 12 Hai Ba Trung.
Tel: 822 079; Fax: 821 039.
Located in the centre of Can Tho
town near the market, this is a
popular mid-range choice with many
Western tourists. Rooms are basic
with air-conditioning and bath,
though some have balconies with
river views. Restaurants, bar,
meeting room, and the usual
dancing and karaoke facilities. **$–$$**
Saigon Can Tho Hotel, Phan Dinh
Phung Street. Tel: 825 831; Fax:
823 288. A flashy modern hotel
with 46 rooms. Facilities include a
business centre, conference room,
fitness centre with sauna and
massage, and billiard and karaoke
rooms. The restaurant serves
Western, Chinese and Vietnamese
food. **$–$$**
Victoria Can Tho Hotel, Cai Khe
Ward, Can Tho City. Tel: 810 111;
Fax: 829 259;
victoriact@hcm.vnn.vn.
Opened in October 1998, this is
the most luxurious hotel in the
whole Delta. Located on its own
promontory on the banks of the
Hau River several kilometres from
the centre of town, this resort has
88 tasteful rooms and 8 suites.
With full facilities, business centre,
conference rooms, swimming pool,
and its own jetty. Plans call for
developing ecotourism in the area
as a way of attracting guests.
Restaurant offers Western and
Asian cuisine in a classy, pleasant
environment. **$$–$$$**

My Tho

Chuong Duong Hotel, 10, 30/4
Street. Tel: 870 875; Fax: 870 876.
Air-conditioned rooms available. **$**
Cong Doan Hotel, 61, 30/4 Street.
Tel: 874 324. Standard budget
accommodation located on the
riverfront. Car and boat rental. **$**
Dao Dua
Coco Island. No phone available.

Located on a beautiful island in Ben
Tre province, a short boat ride from
My Tho. No air-conditioning. **$**
Rang Dong Hotel, No. 25, 30/4
Street. Tel: 874 400. One of the
nicer places in town, this mini-hotel
next to the river has 21 rooms with
air-conditioning, telephones and hot
water. **$**
Song Tien Hotel, 101 Trung Trac.
Tel: 872 009. Located in the centre
of town, this 8-storey hotel is the
largest in My Tho, with 40 rooms
and a view of the city from the
hotel's terrace. Rooms with fans
run at US$6, those with air-
conditioning range from $10 to 20.
Tien Giang Province Guest House.
On the corner of Hung Vuong
Boulevard and Rach Gam Street. **$**

Rach Gia

Palace Hotel, 41 Tran Phu Street.
Tel: 863 049. Probably the nicest,
most modern hotel in town. Expect
the usual entertainment and
karaoke facilities. **$**
1/5 (First of May) Hotel, 38
Nguyen Hung Son Street. Tel: 863
414. 18 air-conditioned rooms –
when the electrics are working. The
plumbing is also very
temperamental. Very basic and
overpriced accommodation at
US$26 for doubles and US$20 for
singles. 15 other rooms are even
more basic, but so is the price –
US$15 for doubles and US$12
for singles. The food, however,
is good.
To Chau Hotel, 16 Le Loi Street.
Tel: 863 718; Fax: 862 111. An
unremarkable place with large,
adequate rooms. Parking is
available here. Rooms with air-
conditioning and hot water cost
US$11 to 18, those with fan and
cold water are $6.
Binh Minh Hotel, 48 Pham Hong
Thai Street. Tel: 862 154. Basic
budget accommodation near the
market with a small restaurant on
the premises. **$**
Thanh Binh Hotel, 11 Ly Truong
Street. Tel: 863 053. 9 rooms with
fan and bath. **$**
Nha Kach Uy Ban, 31 Nguyen Hung
Son Street. Tel: 863 237. Singles
with shared bath. **$**

Long Xuyen

Cuu Long Hotel, 21 Nguyen Van
Cung. Tel: 843 280; Fax: 843 176.
One of the nicer hotels in town,
which is not saying much. Air-
conditioning and hot water. **$**
Long Xuyen Hotel, 17 Nguyen Van
Cung Street. Tel: 841 659; Fax:
842 483. Basic, but there's
karaoke. **$**
Thai Binh Hotel, 12 Nguyen Hue,
Thi Xa. Tel: 852 184. 32 rooms with
fans, doubles US$6 and air-
conditioned rooms US$8. Good
restaurant and dance hall.

Chau Doc

Chau Doc Hotel, 17 Doc Phu Thu,
Thi Xa. Tel: 866 484. 30 rooms,
double room with fan costs US$6
and air-conditioned costs US$10.
Hang Chau Hotel, 32 Le Loi Street.
Tel: 866 196; Fax: 867 773.
Located on the riverfront close to
the Hau Giang terminal. All rooms
are air-conditioned. **$**
Thanh Tra Hotel, 77 Thu Khoa
Nghia. Tel: 866 788. Basic
accommodation that's popular
with Western tour groups. Parking
available for those who arrive by
private car. Rooms with fan and
attached baths run US$5–8, those
with air-conditioning and cold
water are $9, and the luxury ones
with air-conditioning and hot water
are $17.
Thuan Loi Hotel, 18 Tran Hung Dao.
Tel: 866 134; Fax: 868 447.
Centrally located hotel that caters
to many Western tourists. Rooms
are decent and some come with
fridge and TV. There is a restaurant
on the premises though travellers
seem to prefer to eat their main
meals elsewhere. Rooms with hot
water and fan run at US$12 while
air-conditioning brings the price up
to $17 to $19.

Vinh Long

Cuu Long Hotel, 501 1/5 Street.
Tel: 822 494; Fax: 823 357. The
newer wing of the Cuu Long Hotel,
this is the best hotel in town, which
is not saying much. Located on the
riverfront with facilities including
restaurant, bar, laundry and
karaoke rooms. **$**

Long Chau Hotel, 1, 1/5 Street, Tel: 823 611. A depressing dump of a place. Rates start from US$4 for rooms with fans to $18 for rooms with air-conditioning, attached bath.

In addition, homestays on An Binh and Binh Hoa Phuoc Islands can be arranged through **Cuu Long Tourist**, 1, 1/5 Street. Tel: 823 616; Fax: 823 357.

Ben Tre

Dong Khoi Hotel, 16 Hai Ba Trung. Tel: 822 240. **$**

Ha Tien

Dong Ho Hotel, Corner of To Chau and Dong Ho streets. Tel: 852 141. Very basic accommodation located near the market. There's no hot water here. Rooms with fans are US$5; with air-conditioning and television US$8 to 11.
Ha Tien Hotel. On the corner of Ben Tran Hau and Phuong Thanh streets. **$**
Hai Van Hotel, 646A Lam Son Street. Tel: 852 872. Located a block from the riverfront. Rooms with air-conditioning, hot water and telephone cost US$11 while those with fans only are $6.
Ha Chau Hotel
Trang Cong Street, south of floating bridge. Tel: 852 670. Very cheap, friendly, clean and relatively new. Air-conditioned rooms are available. **$**
To Chau Hotel, Corner of To Chau and Dong Ho Streets. Tel: 852 148. Located near the floating bridge with views of the river. Rooms with fan and attached bath are US$5 while those with bath, air-conditioning and television run at US$10 – 12.

Central Vietnam

Hue

Century Riverside, 49 Le Loi Street. Tel: 823 390; Fax: 823 394. Recently remodelled, the Century commands a stunning view of the Perfume River. Breakfast in the restaurant is excellent. **$$**
Huong Giang Hotel (Perfume River), 51 Le Loi Street. Tel: 822 122; Fax: 823 102. 42 air-conditioned rooms with fridge and telephone. Terrace restaurant,

souvenir shop, post office, telex, Vietnamese massage, tennis, ping pong, billiards, dancing (Saturday evenings), small private jetty, boat trips. **$$–$$$$**
Thuan Hoa Hotel, 7 Nguyen Tri Phuong. Tel: 822 553, 822 576; Fax: 822 470. 78 rooms – 44 air-conditioned, with fridge and telephone. Restaurant, terrace cafe, small boutique. **$–$$**
Hotel Saigon Morin, 30 Le Loi Street. Tel: 823 526; Fax: 825 155. Recently totally refurbished. Spacious rooms with high ceilings and hot water. The courtyard restaurant is also good. **$$**
Dong Phuong Hotel (Nua Thu Hotel), 26 Nguyen Tri Phuong. Tel: 823 929. Excellent restaurant. **$**
Thanh Noi Hotel, 3 Dang Dung Street. Tel: 822 478; Fax: 827 211. Beautifully situated near the Citadel. **$**
San Thuong Tu Hotel, 1 Dinh Tien Hoang Street. **$**
Hang Be Hotel, 173 Huynh Thuc Khang Street. Tel: 823 752. Ground floor restaurant. **$**
Tan My Hotel, Thuan An Beach. Tel: 866 033. Souvenir shop, laundry. **$**
Nha Kach, 11 Ly Thuong Kiet Street. US$16 to 20; 16 Ly Thuong Kiet Street. Tel: 823 679; and at number 18, Tel: 823 889. US$16 to 20. These three small villas on Ly Thuong Kiet Street provide some of the most pleasant accommodation in Hue.

Da Nang

Phuong Dong (the Oriental), 93 Phan Chu Trinh. Tel: 821 266, 822 854. 36 air-conditioned rooms. Restaurant, bar, telex and IDD services, souvenir and craft shop, laundry. **$$**
Da Nang Hotel, 3 Dong Da Street. Tel: 821 986. Great value with rooms starting at US$25. Has the fastest laundry facilities in Vietnam.
Marble Mountain Hotel, 5 Dong Da Street. Next to the popular Da Nang Hotel with comparable facilities but less atmosphere. Located in the far north of town close to the budget traveller's Cafe Lien. **$**
Non Nuoc Hotel, 10 Ly Thuong Kiet, Hua Nghi. Tel: 821 470, 822 137.

Price Categories

Below US$50:	**$**
US$50 to US$100:	**$$**
US$100 to US$200:	**$$$**
More than US$200:	**$$$$**

14 km (9 miles) from Da Nang at the foot of the Marble Mountains, situated on a lovely beach. Advance booking is necessary due to its popularity. Restaurant and bar on the beach. **$$**
The Hai Au Hotel, 177 Tran Phu Street. Tel: 822 722; Fax: 824 165. A modern hotel with air-conditioned rooms. **$$**
The Bach Dang Hotel, 50 Bach Dang Street. Tel: 823 649; Fax: 821 659. Located on the river. **$**

Qui Nhon

Dong Phuong Hotel, 39 Mai Xuan Thuong Street. Probably the most reasonable rates in town. **$**

Nha Trang

Ana Mandara Resort, Beachside, Tran Phu Blvd. Tel: 829 829; Fax: 829 629. Nha Trang's nicest and most luxurious hotel is located in the southern part of town near the airport. Accommodation is in 68 individual villas with open timbered roofs and bamboo furniture. Full facilities including a watersports centre, diving school and private beach. Open-air restaurant serving Vietnamese and international cuisine. **$$$–$$$$**
Bao Dai's Villas, Cau Da. Tel: 881 049; Fax: 881 471. Located 6 km (4 miles) south of Nha Trang, this hotel has 48 rooms in 5 old French colonial villas and 2 newly built, drab concrete blocks. With 2 restaurants, a pleasant garden, great views, and access to a private beach, this appears to be a popular choice with travellers. **$–$$**
Hai Yen Hotel, 40 Tran Phu. Tel: 822 828; Fax: 821 902. This mid-range option by the beach offers 107 unremarkable but adequate rooms and the usual facilities, including a seafood restaurant, dance hall, conference rooms, karaoke, massage, sauna, beauty

parlour and shared swimming pool. Credit cards accepted. **$–$$**

Huu Nghi Hotel, 3 Tran Hung Dao. Tel: 826 703; Fax: 827 416. Even by budget standards, the rooms here are dirty and depressing though the staff tries hard and is friendly enough. You can do better elsewhere. **$**

My A Hotel, 9 Nguyen Thien Thuat Street. Tel: 827 312; Fax: 824 214. Basic budget quarters with restaurant, foreign exchange and ticket-booking services. **$**

Nha Trang Lodge Hotel, 42 Tran Phu. Tel: 810 500; Fax: 828 800; Nt-Lodge@dng.vnn.vn. Nha Trang's other deluxe hotel, this Malaysian joint venture on the beachfront boasts 14 floors and 132 tasteful rooms, each one with an ocean view. Seafood restaurant with Asian and European dishes. Full facilities, business centre, and a swimming pool and tennis courts shared with the Vien Dong and Hai Yen hotels. **$$**

Que Huong Hotel, 60 Tran Phu. Tel: 825 047; Fax: 825 344. One of the newer, and therefore nicer, government-run hotels, the Que Huong is up to the international standards of a 3-star hotel. Rooms are comfortable and equipped with satellite TV and IDD phones. The usual entertainment facilities, swimming pool and tennis courts. Popular with Western tour groups. **$$–$$$**

Thanh Thanh Hotel, 98A Tran Phu. Tel: 824 657; Fax: 823 031. Located somewhat inconveniently on the southern edge of town, this no-frills mini-hotel nevertheless gets good reviews from travellers for its clean rooms, many with balconies and ocean views, friendly service and proximity to the beach. Rooms from US$18 for double, US$15 for single. A good choice if you don't mind being a bit further from town.

Thong Nhat Hotel, 18 Tran Phu Blvd. Than Pho. Tel: 822 966. Opposite the beach. 70 rooms. **$**

Thang Loi Hotel, 4 rue Pasteur, Thanh Pho. Tel: 822 226, 822 241. 70 rooms. Restaurant, souvenir shop, money changing, laundry. **$**

Vien Dong Hotel, 1 Tran Hung Dao.

Price Categories

Below US$50:	**$**
US$50 to US$100:	**$$**
US$100 to US$200:	**$$$**
More than US$200:	**$$$$**

Tel: 821 606; Fax: 821 912. An old standby with travellers, this government-run hotel has seen better days. Dark and dank rooms are made more tolerable by the swimming pool, sauna and nightly musical performances featuring traditional Vietnamese song and dance. Poolside dining. **$**

Phan Thiet

Bamboo Village Resort, Km 11, 8 Ham Tien. Tel: 847 007; Fax: 847 095; dephan@netnam2.org.vn. The advertisement for its beach reads: "no beggars, no vendors, no students practising English". Need we say more. This new kid on the block offers a pleasant all-bamboo environment. Accommodation is in thatched-roof bungalows. A restaurant serving Western and Asian cuisines, volleyball courts and a children's playground are here too. **$**

Chez Nina, Km 12, Ham Tien. Tel: 847 177. A small, charming, family-run hotel right on the beach, Chez Nina has 2 bungalows and 2 rooms in the main house. Western and Asian food served. Friendly and efficient service. **$**

Hotel 19/4, 1 Tu Van Tu, Phan Thiet Town. Tel: 821 794; Fax: 825 184. Located in the heart of town (read: no beach access), this large, depressing place offers basic accommodation in air-conditioned rooms. Restaurant on the premises. Yes, they have massage, sauna and karaoke facilities. **$**

Coco Beach Hai Duong Resort, Km 12.5 Ham Tien. Tel: 847 111; Fax: 847 115; cocobeach@saigonnet.vn. A lovely, secluded resort with only 15 bungalows and villas, this hotel offers all the usual amenities except for karaoke. In compensation, there's a small video library. A variety of sea sports are offered here. **$$–$$$**

Ocean Dunes Resort, 1 Ton Duc Thang. Tel: 822 393; Fax: 825 682; novpht@bdvn.vnmail.vnd.net. This large Club Med-style hotel with 123 rooms is surrounded on three sides by the 18-hole Ocean Dunes Golf Course. Facilities include two pools, a private beach, tennis courts, conference rooms. Daily programme of recreational activities. **$$–$$$**

Phan Thiet Tourist Hotel, 40 Tran Hung Dao, Thi Xa. Tel: 822 573. Air-conditioned rooms. **$**

Victoria Phan Thiet Resort, Km 9 Phu Hai. Tel: 847 170; Fax: 847 174; victoriaPT@bdvn.vnd.net. The most luxurious of the resorts, the Victoria features 50 cottages, all with a sea view. Family cottages are also available. Full facilities, conference room, bike and car rentals, private beach, freshwater pool and Jacuzzi, it's all here. Restaurant serves Western, Asian and local cuisine. Transfer to and from Ho Chi Minh City. **$$–$$$**

Vinh Thuy Hotel, Duong Nguyen Tat Thanh, Thi Xa. Tel: 821 294, 822 394. With 66 rooms, double rooms with air-conditioning cost US$27 to 34. Very good restaurant and swimming beach. **$–$$**

Da Lat

Anh Dao Hotel, 50–52 Hoa Binh Square. Tel: 823 577; Fax: 823 570. Located in the centre of Da Lat, this rather tired-looking hotel is nevertheless still a popular choice. Basic rooms with hot water, phone, minibar and TV. Some rooms have a view of the lake. Also available are Thai massage, karaoke and dancing. Credit cards accepted. **$**

Camdo Hotel, 81 Phan Dinh Phung Street. Tel: 822 482; Fax: 830 273. No frills budget accommodation. Restaurant on premises. **$**

Golf 3 Hotel, 4 Nguyen Thi Minh Khai Street. Tel: 826 042; Fax: 830 396. This newly opened hotel in the centre of the city is a good mid-range choice. With 7 floors and 78 posh rooms, a restaurant serving Asian, European and local food, the usual entertainment facilities, and the open-air Sky View Cafe on the top floor. **$$–$$$**

Hai Son Hotel, 1 Nguyen Thi Minh Khai Street. Tel: 822 379; Fax: 822 623. Centrally located across from the market, this rather dull hotel with tacky furnishings offers basic but comfortable rooms, restaurant, shops, entertainment rooms and parking. **$**

Mimosa Hotel, 170 Phan Dinh Phung Street. Tel: 822 656. Popular budget accommodation that's a bit of a hike from the centre of town. 30 rooms with hot water. **$**

Minh Tam Hotel, 20A Khe Sanh. Tel: 822 447; Fax: 824 420. Located 3 km (2 miles) from the centre of town, this hotel is set on a large, well-kept garden and has 48 rooms. **$**

Nam Ky Hotel, 11 Nam Ky Khoi Nghia. Tel: 824 493. One of the few mini-hotels in Da Lat authorised to accept foreigners. Centrally located with clean rooms and friendly staff. Though their own karaoke facilities remain relatively quiet, be warned that it can get awfully noisy with neighbouring karaoke joints competing against each other.

Ngoc Lan Hotel, 42 Nguyen Chi Thanh Street. Tel: 822 136, 824 032. This bright, 2-star hotel overlooks Xuan Huong Lake and is very popular with Vietnamese tour groups. Restaurant, dance hall, conference room. **$**

Novotel Da Lat, 7 Tran Phu Street. Tel: 825 777; Fax: 825 888; novotel@netnam2.org.vn. Formerly the Du Parc Hotel, this hotel was renovated in 1997 and is now managed by the same company that manages its neighbour the Sofitel Palace. Elegant rooms. The one disadvantage of this hotel is that it shares many of its facilities, including the restaurants and bar, with the Sofitel, all of which are on the Sofitel's premises. **$$$**

Sofitel Da Lat Palace, 12 Tran Phu Street. Tel: 825 444; Fax: 825 666; sofitel@netnam2.org.vn. The only 5-star hotel in Da Lat, this magnificent sprawling palace overlooking Xuan Huong Lake is one of the top luxury hotels in Vietnam. Renovated in classic French colonial-style, the hotel boasts 43 tastefully furnished rooms, a gourmet French restaurant, the usual full facilities, as well as 2 tennis courts and easy access to the 18-hole Da Lat Golf Course. **$$$–$$$$**

Thanh Binh Hotel. Tel: 822 909. Opposite central market. **$**

Phu Hoa Hotel. 16 Tang Bat Ho Street. Rooms from US$5 to 10.

In addition, visitors can stay in **Bao Dai's Summer Palace**, the former Governor General's residence, or one of the many newly renovated villas on Tran Hung Dao. Reservations should be made through Lam Dong Tourist Company.

The North

HANOI

Bodega Cafe & Guesthouse, 57 Trang Tien Street. Tel: 826 7784. This place is always full, but if you can get a room they are a good value, clean and tidy. **$**

Daewoo Hotel, 360 Kim Ma. Tel: 831 5000; Fax: 831 5500. Immense complex in western Hanoi with every conceivable facility for the international traveller. Large and comfortable rooms, airy. **$$$$**

Dan Chu Hotel, 29 Trang Tien Street, Tel: 84-8 825 3323. Fax: 826 6786. It looks a little depressing from the street, but the rooms are quite nice in this one-time French hotel. **$$–$$$**

De Syloia, 17A Tran Hung Dao. Tel: 824 5346; Fax: 824 1083. An international-quality hotel, with an excellent restaurant and gym. **$$$**

Dragon Hotel, 9 Tay Ho Road. Tel: 829 2954; Fax: 829 4745. On West Lake. **$–$$**

Especen, 79-E Hang Trong. Tel: 826 6856. Fax: 826 9612. 66 rooms at 10 small inns around the Old Quarter. Spare, but clean rooms, with private baths. **$**

Flower Hotel, 97 Nguyen Truong To. Tel: 823 7025. A bit out of the way, the rooms are decorated with rosewood Oriental furniture and are quiet. There are several other mini-hotels located nearby. **$$**

Galaxy Hotel, 1 Phan Dinh Phung. Tel: 828 2888; Fax: 828 2466. Well-appointed rooms (for the price)

Hanoi Hotels

Hanoi is now glutted with hotel rooms of all standards, the whole year-round. Feel free to bargain. The hotels listed below typically post rack rates of about US$100 for a single room; negotiating a 50 percent discount should not be difficult. Most welcome has been the explosion of countless "mini-hotels" in the Old Quarter and other areas close to Hoan Kiem Lake. Rather like European pensions, many are family-run and located in appealing colonial-style buildings but lack restaurants. A top-end room in a mini-hotel costs about US$30 and includes a bathroom with hot shower, air-conditioning, balcony, refrigerator, telephone and Vietnamese-language TV. The atmosphere is charming, but with the charm comes noise.

and excellent staff. **$$–$$$**

Green Bamboo, 42 Nha Chung. Tel: 826 8752. Fax: 826 4949. Has 7 rooms. Quiet rooms in the back of a restaurant and tourist company office. A bit on the rugged side, this inn is designed for backpackers. **$**

Hanoi Horizon Hotel, 40 Cat Linh Street. Tel: 733 0808. Fax: 733 0888. Pleasant 5-star hotel with cosy and well-designed rooms. Pleasant atmosphere in public places. **$$$$**

New World Hotel, 21 Chau Long. Tel/Fax 829 2815. Situated to the north of the city, near the Truc Bach and West lakes. **$**

Prince Hotel, 78 Hang Ga. Tel: 828 1332; Fax: 828 0156. Several locations in the Old Quarter. **$$**

Royal, 20 Hang Tre. Tel: 824 4230; Fax: 824 4234. A popular disco downstairs; visitors say they aren't bothered by loud music. Rooms are reminiscent of Holiday Inns. **$$$**

Sofitel Metropole, 15 Ngo Quyen. Tel: 826 6919; Fax: 826 6920. The Metropole, or Thong Nhat as it was known before, was renovated in 1992. The Metropole is the centre of international business in Hanoi,

and its guests are primarily American, French and Asian business people. **$$$$**
Thuy Tien Hotel, 1C Tong Dan. Tel: 824 4775; Fax: 824 4784. Newly built with modern facilities on a street nicely located near the centre of town and near the Old Quarter. **$$**

Hai Phong
Hotel Du Commerce, 62 Dien Bien Phu. Tel: (031) 842 706; Fax: 842 560. Colonial-style accommodation redolent of the French era. recently refurbished; friendly staff. **$–$$**
Huu Nghi, 60 Dien Bien Phu. Tel: (031) 823 244; Fax: 823 245. Offers top-quality accommodation at high prices, but lacking the period charm of the Hotel du Commerce. **$$–$$$$**

Ha Long Bay
Ha Long Hotel, Ha Long Road, Bai Chay. Tel: 846 320; Fax: 846 318. Renovated colonial hotel. **$–$$**
Son Long Hotel, Bai Chay. Tel: 846 274. Rather run down and scheduled for rebuilding or improvement. Popular with Chinese tourists. **$–$$**
Vuon Dao Hotel, Ha Long Road. Bai Chay. Tel: 846 455; Fax: 846 287. Large, rambling and inefficient, but with fine views over Halong Bay. **$–$$**

Sa Pa
Sa Pa does not have street names. With the exception of the Victoria Sa Pa, Sa Pa's accommodation consists of guesthouses and small hotels. A rate for a single room is typically US$7 – 10 whether there are one, two, or three occupants. Rates may jump by one-third on summer weekends when tour groups from Hanoi descend.
Dang Trung Auberge, Sa Pa, Lao Cai Province. Tel: 020 87 1243;

Fax: 020 87 1282. Known for its cuisine, including wildlife entrees.
Green Bamboo Hotel, Sa Pa, Lao Cai Province. Tel: 020 87 1214; Fax: 020 87 1411; bamboo@netnam.org.vn.
Victoria Sa Pa Hotel, Sa Pa, Lao Cai Province. Tel: 020 87 1522; Fax: 020 87 1539; victoriasapa@fpt.vn. New, French-run. Heaters, IDD telephones, satellite TV, swimming pool. Room rates start at US$50, but bargaining is recommended.

Thanh Hoa
Khach San Thanh Hoa. Located on Highway 1 in the centre of town. **$**

Sam Son
There are numerous government hotels along the beach. Expect to pay at least US$10 for a comfortable room. In the summer it can be impossible to find space.

Vinh
The Hotel Huu Nghi, Le Loi Street. Rooms are available from US$15.

Dong Hoi
The Hoa Binh Hotel. Rooms run between US$15 and US$25.

Dong Ha
Nha Khach Dong Ha, Tran Phu Street. Comfortable rooms are US$15.

Eating Out

General
Vietnamese cuisine offers the visitor a wide variety of fine dishes, delicately flavoured with fresh herbs, spices and *nuoc mam* (fish sauce), usually accompanied by *nuoc cham*, a condiment sauce of *nuoc mam*, lime juice, a little grated carrot, chilli, garlic and sugar. Steamed rice *(com)* and soup are eaten at every meal. Different regional specialities lend even more variety to this varied menu. Ask the locals for recommendations and they will be very happy to initiate you.

Due to the highly inflated price of meat, seafood and river fish play an important part in the Vietnamese menu, particularly in the south. The lobsters, flower crabs and oysters, in particular, are excellent. Pork, chicken, beef, duck and pigeon also feature widely on the menu, plus a wide variety of vegetables and tropical fruit. A leftover from the colonial era, French bread, is available throughout the country. Baguettes with local pate and salad make an excellent snack.

The famous national dish, *cha gio* is made from crab and pork, mushrooms, prawns, rice vermicelli and bean sprouts, rolled in a thin rice pancake then deep-fried. These delicious crisp rolls are eaten wrapped in a lettuce leaf with fresh herbs and dipped in sauce. *Go cuon*, another national favourite, is made without pork and eaten raw. Look out for *chao tom*, a dish made of fried minced crab and pork on sugarcane, served with vermicelli, vegetables and coriander leaves.

Another celebrated dish is *cha ca* – fish marinated with *nuoc mam* and *saffron* then barbecue grilled and served with rice vermicelli, herbs, grilled peanuts and a special sauce. One of Hanoi's oldest streets is named after this delicious speciality.

For the more adventurous some speciality restaurants serve turtle, snake, eel, bat and wild game. Numerous restaurants specialise in French and Chinese food. Note that Vietnamese restaurants often do not list prices next to menu items. Always determine the price first – it doesn't hurt to go as far as writing the figure down and ensuring the waiter's agreement.

Where to Eat

Ho Chi Minh City (Saigon) and Hanoi's large hotel restaurants offer both Vietnamese specialities and Western dishes, particularly French, but be sure to check on the hours and book in advance if you're not a guest. Wherever you are in the country, don't hesitate to frequent the small local eating places serving a variety of Vietnamese dishes at any hour; you will be in for some delicious surprises.

HO CHI MINH CITY

Vietnamese

Bo Tung Xeo Restaurant, 31 Ly Tu Trong St. Dist 1. Though the menu (available in English) is extensive, the speciality here seems to be barbecue, Vietnamese-style. A popular favourite with locals. Even if grilled frog legs aren't to your liking, come and soak in the always festive, sometimes raucous atmosphere, especially on weekend nights or when the power goes out. **$$**
Lemon Grass, 4 Nguyen Thiep Street, Dist 1. Tel: 822 0496. A consistent favourite for delicious and inventive Vietnamese food. The chicken salad is especially good. The tasteful bamboo decor is not bad either. Special luncheon menus afford a chance to sample different items. **$$–$$$**
Mandarine, 11A Ngo Van Nam St. Dist Tel: 822 9783. Traditional dishes at reasonable prices. **$$**
Ngoc Suong, 176/7 Le Van Sy Street, Dist 3. Tel: 844 8831.

Excellent inexpensive Vietnamese seafood worth seeking out. **$**
Vietnam House, 93–95 Dong Khoi, Dist 1. Tel: 829 1623. Moderately-priced favourite with tourists. **$$**

Asian/Chinese

Ashoka, 17/10 Le Thanh Ton, Dist 1. Tel: 823 1372. A popular place for authentic Indian cuisine. **$$**
Continental Palace, 132–134 Dong Dhoi, Dist 1. Tel: 829 9255. A classy Chinese restaurant in the Continental Hotel with an extensive menu. **$$$**
Dynasty Restaurant, New World Hotel, 76 Le Lai, Dist 1. Tel: 822 8888. Serves dim sum and Cantonese cuisine. **$$**
Golden Phoenix, Equatorial Hotel, 242 Tran Binh Trong, Dist 5. Tel: 839 0000. Considered to be Saigon's best Chinese restaurant. **$$**
Nishimura, Omni Saigon Hotel, 251 Nguyen Van Troi, Phu Nhuan District. Tel: 844 9222. Offers a variety of Japanese dishes, including sushi and tepanyaki prepared by Japanese chefs. Quality and prices here can match top Japanese restaurants anywhere. **$$$**

International/Western

Annie's Pizza, 21 Bui Thi Xuan, Dist 1. Tel: 839 2577. A Saigon standby offering pizzas and burgers. **$**
Augustin, 10 Nguyen Thiep, Dist 1. Tel: 829 2941. Classic French cuisine at reasonable prices. **$**
Brodard Cafe and Restaurant, 131 Dong Khoi Street, Dist 1. Tel: 822 3966. Open 6.30am–11pm. An old

favourite for French food though the rest of the international menu, especially the lasagne, is not bad either. A good selection of pastries. Nice ambience. **$$**
Cafe Latin, 25 Dong Du, Dist 1. Tel: 822 6363. Open 11am–2pm; 5pm–1am. Tapas bar. Also serves pasta and international entrees. **$$**
Cafe Phap (Le Bistro), Corner of Hai Ba Trung Street and Le Thanh Ton Street. For Francophiles and the French community. Cafe Phap offers an inexpensive French country menu featuring flown-in cheese and wine. **$**
Chez Guido Ristorante, Continental Hotel. Tel: 829 9201. Moderately priced Italian dishes and pizza. **$$**
Ciao Café, 72 Nguyen Hue Street, Dist 1. Tel: 825 1203. Also at 21–23 Nguyen Thi Minh Khai Street, Dist 1. Tel: 822 9796. Open 7am–11pm. Popular place serving a variety of reasonably priced sandwiches, pastas and excellent pizzas. Finish by choosing from a selection of desserts and ice cream. **$**
Gartenstadt, 34 Dong Khoi Street, Dist 1. Tel: 822 3623. A favourite expatriate haunt featuring German and European cuisine. **$$**
Givral, 169 Dong Khoi Street, Dist 1. Tel: 824 2750. A popular old standby for tourists. European and Vietnamese cuisine in a coffee-

Soup Specialities

Most localities have their particular noodle soups, which vary in the noodles and meat used and the use of spices and herbs. The most celebrated dish in the north is *pho*, a delicious soup of rice noodles, beef stock, and ginger, to which beef, bean sprouts, fresh coriander, basil, and mint are added at the very last minute. This is one of those universally hearty meals.

In the south, an excellent soup, *ho tieu*, is enjoyed, which is often made with prawns or crabmeat and pork. Another very popular soup is *bun bo*. Rich and spicy, it is eaten with mint, bean sprouts, and a twist of lime.

People from Hue make their own version of this. One of the favourite soups is *canh chua*, made with fish, pineapple, star fruit, okra and fresh herbs.

Floating Restaurants

At the end of Dong Khoi on the Saigon River. Every evening the boats pick up passengers for a slow two-hour dinner cruise on the Saigon River.

shop setting. Pastries are sold next door. **$$**
Gourmet Royale, 105 Dong Khoi Street, Dist 1. Tel: 829 5429. Also at 193 Tran Hung Dao, Dist 1. Tel: 836 7848. Bakery offering a good selection of gourmet sandwiches, pastries and truffles. **$$**
Le Bordeaux, F7–F8, D2 Road, Commune 25, Binh Thanh Dist. Tel: 899 9831. Expensive, outstanding French food worth venturing out to Binh Thanh District for. **$$$**
La Cigale, 158 Nguyen Dinh Chinh, Phu Nhuan District. Tel: 844 3930. First-rate French cuisine with private dining rooms. **$$$**
Maxim's Dinner Theatre, 15–17 Dong Khoi Street, Dist 1. Tel: 822 5554. Though once famous for its rather wild floor shows, this institution is showing its age. Today's visitors (mostly Hong Kong and Taiwanese businessmen) dining on unremarkable European and Asian cuisine are treated to a more sedate floor show of folk dances and traditional Vietnamese music. For those seeking wilder times, there's always karaoke or the nightclub, which is open to 2am. **$$**
Panorama Lounge and Restaurant, Level 32/33, Saigon Trade Center, 37 Ton Duc Thang, Dist 1. Tel: 910 0492. Open from 10am–11pm. Opened in July 1998, Saigon's highest restaurant offers outdoor seating with panoramic views as well as the fusion cuisine *au courant*. Try Justin's Salad or the Streets of Saigon noodles. More traditional fare includes beefburgers, lamb cutlets and chargrilled salmon. A bar and lounge on the 33rd floor offers a daily tea buffet. **$$**
Paloma Café, 26 Dong Khoi Street, Dist 1. Tel: 829 5813. Also at 28 Pham Ngoc Thach Street, Dist 3. Tel: 823 1745. Open 7.30am–

12am. Cafe-style food in an informal setting complete with cable TV and a giant screen. Popular with the younger set. Live music in the evenings. **$**
Restaurant 99 Pasteur, 99 Pasteur Street. This restaurant serves delicious egg crepes stuffed with shrimp and vegetables and marinated beef that you grill at your own table. Don't be put off by the fact that the restaurant is in a bus garage – it is probably the best family restaurant in Saigon. **$$**
The Rex Hotel Restaurant. The rooftop restaurant at the Rex is an international community favourite where you can dine gazing at the Saigon skyline surrounded by tropical bird cages and festive outdoor lighting. The extensive Vietnamese and Chinese menu is supplemented

Nightlife in Ho Chi Minh City

Apocalypse Now, 2C Thi Sach, Dist. 1. Tel: 824 1463. Its reputation as one of the loudest and rowdiest of bars still holds.
Gecko Bar, 74/1A Hai Ba Trung, Dist. 1. Tel: 824 2754. Popular expat haunt offering billiards, darts, satellite TV, and good food and music.
Marine Club, 17A 4 Le Thanh Ton, Dist. 1. Tel: 829 2249. A popular hangout with the young, hip crowd. French food and drinks served.
Q Bar, 7 Lam Son Square, Dist. 1. Tel: 823 5424. Open 6pm–2am. Located on the side of the Municipal Theatre across from the Delta Caravelle Hotel. Despite competition from other bars, this is still one of the coolest places for the hip to see and be seen. With an extensive selection of alcohol and a good jazz collection.
Saigon Saigon Rooftop Bar, Delta Caravelle Hotel, 19 Lam Son Square, Dist. 1. Tel: 823 4999. The new kid on the block, this pleasant place offers bar food, drinks, and fantastic views of downtown Ho Chi Minh City.

by an equally impressive European menu that includes the best steaks in Vietnam. **$$**

HANOI

Every large hotel has a restaurant where a variety of Vietnamese and Chinese dishes are served. Hanoi is famous for its delicious *pho*, a thin noodle soup served with mint, lime and bean sprouts. This is most evident at breakfast time, where many pavement restaurants serve it.

Al Fresco's, 23L Hai Ba Trung. Tel: 826 7782. A variety of steaks, pizzas, pastas and fresh salads. **$$**
Le Beaulieu, Sofitel Metropole, 15 Ngo Quyen. Tel: 826 6919. Hanoi's most famous hotel, but the Vietnamese and European menu is quite unimaginative. Every morning there is a large breakfast buffet featuring freshly baked goods. **$$$**
Bia Hoi, Trade Union Guest House, 1 Tang Bat Ho. Tel: 821 3112. "Bia Hoi" means draught beer. A cheap, friendly beer garden that springs up nightly on the grounds of an old colonial administrative building. The natives are friendly. **$**
The Cha Ca La Vong, 14 Ca Ca Street. Tel: 825 3929. The name means fried freshwater fish and that's what it serves. A few years ago, this was one of the few restaurants in town. It has been substantially refurbished, but it's questionable whether the quality has kept pace with prices. **$$**
E-motion Cafe, 52 Ly Thuong Kiet. Tel: 934 1066. Quiet bar and cafe with inexpensive Internet fees. Favourite of expats and business travellers. Conveniently situated for the Hanoi Hilton. **$–$$**
Lotus Restaurant. At the intersection of Trang Tien and Ngo Quyen Street. The menu is Vietnamese and Chinese with some Western dishes. The restaurant is on the fourth floor of an art gallery that is well worth a look. **$$**
Met Pub, 56 Ly Thai To. Tel: 826 6919. Expensive French pub. **$$**
Piano Restaurant, 50 Hang Vai Street. Tel: 823 2423. Vietnamese

Hanoi Hotspots

Since the early 1990s, when there literally were only a handful, the number of private restaurants, cafes, beer gardens, and pubs has mushroomed. Many have karaoke lounges. Fertile hunting grounds are around the Old Quarter, the Municipal Theatre, Hoan Kiem Lake, Nguyen Thai Hoc Street, and Ly Thuong Kiet Street.

menu with live music on most nights. **$$**
Restaurant 202, 202 Pho Hue. A French and Vietnamese menu is served here and the prices are very reasonable. **$**
Seasons of Hanoi, 95B Quan Thanh. Tel: 843 5444. Classic Vietnamese cuisine in a beautiful French-style villa. **$$**
Tin Tin Bar & Cafe, 14 Hang Non Street. Tel: 826 0326. Strictly for tourists, but a friendly little closet nonetheless. **$**
Verandah Bar & Cafe, 9 Nguyen Khac Can Street. Tel: 825 7220. Meet the expat community. **$$**

HUE

Hoa Mai and Royal Restaurant, Huong Giang Hotel, 51 Le Loi Street. Menu includes seafood, Vietnamese and Western dishes, and Hue specialities. **$–$$**
Song Huong Floating Restaurant, 3–2 Le Loi. Tel: 826 655. Situated on the Perfume River between the Huong Giang Hotel and the old Clemenceau Bridge. **$–$$**
Lac Thanh Restaurant, Dien Tien Hoang Street. This small restaurant is well known for its *banh khoai*, crepes stuffed with pork, shrimp and bean sprouts topped with a spicy peanut sauce. For dessert have fresh coffee with a delicious creme caramel. **$**
Lac Thien Restaurant, Dien Tien Hoang Street. Certainly some of the best food in Hue. Try the dried noodles with beef. Lively atmosphere. **$**

Attractions

Museums

Please note that many museums charge extra to bring in a camera or video camera.

Hanoi

Most museums are closed on Mondays. There are a few exceptions. Quoted admission fees apply to foreigners. Fees for Vietnamese are generally at least 50 percent lower, if not free of charge.

Air Force Museum (Bao Tang Khong Quan), Truong Chinh, Dong Da District. Open daily 7.30–11.00am, 1.30–4.30pm. Admission: about 50 US cents. While this museum is supposed to be open daily, you will be lucky to find it open. Fortunately, you can still wander, at no charge, among the rusty Russian, French, Chinese and US planes and tanks strewn about the grounds. Far-flung location on edge of town.
Army Museum (Vien Bao Tang Quan Doi), 28-A Dien Bien Phu. Tel: 823 4264. Open daily, 8.30–11.30am and 1.30–4.00pm. Admission: about US$1. From the crumpled metal of a B-52 shot down over Hanoi to a pistol belonging to former South Vietnamese President Nguyen Van Thieu, the Army museum displays a range of war souvenirs from Vietnam's battles against the French and Americans. No mention of the 1979 war with China or the invasion of Cambodia.
Fine Arts Museum (Vien Bao Tang My Thuat), 66 Nguyen Thai Hoc. Open Tuesday–Sunday, 8–11am and 1–4pm. Admission: about US$1. Beginning with 10,000-year-

old Dong Noi stone carvings, includes Cham statues, dinh house carvings, lacquer Buddha statues and the Impressionism and Post-Impressionism of the present day. Along with the History Museum, for information and quality of exhibits, this is Hanoi's best museum. Alas, the crudest propaganda paintings of yesteryear have been removed.
Geology Museum (Vien Bao Tang Dia Chat), 6 Pham Ngu Lao. Tel: 826 6802. Open Monday–Saturday, 8am–noon and 1.30–4.30pm. Details the processes behind many of Vietnam's unique geological features.
History Museum (Vien Bao Tang Lich Su), 1 Pham Ngu Lao. Tel: 825 3518. Open Friday–Wednesday, 8.15–11.45am and 1.30–5pm. Admission: about US$1. Exhibits cover every era of Vietnam's fascinating and complex history. The archaeological collection dates from the Paleolithic and Neolithic eras, including relics from the era of the Hung kings, Neolithic graves, bronze age implements, the beautiful bronze drums of Ngoc Lu and Mieu Mon, Cham relics, stelae,

"Hanoi Hilton"

Hoa Lo Prison, 1 Hoa Lo. Admission: about US$1. Open Tuesday–Sunday, 8–11.30am, 1.30–4.30pm. Built in 1896, Hoa Lo was the prison home and execution site for many revolutionaries under the French. After 1954, it was used by the Vietnamese state to "imprison legal violators". It was dubbed the "Hanoi Hilton" by US prisoners-of-war held here during the American war. In the mid-1990s, virtually the entire prison was torn down to make way for the construction by foreign capitalists of an enormous, curtain-glass, imperialist-style shopping-office-hotel complex – which remains virtually vacant. The "historic relic" consists of a few cells, stocks, and a guillotine employed by the French and vintage rhetoric.

statues, ceramics, and an eerie sculpture of the goddess Quan Am with her one thousand eyes and arms. One room features an ornate throne, clothes and artefacts belonging to the thirteen kings of the Nguyen Dynasty. This and the Fine Arts Museum are the best two museums in town, even if history stops at 1975. Originally the museum of the French School of the Far East, the 1930 structure is a blend of East and West.

Ho Chi Minh Mausoleum (Lang Chu Tich Ho Chi Minh), Ba Dinh Square, near Hung Vuong Street. Tel: 845 5124. Open daily except Monday and Friday, 8.30–11.30am. Often closed from September to December. Admission: free.

Memorial House, 48 Hang Ngang. Open daily, 8am–6pm. Admission: free. Yet another shrine-cum-souvenir stand in honour of Uncle Ho. This is a modest shophouse where Ho supposedly drafted Vietnam's independence declaration. Don't bother unless in the Old Quarter.

Ho Chi Minh Museum (Vien Bao Tang Ho Chi Minh), 3 Ngoc Ha Street. Tel: 846 3752. Open Tuesday–Sunday, 8–11.30am and 1.30–4pm. Admission: about US 25 cents. Its reputation as a truly bizarre museum is not exaggerated.

Revolutionary Museum (Vien Bao Tang Cach Mang), 25 Tong Dan. Tel: 825 4151. Open daily, 8–11.30am and 1.30–4.30pm. Admission: about US 50 cents. The museum documents the struggles of the Vietnamese people from 2,000 years ago until 1975. Among the exhibits are some of the long wooden stakes used to cripple the Mongol fleet during the battle of Bach Dang in Ha Long Bay and an enormous bronze war drum dating from 2,400BC.

Temple of Literature (Van Mieu), Quoc Tu Giam Street, between Van Mieu and Ton Duc Thang streets. Tel: 845 2917. Open daily, 7.30am–5.30pm. Admission: about US$1. Tablets engraved with the names of scholars from Vietnam's Confucian era are the highlight of this ancient temple in a pleasant,

The Tunnels in Cu Chi

Some foreigners call the tunnels Cong World, a theme park built in and around the tunnels that helped the Communist Viet Cong win the war against America.

As much as Vietnam says it wants to forget about the war, it is at the same time busily sprucing up war battlefields.

About 75 km (45 miles) northwest of Ho Chi Minh City, the Cu Chi Tunnels provide vivid testament to the tenacity and ingenuity that helped Vietnam win the war against a superpower like the United States. Nationalist soldiers fighting French colonialists originally dug the first of the tunnels in the 1940s. The system was expanded in the early 1960s; eventually, the tunnels with their many tributaries ran for over 240 km (150 miles).

Built on three levels, soldiers and sometimes villagers lived in the tunnels. There are cooking rooms, ventilated through small holes and tunnels that masked the source of the smoke. There were booby traps, such as floors that gave way, causing intruders to fall into a pit with sharpened bamboo stakes. There were escape tunnels that ended at a river, where guerrillas would swim to safety.

The subterranean garrison gave the communists a toehold within 20 miles of Saigon. Some of the tunnels even ran underneath the headquarters of the US Army's 25th Division.

Today, only some of the tunnels are open to visitors. They have been enlarged – eight inches higher and eight inches wider – to accommodate the larger frames of western tourists. Small lights have been strung along the floor to help visitors find their way, but guides will switch them off to give a sense of what the darkened existence was like for soldiers. Visitors can even eat a staple of the Cu Chi Tunnel diet, tapioca.

Some guides working at Cu Chi are veterans of the war who lived in the tunnels. The bombing of the area, they say, was constant, and by the late 1960s, US carpet-bombing had finally destroyed much of the network. But the effectiveness of the tunnels – allowing VC guerrillas to virtually appear out of nowhere – is quite evident.

Strangely, the sound of gunfire still fills the air at Cu Chi. Tourists can fire AK-47s or M-16s, at $1 a clip, at a shooting range with paper targets of tigers and crocodiles.

outdoor park setting. Traditional musicians perform hourly in a recently renovated area.

Vietnam Museum of Ethnology (Bao Tang Dan Toc Hoc), Duong Nguyen Van Huyen. Tel: 836 0351, 756 2193; Fax: 836 0351. Open Tuesday–Sunday, 8.30–11.30am, 1.30–4.30pm. Admission: about US$1. Built with French funds, this is Vietnam's newest, superficially most modern museum. Its suburban location perhaps discourages visitors. Videos, full-scale models, crafts and musical instruments are impressive, but relatively few of the 54 ethnic groups are represented. And there's no treatment of the

destructive and genocidal policies regarding minorities carried out by both the French and Vietnamese.

Women's Museum (Bao Tang Phu Nu), 36 Ly Thuong Kiet. Open daily, 8.30–11.30am, 1.30–4pm. Admission: about US$1. Those who have had their fill of bizarre kitsch in the Ho Chi Minh Museum should proceed to the interesting 4th-floor exhibits of the female dress of various ethnic groups.

Ho Chi Minh City
Reunification Palace (Dinh Thong Nhat), Nam Ky Koi Nghia Street at Le Duan; visitors can enter from 106 Nguyen Du or from 133 Nam Ky Hoi Nghia. Tel: 822 3652. Open

daily 7.30–11am and 1–4pm. Admission: 50,000d or about US$4. A fascinating look at the official residence of the former Presidents of South Vietnam. Guided tours in English and French will take you from underground war-planning and communications rooms to cavernous banquet rooms and reception halls, to grand sitting and dining rooms, libraries, a theatre, finally landing you on the rooftop helipad complete with non-working helicopter.

War Remnants Museum (Bao Tang Chung Tich Chien Tranh), 28 Vo Van Tan, Dist 3. Tel: 829 0325. Open daily, 7.30–11.45am and 1.30–4.45pm. Admission: 10,000d (less than US$1). One of the most visited museums in Saigon, this place offers a sobering, if somewhat one-sided view of the legacy of the Vietnam War. On display here are American military hardware including tanks and fighter planes, pictures of American war atrocities, graphic exhibits of the effects of Agent Orange, an original French guillotine, and tiger cages from the prison island of Con Son.

Fine Arts Museum (Bao Tang My Thuat), 97-A Duc Chinh Street, Dist 1. Tel: 829 4441. Open Monday–Saturday 8–11.30am and 1.30–4.30pm. Admission is free. Features ancient Cham and Khmer relics, Revolutionary-era art and sculpture, and contemporary Vietnamese paintings.

History Museum (Bao Tang Lich Su), 2 Nguyen Binh Khiem Street, Dist 1. Tel: 829 8146. Open Monday–Saturday, 8–11.30am and 1.30–4.30pm; Sundays and holidays 8.30am–4.30pm. Admission: 10,000d (less than US$1). Located just inside the entrance gate to the zoo, this museum houses a good collection of artefacts tracing the evolution of Vietnam from the Bronze Age Dong Son Culture through the ancient Oc Eo culture to the coming of the Chams, Khmers and Vietnamese. Also on display here is a collection of Buddhas from different Asian countries.

Military Museum (officially called the Ho Chi Minh Campaign Museum), Bao Tang Chien Dich Ho Chi Minh), 2 Le Duan, Dist 1. Tel: 822 9387. A tired, forsaken place looking like it belongs in a museum. Exhibits include American, Soviet and Chinese military hardware as well as the tank that crashed through the gates of Reunification Palace in April 1975.

Ho Chi Minh Museum, 1 Nguyen Tat Thanh St, Dist 4. Tel: 829 1060. Open daily except Monday and Friday mornings, 7.30–11.30am and 1.30–4.30pm. Admission: 10,000d (less than US$1). Documents, letters and photographs charting Ho Chi Minh's life and rise to power are all displayed in this salmon-coloured edifice. Originally a customs house, this was where the young revolutionary set sail from Vietnam in 1911 as a cook on a French ship.

Revolutionary Museum (Bao Tang Cach Mang), 65 Ly Tu Trong, Dist 1. Tel: 829 8250. Formerly the Gia Long Palace and most recently renovated in 1998, this museum houses photographs, maps and relics from the French and American wars. There are also underground tunnels here leading all the way to the Reunification Palace.

Hue

Imperial Museum (Vien Bao Tang Hue), 11 Le Loi St. Tel: 822 489. Open daily except Sunday, 7.30–11.30am and 2–4.30pm. Admission: about US$1.

Military Museum (Vien Bao Tang Quan Su), 6 Le Loi St. Tel: 822 152. Open daily except Sunday, 7.30–11.30am and 2–4.30pm. Admission: US$1.

Festivals

Traditional and Religious Festivals

Many traditional and religious festivals take place in Vietnam, particularly in the north in and around Hanoi during Tet. Dates, unless otherwise stated, fall in the first lunar month.

Dong Ky Festival, a firecracker competition festival, held on the 15th in Dong Ky village, Tien Son District. One of the largest and most spectacular festivals. Tape recordings take the place of the real thing since the government banned firecrackers in 1995.

Mai Dong Festival, which takes place from the 4th to 6th at the Mai Dong Temple in Hai Ba Trung District, Hanoi, is held in honour of Le Cham, the Trung Sisters' brave female general who fought against the Chinese in the first century.

Dong Da Festival, held on the 5th, in Hanoi's Dong Da District, commemorates King Trung Quang's victory at Dong Da and those who died in this battle against the Tsing in 1789.

An Duong Vuong Festival occurs between the 6th and 16th, in the temple of the same name in Co Loa village near Hanoi. Held in memory of King Thuc An Duong Vuong, one of the founders of ancient Vietnam who built the Co Loa Citadel.

Le Phung Hieu Festival, on the 7th, at the temple of the same name in Hoang Hoa district, Thanh Hoa Province.

Lim Festival, held on the 13th in the Lim village pagoda, Ha Bac Province. Features singing and a wide range of cultural and artistic activities.

Ha Loi Festival, on the 15th at Ha Loi Temple in the Me Linh suburb of Hanoi. Commemorates the Trung Sisters.

Den Va Temple Festival, dedicated to Tan Vien, God of the Mountain, held in the Bat Bat suburb of Hanoi on the 15th.

Ram Thang Gieng, the most important Buddhist festival, takes place on the 15th.

Van Village Festival, celebrated in Hanoi's Viet Yen District from the 17th to the 20th.

Khu Lac and Di Nau Festival, occurs on the 7th and 26th in Tam Thanh District, Vinh Phu Province.

Lac Long Quan Festival, from the 1st to 6th days of the third lunar month, at Binh Minh village, Ha Tay Province. Dedicated to Lac Long Quan, the quasi-legendary ancestor of the Vietnamese people. Features traditional music, elders dressed in traditional silk robes, firework displays, and a stunning display of young ladies carrying altars laden with fruit and flowers through Binh Minh's narrow streets.

Huong Tich Festival, held throughout the Spring in the spectacular Huong Son mountains west of Hanoi in Ha Tay Province. This festival can be visited at the same time as Lac Long Quan Festival.

The Buffalo Immolation Festival, held during Spring in the Tay Nguyen Highlands.

Thay Pagoda Festival, held on the 7th day of the 3rd lunar month in Quoc Hai, Ha Tay Province, is dedicated to To Dao Hanh, a revered Buddhist monk and teacher. An excellent opportunity to see the traditional water puppet theatre in an historical and idyllic setting. Also features rowing contests and mountain climbing.

12th March, the Den Festival takes place at the site of the ancient capital of Hoa Lu in Ha Nam Ninh Province. The festival commemorates King Dinh Bo Linh and General Le who fought against the Sung invaders.

16th March, De Tham Festival in Hanoi's Yen The district.

8th April, the Dau Pagoda festival in Thuan Thanh.

Easter, this is celebrated more in the south than in the north of the country.

12th April, the anniversary of Vietnam's first King, Hung Vuong.

15th May, Buddha's birth, enlightenment and death, celebrated in pagodas, temples, and private homes throughout the country.

July/August, on the first day of the 7th lunar month. Offerings of food and gifts are made in homes and temples for the wandering souls of the dead.

September/October, the Mid-Autumn Festival on the day of the full moon in the 8th lunar month. Celebrated with sticky rice mooncakes filled with lotus seeds, salted duck egg yolks, peanuts and melon seeds. Brightly coloured lanterns depicting all manner of things, including dragons, boats and butterflies, are carried by children in evening processions.

The Kiep Bac Temple Festival, held in Hai Hung Province on the 20th day of the 8th lunar month, commemorates the national hero Tran Hung Dao who wiped out the invading Mongol forces in the 13th century.

25th December, Christmas.

Shopping

What to Buy

Traditional Vietnamese handicrafts offer a wide variety of wares to choose from. These include lacquerware, mother-of-pearl inlay, ceramics, pottery, precious wood, tortoise shell, embroidery, silk paintings, bamboo and wickerware, baskets, wool carpets, sculpture, wood, marble and bone carvings, jewellery, jade, engraving, silk and brocade. You may like to add a *non la*, the famous Vietnamese conical hat and an *ao dai*, the traditional costume worn by the Vietnamese fairer sex, to your wardrobe. Green pith helmets, worn by soldiers during the war and by cyclo drivers and labourers today, are sold, as well as the old-fashioned "Uncle Ho" sandals made from used tyre treads. In Ho Chi Minh City, popular items are helicopters, airplanes and cyclos made out of Coca-Cola and Tiger beer cans.

Heavy taxation has discouraged the sale of antiquities, which has become almost clandestine and very limited in the north and strictly controlled in the south. Only after inquiring of the proprietor will you discover all that may be available, as the best pieces are never displayed. Antique shops in the centre of Ho Chi Minh City and the old town of Hanoi sell Vietnamese wood or Laotian bronze Buddhas, old porcelain, objects in silver and ivory, small jade statuettes and objects used by the various cults. Prices are in US dollars and subject to bargaining.

Russian vodka, caviar and even French champagne may be found at very reasonable prices. Clothing is cheap and tailors can quickly produce well-made garments.

HO CHI MINH CITY

Books/Newspapers

Bookazine, 28 Dong Khoi, Dist 1. Tel: 829 7455. Excellent for large-format arts and culture books, and foreign magazines.

Fahasa Bookshop, 1st Floor, 40 Nguyen Hue. Tel: 822 5796. Books in English, French, Vietnamese and Russian.

Xuan Thu Bookshop, 185 Dong Khoi Street, Dist 1. Tel: 822 4670; Fax: 822 5795. One of the largest bookstores in Saigon carrying English and French books.

Viet My – Stern's Books, 2A Le Duan, Dist 1. Tel: 822 9650; Fax: 823 4542.

Lacquerware/Handicrafts

Artexport (state-run), 159 Dong Khoi. Objets d'art and antiquities.

Cultrimex (state-run), 94 Dong Khoi. Tel: 829 2574, 829 2896. Handicrafts, paintings, lacquer work, reproductions of antiquities.

Cuu Long, 177 Dong Khoi. Ao dai and fabrics.

"47", 47 Dong Khoi. Antiquities and objets d'art.

Hoang Oanh, 45 Dong Khoi. Antiquities and objets d'art.

Phuong Nam Lacquerware, 219 Nguyen Trai Street, Dist 1. Tel: 837 0434; Fax: 837 0435. Good-quality lacquerware, wooden carvings, interior decorations and handicrafts.

Sodasy, 115 Le Than Ton. Tel: 829 7752. Produces natural shell and ivory articles.

Tay Son, 198 Bo Thi Sau St, Dist 3. Tel: 820 2524; Fax: 820 2526.

Gift Shop, 30 Ngo Duc Ke, Dist 1.

Bear in mind that it is forbidden to export certain objects and, in principle, clearance must be obtained before you take antiquities out of the country. Obtaining this permission from officials can take weeks. An antique is defined as any object more than 30 years old.

Tel: 829 8784.

Made in Vietnam, 26B Le Thanh Ton, Dist 1. Tel: 822 0841.

Fashion/Clothing/Tailors

Catinat Fashion, 2–4–6 Dong Khoi, Dist 1. Tel: 829 1074. Imported designer clothes.

Fadin, Fashion Design Institute, 41 Ben Choung Duong, Dist 1. Tel: 829 7226.

Lac Long, 143 Le Than Ton. Leather and skin goods.

Vietsilk, 19–21 Dong Khoi, Dist 1. Tel: 823 4860.

Zakka, 23 Dong Khoi, Dist 1. Tel: 829 8086.

Art Galleries

There are many galleries offering the works of masters and younger Vietnamese artists. Below is just a sampling. In addition, there are also some galleries in the basement of the Fine Arts Museum.

Bac Art Gallery, 49 Dong Khoi, Dist 1. Tel: 829 1655.

Blue Space Gallery, 1A Le Thi Hong Gam, Dist 1. Tel: 821 3695; Fax: 821 3693.

HCMC Fine Arts Association, 218A Pasteur, Dist 1. Tel: 823 0025.

Phuong Dong Gallery, 135 Nam Ky Hoi Nghia, Dist 1. Tel: 822 1716.

Saigon Art Gallery, 5 Ton Duc Thang St, Dist 1. Tel: 829 7102.

Xuan Gallery, 32 Vo Van Tan, Dist 3. Tel: 829 1277. Exhibits and sells contemporary paintings by Vietnamese artists.

Supermarkets:

Citimart, Regency Chancellor Court, 21–23 Nguyen Thi Minh Khai, Dist 1. Tel: 824 4818.

PNJ Mart, 106 Le Van Sy, Phu Nhuan District. Tel: 844 3273.

Other Shopping Areas

Binh Tay Market, Cho Lon's main marketplace located on Hau Giang Blvd. The usual plethora of household goods and food items are on sale here, though there is a significant amount of wholesale business too.

Ben Thanh Market, at the intersection of Ham Nghi, Le Loi, Tran Hung Dao and Le Thanh Ton streets, is the city's central market, where fruit, vegetables, rice and meat are sold, as well as electronics, clothes, household goods and flowers. There are also some small food stalls selling soup and rice dishes.

Le Thanh Ton Street. Several shops sell embroidery and silk clothes in Western styles. A shop across from the Norfolk Hotel sells modern glass, ceramics, linens and wood items, all made in Vietnam. Near the New World Hotel a shop sells glass, ethnic fabrics and ceramics of good quality.

Saigon's main antique street is Le Cong Kieu. Dong Khoi Street also has a number of stores selling everything from old furniture to trinkets. As always, beware of fakes, which are a real possibility.

Dan Sinh Market, at the corner of Yersin and Nguyen Thai Binh streets. Once known as the American market, this place now only has a few stalls in the back selling paraphernalia related to the Vietnam War: army fatigues, combat boots, dog-tags (fake, no doubt), gas masks and the like. Most of the other stalls offer items for daily living: housewares, household tools, machinery, clothing and electronics.

HANOI

Crafts and Bookshops

Souvenirs of Vietnam, 30A Ly Thuong Kiet. Vietnamese handicrafts

Cultrimex Gallery, 22B Ha Ba Trung. Silk paintings, paintings and antique reproductions.

Xunhasaba, 32 Hai Ba Trung. Ministry of Culture-sponsored society for the sale and export of books, periodicals, reproductions of objets d'art and handicrafts. Foreign-language publications are also available.

Souvenir Shop, 89 Dinh Thien Hoa.

Rong Dat, 105 Hang Gai. Embroidery.

Han Art, 43 Trang Tien Street. Tel: 824 0038. Ceramics, lacquerware.

Hanoi Gallery, 61 Trang Tien Street.

International Bookshop, 61 Trang Tien Street. Tel: 824 8914.

Book Sach, 57 Trang Tien. Foreign-language publications.

Vietnamese Bookshop, On the corner of 19 Ngo Quyen and 40 Trang Tien. A few foreign-language publications.

Hanoi Foreign Trade Company, 56 Trang Tien Street.

Souvenir Shop, 89 Dinh Thien Hoang.

Markets

These sell all manner of goods, including fresh fruits and vegetables, meat and eggs, as well as packaged goods. Some sell electronics, household goods and clothing.

Cho Hang Da, at the corner of Dau Duong Thanh and Hang Dieu. Tel: 825 7104.

Cho Hoa Binh, at the corner of Tran Nhan Tang and Pho Hue. Tel: 826 2191.

Cho Hom, at the corner of Tran Xuan Son and Pho Hue. Tel: 825 6172.

Cho Long Bien, near the Long Bien Bridge. Tel: 825 8708.

Cho Mo, at the corner of Truong Dinh and Minh Khai. Tel: 863 3023.

Cho Hang Be, 2 Da Ngu. Tel: 825 7032.

Cho Cua Nam, on Cua Nam. Tel: 824 6352.

Cho 19–12 (or Cho Ma), 41 Hai Ba Trung. Tel: 826 2910.

Silk and embroidery

There are many shops on Hang Gai and Hang Bong Streets to be found in the Old Quarter.

Tailoring

The upmarket garment shops of Hang Gai and Hang Bong Streets will also make clothes with fabric brought from elsewhere. Quality is good, but bargain hard.

Musical instruments

Wooden percussion instruments, stringed instruments and bamboo xylophones are sold in several shops in the Old Quarter on Hang Non Street.

Antiques

Several shops on Le Duan Street, near Lenin Park and Tran Tien sell antiques.

Fine Art

Hanoi boasts scores of art galleries. Below are most of the finer ones, where works by the contemporary painters that have recently drawn international attention to Vietnam can be found. Beware, though, that works by masters will often be hung amidst the purest dross – poor imitations of Impressionists, Post-Impressionists, Picasso and Dali. Moreover, artists don't have exclusive relationships with galleries; the works of some (such as Thanh Chuong and Dinh Quan) can be found in many galleries, state and private.

Apricot Gallery, 40B Hang Bong. Tel: 288 8965; Fax: 828 7304.

Codo Gallery, 46 Hang Bong. Tel/Fax: 825 8573. Sculptures, ceramics, paintings.

Co Xanh (Green Palm), 51 Hang Gai. Tel: 826 7116; Fax: 828 9293.

Dong Son, 47 Le Dai Hanh. Tel/Fax: 821 8876.

Hanoi Studio, 33 Tran Quoc. Tel: 943 1106; Fax: 847 0823. The city's slickest space.

Mai Hien–Anh Khanh, 99 Nguyen Thai Hoc. Tel: 846 9614; Fax: 823 0886. This well-known painting couple run their own gallery.

Nam Son, 41 Trang Tien. Tel: 826 2993; Fax: 825 9224, 893 3471. The best of the state-owned galleries in this neighbourhood.

Salon Natasha, 30 Hang Bong. Tel: 826 1387. Up-and-coming artists. Includes sculpture, installations.

Thang Long Gallery, 15 Hang Gai. Tel: 825 0740; Fax: 828 8955.

Trang An Gallery, 15 Hang Boum, Tel: 826 9480; Fax: 829 5296.

Language

General

Vietnamese, the national language, is spoken by practically all the population. Variations in dialect, accent and pronunciation exist between the north, south and centre and among the ethnic minorities who have their own dialects. The Vietnamese language has its origins in the Austro-Asiatic languages and has been influenced by the Sino-Tibetan Tai language. Through the centuries of Chinese occupation the Vietnamese adopted the Han characters. In the 13th century they developed their own written language – Nom. In the 18th century, on the initiative of a French Jesuit priest, Alexandre de Rhodes, missionaries translated the language into its Romanised form, Quoc Ngu, which was first used by the Catholic church and the colonial regime's administration. Gradually its use spread, replacing the old written form in the 20th century. Variations of spelling, particularly noticeable in place names, are common. The languages of Vietnam's ethnic minority groups are drawn from the many Southeast Asian linguistic groups of Austro-asiatic, Austronesian or Malayo-Polynesian, Tibeto-Burman, Kadai and Miao.

Pronunciation

Vietnamese is not an easy language to pronounce. The syllable is the language's base unit. Most syllables have their own particular meaning and each syllable can be pronounced in six different tones to convey six meanings. They bear no relationship to one another, either. In the Romanised written form these tones are expressed by five diacritical accents and one atonic, where the syllable has no accent. For example the syllable "bo" can mean a children's toilet, father, lover, to chop, impolite, or a government ministry. Obviously that leaves much room for confusion for any novice and anyone on the receiving end of a beginner's efforts. (You might accidentally call someone's father his lover, for example, or worse yet, his toilet.)

French is still spoken by many of the older, educated generation in Vietnam. English is spoken by more and more young people, and a fair amount of middle-aged people, particularly in the south.

Greetings

The basic hello – *chao*, is always followed by another word that varies depending on the age and sex of whom you address.

for an old lady/*Chao ba*
for a young lady/*Chao co*
for an older lady/*Chao chi*
for an old man/*Chao ong*
for a young man/*Chao anh*
for an older man/*Chao bac*
for a young person/*Chao em*
goodbye/*Tam biet*
See you again/*Hen gap lai*
I am sorry/*Xin loi*
please/*Xin moi*
thank you/*cam on*
yes/*da*
no/*khong*
My name is .../*Toi ten la ...*
What's your name?/*Ten ong la gi?* (pronounced zee)
How are you?/*Bac co khoe khong?*
Fine thank you/*Cam on binh thuong*
I/*toi*
a little/*it*
how much?/*bao nhieu?*
today/*hom nay*
tomorrow/*ngay mai*

Asking For Directions

O dau? – where?, comes at the end of the sentence directly after the noun. For example if you want to ask for the Post Office – *Buu dien, Buu dien o dau?*

Further Reading

Non-Fiction

A Dragon Apparent – Norman Lewis. Eland, London, 1951, 1982. Travels through Indochina in the waning days of the French empire.
Dispatches – Michael Herr. Avon, New York, 1978. A new kind of war reportage.
Free in the Forest: Ethnohistory of the Vietnamese Central Highlands, 1964–1976 – Gerald C. Hickey. Yale University Press, New Haven, 1982. One of many volumes by a top expert on ethnic minorities.
The Refused – Barry Wain. Simon and Schuster, New York, 1981. Boat people and fellow travellers.
The Smaller Dragon: A Political History of Vietnam – Joseph Buttinger. Praeger, New York, 1958. Pre-history through the French conquest by a pioneering and talented writer.
Tradition on Trial 1920–1945 – David G. Marr. University of California Press, Berkeley, 1981. Engrossing thematic approach.
Vietnam: A Dragon Embattled (Vol 1): From Colonialism to the Vietminh – Joseph Buttinger. Praeger, New York, 1967. A lacerating indictment of the destruction of traditional Vietnamese society and economy.
Vietnam: A History – Stanley Karnow. Viking Press, New York, 1983. Comprehensive account of the American War.
Vietnam Notebook – Murray Hiebert. Review Books, Hong Kong, 1996. An insightful collection by a Vietnamese-speaking journalist, among the first Westerners in Hanoi after the onset of *doi moi*.
Vietnam: Revolution in Transition – William J. Duiker. Westview Press, Boulder, 1995. Politics, economics, culture since 1975. Very academic.

Why Vietnam? – Archimedes L. Patti. University of California Press, Berkeley, Los Angeles & London, 1980. Patti was the US major that assisted Ho in writing Vietnam's declaration of independence.
A Bright Shining Lie – Neil Sheehan. Vintage Books, New York, 1988.
Romancing Vietnam – Justin Wintle. Penguin Group, 1991. Wintle travels from the Chinese frontier to the Mekong Delta.
Fire in the Lake – Frances Fitzgerald. Vintage Books, New York, 1972. A classic on Vietnam War.
River Journeys – William Shawcross. Describes the author's Mekong River trip made in 1983.

Vietnamese Authors

A Vietcong Memoir – Truong Nhu Tang. Harcourt, Brace, San Diego, 1985. The voyage of a scion of the Saigon bourgeoisie to the jungle, to victory and finally to escape as a boat person.
Novel Without a Name – Duong Thu Huong. Morrow (US English-language edition), New York, 1995. The writer has been imprisoned for her writings that included veiled criticisms of the government.
Paradise of the Blind – Duong Thu Huong. Morrow, New York, 1988. Fictional account of a rural family ruined by the vicious 1950s' land reform campaign.
The Sorrow of War – Bao Ninh. Pantheon (US English-language edition), 1995. A North Vietnam war veteran who writes one of the first realistic novels from a northern soldier's perspective.
The Tale of Kieu – Nguyen Du. English translations sold in Vietnam bookstores.
When Heaven and Earth Changed Places – Le Ly Hayslip. Doubleday, New York. The peasant girl who became an American businesswoman spares neither the Americans nor the Vietcong.
The Will of Heaven – Nguyen Ngoc Ngan. Dutton, New York, 1981. One of several memoirs by survivors of Communist re-education camps.

ART & PHOTO CREDITS

Dieulefils, Pierre 18/19, 36/37, 39, 40, 78, 79
Dinh Duc, Trinh 41
Dugast, Jean-Leo 107, 140, 143, 158, 209, 304/305
Evrard, Alain 177, 330
Farnay, Rachel 110L, 113
Holmes, Jim spine, front flap top, back cover right, back flap top, 54, 60, 65, 88, 101, 124, 134, 146M, 148M, 148, 153M, 164M, 170, 180M, 198, 200, 202M, 208M, 208, 211, 224M, 224, 225, 231, 236, 240M, 242M, 245M, 254M, 256M, 256, 257, 258, 261, 264, 270, 272M, 273, 276M, 279, 280M, 280, 281M, 284M, 285, 289, 292L/R, 293L, 294M, 295M, 300L/R, 301L, 306, 310M, 315, 320M, 322M, 326M, 336
Karnow, Catherine 8/9, 12/13, 17, 22/23, 43, 48, 50, 52, 53, 58/59, 61, 64, 66/67, 71, 72, 89, 94/95, 96, 106, 114, 120/121, 122, 123, 125, 128/129, 132/133, 138/139, 145, 147, 149, 150M, 150, 151, 152, 153, 155M, 155, 156M, 156, 157, 163, 164, 165, 166, 167L/R, 168, 171M, 171, 176, 180, 181, 182M, 182, 183, 184M, 184, 185, 188/189, 191, 194, 195, 196, 204, 206, 214/215, 216, 218, 219, 220, 221, 222, 223, 226, 227, 228, 232/233, 242, 244, 245, 252, 254, 262/263, 268/269, 286/287, 290, 291M, 291, 293R, 295, 296M, 301R, 302, 303, 308R, 318, 322

Lynch, Joseph front flap bottom, 6/7, 68, 69, 70, 80/81, 84L, 91, 100, 116, 210, 230, 298, 308L, 312, 313, 314, 320L, 326, 327, 331, 332, 333
Naylor, Kim back cover centre, 20, 62L, 84R, 169R, 174, 203, 229, 237, 241, 253, 272, 274, 275, 277, 282, 283, 311, 324
Page, Tim 25, 30L, 49, 56/57, 74, 75, 77L/R, 82, 83, 85L/R, 87, 90, 169L, 172, 173, 175, 179, 192, 193L/R, 197, 199, 201, 217, 243, 246, 247, 250/251, 255, 259, 278, 284, 334, 335
Photobank 10/11, 24, 26, 51, 55, 98, 105, 115, 127, 190
Rutherford, Scott 109, 111, 112
Thoma, Zdenka 126
Turnnidge, Brenda 99
Van Cappellen, Wim 14, 202, 205
Wassman, Bill back cover bottom, 62R, 130/131, 146, 159, 207, 239
Westlake, Martin back flap bottom, 73, 86, 154, 238M, 294, 296, 297, 299M, 299, 300M, 307, 309M, 309, 310, 312M, 316/317, 319, 320R, 321, 323, 325, 328, 329
New York Public Library Picture Collection 38
Plum Blossoms Gallery 102/103, 104, 110R
U.S. National Archives 21, 42, 46L/R, 76
Vietnam News Agency 44, 45, 47, 144
Vietnam Tourism 63, 97, 160/161, 238, 240

Picture Spreads

Pages 92/93: Top row from left to right: Jim Holmes; Jim Holmes; Liba Taylor; Jim Holmes. Bottom row from left to right: Trip/Viesti Collection; Jim Holmes; Jim Holmes; Jean-Leo Dugast; Jean-Leo Dugast.
Pages 118/119: Top row from left to right: Jim Holmes; Jim Holmes; Trip/R Nichols; Jim Holmes. Centre row from left to right: Trip/W Jacobs; Jean-Leo Dugast. Bottom row from left to right: Tibor Bognar; Jim Holmes; Tibor Bognar; Trip/R Nichols.
Pages 208/209: Top row from left to right: Jim Holmes; Jean-Leo Dugast; Jim Holmes; Panos Pictures. Centre row from left to right: Trip/J Sweeney; Panos Pictures. Bottom row from left to right: Jim Holmes; Jean-Leo Dugast; Peter Barker; Jim Holmes.
Pages 244/245: Top row from left to right: Jim Holmes; Jim Holmes; Trip/W Jacobs; Trip/R Nichols. Bottom row from left to right: Tibor Bognar; Tibor Bognar; Jean-Leo Dugast; Trip/W Jacobs; Trip/B Vikander.

Maps Cosmographics
© 2003 Apa Publications GmbH & Co. Verlag KG (Singapore branch)

INSIGHT GUIDE
Vietnam

Cartographic Editor **Zoë Goodwin**
Production **Caroline Low**
Design Consultants
Carlotta Junger, Graham Mitchener
Picture Research **Hilary Genin**

Index

a

Agent Orange 64, 294
Ambassadors' Pagoda (Chua Quan Su) 149
An Giac 208
An Hiep 323
An Nam 28
ancestor worship 79, 89
Ankroet 284
anti-Catholic policies 39, 85
ao dai 206
Army Museum (Bao Tang Quan Doi) 154
art 109–15
Association of South East Asian Nations (ASEAN) 21, 50, 52
Au Lac 20, 26, 143
Au Viet 26
August Revolution 42

b

Ba Be National Park 205
Ba Chieu 310
Ba Chuc 327
Ba Ho 275
Bac Cam Chau 194
Bac Ha 202
Bac Lieu 334
Bac Ninh 174
Bai Bien Non Nuoc (China Beach) 257
Bai Chay 182
Bai Dau 313, 314
Bai Duong 330
Bai Sau 313
Bai Truoc 313
Bali 25
Ban Doc 208
Ban Mong 194
Bao Dai 40, 42, 45, 274, 281
Bao Loc 284
Bao Ninh 105
Bao Tang Cach Mang (Revolutionary Museum) 148
Bao Tang Dan Toc Hoc Viet Nam (Vietnam Museum of Ethnology) 158
Bao Tang Ho Chi Minh (Ho Chi Minh Museum) 155
Bao Tang Lich Su (History Museum) 148
Bao Tang Lich Su (National History Museum) 298
Bao Tang My Thuat (Fine Arts Museum) 153, 296
Bao Tang Quan Doi (Army Museum) 154
Bao Tang Quan Doi (Military Museum) 298
Bao Tang Son La (Son La Prison) 194
Bao Tang Thuan Thien-Hue (Hue Provincial Museum) 241
Bat Trang 171
Ben Hai 246
Ben Tre 323
Bien Dong (South China Sea) 61, 177
Bien Hoa 311
Biet Dien Quoc Truong (Summer Residence) 281
Binh San 332
Binh Son Tower (Chua Vinh Khanh) 169
bodhisattva 88
Botanical/Zoological Gardens (HCMC) 297
British 42
Buddhism 29, 30, 46, 84, 86, 281, 314
Buon Ma Thuot 284
Bush, Pres. George 52

c

Ca Mau 334
cai luong 100
Cam Ly 282
Cam Ranh Bay (Vinh Cam Ranh) 276
Cambodia 21, 25, 45, 49, 61, 308, 326
Can Thanh 240
Can Tho 324
Can Vuong 39
Cao Bang 206
Cao Dai sect 86, 309, 333
Cao Lanh 324
caphe cut chon (fox-dung coffee) 278
casino 179
Cat Ba 184
Cat Ba archipelago 184
Cat Tien 312
Catholicism 33, 39, 85, 89, 217, 226, 272
Cau Da 274
Cau Nhat Ban (Japanese Covered Bridge) 260
Cau Trang Tien (Trang Tien Bridge) 240
cay neu (signal tree) 87
Central Highlands 284

ceramics 171
Cham 73, 247, 255, 273
Cham Tam Church 300
Cham towers 256, 277
Champa 25, 30, 32, 71, 245, 255, 276, 308
Chau Doc 325
Chau Giang Mosque 326
chemical defoliants 64
Chi Lang 209
China 20, 21, 26, 28, 40, 44, 49, 54, 61, 174, 178, 202, 206, 255
China Beach (Bai Bien Non Nuoc) 257
Chinese 25, 27, 31, 33, 42, 69, 73, 123, 177, 260, 276, 290, 311
Chinese invasion 209
Chinese language 78
Cho Ben Thanh 296
Cho Binh Tay 300
Cho Da Lat 280
Cho Dam 273
Cho Dan Sinh 297
Cho Dong Ba 241
Cho Dong Xuan 152
Cho Hoi An 260
Cho Lon 300
Cho Lon Mosque 301
Cho Quan Church 300
Christianity 89
chu nom (script) 105
Chua Ba Da 149
Chua Bich 222
Chua But Thap 173
Chua Co 324
Chua Con Son 174
Chua Dat Set 334
Chua Dau 173
Chua Doi 334
Chua Giac Lam 302
Chua Giac Vien 302
Chua Hang 330
Chua Huong (Perfume Pagoda) 170
Chua Keo 218
Chua Lam Ty Ni 282
Chua Lien Phai 158
Chua Linh Son 281, 309
Chua Long Son 272
Chua Ly Trieu Quoc Su 149
Chua Mot Cot (One Pillar Pagoda) 154
Chua Ngoc Hoang (Emperor of Jade Pagoda) 299
Chua Ong 301
Chua Phat Lon (Big Buddha Pagoda) 329

Chua Pho Mieu 301
Chua Phu Tay Ho 157
Chua Quan Su (Ambassadors' Pagoda) 149
Chua Tay Phuong 164
Chua Thay 163
Chua Thien Mu 241
Chua Thien Vuong (Chua Dao) 282
Chua Tran Quoc 157
Chua Vinh Khanh 169
Chua Vinh Nghiem 299
City Hall (UBND Thanh Pho) 294, 295
civet cat 278
climate 62
Clinton, Pres. Bill 52
Co Loa 26, 28, 143, 159
coal mines 183
Coconut Monk (Ong Dao Dua) 321
coffee 278
communal houses (*dinh*) 83
Communist Party 20, 21, 40, 42, 47, 49, 52, 106, 194
Con Dao 314
Con Phung 321
Con Son 314
Confucianism 29, 30, 85
Confucius 85, 97
Cong Vien Le Nin (Lenin Park) 150
Cong Vien Quoc Gia Ba Be (Ba Be National Park) 205
Cong Vien Quoc Gia Cuc Phuong (Cuc Phuong National Park) 224
Cong Vien Van Hoa 293
corruption 54, 72
cosmology 83
Cot Co (Flag Tower) 154
crafts 115–16
Cu Chi 307
Cu Lao Dat 323
Cu Lao Pho 311
Cua 218
Cuc Phuong National Park 224
cuisine 123–26
Cuu Dinh 239
Cuu Long (Mekong River) 319

d

Da Lat 278–84
Da Nang 21, 33, 39, 253, 302
Da Tanla 284
Dai Co Viet 28, 220
Dai Noi (Great Palace/Imperial City) 238

Dai Viet 28, 30, 31
Dao Phu Quoc 333
Daoism 88
de Behaine, Pigneau 33, 333
de Genouilly, Charles Rigault 302
de Rhodes, Alexandre 117
deforestation 193
Demilitarised Zone (DMZ) 227, 246
Den Bach Ma 152
Den Dinh Tien Hoang 221
Den Ha 168
Den Hai Ba Trung 158
Den Hung 169, 298
Den Kiep Bac 174
Den Le Hoan 222
Den Ngoc Son 146
Den Quan Thanh 157
Den Thuong 169
Deo Ca (Ca Pass) 276
Deo Hai Van (Hai Van Pass) 253
Devil's Island (Poulo Condore) 314
Dien Bien Phu 44, 195
Dien Thai Hoa (Thai Hoa Palace) 238
Dien Tho 239
Dinh Bo Linh 28
Dinh Co 312
Dinh dynasty 20, 28
Dinh Than Chau Phu 325
Dinh Thong Nhat (Reunification Palace) 291
Dinh Tien Hoang 221
Do Son 179
Doc Let 275
doi moi 21, 50, 53, 111
Dong Dang 210
Dong Duong 255
Dong Ho 174
Dong Ky 171
Dong Son culture 25, 227, 276
Dong Son drums 70, 97
Dong Tam 322
Dong Thap Muoi 324
Doumer, Paul 314
Du Hang 179
Duong Dong Khoi 293
Duy Tan 39
dynasties
  Dinh 20, 28
  Ho 20, 30
  Hung 20
  Hung Vuong 26
  Le 20, 31, 97, 107
  Ly 20, 28, 29
  Mac 20, 32

Ngo 20, 28
Nguyan 20
Nguyen 33, 237, 243
Tien Le 20, 29, 98
Tran 20, 30, 100, 217
Trieu 26

e – f

Eastward Movement 20, 39
Emperor of Jade Pagoda (Chua Ngoc Hoang) 299
environment 64
ethnic minorities 73–78, 158, 191, 203, 212–13, 227, 281, 284
Faifo (Hoi An) 255, 258
family names 75
family registries 76
Fan Si Pan 61, 199
festivals 92–93
Fine Arts Museum (Bao Tang My Thuat) 153
Fine Arts Museum (HCMC) 296
firecrackers 171
Five Mounts (Ngu Linh) 27
flora and fauna 63, 224
Flower Gardens (Da Lat) 280
folk art and crafts 115
Forbidden City (Hue) 239
forests 63
fox-dung coffee (*caphe cut chon*) 278
French 20, 33, 39, 41, 145, 165, 166, 167, 177, 196, 203, 217, 219, 237, 243, 278, 289, 302, 320, 329, 333

g

galleries 114
Geneva accord 21
Geneva Agreement 46
Geneva Conference 246
Gia Long 32, 34, 35, 107, 144, 238, 242, 243, 331
Gia Long tomb 246
Giao Chi 27
Go Den 320
Go Dong Da 158
Gougah 284
Guangzhou (Canton) 26
guerrillas 44, 210, 307
guillotine 149
Gulf of Tonkin (Vinh Bac Bo) 217
Gulf of Tonkin Resolution 229

h

Ha Dong 163
Ha Long 182
Ha Long Bay (Vinh Ha Long) 180–83
Hanoi 143–58
Hanoi Hilton (Hoa Lo) 149
Ha Tien 331
Hai Phong 43, 177–79
Hai Van Pass 253
Ham Nghi 20, 39
Hang Dau Go 181
Hang Hanh 182
Hang Kenh 179
Hang Mo So 331
Hang Thien Cung 182
Hang Tien (Coin Grotto) 330
hat cheo 100
helicopters 45
Hien Lam Cac 239
hill tribes See ethnic minorities
Hinduism 84
History Museum (Bao Tang Lich Su) 148
Hmong 76, 203
Ho Ba Be 205
Ho Ba Om 323
Ho Bay Mau 150
Ho Cam Son 208
Ho Chi Minh 20, 21, 40, 47, 155, 169, 207, 208, 230, 297
Ho Chi Minh City 289–302, 307
Ho Chi Minh House (Nha San Bac Ho) 155
Ho Chi Minh Mausoleum (Lang Chu Tich HCM) 155
Ho Chi Minh Museum (Bao Tang HCM) 155
Ho Chi Minh Trail 21, 45
Ho Da Thien 283
Ho Dong 332
Ho dynasty 20, 30
Ho Hoan Kiem 145
Ho Qui Ly 144
Ho Tay (West Lake) 156
Ho Than Tho 283
Ho Thien Quang 150
Ho Truc Bach (White Silk Lake) 157
Ho Xuan Huong 280
Ho, Stanley 179
Hoa Binh 165, 191
Hoa Hao sect 328
Hoa Lo ("Hanoi Hilton") 149
Hoa Lu 220
Hoang Lien Son 200

Hoang Thanh (Yellow Enclosure) 238
Hoang Tru 230
Hoi An 247, 258–60
Hoi Tuong Te Nguoi Hoa (Ong Bac De) 329
Hon Chen 245
Hon Chong 274, 330
Hon Gai 183
Hon Giang 333
Hon Lao 275
Hon Mieu 274
Hon Tre 275
Hotel de Ville See City Hall
Hue 237–49
Hung dynasty 20
Hung Vuong 26
Huynh Phu So 327

i – j

I Ching (Book of Changes) 88
Imperial City (Dai Noi/Hue) 238
Independence Museum 151
investment 51, 52
Islam 90
Jade Emperor 87, 299, 329, 332
Japanese 20, 35, 147, 207, 299
Japanese Covered Bridge (Cau Nhat Ban) 260
Johnson, Pres. Lyndon 46

k

karst 223
Kenh Ga 223
Kh'leng 333
Khai Dinh 39, 40
Khai Dinh tomb 245
Khmer 73, 255, 319, 323, 333
Khmer Rouge 49, 50, 327, 329, 333
Khu Luu Niem Bac Ho (Dragon House) 297
Khuong Viet 29
Kim Lien 230
Kim Son 226
kingdoms
   An Nam 28
   Au Lac 20, 26, 143
   Dai Co Viet 28, 220
   Dai Viet 28, 30, 31
   Giao Chi 27
   Lac Viet 26
   Nam Viet 20, 26
   Van Lang 20, 26, 35, 163

Van Xuan 20
   Viet Nam 34
   Xich Qui 26
kings/emperors
   Bao Dai 40, 42, 45, 274, 281
   Dinh Bo Linh (Tien Hoang) 20, 28
   Duy Tan 39
   Gia Long 32, 34, 35, 107, 144, 238, 242, 246, 310, 331
   Ham Nghi 20, 39
   Ho Qui Ly 144
   Khai Dinh 39, 40, 245
   Le Dai Hanh 29
   Le Loi 44, 174
   Le Qui Ly 30
   Le Thai To (Le Loi) 31, 145
   Le Thai Tong 32
   Le Thanh Tong 32, 276
   Ly Bon 28
   Ly Thai To (Ly Cong Uan) 29, 101, 155, 158, 163
   Ly Thai Tong 172
   Ly Thanh Ton 30
   Mac Dang Dung 32
   Mac Mau Hop 20, 32
   Minh Mang 34, 39, 85, 206, 239, 242, 246, 310
   Ngo Quyen 28
   Nguyen Anh 33
   Quang Trung (Nguyen Hue) 33
   Thien Tri 244
   Tran Canh 30
   Trieu Da 26
   Tu Duc 244
   Vu Vuong 237
Kissinger, Henry 47
Kontum 284
Krempf, Armand 274
Krong Pha 277
Kublai Khan 30, 181

l

l'Esperance 320, 329
Lac Viet 26
lacquer ware 115
Lai Chau 197
lakes *(ho)*
   Ba Om 323
   Bay Mau 150
   Cam Son 208
   Da Thien 283
   Hoan Kiem 101, 145
   Tay 156
   Than Tho 283
   Thien Quang 150

Truc Bach 157
Xuan Huong 280
Lam Kinh 229
Lam Son 228
Lang Ca Ong 313
Lang Chu Tich Ho Chi Minh (Ho Chi Minh Mausoleum 155
Lang Co 253
Lang On Ba Chieu 310
Lang Son 209
language 78, 117
Lao Cai 202
Laos 25, 45, 54, 61
Lat 284
Le Chan 179
Le Dai Hanh 29
Le Duan 50, 194
Le Duc Tho 47
Le dynasty 20, 31, 97, 107
Le Loi 31, 44, 174
Le Mat 172
Le Qui Ly 30
Le Thai To 145
Le Thai To (Le Loi) 31
Le Thai Tong 32
Le Thanh Tong 32, 276
Le Van Duyet 310
Liem Tuc 218
Lien Khuong 284
Lim 173
Linh Ung 257
literacy 107
literature 105–09
Literature Temple (Van Mieu) 153
Long Bien Bridge (Doumer Bridge) 152
Long Hai 312
Long Xuyen 325
Luang Prabang 196
Luong Ngoc Quyen 204
Ly Bon 28
Ly Cong Uan 29
Ly dynasty 20, 28, 29
Ly Nguyen Cat 100
Ly Thai To 30, 155, 158, 163
Ly Thai Tong 172
Ly Thanh Ton 30

m

Mac 217
Mac Cuu 331
Mac Dang Dung 32
Mac dynasty 20, 32
Mac Mau Hop 20, 32
Maddox, U.S.S. 229
Mai Chau 192
Malte-Burn, Konrad 35

mangrove forest 334
Marble Mtns (Ngu Hanh Son) 257
Mariamman Hindu Temple 296
Mausoleum, Ho Chi Minh 155
Mekong (Cuu Long) 319
Mekong River (Cuu Long Giang) 62
Metropole Hotel 146
Mieu Ba Chua Xu 327
Mieu Than Dong Co 228
Ming dynasty (China) 31, 243
Minh Mang 34, 39, 85, 90, 206, 239, 242, 310
Minh Mang tomb 246
Minh Thanh 246
Moc Chau 192
Mong Cai 210
Mongols 30, 148, 174, 177, 183, 217
Mui Ne 277
Municipal Theatre (Nha Hat Lon) 147
Municipal Theatre (Nha Hat Thanh Pho) 295
Museum of Cham Sculpture 256
Museum of Royal Fine Arts (Hue) 240
museums (Hanoi)
    Army (Bao Tang Quan Doi) 154
    Ethnology (Bao Tang Dan Toc Hoc Viet Nam) 158
    Fine Arts (Bao Tang My Thuat) 153
    History (Bao Tang Lich Su) 148
    Ho Chi Minh (Bao Tang Ho Chi Minh) 155
    Ho Chi Minh House (Nha San Bac Ho) 155
    Hoa Lo ("Hanoi Hilton") 149
    Revolutionary (Bao Tang Cach Mang) 148
museums (Ho Chi Minh City)
    Fine Arts (Bao Tang My Thuat) 296
    Military (Bao Tang Quan Doi) 298
    National History (Bao Tang Lich Su) 298
    Reunification Palace 292
    Revolution (Vien Bao Tang Cach Mang) 294
    War Remnants 293
museums (other)
    Cham Sculpture (Da Nang) 256

Ethnic Minority (Da Lat) 281
    Hoi An 260
    Royal Fine Arts (Hue) 240
music 97, 276
Muslims 301, 326
My Khe 257
My Lai massacre 21
My Son 247, 255
My Tho 321

n

Nam Dinh 217
Nam Giao Dan 242
Nam Viet 20, 26
National History Museum (HCMC) 298
National Liberation Front 21, 46, 333
national parks
    Ba Be 205
    Cuc Phuong 224
nationalism 40
Ngo Dinh Diem 21, 45, 85, 237, 292, 300, 333
Ngo dynasty 20, 28
Ngo Minh Chieu 309
Ngo Quyen 177
Ngo Viet Thu 292
Ngu Hanh Son (Marble Mountains) 257
Nguyen Ai Quoc *See Ho Chi Minh*
Nguyen Anh 33
Nguyen Dinh Chieu 323
Nguyen Du 107, 230
Nguyen dynasty 20, 33, 243–46, 326
Nguyen Gia Tri 110
Nguyen Hoang 237, 241
Nguyen Phan Chanh 110
Nguyen Thanh 34
Nguyen That Thanh *See Ho Chi Minh*
Nguyen tombs 243
Nguyen Trai 174
Nguyen Trung Truc 329
Nguyen Van Linh 50
Nguyen Van Thieu 281
Nha Hat Lon (Municipal Theatre/Opera House) 147
Nha Hat Thanh Pho (Municipal Theatre) 295
Nha San Bac Ho (Ho Chi Minh House) 155
Nha Tho Con Ga (Da Lat Cathedral) 281
Nha Tho Duc Ba (Notre Dame) 293

Nha Tho Lon (St Joseph's Cathedral) 148
Nha Tho Phanxico Xavia (Cham Tam Church) 300
Nha Trang 247, 271–77
Nha Trang Huu Duc (Po Nagar) 273
Nha Trung Bay Toi Ac Chien Tranh (War Remnants Museum) 293
Nhat Tao 320
Niet Ban Tinh Xa 314
Ninh Binh 219
Nixon, Pres. Richard 47
Nobel Prize 47
Norodom Sihanouk 50
North Vietnam 21, 45
Notre Dame (Nha Tho Duc Ba) 293
Nui Ba Den 309
Nui Lon 314
Nui Sam 326
nuoc mam (fish sauce) 123, 253

o

Oc Eo 328
Oceanographic Institute (Nha Trang) 274
oil-and-gas industry 53
Old Quarter (36 Pho Phuong) 150
One Pillar Pagoda (Chua Mot Cot) 154
Ong Dao Dua (Coconut Monk) 321
Opera House (Municipal Theatre/Nha Hat Lon) 147

p

Pac Bo 208
pagodas *(chua)* 83, 118–19
   See listings under temples/pagodas
painting 109–15
Paracel Islands (Hoang Sa) 61
Paris Peace Agreement 21, 47
Pasteur Institute 272
Perfume Pagoda (Chua Huong) 170
Perfume River (Song Huong) 237
Phan Boi Chau 39, 230
Phan Chu Trinh 39
Phan Dinh Phung 20, 39
Phan Rang 276
Phan Thiet 277

Phat Diem Cathedral 226
Phat Tich 174
pho 125
Pho Minh 217
Phong Tho 198
Phu Dung 332
Phu Nam 324
Phu Nam (Funan) 328
Phu Tan 327
Phuc Thanh 260
Phung Nguyen culture 20
Phuoc Duyen 241
Phuoc Hai Tu 299
Phuoc Kien 260
Phuoc Nhia 225
Pleiku 284
Po Klong Garai 277
Po Nagar 74, 245
Po Nagar (Nha Trang Huu Duc) 273
Po Ro Me 277
poetry 98, 105
Pol Pot 21
political reform 54
Polo, Marco 35
Pongour 284
Portuguese 35, 258, 313
Poulo Condore (Devil's Island) 314
Prenn (Thien Sa) 284
preservation 247
Presidential Palace 156
Prince Canh 34
Ptolemy 35

q – r

Quan Chuong 152
Quang Trung 33
quoc ngu (script) 117
Quy Quan Mon 209
Rach Gia 329
reforestation 64
religion 83–90
   ancestor worship 89
   Buddhism 86
   Cao Dai 86, 309
   Catholicism 217
   Christianity 89
   Confucianism 85
   Daoism 88
   Hinduism 84
   Islam 90
reunification 21, 25, 49
Reunification Palace (Dinh Thong Nhat) 292
Revolutionary Museum (Bao Tang Cach Mang) 148
Rex Hotel 295

rice 123
rivers *(song)*
   Cam Ly 278
   Chai 277
   Cuu Long Giang (Mekong) 62, 319
   Da (Black) 166, 197
   Da Rang 273
   Day 165
   Dong Nai 311
   Gian Thang 331
   Han 253
   Hau Giang 325
   Hong (Red) 61, 69, 143, 163, 177, 191
   Huong (Perfume) 237
   My Tho 321
   Nha Trang 273
   Sai Gon (Saigon) 289, 307
   Vam Co Dong 320
Roi Nuoc Thang Long (Thang Long Water Puppet Theatre) 151
Rung Tram 324

s

Sa Dec 324
Sa Pa 199–202
Sai Son 163
Saigon Trade Centre 297
sailing (Ha Long) 183
salt 219
Sam Son 229
script 33, 84
silk 284, 326
snake cuisine 172
snakes 172, 322
Soc Trang 333
Son La 193
Son La Prison (Bao Tang Son La) 194
Song Cam Ly (Cam Ly River) 278
Song Chai 277
Song Da (Black River) 166, 197
Song Da Rang 273
Song Day (Day River) 165
Song Dong Nai (Dong Nai River) 311
Song Gan Hao 334
Song Gian Thang 331
Song Han (Han River) 253
Song Hau Giang 325
Song Hong (Red River) 25, 61, 69, 143, 163, 177, 191
Song Huong (Perfume River) 237

Song My Tho 321
Song Sai Gon (Saigon River) 289, 307
Song Thu Bon 259
Sorrow of War, The 105
South China Sea (Bien Dong) 177
South Vietnam 21, 45, 237, 289, 333
Soviet Union 21, 49
Spratly Islands (Truong Sa) 54, 61
standard of living 71
State Guest House 146
Sun Yat-sen 39

t

Tale of Kieu, The 107, 108, 230
Tam Bao 332
Tam Coc 222
Tam Dao 168
Tam Ta Toong 195
Tam Thanh 210
Tam Thi 257
Tan Ky House 260
Tan Trao 169
Tay An 327
Tay Giai 228
Tay Ninh 308
Tay Phuong (pagoda) 164
Tay Son 333
Tay Son Uprising 20, 32, 33, 237, 243
Temple of Literature (Van Mieu) 153
temples/pagodas (Hanoi)
Chua Ba Da 149
Chua Lien Phai 158
Chua Ly Trieu Quoc Su 149
Chua Mot Cot (One Pillar) 154
Chua Phu Tay Ho 157
Chua Quan Su (Ambassadors' Pagoda) 149
Chua Tran Quoc 157
Den Bach Ma 152
Den Hai Ba Trung 158
Den Ngoc Son 146
Den Quan Thanh 157
Thap Rua 146
Van Mieu 29, 153
Voi Phuc 158
temples/pagodas (Hanoi Environs)
Chua But Thap 173
Chua Con Son 174
Chua Dau 173
Chua Huong (Perfume Pagoda) 170
Chua Tay Phuong 164
Chua Thay 163
Chua Vinh Khanh 169
Den Ha 168
Den Hung 169
Den Kiep Bac 174
Den Thuong 169
temples/pagodas (north)
Chua Bich 222
Chua Keo 218
Den Dinh Tien Hoang 221
Den Le Hoan 222
Mieu Than Dong Co 228
Phuoc Nhia 225
temples/pagodas (Hue)
Chua Thien Mu 241
Hon Chen (Ngoc Tran Dien) 245
Minh Thanh 246
Nam Giao Dan 242
Phuoc Duyen 241
temples/pagodas (Da Nang/Hoi An)
Mieu Quan Cong 260
Phuc Thanh 260
Phuoc Kien 260
temples/pagodas (Ho Chi Minh City)
Chua Giac Lam 302
Chua Giac Vien 302
Chua Ngoc Hoang (Jade Emperor) 299
Chua Ong 301
Chua Pho Mieu 301
Chua Vinh Nghiem 299
Den Hung 298
Mariamman (Hindu) 296
temples/pagodas (HCMC Environs)
Chua Linh Son 309
Lang Ca Ong 313
Lang On Ba Chieu 310
Niet Ban Tinh Xa 314
temples/pagodas (south)
Chua Co 324
Chua Dat Set 334
Chua Doi 334
Chua Hang 330
Chua Phat Lon (Big Buddha) 329
Mieu Ba Chua Xu 327
Nguyen Dinh Chieu 323
Nguyen Trung Truc 329
temples/pagodas (other)
Chua Lam Ty Ni 282
Chua Linh Son 281
Chua Long Son 272
Chua Thien Vuong 282
Du Hang 179
Nha Trang Huu Duc (Po Nagar) 273
Thach Dong Thon Van 332
Tet Nguyen Dan (Tet New Year) 87
Tet Offensive 21, 46, 237, 240, 293
Thac Xa 164
Thach Dong Thon Van 332
Thai Ngoc Hau 326
Thai Nguyen 204
Thang Vang 217
Thanh Hoa 227
Thanh Pho Ho Chi Minh (Ho Chi Minh City) 289–302
Thao Cam Vien (Botanical and Zoological Gardens) 297
Thap Rua (Tortoise Tower) 146
The Doc Cuoc 229
The Sorrow of War 105
The Tale of Kieu 107, 108, 230
theatre 98–100
Thich Ca Phat Dai 314
Thich Quang Duc 46
Thien Hau 301
Thien Mu Pagoda (Hue) 241
Thien Vien Truc Lam (Bamboo Forest Meditation Centre) 283
Thieu Tri tomb 244
36 Pho Phuong (Old Quarter) 150
Thong Nhat (Reunification Express) 296
Thu Duc 310
Thung Lung Tinh Yeu (Valley of Love) 283
Tien Le dynasty 20, 29
Toa An Nhan Dan (People's Court) 294
tombs (Hue/Nguyen) 242–46
Gia Long 246
Khai Dinh 245
Minh Mang 246
Thieu Tri 244
Tu Duc 244
totemism 77
Tra Kieu 255
Tra Vinh 323
trade embargo 21, 52
Tran dynasty 20, 30, 217
Tran Hung Dao 174, 183
Treaty of Saigon 20
Tri Nguyen Aquarium 274
Trieu Da 26
Trieu dynasty 26
Trieu Thi Trinh 229
Trinh family 20, 243

Trinh Nu 181
Trung Sisters (Hai Ba Trung) 20, 26, 27, 179
Truong Chinh 194
Tu Cam Thanh (Forbidden Purple City) 239
Tu Duc 244
Tuan Chau 182
Tuan Giao 195
tunnels 246, 307

u

U Minh 334
U.S. embassy 293
U.S.S. Maddox 229
UBND Thanh Pho (People's Committee/City Hall) 294
UNESCO 247, 259
UNESCO World Heritage Site 180
United Nations 50
United States 21, 45, 178, 229

v

Van Lan 223
Van Lang 20, 26, 35, 163
Van Mieu (Temple of Literature) 29, 153
Van Thanh Mieu 323

Van Xuan 20
Vien Bao Tang Cach Mang (Museum of the Revolution) 294
Viet Cong 21, 45, 46, 64, 237, 278, 293, 307, 333
Viet cosmology 27
Viet Hai 184
viet kieu 290
Viet Minh 20, 41, 44, 147, 165, 166, 167, 169, 177, 195, 206, 219, 307, 333
Viet Nam 34
Vietnam Quoc Dan Dang Party 39
Vietnam War 21, 43–47, 51, 229, 241, 246, 253, 256, 276, 307, 322
Vietnamese calendar 197
Vietnamese language 117, 258
Vietnamese zodiac 197
Villa Blanche (White Villa) 314
Vinh 230
Vinh Bac Bo (Gulf of Tonkin) 217
Vinh Cam Ranh (Cam Ranh Bay) 276
Vinh Ha Long (Ha Long Bay) 180–183
Vinh Long 323

Vinh Muoc 246
Vinh Trang 321
Vinh Yen 167
Vo Nguyen Giap 40, 42, 167, 196, 207
Voi Phuc 158
Vu Vuong 237
Vung Tau 313

w – z

War Remnants Museum (HCMC) 293
Water Puppet Theatre (Roi Nuoc Thang Long) 151
water puppets 101, 151
whale cult 313
White Horse Temple (Den Bach Ma) 152
White Villa (Villa Blanche) 314
woodcuts 115
World War II 20, 41, 147
Wudi 26
Xeo Quit 324
Xich Qui 26
Xom Bong 273
Yen Bai 203
Yersin, Dr Alexandre 272
zodiac, Vietnamese 197

A
B
D
E
F
G
H
I
J
a
b
c
d
e
f
g
h
i
,
k
l

Insight Guides Website
www.insightguides.com

*Don't travel the
planet alone.
Keep in step with
Insight Guides'
walking eye,
just a click away*

Insight Guides Website

Insight Guide
South Africa

This 370-page book includes a section detailing South Africa's history, 22 features covering aspects of the country's life and culture, ranging from living without Apartheid to spectacular wildlife, a region by region visitor's guide to the sights, and a comprehensive Travel Tips section packed with essential contact addresses and numbers. Plus many quality photographs and 15 maps.

UK: £16.99 ISBN: 981-234-223-0
US: $22.95 ISBN: 0-88729-445-6

(Note: cover shown may differ in some markets.)

Close Window

INSIGHT GUIDES

The classic series that puts you in the picture

Alaska
Amazon Wildlife
American Southwest
Amsterdam
Argentina
Arizona & Grand Canyon
Asia, East
Asia, Southeast
Australia
Austria
Bahamas
Bali
Baltic States
Bangkok
Barbados
Barcelona
Beijing
Belgium
Belize
Berlin
Bermuda
Boston
Brazil
Brittany
Brussels
Buenos Aires
Burgundy
Burma (Myanmar)
Cairo
California
California, Southern
Canada
Caribbean
Caribbean Cruises
Channel Islands
Chicago
Chile
China
Continental Europe
Corsica
Costa Rica
Crete
Cuba
Cyprus
Czech & Slovak Republic
Delhi, Jaipur & Agra
Denmark

Dominican Rep. & Haiti
Dublin
East African Wildlife
Eastern Europe
Ecuador
Edinburgh
Egypt
England
Finland
Florence
Florida
France
France, South West
French Riviera
Gambia & Senegal
Germany
Glasgow
Gran Canaria
Great Britain
Great Railway Journeys
   of Europe
Greece
Greek Islands
Guatemala, Belize
   & Yucatán
Hawaii
Hong Kong
Hungary
Iceland
India
India, South
Indonesia
Ireland
Israel
Istanbul
Italy
Italy, Northern
Italy, Southern
Jamaica
Japan
Jerusalem
Jordan
Kenya
Korea
Laos & Cambodia
Las Vegas
Lisbon

London
Los Angeles
Madeira
Madrid
Malaysia
Mallorca & Ibiza
Malta
Mauritius Réunion
   & Seychelles
Melbourne
Mexico
Miami
Montreal
Morocco
Moscow
Namibia
Nepal
Netherlands
New England
New Orleans
New York City
New York State
New Zealand
Nile
Normandy
Norway
Oman & The UAE
Oxford
Pacific Northwest
Pakistan
Paris
Peru
Philadelphia
Philippines
Poland
Portugal
Prague
Provence
Puerto Rico
Rajasthan

Rio de Janeiro
Rome
Russia
St Petersburg
San Francisco
Sardinia
Scandinavia
Scotland
Seattle
Sicily
Singapore
South Africa
South America
Spain
Spain, Northern
Spain, Southern
Sri Lanka
Sweden
Switzerland
Sydney
Syria & Lebanon
Taiwan
Tenerife
Texas
Thailand
Tokyo
Trinidad & Tobago
Tunisia
Turkey
Tuscany
Umbria
USA: On The Road
USA: Western States
US National Parks: West
Venezuela
Venice
Vienna
Vietnam
Wales
Walt Disney World/Orlando

✵ INSIGHT GUIDES

The world's largest collection of visual travel guides & maps